CATHOLIC SURVIVAL IN PROTESTANT IRELAND, 1660–1711

Irish Historical Monograph Series

ISSN 1740-1097

Series editors
Marie Therese Flanagan, Queen's University, Belfast
Eunan O'Halpin, Trinity College, Dublin
David Hayton, Queen's University, Belfast
Fearghal McGarry, Queen's University, Belfast

Previous titles in this series

I. Ruling Ireland 1685–1742: Politics, Politicians and Parties, *D. W. Hayton*, 2004

II. Lord Broghill and the Cromwellian Union with Ireland and Scotland, *Patrick Little*, 2004

III. Irish Migrants in New Zealand, 1840–1937: 'The Desired Haven', *Angela McCarthy*, 2005

IV. The Fenian Ideal and Irish Nationalism, 1882–1916, *M. J. Kelly*, 2006

V. Loyalism in Ireland, 1789–1829, *Allan Blackstock*, 2007

VI. Constructing the Past: Writing Irish History, 1600–1800, *edited by Mark Williams and Stephen Forrest*, 2010

VII. The Making of the Irish Protestant Ascendancy: The Life of William Conolly, 1662–1729, *Patrick Walsh*, 2010

VIII. The Militia in Eighteenth-Century Ireland: In Defence of the Protestant Interest, *Neal Garnham*, 2012

IX. The Anglo-Irish Experience, 1680–1730: Religion, Identity and Patriotism, *D. W. Hayton*, 2012

X. The Presbyterians of Ulster, 1680–1730, *Robert Whan*, 2013

XI. The Welsh and the Shaping of Early Modern Ireland, 1558–1641, *Rhys Morgan*, 2014

XII. The Irish in the Spanish Armies in the Seventeenth Century, *Eduardo de Mesa*, 2014

XIII. Consumption and Culture in Sixteenth-Century Ireland: Saffron, Stockings and Silk, *Susan Flavin*, 2014

XIV. Elite Women in Ascendancy Ireland, 1690–1745: Imitation and Innovation, *Rachel Wilson*, 2015

XV. The Stuart Restoration and the English in Ireland, *Danielle McCormack*, 2016

XVI. Charity Movements in Eighteenth-Century Ireland: Philanthropy and Improvement, *Karen Sonnelitter*, 2016

XVII. Hugh de Lacy, First Earl of Ulster: Rising and Falling in Angevin Ireland, *Daniel Brown*, 2016

CATHOLIC SURVIVAL IN PROTESTANT IRELAND 1660–1711

Colonel John Browne, Landownership and the Articles of Limerick

Eoin Kinsella

THE BOYDELL PRESS

First published 2018
The Boydell Press, Woodbridge

ISBN 978-1-78327-316-4

The Boydell Press is an imprint of Boydell & Brewer Ltd
PO Box 9, Woodbridge, Suffolk IP12 3DF, UK
and of Boydell & Brewer Inc.
668 Mt Hope Avenue, Rochester, NY 14620–2731, USA
website: www.boydellandbrewer.com

A CIP catalogue record for this title is available from the British Library

The publisher has no responsibility for the continued existence or accuracy of URLs for external or third-party internet websites referred to in this book, and does not guarantee that any content on such websites is, or will remain, accurate or appropriate

This publication is printed on acid-free paper

This book is dedicated to my parents

Contents

List of Illustrations	ix
Acknowledgements	x
List of Abbreviations	xii
Editorial Note	xiv
Glossary	xv
Introduction	1
Part I: The Rise and Fall of the 'New Interest'	15
1. 'I hope all will end well with our New Interests': The rise and fall of a 'new interest' landowner, 1666–89	17
2. 'You must engage your plate, your credit, and all is at stake': Jacobite colonel, ironmaster and negotiator, 1689–91	41
Part II: The Articles of Surrender	63
3. 'They were drawn by some furious lawyer': Implementing the minor articles of surrender, 1691–1704	65
4. 'With justice but not favour': Implementing the articles of Limerick, 1691–1704	95
5. 'The same was refused to the Galway men': Implementing the articles of Galway, 1691–1704	123
Part III: Article 13 of Limerick	145
6. 'This clause was surreptitiously obtained': Implementing article 13 of Limerick, 1691–8	147
7. 'I fear a bill relating to me be gone for England': Implementing article 13 of Limerick, 1698–1708	178
8. 'I am plagued with a quarrel': The Browne family and the gentry of Connacht, 1692–1711	210
Conclusion	236

CONTENTS

Appendix A: Articles of Surrender, 1690–91   247

Appendix B: Hearings scheduled for adjudication under the articles of Limerick, 1694   262

Appendix C: Proclamations of 7 July & 1 August 1691; 'A copy of and answers to several complaints made by the Irish by their agent Mr Cockly'   274

Bibliography   287

Index   309

Illustrations

Plates

1. Portrait of Colonel John Browne, n.d. (Westport House)   16

2. Silver chamber candlestick presented to Colonel John Browne by Patrick Sarsfield, 1691 (Westport House)   56

3. *The case of all persons comprized in the articles or capitulations of Waterford ...* [1700]   64

4. *A diary of the siege and surrender of Lymerick* (1692)   96

5. *The articles of Galway exactly printed from the letters-patents* (1692)   124

6. *The state of the case of Denis Daly, and Edmund Malone, Esqrs* [1696]   126

Tables

1: Numbers of Successful Claimants to Articles and Estates Restored by Articles   79

2: Methods of Implementing the Articles   118

3: Total acreage and sales of Browne's estate by April 1704 in Co. Galway   192

4: Total acreage and sales of Browne's estate by April 1704 in Co. Mayo   193

5: Sale of John Browne's Estate in Co. Galway, 1699–1700   194

6: Sale of John Browne's Estate in Co. Mayo, 1698–1707   196

7: Sale of John Browne's estate, April 1704 – July 1708   200

8: Principal purchasers of John Browne's estate   203

The author and publishers are grateful to all the institutions and individuals listed for permission to reproduce the materials in which they hold copyright. Every effort has been made to trace the copyright holders; apologies are offered for any omission, and the publishers will be pleased to add any necessary acknowledgement in subsequent editions.

Acknowledgements

During a postgraduate seminar led by James McGuire at the Department of History, University College Dublin, a passing comment caught my attention. James mentioned the ambiguous allegiances of the Catholic 'new interest' during the Williamite war of 1689–91. Intrigued, I asked who the 'new interest' were, and what had happened to them after the surrender of Limerick in 1691. James simply replied that perhaps I might answer those questions myself. The process he set in train that day has led, via a slightly circuitous route, to this book. It is the culmination of more than a decade of intermittent research, first during my doctoral studies, and then as part of my continuing efforts to understand Catholic politics and society in eighteenth-century Ireland.

I have been fortunate enough to receive funding to support my research, and would like to thank the Micheál Ó Cléirigh Institute for the award of a PhD scholarship. I am also grateful to the Irish Research Council for the award of a postdoctoral fellowship in 2012. The Esme Mitchell Trust generously provided me with a grant in aid of publication. Donough Cahill and David Fleming of the Irish Georgian Society provided logistical assistance.

My thanks to the librarians and archivists of the Bodleian Library, Oxford; the British Library; the National Archives of Ireland; the National Archives of the United Kingdom; the National Library of Ireland; the Royal Irish Academy; Trinity College Dublin; and University College Dublin. At Boydell and Brewer, I am grateful to the series editor, David Hayton, and the commissioning editor, Peter Sowden, for their advice and encouragement.

I am indebted to Lord and Lady Bellew of Barmeath Castle for their hospitality during several research trips to their home, and for permission to cite their family papers. Lord and Lady Kilmaine granted me permission to view their family papers at their home in Alcester, Warwickshire. Anthony Malcomson arranged introductions to several private archives and steered me through questions of etiquette. David Hayton and Michael Page kindly permitted me to use their transcripts of the Brodrick correspondence in the Midleton papers, held at the Surrey History Centre. Evelien Schillern generously provided me with material from Utrecht Archive. Sheelyn Browne, a direct descendant of Colonel John Browne, provided me with digital images of items that belonged to her ancestor and graciously granted permission to reproduce them in the book. Permission to reproduce documents in their collections has also been granted by the Royal Irish Academy and the National Library of Ireland.

ACKNOWLEDGEMENTS

I have enjoyed the advice, assistance and good company of many people while researching and writing this book. My former supervisor, Declan Downey, patiently guided me during my time at University College Dublin. My thanks also to Kate Breslin, Sarah Campbell, Brigid Clesham, Edward Collins, Mary Daly, Selena Daly, Elizabeth Dawson, Coleman A. Dennehy, Aoife Duignan, Mark Duncan, Lindsey Earner-Byrne, Sarah Feehan, Gillian Finan, Mark Jones, James Kelly, Laura Kelly, Michael Kennedy, Emma Lyons, Marian Lyons, John McCafferty, Jason McElligott, William Mulligan, Conor Mulvagh, Eamon O'Flaherty, Tadhg Ó hAnnracháin, Kate O'Malley, Paul Rouse, Sue Schulze, Eiriol Townsend and Patrick Walsh, for reasons academic and otherwise.

David Hayton and James McGuire continue to provide me with invaluable guidance on early modern Ireland, and all matters academic. Ivar McGrath has been a friend and mentor for many years. He read an early draft and later suggested the book's structure, breaking months of writer's block. John Bergin's help, advice and generosity with sources has vastly improved my work. I look forward to the continuation of our scholarly conversation. Neil Johnston and Suzanne Forbes have been in the trenches with me since we met as postgraduates and later established the annual Tudor and Stuart Ireland Conference. Special thanks to Carole Holohan who, apart from being equal parts counsellor and friend for more than fifteen years, read and provided perceptive commentary on the entire manuscript.

Above all, my thanks to my family. My four brothers, Andrew, Lorcan, Séamas and Dónal, amuse and irritate me in equal measure, as all good brothers should do. My wonderful wife, Lily, has lived with the events explored within this book for as long as we are together, and still agreed to marry me. I can think of no better person to have shared this journey with. I cannot adequately express my gratitude to my parents, Pat and Larry, who are constant in their support and encouragement of their family. This book is dedicated to them.

Abbreviations

Bergin, 'Irish Catholic interest'	John Bergin, 'The Irish Catholic interest at the London Inns of Court, 1674–1800' in *E.C.I.*, xxiv (2009), pp 36–61
Bergin, 'Irish legislative procedure'	John Bergin, 'Irish legislative procedure after the Williamite revolution: the operation of Poynings' Law, 1692–1705' (PhD thesis, 2 vols, University College Dublin, 2005)
Bergin & Lyall (eds), *The acts of James II's Irish parliament*	John Bergin and Andrew Lyall (eds), *The acts of James II's Irish parliament of 1689* (Dublin, 2016)
B.L.	British Library
B.L., Add. Ms	British Library, Additional Manuscript
Bodl.	Bodleian Library, Oxford
C.J.	*The journals of the house of commons* [of England]
C.J.I.	*The journals of the House of Commons of the kingdom of Ireland* (4th series, 18 vols, Dublin, 1796–1802), volume ii
Convert Rolls	Eileen O'Byrne & Anne Chamney (eds), *The convert rolls* (revd. ed., Dublin, 2005)
C.S.P.D.	*Calendar of State Papers, domestic series*
C.T.B.	*Calendar of Treasury Books*
D.I.B.	*Dictionary of Irish Biography* (online edition)
E.C.I.	*Eighteenth-Century Ireland*
Hayton, *Ruling Ireland*	D.W. Hayton, *Ruling Ireland, 1685–1742: politics, politicians and parties* (Woodbridge, 2004)
H.I.P.	Edith Mary Johnston-Liik, *History of the Irish parliament, 1692–1800: commons, constituencies and statutes* (6 vols, Belfast, 2002)
H.M.C.	Historical Manuscripts Commission
I.H.S.	*Irish Historical Studies*
J.R.S.A.I.	*Journal of the Royal Society of Antiquaries of Ireland*

Kelly & Lyons (eds), *Proclamations of Ireland*	James Kelly and Mary Ann Lyons (eds), *The proclamations of Ireland, 1660–1820* (5 vols, Dublin, 2014)
K.I.A.P.	Edward Keane, P. Beryl Phair and T. U. Sadlier (eds), *King's Inns admission papers, 1607–1867* (Dublin, 1982)
King, *State of the Protestants*	William King, *The state of the Protestants of Ireland under the late King James's government* (4th ed., London, 1692)
L.J.I.	*The journals of the House of Lords of the kingdom of Ireland* (8 vols, Dublin, 1779–1800)
Maynard, 'Irish membership of the English inns of court'	Hazel Maynard, 'Irish membership of the English inns of court, 1660–1669: lawyers, litigation and the legal profession' (PhD thesis, University College Dublin, 2006)
MP	Member of Parliament
N.A.I.	National Archives of Ireland
N.L.I.	National Library of Ireland
P.R.I.A.	*Proceedings of the Royal Irish Academy*
R.I.A.	Royal Irish Academy
S.H.C.	Surrey History Centre, Woking
Simms, 'Irish Jacobites'	J. G. Simms, 'Irish Jacobites' in *Analecta Hibernica*, 22 (1960), pp 11–230
Simms, *Jacobite Ireland*	J. G. Simms, *Jacobite Ireland, 1685–91* (Dublin, 1969)
Simms, *Williamite confiscation*	J. G. Simms, *The Williamite confiscation in Ireland, 1690–1703* (London, 1957)
S.R.O.	Staffordshire Record Office, Stafford
T.C.D.	Trinity College Dublin
T.N.A.	The National Archives of the United Kingdom, London

Editorial Note

All dates are given in the old style, though the year is taken to begin on 1 January, rather than 25 March. Spelling, punctuation and capitalisation has been modernised in all quotations, except in instances where the meaning or reading of the original is ambiguous.

Glossary of Terms

Definitions are taken from Giles Jacob, *A new law dictionary* (London, 1729); Andrew Lyall with Albert Power, *Land law in Ireland* (3rd ed., Dublin, 2010); and the *Oxford English Dictionary*.

Attachment: an attachment was not an arrest, but the taking into custody of a person in order to ensure they appeared in court on a certain day.

Attainder: Where a person has been convicted of treason, or has had a judgment for **outlawry** given against them. A person who had been attainted was subject to the loss of their property and, though very rarely, to the death penalty.

Bills: In legislative terms, a bill is a proposal for a new act, or a proposal to modify an existing law. A bill becomes an act if presented to and accepted by both houses of parliament.

Chaffery: One of the two principal forges typically found in an ironworks, used for reheating iron and complementing the work done in the finery.

Chattels personal: legally defined as all moveable goods and property, such as money, furniture and livestock.

Chattels real: legally defined as immoveable goods, such as land, buildings and leases.

Conveyance: The transfer of the ownership of land from one person to another. Also refers to the written deed effecting the transfer.
> **Lease and Release**: A form of conveyance involving two transactions. The lease specified a term of duration (usually six months to a year) along with a nominal rent. The release followed a day later, in which the lessor conveyed his right to the specified land to the lessee, or occasionally a trustee, in exchange for the consideration in money. 'Lease and release' agreements thus usually comprise two separate documents.

Custodiam: A grant or lease to a person, for a period of time, of the custody of land or other property that belongs to the crown. The grantee or lessee is given full power to collect and dispose of rents or other profits from the land or property. The grant or lease was granted from the court of Exchequer.

Distraint/Distress: a common procedure in the seventeenth century. It involved the confiscation of a person's goods in order to compel them to honour a debt, bond or other charge, usually rent.

Estate

> **Real**: all of a person's immoveable property. Typically ownership or any other inheritable interest in land, buildings or other immoveable property.
>
> **Personal**: all of a person's property, with the exception of land or any interests in land that is inheritable by his/her heirs.

Finery: One of two principal furnaces typically found in an ironworks, in which pig iron is refined to make steel or wrought iron.

Forfeiture: A punishment for some illegal act, or negligence, whereby the owner of lands loses his interest in those lands. Forfeiture usually arose from a conviction for outlawry.

Jacobite: a supporter of James II and of the right of the Stuart family to the crowns of England, Scotland and Ireland after the 'Glorious Revolution' of 1688.

Messuage: A house with adjoining land and buildings, which are dedicated to the use of the house and its occupants.

Outlawry: Where a person is put outside the protection of the law. All of that person's goods and property were then forfeited to the crown.

Private Act: an act of parliament that applies only to an individual or a small group of individuals. Private acts were usually not formally printed in the era under examination in this book.

Proviso: A special clause inserted into an act of parliament in favour of a specified person or persons, often exempting them from some or all of the implications of the act. Also a specific condition entered into a deed. Also known as a **saving clause**.

Remainder: A right to possession of property (typically land) only when other interests, granted at the same time, expire. Most frequently used when an estate has been conveyed to a person for life, and on their death to another person. The latter person is said to have the estate in remainder.

Saving Clause: See **Proviso**.

Williamite: A supporter of William of Orange, who was declared William III, king of England, Scotland and Ireland, during the convocation parliament of February 1689.

Introduction

This book is a study of Irish Catholic landownership and political lobbying, from the Restoration of Charles II in 1660 to the reign of Queen Anne. The fortunes of Irish Catholics fluctuated dramatically during this period, from the generally benevolent tolerance of Charles II's reign, through the heady days of the Catholic resurgence under James II, on to the beginnings of the penal era after 1691. Divided into three parts, the primary focus is on the rise of the 'new interest' of propertied Catholics after the Restoration, the Jacobite administration during the Williamite war (1689–91), the negotiation of the various articles of surrender that ended the war, and on the protracted and contested progress towards the implementation of these articles in the two decades that followed.

Part I provides an overview of the life and career of Colonel John Browne, an Irish Catholic who built one of the largest estates in Ireland in the 1660s and 1670s, as well as the impact of James II's reign on Catholic landowners. Lobbying by Irish Catholics, in Dublin and in London, provides the core focus for Parts II and III. Part II explores the drafting and aftermath of the various articles of surrender, signed during the Williamite war at Drogheda, Waterford, Galway, Inis Boffin, Sligo and Limerick. Those who claimed the benefit of the articles were known as the articlemen. Their political activity during the 1690s and early 1700s concentrated on ensuring that the Irish and English governments honoured the terms of the articles. Part III analyses the implementation and impact of article 13 of Limerick, an extraordinary and disputed addition to the terms that called for a special levy on all Catholic-owned estates to help pay debts owed by John Browne. Article 13 was unique in a number of respects, and it proved to be the only article for which the Irish parliament actively sought to enact legislation. Though the aim of the Jacobite negotiators at Limerick was to safeguard the economic future of Irish Catholics, article 13 was financially punitive to the articlemen and they made strenuous efforts to prevent the collection of the special levy. Article 13 was, however, crucial to any chance John Browne had to emerge from underneath a mountain of personal debt. Supported by his creditors, the majority of whom were Protestant and members of the Irish parliament, Browne lobbied vigorously for the implementation of Article 13 in the 1690s and the first decade of the eighteenth century.

I

Any consideration of Irish Catholic or Jacobite history in the 1690s and early 1700s must first look to the emergence of the Catholic 'new interest' during the reign of Charles II, and their fortunes under James II. This is especially true for Catholic landowners. The repeal of the Restoration land settlement by the 1689 parliament – which was almost entirely Catholic in its composition – had serious implications for the 'new interest' in the event of a Jacobite victory and undermined their commitment to the Jacobite war effort.

For some Catholic landowners, the confiscations of land that followed the war of 1689–91 were merely the latest in a series of struggles to protect landholdings that stretched back to the Cromwellian confiscation of the 1650s. For the 'new interest', who established themselves as landowners after 1660, William III's reign was not much more nerve-wracking than James II's had been. During both, though for very different reasons, landowning Irish Catholics were faced with dispossession.

The amount of Irish land owned by Catholics had declined dramatically during the seventeenth century, beginning with the Ulster plantation and culminating in the Williamite confiscation.[1] This experience was not universal and the estates targeted for confiscation changed from those of the Gaelic Irish to those of the general Catholic population in the mid-seventeenth century.[2] The distinction, though important in tracing the evolution of government policy, is in the broader sense somewhat pedantic. The Gaelic Irish were almost universally Catholic, with the mid-century change of policy prompted by the Confederate wars of the 1640s. The resulting Cromwellian transplantation and confiscation was, of course, targeted at Catholic landowners and was largely confirmed by the Restoration land settlement.

Even so, religion was not an insurmountable obstacle to Catholics who regained estates in the decade after the Restoration thanks to the patronage of

---

[1] The classic accounts for this period are J.A. Froude, *The English in Ireland in the eighteenth century* (3 vols, London, 1872–4), i, 66–207; W.E.H. Lecky, *A history of Ireland in the eighteenth century* (5 vols, London, repr. 1913), i, 21–171. See also T.W. Moody, F.X. Martin & F.J. Byrne (eds), *A new history of Ireland: iii, early modern Ireland, 1534–1691* (Oxford, 1976), pp 187–633; Brendan Fitzpatrick, *Seventeenth-century Ireland: the war of religions* (Dublin, 1988); Raymond Gillespie, *Seventeenth-century Ireland: making Ireland modern* (Dublin, 2006); Pádraig Lenihan, *Consolidating conquest: Ireland, 1603–1727* (Harlow, 2008). Survey treatments of the second half of the century are found in Seán Connolly, *Religion, law and power: the making of Protestant Ireland, 1660–1760* (Oxford, 1992); idem, *Divided kingdom: Ireland, 1630–1800* (Oxford, 2008); David Dickson, *New foundations: Ireland, 1660–1800* (2nd ed., Dublin, 2000).
[2] Simms, *Williamite confiscation*, p. 13.

2

Charles II and James Butler, duke of Ormond, or who were able to prove their 'innocence' at the court of claims of 1663.[3]

After the Restoration a new landowning interest was formed among Irish Catholics: men who had held no land prior to the upheavals of the 1640s and 1650s, or those who were dispossessed yet able to acquire new estates. Their 'new interests' consisted of land purchased from Cromwellian soldiers and Irish Protestants, or Irish Catholics who, though they regained their estates, became heavily indebted in the process and were forced to sell their land.[4] Perhaps 29% of profitable land in Ireland was in Catholic hands by the mid-1670s, in number a little over 1,300 landowners. West of the Shannon, Catholic landownership remained strong in the counties of Mayo, Galway and Roscommon, as it did in the counties of the Pale.[5] These landowners were as reliant as their Protestant counterparts on the Restoration land settlement – which had its legal foundations in the acts of settlement (1662) and explanation (1665) – for the security of their land. So too were the beneficiaries of Ormond's and Charles II's patronage and the 'innocents' of the court of claims.[6]

The emergence of the Catholic 'new interest' complicates the traditional historiographical tendency to identify and emphasise tensions between discrete Catholic, Protestant and Dissenter interests, invariably at odds over land

---

[3] For a summary of the historiography of the Restoration land settlement, see Michael Perceval-Maxwell, 'The Irish Restoration land settlement and its historians' in Coleman A. Dennehy (ed.), *Restoration Ireland: always settling and never settled* (Aldershot, 2008), pp 19–34. See also John Cunningham, *Conquest and land in Ireland: the transplantation to Connacht, 1649–1680* (London, 2011); Jane Ohlmeyer, *Making Ireland English: the Irish aristocracy in the seventeenth century* (London, 2012), pp 300–46; Margaret Anne Creighton, 'The Catholic interest in Irish politics in the reign of Charles II' (Ph.D. thesis, Queen's University Belfast, 2000).

[4] The term 'new interest' was originally used to refer to English Protestants who had arrived in Ireland after 1649. The term evolved to encompass any person who had purchased land after the Irish parliament approved the act of settlement in 1662. For a general analysis of the emergence of the Catholic 'new interest' during the reign of Charles II, and their political activities during the reigns of Charles II and James II, see Eoin Kinsella, '"Dividing the bear's skin before she is taken": Irish Catholics and land in the late Stuart monarchy, 1683–91' in Dennehy (ed.), *Restoration Ireland*, pp 161–78. See also Sheila Mulloy, 'Galway in the Jacobite war' in *J.G.A.H.S.*, xl (1986), pp 1–19; eadem, 'The transfer of power: Galway, 1642–1702' in Gerard Moran (ed.), *Galway: history and society* (Dublin, 1996), pp 223–4.

[5] By 1675 Protestant and Catholic shares of landownership in Ireland had completely reversed from their standing in 1641: from 30% to 67% and 66% to 29% respectively (Kevin McKenny, 'The Restoration land settlement in Ireland: a statistical interpretation' in Dennehy (ed.), *Restoration Ireland*, pp 35–52).

[6] The Restoration land settlement was given legislative force by the act of settlement (1662) and act of explanation (1665). See K.S. Bottigheimer, 'The Restoration land settlement: a structural view' in *I.H.S.*, xviii (1972–3), pp 1–21; L.J. Arnold, *The Restoration land settlement in County Dublin, 1660–1688: a history of the administration of the acts of settlement and explanation* (Dublin, 1993); idem, 'The Irish court of claims of 1663' in *I.H.S.*, xxiv (1985), pp 417–30; Geraldine Tallon (ed.), *Court of claims: submissions and evidence, 1663* (Dublin, 2006).

and religious policy.[7] The Catholic 'new interest' had much in common with Protestant counterparts who had similarly benefited from the Restoration land settlement, and who feared any attempt to revisit the land question. The 'new interest' constituted a powerful and wealthy new Catholic polity, distinguished from the majority of the Catholic population by their determination to preserve the status quo in land ownership.

The rapid rise of the Catholic 'new interest' during the 1660s and 1670s has largely been painted in broad brush strokes, with little attention paid to the processes whereby they actually acquired their estates. They had little standing with co-religionists who suffered dispossession in the 1650s and regarded the 'new interest' as having 'purchased from usurpers the inheritance of their own countrymen'.[8] Often they benefited from the misfortune of family members, as did John Browne, an exemplar of the rise of the 'new interest'. Originally from the Neale, County Mayo, Browne later established himself at Westport (Cahernamart) on land previously owned by the Viscounts Mayo. He took advantage of his wife's family's financial difficulties to acquire an enormous estate in Counties Mayo and Galway, and was a well-known and influential figure within Connacht society. Tracing his rise to prominence, alongside that of the wider 'new interest', provides essential background for the activities of Catholic landowners during the Williamite war and the two decades that followed. When contextualised alongside those of his 'new interest' contemporaries, Browne's career provides a wealth of insights into Catholic landownership and politics in the late seventeenth and early eighteenth centuries.[9]

Browne personified many of the key attributes of the 'new interest', including a shrewd and advantageous marriage, education at the London inns of court

[7] For important exceptions, see Anne Creighton, 'The Remonstrance of December 1661 and Catholic politics in Restoration Ireland' in *I.H.S.*, xxxiv (2004–5), pp 16–41; eadem, '"Grace and favour": the Cabal ministry and Irish Catholic politics, 1667–73' in Dennehy (ed.), *Restoration Ireland*, pp 141–60; Hayton, *Ruling Ireland*, pp 16–18.

[8] Charles O'Kelly, *Macariae Excidium, Or, The Destruction of Cyprus; Being a Secret History of the War of the Revolution in Ireland*, ed. J.C. O'Callaghan (Dublin, 1850), p. 71.

[9] Though he merited an entry in the *Dictionary of Irish Biography*, Browne has received almost no scholarly attention. His rental accounts were utilised in Raymond Gillespie's examination of the economic development of County Mayo in the seventeenth century, while J.G. Simms briefly noted that Browne established himself as a landowner of considerable influence after the Restoration. Neither scholar appears to have had access to the majority of John Browne's papers, formerly in Westport House and now in the National Library of Ireland. The Westport papers (which were formerly known as the Sligo papers) are a source of exceptional quality and importance for the history of the Catholic landed class of Connacht in the late seventeenth century (Raymond Gillespie, 'Lords and commons in seventeenth-century Mayo' in Raymond Gillespie and Gerard Moran (eds), 'A various county': essays in Mayo history, 1500–1900 (Westport, 1987), pp 44–66; J.G. Simms, 'Mayo landowners in the seventeenth century' in *J.R.S.A.I.*, 95 (1965), pp 237–47; idem, 'Connacht in the eighteenth century' in *I.H.S.*, xi (1958–9), pp 116–33; Brigid Clesham, 'The Westport estate papers' in *Cathair na Mart*, 26 (2008), pp 90–105).

and a reputation as an excellent lawyer.[10] By the 1680s his estate was one of the largest in the kingdom. Browne also embarked on a disastrous attempt to establish himself as an entrepreneur and ironmaster during the 1670s. It was perhaps ironic that Browne, who had profited so handsomely from the financial distress of others, was himself heavily indebted by the time of James II's accession in 1685.[11] While in some ways unique, Browne's case nonetheless throws many sidelights on seventeenth-century estate management and the private finances of an Irish landowner.[12] As with the other members of the 'new interest', the future ownership of Browne's estate was plunged into uncertainty following the accession of James II and William of Orange's subsequent invasion of England in 1688. The decision by James II's Irish parliament of 1689 to pass an act reversing the Restoration land settlement, and the partial implementation of that act, tested the loyalty of the 'new interest' and gravely undermined the Jacobite war effort.

Though the political and military aspects of the Williamite war have been studied extensively, very little is known of James II's wartime administration, or the manner in which his army was supplied. It has, for example, gone entirely unnoticed that John Browne (now with the rank of Colonel) was one of the Jacobite army's principal suppliers of materiel.[13] Browne does feature in most modern accounts of the Williamite war, though only in passing

[10] For a skilful reconstruction of the career of Sir Richard Nagle, who was a contemporary of John Browne's at Gray's Inn and later served as James II's attorney general in Ireland, see James McGuire, 'A lawyer in politics: the career of Sir Richard Nagle, c.1639–1699' in H.B. Clarke & Judith Devlin (eds), *European encounters: essays in memory of Albert Lovett* (Dublin, 2003), pp 118–31; repr. in N.M. Dawson (ed.), *Reflections on law and history: Irish Legal History Society discourses and other papers, 2000–2005* (Dublin, 2006), pp 18–31.

[11] The discussion of Browne's iron making business is placed within the parameters established in T.C. Barnard, 'An Anglo-Irish industrial enterprise: iron-making at Enniscorthy, Co. Wexford, 1657–92' in *P.R.I.A.*, 85C (1985), pp 101–44; idem, 'Sir William Petty as Kerry ironmaster' in *P.R.I.A.*, 82C (1982), pp 1–32; J.H. Andrews, 'A note on the later history of the Irish charcoal iron industry' in *J.R.S.A.I.*, lxxxvi (1956), pp 217–9; idem, 'Notes on the historical geography of the Irish iron industry' in *Irish Geography*, 3 (1956), pp 139–49; H.F. Kearney, 'Richard Boyle, ironmaster: a footnote to Irish economic history' in *J.R.S.A.I.*, lxxxiii (1953), pp 156–62.

[12] The scholarship concerning private finances in seventeenth-century Ireland is not extensive: see Patricia Stapleton, '"In monies and other requisites": the 1641 depositions and the social role of credit in early seventeenth-century Ireland' in Eamon Darcy, Annaleigh Margey & Elaine Murphy (eds), *The 1641 depositions and the Irish rebellion* (London, 2012), pp 65–78; Jane Ohlmeyer & Éamonn Ó Ciardha (eds), *The Irish statute staple books, 1596–1687* (Dublin, 1998); Michael MacCarthy-Morrogh, 'Credit and remittance: money problems in early seventeenth-century Munster' in *Irish Economic and Social History*, xiv (1987), pp 5–19. Chapter 1 draws upon scholarship on private finances in early modern England to supply an interpretive framework.

[13] The most recent, and fullest account of the war, makes no mention of Browne. See John Childs, *The Williamite wars in Ireland, 1688–91* (London, 2007). Detailed as this study is, its usefulness is hampered by its reliance on printed sources and failure to utilise any of the available manuscript sources in Ireland.

reference to the mysterious circumstances surrounding the inclusion of article 13 in the terms of surrender signed at Limerick. Despite their importance to the history of Catholic Ireland over the next 140 years, the negotiation of the articles of Limerick has been similarly neglected in recent historiography. This is especially true of article 13, negotiated specifically for the benefit of Browne and his creditors, to whom he became indebted *before* the outbreak of the war.[14]

II

Irish Catholics who went into exile on the continent after 1691 have been the subject of many studies, especially those who pursued military careers or attended the vibrant Irish colleges. The mentalités of these displaced elites have been convincingly mapped.[15] Catholics who had their lands confiscated, and those who voluntarily or otherwise went into exile, are properly an important part of most historical accounts. Less well known are the lives and fortunes of Catholics who chose to remain in Ireland and sought to enjoy their estates and the rights promised them in the articles of surrender.[16] Formerly members of the 'new interest', they became known as the articlemen. The importance of the articles of Limerick and of Galway to the survival of a reduced Catholic landowning class has long been recognised. The practicalities of that survival have nonetheless never been laid out in detail, while the other articles of surrender have largely disappeared from the historical memory.[17] Catholic political activity in the two decades that followed the surrender of Limerick was of a scale that has not fully been appreciated, as the articlemen sought the implementation of the articles and later fought to prevent the enactment and enforcement of the penal laws. The overall experience of Catholic landowners at the turn of the eighteenth century has

---

[14] The origins of article 13 have been mentioned briefly in the historiography, but never given extensive treatment. See J.G. Simms, 'The original draft of the civil articles of Limerick, 1691' in *I.H.S.*, viii (1952–3), p. 44; James McGuire, 'The Treaty of Limerick' in Bernadette Whelan (ed.), *The last of the great wars: essays on the war of the three kings in Ireland* (Limerick, 1995), p. 129.

[15] Patrick Kelly, '"A light to the blind": the voice of the dispossessed élite in the generation after the defeat at Limerick' in *I.H.S.*, xxiv (1984–5), pp 431–62; idem, 'The improvement of Ireland' in *Analecta Hibernica*, 35 (1992), pp 45–84; Vincent Geoghegan, 'Thomas Sheridan: toleration and royalism' in D.G. Boyce, Robert Eccleshall & Vincent Geoghegan (eds), *Political discourse in seventeenth- and eighteenth-century Ireland* (Basingstoke, 2001), pp 32–61.

[16] T.C. Barnard, 'Historiographical review: farewell to old Ireland' in *Historical Journal*, 36 (1993), pp 914–15.

[17] The wider context is laid out in Simms, *Williamite confiscation*. For a case study of one family, see W.A. Maguire, 'The estate of Cú Chonnacht Maguire of Tempo: a case history from the Williamite land settlement' in *I.H.S.*, xxvii (1990–91), pp 130–44.

also remained obscure, particularly when compared with the depth and range of the historiography of eighteenth-century Irish Protestantism.[18] Though this can be partly explained by the scarcity of sources, the more pertinent factor is that the history of those 'worsted in the game' is rarely attractive as an avenue of research.[19] As a result, Irish Catholic politics and society remain largely unexplored.[20]

The articlemen adopted a pragmatic attitude towards the Williamite government. They were Catholics who, though initially ardent supporters of and active participants in James II's reign, eventually adopted accommodationist tactics rather than exile. Several retained contacts with the Jacobite court in France after 1691.[21] Yet their decision to engage with the Williamite administration was informed by the certain prospect of the loss of their estates in the event of the return of James II to the throne.[22] Part II of this book examines the articlemen, including John Browne, through the prism of their interaction with the Irish and English governments. Despite the readily accessible nature of many of the sources for this examination, the place of the articlemen in the history of the 1690s and early decades of the eighteenth century has remained largely ignored. Catholic Ireland has long been regarded as moribund in the decades after the defeat of the Jacobite army, a casualty of the consensus view

---

[18] See, for example, Patrick Walsh, *The making of the Irish Protestant ascendancy: the life of William Conolly, 1662–1729* (Woodbridge, 2010); D.W. Hayton, *The Anglo-Irish experience, 1680–1730: religion, identity and patriotism* (Woodbridge, 2012). The most authoritative accounts of the broader contours of the Protestant polity during William III's reign are C.I. McGrath, *The making of the eighteenth-century Irish constitution: government, parliament and the revenue, 1692–1714* (Dublin, 2000), pp 15–192; Hayton, *Ruling Ireland*, pp 35–105.

[19] Ciarán Brady, 'Introduction: historians and losers' in idem, (ed.), *Worsted in the game: losers in Irish history* (Dublin, 1989), pp 3–4.

[20] Recent doctoral scholarship has also begun to address this deficit. See Frances Nolan, 'Jacobite women and the Williamite confiscation: the role of women and female minors in reclaiming compromised or forfeited property in Ireland, 1690–1703' (PhD thesis, University College Dublin, 2015); Philip Walsh, 'The Blakes of Ballyglunin: Catholic merchants and landowners of Galway town and county in the seventeenth and eighteenth centuries' (PhD thesis, University College Dublin, 2017), pp 66–86.

[21] *C.J.*, xii, pp 186–7.

[22] It is worth noting that, in a proclamation issued in April 1693, James II promised to respect the land settlement in Ireland, implicitly disowning the 1689 act of repeal. In a letter explaining this pronouncement to an outraged Justin McCarthy, Viscount Mountcashel, the earl of Middleton reassured Mountcashel that James II would compensate Catholics who had suffered by the Restoration land settlement: 'I mean those who have served him; and not only those here, but all who were included in the capitulation of Limerick, which will be a better security for them, than what they have by the acts of the Dublin Parliament'. Middleton's promises demonstrate that James II had not learned the lessons apparent from Charles II's failure to resolve the land question in Ireland after 1660 (Bodl., Ms Carte 181, f. 525; James Macpherson (ed.), *Original papers, containing the secret history of Great Britain, from the Restoration, to the accession of the House of Hannover* (2 vols, London, 1775), i, 446).

of Irish historians that Catholic society was stripped of all of its natural leaders with the flight of the wild geese in late 1691.[23]

Some of the most prominent Catholics of the Jacobite administration chose to remain in Ireland after Limerick, a fact that has been ignored by historians who have struggled to identify the fractures within Irish Jacobitism.[24] Éamonn Ó Ciardha's examination of Irish support for the Stuarts includes an extensive discussion of Catholic society in the 1690s, but there is little sense within his analysis that there were tensions within the Irish Catholic community.[25] Some landowning Catholics viewed the prospect of a Stuart restoration with unease, while others simply repudiated Jacobitism. During James II's reign Catholic landowners, merchants and lawyers had been appointed to the judiciary, the Irish privy council and, for the first time in a generation, admitted as members of corporations and elected as MPs to an Irish parliament. Not all remained in Ireland after 1691, of course, but very many did. They feature little in accounts of post-Revolution Irish Jacobitism. The articlemen remain outside Ó Ciardha's analysis of Jacobitism in the aftermath of Limerick, despite their status as leaders of the landed Catholic elite. There is, it seems, no place in the historiography for Catholics who do not fit neatly into the archetype of dispossession, discontent and resistance. By concentrating on Catholics dispossessed of their land, either during the 1650s or the 1690s, the recent historiography of Irish Jacobitism does little to acknowledge the more complex milieu of Catholic loyalty and political activity that was apparent during William's reign and, indeed, throughout the eighteenth century.

Despite their evident willingness to co-operate with the Williamite regime, rumours of Jacobite plotting regularly dogged the articlemen, leading to their occasional imprisonment. Some articlemen certainly plotted or corresponded with the exiled Stuart court. The analysis presented here nevertheless brings to mind Lecky's conclusion that, mindful of their treatment by Charles II and James II, the Irish Catholic nobility and gentry had no wish to put their estates in jeopardy again by supporting James II's restoration to the throne after 1691.[26]

[23] For a summary of the views of Irish historians regarding the Catholic population in the decade after the Jacobite surrender see Éamonn Ó Ciardha, *Ireland and the Jacobite cause, 1685–1766: a fatal attachment* (Dublin, 2002), pp 24–5.

[24] For surveys on Irish Jacobitism, see Ó Ciardha, *Ireland and the Jacobite cause*; Vincent Morley, *Irish opinion and the American Revolution, 1760–1783* (Cambridge, 2002); idem, *The popular mind in eighteenth-century Ireland* (Cork, 2017); Breandán Ó Buachalla, *Aisling ghéar: na Stíobhartaigh agus an taos léinn, 1603–1788* (Dublin, 1996); idem, 'James our true king: the ideology of Irish royalism in the seventeenth century' in D.G. Boyce, Robert Eccleshall & Vincent Geoghegan (eds), *Political thought in Ireland since the seventeenth century* (London, 1993), pp 7–35.

[25] Ó Ciardha, *Ireland and the Jacobite cause*, pp 87–111. See also idem, '"A lot done, more to do": the restoration and road ahead for Irish Jacobite studies' in Paul Monod, Murray Pittock & Daniel Szechi (eds), *Loyalty and identity: Jacobites at home and abroad* (Basingstoke, 2010), pp 57–81.

[26] Lecky, *A history of Ireland in the eighteenth century*, i, 413.

J.G. Simms has examined the progress and outcome of the Williamite confiscation extensively.[27] Aside from his seminal study of the land question in the 1690s, the breadth of Simms' scholarship on Jacobite and Catholic Ireland looms large on the historiographical landscape. Few other scholars have done as much to illuminate the history of Catholic Ireland between the Restoration and the Hanoverian succession.[28] While his *Williamite confiscation* discussed the articlemen and provided vignettes of the attempts by several individuals to prove their eligibility to the articles, Simms' primary focus lay on the complex processes of outlawry and attainder and the act of resumption of 1700. That focus had the unintended consequence of deflecting attention from the vibrancy of Irish Catholic lobbying in Dublin and London. The detailed analysis of the articlemen and their lobbying presented here reveals the speed with which the Irish Catholic elite transferred their energies and resources from the military to the political arena. It enables an upwards revision of the number of Catholics who claimed the benefit of the articles of surrender, as well as those who were eventually adjudicated within the articles.[29] It also allows for a major reassessment of Catholic political activity in the 1690s, and of the overall vitality of Catholic Ireland in the two decades after Limerick.

From the early nineteenth century the surrender signed on 3 October 1691 became known as the 'Treaty of Limerick', a term that has become established in the Irish cultural lexicon and has led to the christening of Limerick as the Treaty City. It is, however, technically incorrect.[30] The surrender was never recognised as a formal treaty between sovereign entities. It was, rather, regarded as a bargain made between a king and his rebellious subjects. The terms of surrender were most commonly referred to as 'articles' or 'capitulations' in the 1690s; only rarely does the term 'treaty' appear.[31] Simms also spent considerable time considering the Irish and English governments' attitudes towards

---

[27] Simms, *Williamite confiscation*. This study of the Williamite confiscation, which arose from Simms' doctoral dissertation, was the only substantive engagement with this issue for more than sixty years.
[28] Simms, *Jacobite Ireland*. For a select bibliography of his shorter works, see J.G. Simms, *War and politics in Ireland, 1649–1730*, eds. D.W. Hayton and Gerard O'Brien (London, 1986), pp 15–21. See also Gerard O'Brien (ed.), *Catholic Ireland in the eighteenth century: collected essays of Maureen Wall* (Dublin, 1989).
[29] I have made no attempt to re-examine Simms' figures in relation to Catholic land possession in the 1690s. Simms' estimation of the extent of Catholic landownership in 1688 has, however, been challenged recently: cf J.G. Simms, 'Land owned by Catholics in Ireland in 1688: historical revision ix' in *I.H.S.*, vii (1950–1), pp 180–90; Kevin McKenny, 'Restoration land settlement in Ireland'.
[30] McGuire, 'Treaty of Limerick', pp 132–3.
[31] See for example *C.S.P.D., 1691–2*, pp 118–19. Sir William Trumbull made a rare use of the word treaty when he referred to them as the 'articles of the treaty of Limerick' (Trumbull to Sir Charles Porter, 12 Sep. 1695 (H.M.C., *Downshire Mss*, i, 548)).

the various articles of surrender, particularly those of Limerick. His assessment was overly generous, swayed perhaps by the fact that so few of the articlemen's claims to their estates were rejected.[32] In reality, many claimants to articles may simply have never appeared before the courts, either aware that the government had built convincing cases against them or simply unable to meet the excessive costs associated with the courts. The Irish government generally sought to interpret the articles as narrowly as possible, and grudgingly inched towards a piecemeal implementation.

What success the articlemen did meet with was largely due to their own efforts. F.G. James has previously outlined the work of a Protestant lobby in London in the first half of the eighteenth century, funded and directed from Ireland.[33] The constraints imposed by Poynings' Law on the Irish parliament meant that London was often the best place to influence legislation proposed by, or to be sent to, the Dublin administration. Irish Catholics likewise gravitated to London in the 1690s, lobbying at the privy council and before parliament as their circumstances dictated. Individual Catholics lobbied according to their needs. The articlemen often worked together under their discrete terms of surrender, sending money and instructions to their agents. On rare but significant occasions lobbyists appeared on behalf of all of the articlemen. Their goal was to initiate, modify or suppress proposed legislation, either to ensure that the articles of surrender were implemented or at least that they were not contravened by acts of parliament. When the efforts of Irish Catholics to prevent the early penal laws of the 1690s are considered, it is fair to say that they 'met with small success'.[34] On the other hand, concessions for individuals and small groups such as the articlemen were possible and Catholics consistently engaged with the administrative machinery of the Williamite state. Intensive lobbying and occasional bribery of Irish politicians was matched by similar activity in London. Poynings' Law provided, for all kinds of interests, a second forum where bills could be altered to an individual's or group's advantage.[35] Lobbying

---

[32] *Williamite confiscation*, pp 45–55; *The Treaty of Limerick* (Dundalk, 1961). The latter is reprinted in Simms, *War and politics*. Simms' analysis of the articles of Limerick has also been supplemented by James McGuire and Wouter Troost (James McGuire, 'The Treaty of Limerick', pp 127–38; Wouter Troost, 'William III and religious tolerance' in Whelan (ed.), *The last of the great wars*, pp 39–54).

[33] F. G. James, 'The Irish lobby in the early eighteenth century' in *English Historical Review*, 81 (1966), pp 543–57. The terms 'lobbying' and 'lobby' properly have no place in a discussion of the seventeenth century as they did not acquire their modern meanings until the nineteenth century (ibid., p. 543). The contemporary terms were to 'solicit' or 'manage' the affairs of petitioners before the Irish and English administrations or individual ministers. However, for ease of reference, 'lobby' and 'lobbying' have been used throughout this book to describe such activity.

[34] Ibid., p. 545.

[35] For Poynings' law as it related to the period under review in this book, see Bergin, 'Irish legislative procedure', *passim*; C.I. McGrath, 'Government, parliament and the constitution:

in London was, however, possible only for those with the money to support agents and to bribe officials.[36]

III

Colonel John Browne used his position as one of the Jacobite negotiators at Limerick to include article 13 in the terms of surrender, an article that existed solely for the benefit of Browne and his creditors. The vast majority of these creditors were Protestant, with the money they were owed arising from transactions completed before the outbreak of the war. According to Browne, by the war's end he was owed significant sums of money by the Jacobite administration. Under the terms of article 13, every estate retained by Catholics by virtue of the articles of surrender was subject to a special levy to make up the Jacobite administration's debt to Browne. That levy was payable to Browne's creditors. Part III of this book focuses on the several attempts by the Irish government to implement article 13 of Limerick and to distribute the levy to those creditors.

While Browne was in many ways a quintessential representative of the Catholic 'new interest' in the Restoration period, his personal circumstances after 1691 mark him as a unique figure. The Jacobite administration owed large sums of money to a multitude of its supporters, yet no other Irish Catholic was able to use the articles of surrender to recoup such debts. Article 13 was financially punitive to landowning Catholics. Collection of the levy was vigorously opposed by the articlemen, creating a unique situation where they actually lobbied against the implementation of one of the articles of surrender.

Despite its impact upon the wider Catholic population, and the Irish government's repeated engagement with the issue, the implementation of article 13 of Limerick has not featured in any discussion of the Williamite settlement in Ireland. It was the only one of the articles for which the Irish parliament actively sought to legislate, and no less than ten separate measures relating to

the reinterpretation of Poynings' law, 1692–1714' in *I.H.S.*, xxxv (2006–7), pp 160–72; Kelly, *Poynings' law*, pp 48–156.

[36] The analysis of Catholic lobbying in London presented in Parts II and III of this book forms part of an emerging field of scholarship on the Irish in eighteenth-century London. See also John Bergin & Eoin Kinsella, 'Hurling matches in London (1733–1818) and New York (1781–2)' in *Archivium Hibernicum*, lxviii (2015), pp 19–67; David O'Shaughnessy (ed.), *Networks of aspiration: the London Irish of the eighteenth century* (*Eighteenth-Century Life* special issue, 39:1 (2015)); Bergin, 'Irish Catholic interest'; Ian McBride, 'Catholic politics in the penal era: Father Sylvester Lloyd and the Delvin address of 1727' in Bergin *et al* (eds), *New perspectives on the penal laws*, pp 115–47; Nolan, 'Jacobite women and the Williamite confiscation'.

the levy (and John Browne's debts) were introduced to the Irish parliament, or considered by the Irish and English privy councils, between 1692 and 1709. Two were approved by parliament as private acts.[37] These private acts also included provisions designed to regulate the sale of Browne's estate to raise enough additional funds to clear all of his debts. By 1711 Browne had paid out more than £60,000 to his creditors, most of which was raised through the sale of more than 150,000 acres, but he remained in debt at the time of his death. The process whereby Browne pursued legislation for the sale of his estate and managed the settlement of his debts, though complicated by the articles of surrender, sheds light on estate management in the late seventeenth and early eighteenth centuries. It highlights the central role of the courts in recording debts and regulating the financial system, as well as the importance of private acts to debtors who sought legislative backing for agreements negotiated with their creditors.

John Browne was among the most prominent of the articlemen, a figure well-known to the Irish government and to wider Irish society. He had the benefit of the tacit support of his Protestant creditors, an influential if self-interested group. Yet as a Catholic and as a former Jacobite, Browne was not above suspicion. On two separate occasions he was accused of masterminding Jacobite plots, both of which were entirely fabricated and politically motivated. These incidents, which also implicated other leading articlemen, illustrate the vulnerable position in which Irish Catholics found themselves as the Irish government and parliament set about securing the Protestant interest.[38]

The final chapter of this book shifts the focus away from article 13 to consider the wider impact of Browne's debts on his familial and professional networks in Connacht. The last two decades of Browne's life were dominated by the sale of his estate and attempts to discharge his debts. Browne's four youngest children were largely peripheral to the management of the family's affairs. However, the marriages of two of his three daughters and the requisite dowries placed further financial burdens on Browne, bringing him into conflict with their husbands: Edward Bermingham, Baron Athenry, and Theobald Bourke, Viscount Mayo. Browne's debt did have a notable impact on the plans of his eldest son, Peter, who was forced to abandon his training in London for a career in the law. Called home to assist with the sale of the estate, Peter Browne witnessed his substantial inheritance dwindle away during the 1690s. From 1698 he increasingly shouldered the burden of managing his father's financial affairs, while concurrently rebuilding the family's fortunes.

---

[37] For a discussion of private legislation in this era, see Bergin, 'Irish legislative procedure', i, 9–11; Kelly, *Poynings' law*, pp 75–160.
[38] C.I. McGrath, 'Securing the Protestant interest: the origins and purpose of the penal laws of 1695' in *I.H.S.*, xxx (1996–7), pp 25–46.

John Browne's nephew, Edmund Malone, acted as his legal representative in the 1690s and 1700s and played a prominent role in the management of the Browne family's business. Malone's work as London agent for a variety of families, including the Brownes of Westport, the Brownes of the Neale, and the Veseys, is particularly well documented. His correspondence offers a rare glimpse of the process whereby Catholics petitioned for personal pardons from William III, as well as the associated costs. Malone's career also provides one of the earliest examples of the eighteenth-century phenomenon of Irish Catholic lawyers acting as agents and lobbyists in London for Irish clients, of all denominations.[39] While in Dublin in 1707, Malone was one of a number of family members who were appalled by the conversion to the Church of Ireland of Francis Bermingham, later Baron Athenry and one of John Browne's grandsons. Bermingham was one of at least three of Browne's grandchildren who converted to the established church. His circumstances provide an early case study of the pressure brought to bear on the Catholic nobility and gentry – especially the heirs of the articlemen – by the imposition of penal legislation that targeted their property and gradually eroded the protections enshrined in the articles of surrender.

IV

This book presents for the first time a detailed analysis of the life of an Irish Catholic landowner in the late seventeenth and early eighteenth centuries. It seeks to understand the emergence of the Catholic 'new interest' in the reign of Charles II, and their reaction to the threat posed to the Restoration land settlement during James II's reign. By reconstructing the manner in which the articlemen negotiated their way through the Williamite settlement, what follows is intended to provide an insight into the economic, legal and political circumstances in which surviving Catholic landowners found themselves after the Jacobite surrender. In doing so, it offers a view into a world that has hitherto lain outside the historiography. In particular, it contextualises the rise and fall of John Browne, and of the 'new interest', within the conflicted politics and society of late Stuart Ireland. Browne was an unusual figure but his experience nonetheless reflects those of his co-religionists who sought to retain their property and social position after the collapse of the Jacobite regime. His life

---

[39] Bergin, 'Irish Catholic interest'; idem, 'Irish Catholics and their networks in eighteenth-century London' in O'Shaughnessy (ed.), *Networks of aspiration*, pp 66–102; idem, 'The world of Richard Lahy, an Irish law agent in eighteenth-century London' in Raymond Gillespie & Roy Foster (eds), *Irish provincial cultures in the long eighteenth century: essays for Toby Barnard* (Dublin, 2012), pp 75–92.

and career enables us to examine the remnants of Catholic landed society at the beginning of the long eighteenth century. The attempts of the articlemen to safeguard their economic future, as they first sought the implementation of the articles of surrender and later opposed their progressive dismantling by the Irish parliament, were instrumental to the survival of the Catholic nobility and gentry in eighteenth-century Ireland.

Part I

The Rise and Fall of the 'New Interest'

Plate 1: A portrait of Colonel John Browne, attributed to Godfrey Kneller (n.d.). The portrait currently hangs in the entrance hallway of Westport House. Reproduced by kind permission of Westport House.

1

'I hope all will end well with our New Interests': The rise and fall of a 'new interest' landowner, 1666–89[1]

John Browne of Westport, County Mayo, was the quintessential representative of the Catholic 'new interest'. Called to the Irish bar in 1669, he was a self-made man. As one of the greatest beneficiaries of the upheaval caused by the Restoration land settlement, between 1666 and 1685 Browne accrued an enormous estate in Galway and Mayo of more than 155,000 acres (with over 39,000 acres classed as profitable), as well as property in Counties Sligo, Roscommon, Clare and Dublin. He was an ambitious man who used family connections to great advantage. Married to a daughter of the 3rd Viscount Mayo, Browne was also linked by his siblings' marriages to several prominent families, both Catholic and Protestant, including the Dillons of Roscommon, the Malones of Westmeath, the Binghams of Mayo and the Talbots of Dublin. At least one of his nephews, George Browne, was commissioned in the regiment John raised for James II in 1689. Two other nephews were prominent lawyers: Garrett Dillon in the reign of James II, and Edmund Malone from the 1680s until the 1720s. Both were intimately acquainted with Browne's financial affairs – Dillon became a business partner with his uncle in the 1680s, while Malone proved an important lobbyist for Browne and others in Dublin and London during the 1690s and beyond.

During the Williamite war Browne established himself as one of the most important Irish Jacobites and acted as a negotiator and signatory of the articles of Limerick. He used this position to secure a controversial article, which ensured that liability for his personal debts – at least £30,000, incurred *before* the outbreak of the war and owed mostly to Irish Protestants – was not to be borne by him alone, but shared with all Catholics who retained their land under the various articles of surrender. Nonetheless, the settlement of these debts eventually stripped Browne of almost his entire estate, a process that took more than two decades and was still not complete at the time of his death.

This chapter surveys Browne's rise to prominence as a landowner and lawyer, and his attempts to establish himself as an ironmaster. As with many of his

---

[1] The quotation is taken from Thomas Sisson to John Browne, 1 May 1686 (N.L.I., Ms 40,898/5/1).

'new interest' contemporaries, Browne's training at the inns of court in London equipped him to explore opportunities for investment in land. The recovery of estates during the Restoration land settlement strained the finances of many Catholic families, allowing the 'new interest' to gain a foothold in Irish landownership through purchases and mortgages. Browne exemplifies the type. Yet by the time of James II's accession in 1685 Browne was mired deep in debt and excluded from the Catholicisation of the Irish government by Richard Talbot, earl of Tyrconnell. The 1689 Act of Repeal threatened the 'new interest' with the loss of their estates; its implementation in late 1689 and early 1690 damaged their morale at a crucial juncture for the Jacobite cause.

I

The first Browne to settle at the Neale, County Mayo, was John Browne, mapmaker to Sir Richard Bingham in the 1580s, establishing a connection between the two families that would endure for the next century.[2] Browne claimed to have been the first Englishman to settle in County Mayo, though it seems that he was related to the Brownes of Kilpatrick, County Westmeath, and of Old English descent.[3] Browne twice served as sheriff of County Mayo and in 1585 as a commissioner for the composition of Connacht, in the process gathering a personal estate in the Neale. Four years later he received a military commission from Bingham to help suppress rebellion in Mayo, an appointment that proved to be his last. Browne was killed in a small skirmish with the Burke and Joy families near Burrishoole, County Mayo, in February 1589.[4] His only son Josias married Joan Birmingham of County Kildare and served as high sheriff of County Mayo in 1622. Their eldest son, also named John, married Mary Browne, daughter of Sir Dominick Browne of Castlemagarrett, County Mayo.[5]

[2]   Sir Richard Bingham (1528–99) established the Bingham family in County Mayo during his tenure as chief commissioner of Connacht, bringing his brother George to serve with him. George served as sheriff of County Sligo, died in Dublin in 1599 and is the direct lineal ancestor of the current earls of Lucan and the barons of Castlebar, which title merged with that of Lucan in 1795 (D.I.B.).

[3]   J.H. Andrews, 'Sir Richard Bingham and the mapping of western Ireland' in P.R.I.A., 103C (2003), pp 61–95; M.J. Blake, 'A map of part of the county of Mayo in 1584' in Journal of the Galway Archaeological & Historial Society, iv (1908), pp 145–8. Browne's claim may have related to his belief that he was the first man of English descent to settle in Mayo.

[4]   Sir George Carew to Sir Thomas Heneage, 18 Mar. 1589 (J.S. Brewer and William Bullen (eds), Calendar of Carew manuscripts, 1589–1600 (London, 1869), pp 2–3); Sir William Fitzwilliam to William Cecil, 31 Mar. 1589 (Calendar of State Papers Ireland, 1588–92, p. 140).

[5]   Sir Dominick Browne (c.1585–c.1656) was a convicted murderer who bought his pardon for £5. He sat in the Irish parliament of 1634 and was knighted by Thomas Wentworth in 1635. He married Anastase Darcy, daughter of James Riveagh Darcy, thus making him granduncle to Denis Daly of Carrownekelly, justice of the common pleas during the reign of James II.

In June 1636, John Browne was granted the Scottish baronetcy of Nova Scotia but never assumed the title, probably due to the financial requirements.[6]

A modern commemorative plaque in Holy Trinity Church, Westport, gives a birth date of 1640 for John Browne's second son, also John, and the main subject of this book.[7] Nothing is known of this John Browne's early life. A child of the 1640s, he grew to maturity in an 'unpropitious time' for Irish Catholics.[8] His father was indirectly connected with the massacre of a Protestant convoy at Shrule, County Mayo, in February 1642. The convoy was under the protection of Miles, Viscount Mayo, who was unfit to accompany it following a night of heavy drinking at the Browne house. Like Viscount Mayo, John senior was a reluctant participant in the 1641 rebellion, eventually joining the Confederates and thus probably converting to Catholicism. He suffered local transplantation under the Cromwellian regime as a result, receiving c.700 profitable Irish acres in the Mayo barony of Kilmaine, where he had held 1,031 profitable acres in 1641.[9] Nevertheless, Viscount Mayo's grandson Theobald and John senior each obtained saving clauses in the Act of Settlement, with evidence suggesting that both men actually expanded their estates during the turmoil of the 1640s and 1650s.[10]

As a second son, John Browne was expected to 'toil out for his living'.[11] His chosen profession was the law, and Browne was admitted to Gray's Inn, London, on 17 April 1662.[12] Attendance for a year or two at an inn of court

---

6 G.E. Cokayne, *Complete baronetage* (5 vols, Exeter, 1900–06), ii, 419. For the baronetage of Nova Scotia see Michael Perceval-Maxwell, 'Sir William Alexander of Menstrie (1567–1640)' in *International Review of Scottish Studies*, xii (1982), pp 14–25.

7 Holy Trinity Church was built for the Church of Ireland between 1868 and 1872, on land donated by George John Browne, 3rd marquess of Sligo – a direct descendant of Col. John Browne (Caitríona Hastings, 'A history of Holy Trinity Church, Westport' in *Cathair na Mart*, 27 (2009), pp 5–27).

8 James McGuire, 'A lawyer in politics: the career of Sir Richard Nagle, c.1636–1699' in Howard Clarke & Judith Devlin (eds) *European encounters: essays in memory of Albert Lovett* (Dublin, 2003), p. 119. All references to John Browne from this point are to the main subject of this study. Namesakes will be clearly distinguished.

9 R.C. Simington, *The transplantation to Connacht, 1654–58* (Dublin, 1970), p. 218. 121 Irish acres was the equivalent of 199 statute acres, making Browne's allocation c.1,150 statute acres. Browne's estate in 1641 in County Mayo consisted of c.2,180 profitable acres (R.C. Simington (ed.), *Books of survey and distribution, ii: Co. Mayo* (Dublin, 1956), *passim*).

10 14 & 15 Chas. II, c.2, ss xxv, ccxxv. See also *Calendar of State Papers Ireland, 1660–2*, p. 366; Raymond Gillespie, 'Mayo and the rising of 1641' in *Cathair na Mart*, 5 (1985), p. 42; idem, 'Lords and commons in seventeenth-century Mayo' in Gillespie & Moran (eds), *A various country: essays in Mayo history, 1500–1900* (Westport, 1987), pp 55–7.

11 A phrase used in 1623 by Lord Clanricarde when advising Sir Henry Lynch on the education of his second son (Bernadette Cunningham, 'Clanricarde letters' in *Journal of the Galway Archaeological & Historical Society*, xlviii (1996), p. 183).

12 Joseph Foster, *The register of admissions to Gray's Inn, 1521–1889* (London, 1889), p. 293; Maynard, 'Irish membership of the English Inns of Court', p. 392.

was considered a desirable part of a young gentleman's education, and not all who entered the inns had set their sights on a career at the bar.[13] Browne did not have the luxury of such a choice, completing his studies at Gray's Inn before being called to the Irish bar on 5 February 1669.[14] He quickly established a good practice in Ireland and has been described as 'particularly prominent' in the court of chancery during the 1670s.[15] Browne probably began his career at the presidency court of Connacht, until its abolition in 1672 forced Connacht lawyers to appear more regularly at the superior courts in Dublin.[16]

The attendance of Irish Catholics at the inns of court during the 1640s and 1650s had declined dramatically.[17] Browne's admission to Gray's Inn in 1662 marked him as one of the first of a new wave of Irishmen, Catholic and Protestant, who saw opportunities in the study of the law. Profitable possibilities lay in the uncertainty surrounding the land settlement. The multiplicity of changes to land ownership in the preceding twenty years, together with the determined efforts of many dispossessed Catholics to recover their land (and the equally determined defence by incumbents), ensured that knowledge of the law became a much-prized attribute. Irish families with no previous tradition of legal education began to send their sons to the inns of court.[18] However, familiarity with the intricacies of Irish land law was not guaranteed by attendance at the inns, suggesting that the more successful newly qualified Irish lawyers first clerked for more senior colleagues.[19] Denis Daly, a member of the Connacht 'new interest' who was appointed judge of the common pleas in 1686, was clerk to Patrick Darcy before his admission to the Middle Temple.[20] The speed with

---

[13] Irishmen who wished to pursue a career as a barrister were required by the Statute of Jeofailles (1542) to spend at least eight terms at one of the four English inns of court, before they could be called to the Irish bar. See Hazel Maynard, 'The Irish legal profession and the Catholic revival, 1660–89' in James Kelly, John McCafferty and C.I. Mcgrath (eds), *People, politics and power: essays on Irish history, 1660–1850, in honour of James I. McGuire* (Dublin, 2009), pp 3, 29.

[14] *K.I.A.P.*, p. 57. Many of Browne's contemporaries were called to the Irish bar within five or even four years of their admission to the inns of court (despite a requirement that candidates should have spent five years at one of the London inns). It is unclear why Browne's call did not occur until seven years after his admission to Gray's Inn.

[15] Maynard, 'Irish membership of the English inns of court', pp 46, 270.

[16] Liam Irwin, 'The Irish presidency courts, 1569–1672' in *Irish Jurist*, n.s., xii (1977), pp 113–14; idem., 'The suppression of the Irish presidency system' in *I.H.S.*, xxii (1980–81), pp 21–32; O.J. Burke, *Anecdotes of the Connaught circuit* (Dublin, 1885) p. 55.

[17] Colum Kenny, 'The exclusion of Catholics from the legal profession in Ireland' in *I.H.S.*, xxv (1986–7), pp 349–50; Maynard, 'Irish legal profession', p. 30. The number of Catholics admitted to the inns of court between 1660 and 1699 was about the same as the number admitted between 1600 and 1641 (Maynard, 'Irish membership of the English inns of court', p. 21).

[18] Maynard, 'Irish membership of the English inns of court', pp 21–2.

[19] T.C. Barnard, 'Lawyers and the law in seventeenth-century Ireland' in *I.H.S.*, xxviii (1992–3), p. 260.

[20] S.W. Singer (ed.), *The correspondence of Henry Hyde, earl of Clarendon, and of his brother,*

which Browne established his own practice suggests that he too served as a clerk before his formal legal education.

Legal expertise was as useful for new acquisitions of land as it was for the defence of existing land titles. The Restoration afforded Catholics not only opportunities to recover ancient patrimonies, but also to build new estates. During the 1670s and, to a lesser extent, the 1680s, John Browne amassed an enormous estate in Connacht, which rivalled and may have surpassed even that of William Bourke, earl of Clanricarde, the regional grandee.[21] The number of transactions completed by Browne in the late 1660s and 1670s ran into the hundreds and comprised purchases or leases from Protestants and Catholics, including Charles Daly; Dr Robert Gorges; Stephen Rice; Walter Bourke; Sir John Thomson; Sir Robert Booth; Pierce Butler, Viscount Ikerrin; the earl of Clanricarde; Sir John Davis; Sir Richard Reynell; Sir John Temple; Michael Boyle, archbishop of Dublin; Theobald, Viscount Dillon and his son Henry.[22]

Of particular interest is the relationship between Browne and the Viscounts Mayo. It was a relationship that established Browne among the upper echelons of elite society in Connacht. If admission to Gray's Inn proved one of the decisive events in Browne's life, another was his marriage in 1669 to Maud Bourke, daughter of Theobald Bourke, 3rd Viscount Mayo, and great-great-granddaughter of the famed noblewoman and sea captain, Gráinne O'Malley. The marriage strengthened the ties between the Browne and Bourke families and, more importantly, provided Browne with the opportunity to acquire vast tracts of the Bourke estate.

Browne's future brother-in-law, Theobald Bourke, 4th Viscount Mayo, became a beneficiary of Charles II's 'grace and favour' after the Restoration, obtaining a saving clause in the act of settlement. His petition to the king in 1661 stated that he had resided in England since 1653, conforming to the Church of England. A private bill for Viscount Mayo was transmitted from Ireland to the English privy council in 1662, though opposition was raised following the council's decision to include provisos for several other nominees.[23]

Laurence Hyde, earl of Rochester (2 vols, London, 1828), i, 361. For Darcy, a well known Confederate lawyer, see his entry in the *D.I.B.*

[21] Clanricarde's estate, with extensive lands in County Clare, consisted of over 145,000 acres in 1675 (Kevin McKenny, 'The Restoration land settlement in Ireland: a statistical interpretation' in Coleman A. Dennehy (ed.), *Restoration Ireland: always settling and never settled* (Aldershot, 2008), p. 47).

[22] N.L.I., Mss 40,889/14/6–7, 12; 40,889/15/5, 9–10; 40,889/16/4–6; 40,889/18/1–6; 40,889/19/1–6; 40,889/20/1, 3; 40,889/21/5; 40,889/32/6–7; 40,889/33/11.

[23] Charles II to the Irish lords justices, 25 Feb. 1661 (*C.S.P.I., 1660–2*, p. 227); 'List of bills transmitted to England and not returned to Ireland', 21 Oct. 1662 (ibid., pp 607–8); warrant relating to Mayo's private bill, [Dec.] 1662 (ibid., p. 670); Roger Boyle, earl of Orrery to Sir James Shaen, 27 Dec. 1662 (*C.S.P.I., 1663–5 & Addenda*, p. 497); Charles II to Ormond, 30 Dec. 1662 (ibid., p. 498).

The bill was dropped and Mayo was still unrestored by mid-1664, prompting the earl of Orrery to write on his behalf to Sir Henry Bennet, the secretary of state.[24] A proviso to the same effect, ordering Mayo's immediate restoration, was included in the act of explanation.[25]

Yet the cost of pursuing his restoration to the family estates put Mayo in a precarious financial position. From 1666 he increasingly leased and released and mortgaged large parts of his estate. Beneficiaries of Viscount Mayo's straitened circumstances included the confederate lawyer Sir Roebuck Lynch and Frances Pullein, widow of Samuel, Church of Ireland archbishop of Tuam.[26] John Porter of Waterford city obtained 488 acres in a lease and release agreement, in return for £300.[27] John Browne's first known foray into land acquisition was the purchase of Shrule castle and associated lands for £300 from William, earl of Clanricarde, in November 1666.[28] The years 1666 and 1669 were pivotal in the formation of Browne's career. The completion of his legal training, his marriage to Maud and first steps into the land market signalled the emergence of a major figure in Connacht society. His marriage alliance, together with his call to the bar, created a powerful momentum that carried Browne through the next fifteen years, as he garnered an excellent reputation as a lawyer and acquired an enormous estate in Connacht.

Success at the bar probably provided Browne with the means to expand his estate. Kinturk townland, mortgaged by Viscount Mayo in September 1666, was in Browne's hands by December 1673. Kinturk was an important purchase, becoming Browne's principal residence until he established himself at Westport. In 1672 and 1673, Browne acquired a large portion of his estate, much of it directly from Viscount Mayo or the viscount's lessees and mortgagees.[29] Two important transactions with Viscount Mayo were completed in August and September 1673. The first saw Browne purchase ten castles, 100 messuages and 500 cottages, along with several thousand acres of land, for £1,060. The second was on a smaller scale, yet demonstrated the extent to which Viscount Mayo now depended on Browne for financial support.[30] The death of Theobald,

---

[24] Orrery to Sir Henry Bennet, 20 June 1664 (*C.S.P.I., 1663–5 & Addenda*, p. 409).

[25] 17 & 18 Chas. II, c. 2, s. cciv; Simington (ed.), *Books of survey and distribution*, ii: *Mayo*, pp xxxviii–xxxix; Jane Ohlmeyer, *Making Ireland English: the Irish aristocracy in the seventeenth century* (London, 2012), pp 319–20.

[26] 2 Apr. 1666 (N.L.I., Ms 40,889/8/5); 5 May 1668 (N.L.I., Ms 40,889/10/7–8).

[27] N.L.I., Mss 40,889/8/6–8; 40,893/4/9; 40,895/1/12; John Cunningham, *Conquest and land in Ireland: the transplantation to Connacht, 1649–1680* (Woodbridge, 2011), pp 130–31. This is probably the same John Porter who later claimed the benefit of the articles of Waterford.

[28] T.C.D., Kilmaine papers, Box 4, Bundle B.

[29] N.L.I., Ms 40,889/12/4.

[30] N.L.I., Ms 40,889/12/6–7. Three justices of the king's bench, including Sir Robert Booth, acted as witnesses to the first transaction.

the 4th viscount, in 1676 did not change matters. His brother and successor, Miles, proved equally happy to deal with Browne. Several lease and release agreements and mortgages were completed between the two in 1676 and 1677, with Browne advancing at least £700 as mortgagee.[31] In December 1677 Miles released almost 200 townlands to Browne for just 5s. Browne also lent considerable sums to Viscount Mayo, acknowledged by the viscount's agreement to levy a fine on several thousand acres of land and other property in December 1679, in return for which the viscount was to have an annual rent of £76 and a parcel of land.[32] Browne's knowledge of the other debts of the Viscounts Mayo also proved advantageous. John Yeadon, described as a clothier based in Boyle, County Roscommon, advanced £460 to Viscount Mayo between 1666 and 1669 as mortgagee and purchaser of various lands in the barony of Carra.[33] Browne negotiated the conveyance of Yeadon's interest in some of this land to himself in September 1678, eventually purchasing Yeadon's entire interest in Viscount Mayo's estate in October 1680 for £200.[34]

Purchases from the Viscounts Mayo probably account for Charles II's grant of more than 16,000 acres to Browne in 1677 and 1681 after his appearance before the commission for hearing the claims of transplanted persons in Connacht. Viscount Mayo was granted more than 54,000 acres in 1680; by that time most if not all of this land was in Browne's hands.[35]

Given Browne's relentless acquisition of the Bourke estate, it was perhaps inevitable that relations with one member of the Bourke family soured in 1681. Luke, son of the 3rd Viscount and his second wife Elinor (and so half-brother to Browne's wife), opposed Browne's efforts to have these letters patent passed. An impressive array of counsel appeared on both sides. The prime serjeant, John Osborne, and Peter Wybrantz represented Bourke, while the solicitor general, Sir John Temple, Mr Nugent, and Messrs Whitfield, Burne, Shapcote and Beckett all appeared for Browne, with a Mr Warburton acting as Browne's clerk.[36] A petition from Browne to Ormond defended his purchases from the

31 N.L.I., Ms 40,889/13/4–5, 8–9.
32 N.L.I., Mss 40,886/2/2; 40,889/15/11. Miles's son, Theobald, later accused Browne of defrauding Miles of the estate. By the time of the accusation, Theobald had become Browne's son-in-law. See below, pp 221–4.
33 N.L.I., Mss 40,889/9/3; 40,889/11/1–4; 40,893/2/17.
34 N.L.I., Ms 40,889/17/4–5.
35 N.L.I., Mss 40,885/3–4; 40,889/1/2; 40,889/2/1; 40,889/4/5; *The Eleventh, Twelfth, and Thirteenth, and the Fourteenth and Fifteenth reports from the Commissioners … respecting the public records of Ireland* (London, 1825), pp 243–4, 249, 267–9. For the operation of this commission, see John Cunningham, *Conquest and land in Ireland*, pp 141–9.
36 Peter Wybrantz entered Lincoln's Inn in November 1669, though he does not appear in the King's Inns admission lists. William Beckett is the only man of that surname in the King's Inns admission lists, having been called to the Irish bar in 1659. 'Mr Burne' was probably John Byrne who, along with his brother Gregory, entered Gray's Inn in 1662, just a few months after Browne's

4th and 5th viscounts against Bourke's accusations that they were 'not justly made'.[37] Luke's claims regarding Browne's purchases appear speculative at best, and he failed to produce any evidence to support his case. After almost a year of delaying tactics by Luke's counsel, the case was tried in the court of king's bench in May 1682 and the verdict declared for Browne after a short hearing.[38]

Viscount Mayo died before the trial was completed, leaving his son Theobald, born in January 1682, as his successor. Luke's mother Elinor, dowager viscountess of Mayo, brought a more successful action against Browne later that year. Purchase of the Viscount Mayo's estate brought with it the requirement to honour various entailments and annuities. The 4th viscount had granted £300 annually to his stepmother from 1666, in lieu of her jointure. Her complaint that Browne had failed to honour the charge was vindicated, and he was forced to convey lands in the barony of Carra to the dowager viscountess for the duration of her life. She was to be paid £200 rent out of the lands annually, with £1,000 to be set aside for her heirs.[39]

II

By his fortieth birthday John Browne possessed one of the largest estates in Connacht, yet the 1680s also marked the beginning of his financial troubles. An early indication was his mortgage of extensive lands to Sir Robert Booth and Henry Whitfield in 1680, and to Stephen Rice in 1683 and 1684. Browne continued to expand his estate throughout James II's reign, possibly with the assistance of the £7,200 he borrowed from Rice (£6,000 on mortgage).[40] This money was, however, more likely to have been intended for his ironworks. By the middle of the 1680s, Browne had operational ironworks on his estate at perhaps six different locations; by 1692 his debts totalled approximately

admission. John was called to the Irish bar on 20 June 1666, while Gregory does not appear in the King's Inns admission lists. 'Mr Whitfield' was either Henry or his son Ralph: Ralph would appear more likely, having been admitted to Gray's Inn in 1672. Henry was admitted to Gray's Inn in 1632, though he was not called to the Irish bar until 1661. There is, however, no record of Ralph Whitfield being called to the bar. Three possibilities offer themselves for 'Mr Nugent': Thomas Nugent, future Baron Riverston (admitted to the Inner Temple in 1669, called to the Irish bar November 1674); John Nugent (admitted to Gray's Inn in 1668, called to the Irish bar November 1672) and Francis Nugent (called to the Irish bar in February 1668). A Richard Warburton entered the Middle Temple in May 1683. Shapcote was probably Francis Shapcote, later a creditor to Browne (See Maynard, 'Irish membership of the English inns of court', appendix, for admission dates to the inns of court; *K.I.A.P.*, pp 29, 69, 367–8, 511, 522).

37 Petition of Col. Browne to Ormond, [1681] (N.L.I., Ms 40,896/5/1).
38 N.L.I., Mss 40,896/5/2–23; 40,896/6/1–20.
39 N.L.I., Ms 40,896/7/1–8.
40 N.L.I., Mss 40,885/6; 40,889/21/5; 40,889/22/4, 7–10; 40,897/1/17–20; 40,897/2/7–8; 40,898/1/2, 11–14; 40,898/2/1, 6–7, 12.

£30,000. Though the exact cause of the debt is difficult to gauge, the most plausible explanation lies in the establishment and operation of Browne's ironworks. Ironworks were an expensive enterprise in Ireland during the seventeenth century and few returned substantial profits for investors. There were several prerequisites for success: large amounts of readily available raw materials (especially wood for charcoal), easy access to water supplies, vibrant local markets and 'capital in surprising quantities'.[41] An initial capital investment of between £2,000 and £3,000 was usually necessary to establish a viable ironworks in Ireland. Sir Francis Brewster claimed to have laid out over £30,000 (over an unspecified period) to first set up and then operate ironworks in Kerry before their destruction during the Williamite war.[42] Sir William Petty, operating ironworks near Kenmare, County Kerry in the 1670s, calculated that four years of manufacturing had cost him £10,683, including start-up capital, for a yield of just £11,537.[43] Elsewhere, an English co-operative venture at Enniscorthy, County Wexford, required even greater levels of investment to establish a profitable business. Between 1657 and 1668, some £40,000 was poured into what was actually a successful enterprise. The start-up costs at Enniscorthy were admittedly increased by the investors' purchase of land from Cromwellian grantees in the late 1650s for £8,500, but other costs such as the construction of furnaces and the hiring of specialist workers were consistent with Petty's ironworks and contemporary English enterprises.[44]

Beyond capitalisation, the greatest cost in running an ironworks was the production, including wages, of bar iron – a cost Petty estimated at £13 a ton, including his initial capital, while the ironworks at Enniscorthy had production costs of approximately £10 a ton (excluding capital). Prices obtained for a ton of iron during the 1670s varied from £14 to £15. Profit levels were dependent on frugal production costs. Price was, of course, determined both by demand for and quality of the produce. Demand in the Irish market for indigenous iron surged briefly following the imposition of duties totalling £90 per ton on imported iron in 1664. These duties were relaxed in 1665, and so the success of

41 T.C. Barnard, 'An Anglo-Irish industrial enterprise: iron-making at Enniscorthy, County Wexford, 1657–92' in *P.R.I.A.*, 85C (1985), p. 101. For the establishment and maintenance of ironworks in early modern Ireland, see Barnard, 'Anglo-Irish industrial enterprise'; idem, 'Sir William Petty as Kerry ironmaster' in *P.R.I.A.*, 82C (1982), pp 1–32; J.H. Andrews, 'A note on the later history of the Irish charcoal iron industry' in *J.R.S.A.I.*, lxxxvi (1956), pp 217–19; idem, 'Notes on the historical geography of the Irish iron industry' in *Irish Geography*, iii (1956), pp 139–49; H.F. Kearney, 'Richard Boyle, ironmaster: a footnote to Irish economic history' in *J.R.S.A.I.*, lxxxiii (1953), pp 155–62.
42 *C.S.P.D., 1693*, pp 221–2.
43 Barnard, 'Sir William Petty as Kerry ironmaster', p. 11.
44 Barnard, 'Anglo-Irish industrial enterprise', *passim*.

an iron-making enterprise was far from guaranteed.[45] Of the many challenges facing Irish ironmasters, perhaps the greatest was acquiring high quality iron ore, not generally found in Ireland. Ore was usually imported from the Forest of Dean in Gloucestershire, adding to the costs. For works located in the east and southeast of the country, the acquisition of ore was expensive yet feasible. Petty, however, found to his cost that merchants were generally unwilling to ship ore as far as the west coast, where trade routes to England were not as well established.

Though an account book and other incidental records of expenditure relating to Browne's ironworks survive, they are largely deficient for the years prior to 1692. Fragmentary records of costs and production for the years 1686, 1687 and 1688 are extant, but not comprehensive enough to allow an estimate of the costs of production or of the volume of sales. There are no accounts for the duration of the Williamite war.[46] However, the scale of Browne's borrowings in the late 1670s and early 1680s indicate that a major enterprise was undertaken at this time. The construction of Westport House may have been a contributory factor, though it seems more likely that most of Browne's borrowing, in excess of £15,000, was intended to capitalise several new ironworks.[47] In 1684 Dominick Browne, John's brother, reached an agreement over lands and woods in the baronies of Costello and Gallen with Theobald, Viscount Dillon, and his son Henry. The land was earmarked for the establishment of ironworks, and Dominick immediately assigned his interest to John. The ironworks established here, Gortnagare, were operational by March 1687, when Benjamin Parker was hired as Browne's chief hammer-man and overseer of the works at Gortnagare and Westport.[48] Though agreement for the operation of Gortnagare ironworks specified the right to fell local timber and cord wood for fuel supplies, Browne also contracted with Wicklow colliers for delivery of 500 loads of charcoal annually from 1684.[49] The presence of 'great woods' in counties Mayo and Sligo were probably an incentive to the establishment of Browne's ironworks.[50] However, coppicing of woodlands, a well-established practice at English ironworks and essential for preservation of nearby fuel supplies, had not been adopted in Ireland.[51] A swift exhaustion of

---

[45] Ibid., pp 126–7.

[46] N.L.I., Ms 40,915/3.

[47] Browne's borrowing comprised a mixture of mortgages and loans on the Dublin statute staple, and at least one loan from Sir Abel Ram of £4,100. For Browne's borrowings on the statute staple, see Jane Ohlmeyer & Éamonn Ó Ciardha (eds), *The Irish statute staple books, 1596–1687* (Dublin, 1999), pp 182–3. For his borrowing from Ram, see N.L.I., Ms 40,900/3/19.

[48] N.L.I., Mss 40,897/2/7–8; 40,898/1/1; 40,898/4/16.

[49] N.L.I., Ms 40,897/1/3.

[50] Gerard Boate, *Ireland's natural history* (London, 1652), p. 123.

[51] Andrews, 'Notes on the historical geography of the Irish iron industry', p. 141.

readily accessible fuel supplies inevitably followed, bringing with it escalating production costs due to the necessity of transporting fuel over greater distances, or to outsource supply to independent colliers. A well-managed ironworks would use between five and six loads of charcoal to produce one ton of bar iron, suggesting that Browne's annual production levels may have exceeded 100 tons by 1684. Assuming a profit margin of between £1 and £3 per ton, Browne's ironworks were unlikely to have significantly augmented his income.

Sir William Petty operated ironworks on the west coast of Ireland and faced similar challenges to Browne, allowing for some rough comparisons. Shipment of Petty's iron from Kenmare to Limerick by sea cost 15s. per ton in 1672, but his ironworks failed because of the poor quality of its iron and Petty's inability to establish a foothold in the English market.[52] Browne had greater success. The cost of shipping a ton of iron from Westport to Drogheda, a much longer journey, was negotiated at 20s. per ton in 1683, while the Stantons of Birmingham proved reliable importers of Browne's iron from at least the mid-1680s. Even so, the Stantons were not slow to complain of the occasional poor quality of these imports. Shipments to Drogheda by the Wicklow shipmaster James Murphy were probably intended for the local market, while other vessels were chartered for shipments to Dublin, Bristol and Birmingham. Thomas Sisson, Dublin-based scrivener (and one of Browne's creditors) negotiated rates with Dublin shipmasters on Browne's behalf.[53]

Much of Browne's iron was probably bound for England. Irish exports in general were at a low ebb in 1685, but rebounded in 1686 and 1687. Increased exports were, however, a harbinger of low rent collection. The high rate of exports was fuelled by an abundance of commodities in the market, which drove prices down. Cattle, for example, sold cheaply through 1687 and 1688. The income levels of leaseholders dropped, putting pressure on their ability to pay their rent. The situation was exacerbated by an increase in the Irish population, driving rental rates higher.[54] Sisson, who leased Browne's lands at Darndale, County Dublin, described matters in May 1686:

Business and trade is extreme dull; merchants failing; the price of most commodities extreme low; a cow for a pound or little more at our fairs hereabouts; wool at about six and seven; leather as low as when you were here; corn goods, wheat at eight and nine and people extreme timorous to part with money and most wishing they had it in, to remove their families, many people designing for England, and elsewhere, and

[52] Barnard, 'Sir William Petty as Kerry ironmaster', *passim.*
[53] N.L.I., Ms 40,883/36.
[54] Louis Cullen, 'Economic trends, 1660–91' in T.W. Moody, F.X. Martin & F.J. Byrne (eds), *A new history of Ireland*, iii, *early modern Ireland, 1534–1691* (Oxford, 1976), pp 403–6.

purchases are lessened apace; one may buy for ten [years' purchase] or under. Pray God send us peace and quiet.[55]

Sisson later wrote to complain of the difficulty of collecting rents, noting that his tenants

have the lands at so great a [rental] rate that if they find any hardship by distresses, they will immediately quit it, and the land will be waste … I need not tell you how difficult it is for tenants to make money and of the general fall of rents everywhere. We have several farms here lie waste, so many English being gone for England and more going daily.[56]

Sisson was incensed when he learned that Browne was considering selling the land at Darndale in 1687.[57] The sale does not seem to have gone through, for Sisson wrote in October confirming his fears about unreliable tenants. Those at Darndale had

left not so much as the key under the door and not the value of a penny upon the lands but privately sold all and gone for England. To say the truth the people were undone by the farm, for after they had laid out above six score pounds in bringing it into order, and building a little house, it would not answer so great a rent, especially in these times.[58]

Rents were high but reliable tenants were scarce. The uncertainty and unease introduced by James II's policy in Ireland, and well-founded fears among Irish Protestants for the future of the Restoration land settlement, prompted many to depart for the perceived safety of England. Lacking consistent income, Browne was struggling. The stagnant local economy combined with poor rental incomes to leave him short of the money necessary to meet mortgage repayments and other debts. Many of his correspondents between 1685 and 1688 wrote to chase money, or to advise and sympathise with him on his increasing predicament.[59] Writing from Dublin, Sisson urged Browne to

bestow a few days here for you will find an inconveniency in your long absence. Some people seem to be dissatisfied at it. Whatever you do send up cash to pay interest that there be no complaint for want of that.[60]

---

[55] Sisson to Col. Browne, 18 May 1686; see also same to same, 2 Oct. 1686 (N.L.I., Ms 40,898/5/2–3).

[56] Sisson to Col. Browne, 30 Apr. 1687 (N.L.I., Ms 40,898/5/4). The 'general fall of rents' mentioned by Sisson refers to the difficulty of collecting rents, not the rate at which the lands were set.

[57] Sisson to Ignatius Browne; same to Col. Browne, 30 Apr. 1687 (N.L.I., Ms 40,898/5/4–5).

[58] Sisson to Col. Browne, 27 Oct. 1687 (N.L.I., Ms 40,898/5/7).

[59] For the pursuit of debts, see N.L.I., Ms 40,897/7/1, 3, 10–11.

[60] Sisson to Col. Browne, 18 May 1686 (N.L.I., Ms 40,898/5/2).

Browne, however, seems to have spent most of his time in Mayo, avoiding Dublin for fear of suffering imprisonment for debt or distraint. His son-in-law, Edward Bermingham, Lord Athenry, implored him to keep his spirits high: 'Let me beg of you that you will take no crosses to heart that may prejudice your health, you are not the first that has been indebted.' Athenry urged creativity in generating income. If any of Browne's agents went to France they were to bring back wine: 'French wine is now, at Dublin, sold for eleven pound a hogshead.'[61] In an attempt to invigorate his ironworks and boost profits, Browne imported several thousand animal hides between 1685 and 1688 for maintaining bellows and to provide shoes for his workmen.[62]

Increasing pressures of debt did not prevent Browne from building a house befitting his status as County Mayo's greatest landowner. The construction of Westport House began in the early 1680s, though the project probably only provided brief distraction from the attentions of his creditors.[63] In July 1686, Garrett Dillon leased all of his lands to Browne as security for bonds the two men had entered into with George Kennedy. Between November 1686 and March 1688, Browne and Dillon paid out £3,000 to various creditors. A list of Browne's creditors, compiled in 1688, suggests that by the beginning of 1689 he still owed somewhere between £19,000 and £23,000.[64] Matters were brought to a head in November 1688 (the same month that William of Orange invaded England), when fifteen creditors agreed to Browne's proposal to have the rents from his estate and the profits of his ironworks assigned to a collector, who would oversee their repayment. Under the agreement, the Stantons of Birmingham agreed to pay Browne £13 for each ton of bar iron and £5.5s for each ton of sow iron they received, which would then be distributed among Browne's creditors. The agreement also listed his assets, which included two furnaces, two forges and eight fineries for the production of iron.[65] Of the lands that Browne acquired between 1668 and 1688, only Burrishoole appears to have already had operational ironworks and the cost of fitting out the rest of his premises must be viewed as the primary cause of Browne's debt.[66] Given time, it is possible that these ironworks could have proved as profitable for him as that at Enniscorthy. Time would not, however, prove to be on his side.

---

61 Lord Athenry to Col. Browne, 3 Dec. 1687 (N.L.I., Ms 40,898/5/10).
62 N.L.I., Mss 40,897/1/1–2; 40,897/6/17; 40,898/4/14–16.
63 Ulick Burke to Col. Browne, 18 Jan. 1686 (N.L.I., Ms 40,897/7/10). Browne also kept a house in St Michael's Lane, Dublin.
64 Schedule of Col. Browne's debts, [1688 & 1692] (N.L.I., Ms 40,898/2/9). The actual sum owed in 1688 is difficult to calculate. Several figures have dates beside them denoting the year the debt was first incurred. Some are dated again as 1692. Money owed to Sir Stephen Rice, which was at least £6,000, is not included in the schedule.
65 N.L.I., Ms 40,898/2/11.
66 George Browne to John Browne, senior, 21 Mar. 1666 (H.M.C., *Ormonde Mss*, n.s., iii, 211–12).

III

Untangling the web surrounding Browne's debts is key to understanding his role in the surrender negotiations at Limerick in October 1691, and the resulting article 13, which spread liability for Browne's personal debts among all Catholic landowners in Ireland. Fifty-eight judgments for debt were made against Browne in the courts of chancery, king's bench and common pleas between 1682 and 1695, revealing debts totalling £33,401.[67] Not all the judgments were against Browne alone. Garrett Dillon, Edmund Malone, George Kennedy, Garrett Moore, Valentine Browne (either John Browne's second son or his uncle) and John Bingham are variously listed as bonded with Browne on some judgments. However, the personal judgments against Browne totalled £26,201, £25,101 of which was recorded before the end of 1692. Of the remaining £7,200, he was bound for at least £2,500, and possibly more.[68] Judgments in court were not necessarily an indication that creditors were beginning the process of distraining or dispossessing debtors. Their primary function was to provide undisputed evidence of money owed, allowing the plaintiffs a healthy degree of security. In England, suits for debt accounted for more than 80% of the business of common pleas and king's bench by the 1640s. The trend in Ireland is not as easy to quantify, but the Irish courts probably played a similar role in the 'enforcement of unfulfilled obligations within the credit world'.[69] Suits for distraint were quite common, though they often fell foul of legal complexities.[70] The principle of equity of redemption meant that dispossessions for mortgage debt were rare, with creditors in England finding it difficult to foreclose on defaulted mortgages and assume ownership of the land.[71] The pattern in Ireland is likely to have been the same. Mortgagees often found it preferable to allow interest to accrue, occasionally permitting mortgagors to add the accrued interest to the principal, if significantly in arrears. Mortgagors in Ireland were in a substantially more difficult position than those in England, where the maximum rate of interest had been capped at 6% in 1651, while the

---

[67] N.L.I., Ms 40,900/3/19. It is tempting to attribute the increase in debts from c.£30,000 in 1692 to more than £33,000 in 1695 to the application of a standard rate of interest of 10% over three years. However, judgments entered against Browne up to the end of 1692 totalled £32,301. The suspicion must be that Browne's debts, including interest owed, were closer to £35,000 by 1695.

[68] These figures tally with the debt said to have been owed by Col. Browne to Protestant creditors at the end of the Williamite war. See below, pp 60, 150–1.

[69] Craig Muldrew, 'Credit and the courts: debt litigation in a seventeenth-century urban community' in *Economic History Review*, n.s., xlvi (1993), p. 24.

[70] Gillespie, 'Lords and commons', pp 63–4.

[71] R.C. Allen, 'The price of freehold land and the interest rate in the seventeenth and eighteenth centuries' in *Economic History Review*, n.s., xli (1988), pp 34–5.

market rate fell as low as 4% in the mid 1680s.[72] A standard rate of 10% in Ireland was legislated for in 1634, which remained in place for the next seventy years.[73]

Arrears of interest made up a substantial portion of Browne's debt, and his accounts clearly illustrate the danger of failure to keep up with interest payments.[74] Servicing the mortgage he had agreed with Sir Stephen Rice in 1684 necessitated £600 annually merely to meet the interest repayments. By Trinity term of 1686 the arrears of interest already stood at £900.[75] Though Browne's estate was valued at £4,000 per annum in 1688, returns of between £2,500 and £3,500 per annum were more realistic in the late 1680s and 1690s.[76] Interest payments to Rice alone accounted for approximately 16%–18% of Browne's rental income. By assigning all of his rental and ironworks income to a receiver, the agreement that Browne negotiated with his creditors in November 1688 staved off the threat of the loss of his estate to his mortgagees. Rice, the principal mortgagee, was named as the first recipient of payments made by the receiver.

The radical change in the political landscape of the three kingdoms brought about by the 'Glorious Revolution' of November 1688 and the ensuing war in Ireland ensured that Browne's agreement with his creditors was never implemented. From October 1691 the articles of Limerick protected all of Browne's creditors, and the threat of the loss of his estate to his mortgagees (specifically Stephen Rice) had receded. Rice's debt was now, in fact, more secure than it ever had been, given the prospect of an act of parliament to implement article 13 of Limerick. Rice nonetheless assumed control of some of Browne's land in Counties Mayo and Galway in March 1692, which he then leased to his agent Richard Thompson for twenty-one years with detailed instructions as

---

[72] John Habakkuk, 'The rise and fall of English landed families, 1600–1800: II' in *Transactions of the Royal Historical Society*, 5th series, xxx (1980), pp 206–7; Ohlmeyer and Ó Ciardha (eds), *Irish statute staple*, p. 16.

[73] 10 Charles I, c. 22; Michael MacCarthy-Morrogh, 'Credit and remittance: money problems in early seventeenth-century Munster' in *Irish Economic and Social History*, xiv (1987), p. 7. There were failed attempts in 1697 and 1698 to pass a law reducing the legal rate of interest before an act of 1704 (2 Anne, c.16) reduced it from 10% to 8%. Lower rates could be obtained in private agreements, though Browne does not seem to have been able to do so (H.M.C., *Egmont Mss*, ii, 113).

[74] See, for example, Browne's accounts with Thomas Sisson and a Mr Shuckberg, [May 1692] (N.L.I., Ms 40,900/4/5).

[75] By the terms of the 1684 mortgage, Browne was to make two interest payments of £300 to Rice annually. Richard Thompson, who probably served as agent or collector for Sir Stephen Rice, obtained two judgments against Browne in the exchequer court in Trinity term, for £600 and £300 respectively (N.L.I., Ms 40,900/3/19).

[76] Edmund Malone to Agmondisham Vesey, 14 Oct. 1697 (N.A.I., Sarsfield-Vesey papers); N.L.I., Ms 40,915/1; Gillespie, 'Lords and commons', pp 63–4.

to how the profits of the land should be distributed.[77] Rice's appearance as lessor in this case would ordinarily imply that he was the outright owner of the land in question. However, Browne's consent was explicitly noted in the lease, suggesting Rice preferred a form of joint proprietorship, rather than full possession. Though the articles of Limerick complicated the case, proceedings on Browne's debt to Rice indicate that mortgages were of a more sophisticated nature than has previously been suggested – in this case, default on mortgage payments appears to have allowed Rice a measure of control over the income of the mortgaged lands.[78]

IV

The beginning of Browne's financial problems clearly predated the accession of James II in February 1685, which was followed by a time of generally rising fortunes for Irish Catholics as Tyrconnell led the Catholicisation of the Irish administration and army – first as he undermined the lord lieutenancy of Henry Hyde, earl of Clarendon, and then as lord deputy from January 1687. There are fleeting references in Browne's correspondence to the great changes taking place. Sisson relayed information regarding the elevation of Thomas Nugent, Denis Daly and Stephen Rice (Browne's creditor), all Catholics, to the judicial bench in 1686, while Lord Athenry reported in January 1688 that 'Secretary [Thomas] Sheridan and his family are of a sudden gone for England. They speak variously of him; time will tell'. Two weeks later Athenry confirmed that 'Mr Sheridan is all out of the king's favours and forbid his presence'. The pace of change in the Irish administration unnerved Sisson, who wrote in May 1686: 'It's said there is like to be another reform on the Bench ere long. I hope all will end with our New Interests or else I am sure is destroyed'.[79] As a Catholic, a well-regarded lawyer and one of the most influential men in Connacht, Browne was an obvious candidate to feature in Tyrconnell's transformation of the government of Ireland. The only indication, however, that Browne was ever considered

---

[77] See below, pp 153–4.

[78] MacCarthy-Morrogh, 'Credit and remittance'. Legislation to govern several aspects of mortgage procedure was enacted by the Irish parliament in 1697, while other measures relating to personal debt were considered and sanctioned as parliament sought to compensate for the absence of an effective legislative programme between 1666 and 1695. See Bergin, 'Irish legislative procedure', ii, 90–91, 143, 279–81.

[79] Sisson to Col. Browne, 1 & 18 May 1686; Lord Athenry to Col. Browne, 27 Jan., 11 Feb. 1688 (N.L.I., Ms 40,898/5/1, 2, 12, 14). Thomas Sheridan served as Tyrconnell's secretary from 1686 to January 1688. The relationship between the two men was strained from the beginning, and Tyrconnell had him dismissed on charges of corruption. See John Miller, 'The earl of Tyrconnel and James II's Irish policy' in *Historical Journal*, xx (1977), pp 803–23.

for public office came from Clarendon, in December 1686. Informing Robert Spencer, earl of Sunderland, that one of the justices of the common pleas was dying, Clarendon offered the names of possible replacements:

> I shall take the liberty to inform your lordship of those who are the most considerablest lawyers at the bar, and the fittest to be judges. There are Sir Richard Ryves, Mr [Henry] Echlin and Sir John Meade; these are Protestants. The two first are the king's serjeants; the third is in so good practice, that I believe he will have no mind to come upon the bench. There are likewise Mr Garret Dillon, Mr [Richard] Nagle and Mr [John] Browne; these three are Roman Catholics: Mr Nagle, I believe, has no mind to be a judge, nor I believe, will Mr Dillon, he being in very great practice: he is a very honest gentleman, and it is not fit for me to omit the best men. Mr Browne has a very good reputation, though he be not in so much practice as some of the rest.[80]

If Clarendon's comments on Browne's practice are accurate, it seems likely that the management of his ironworks was then occupying the majority of his time. Clarendon misread the intentions of Dillon and Nagle, who soon after accepted the positions of prime serjeant and attorney general respectively. Peter Martin, a Galway Catholic, filled the vacancy created by Gorges' death.[81] Clarendon's recommendations in this matter were, in any case, useless. His imminent dismissal from the post of lord lieutenant was widely known and Tyrconnell was the arbiter of preferment for Catholics in Ireland. Browne's renown as a lawyer certainly merited serious consideration for a judgeship or another position in the civil administration, while his brother Dominick was married to Barbara Talbot, one of Tyrconnell's nieces. Connacht natives were already well represented in Tyrconnell's administration, which may have militated against Browne's advancement. Or it may be that, as one of the most considerable 'new interest' landowners, he was an unacceptable choice to Tyrconnell. Yet neither of these considerations prevented the advancement of Peter Martin or Denis Daly. The sheer size of Browne's estate, however, possibly dissuaded Tyrconnell – intent as he was on undoing the Restoration land settlement – from bringing so substantial a 'new interest' figure into his circle of advisers.

Even had he been drawn into that circle, Browne could have done nothing to prevent the repeal of the Restoration land settlement by the Irish parliament, summoned by James II in 1689. Tyrconnell engineered Clarendon's recall in late 1686 and was appointed in his place, but with the lesser title of lord deputy. He persuaded James II against issuing a proclamation to preserve the integrity

---

80 Henry Hyde, earl of Clarendon, to Robert Spencer, earl of Sunderland, 23 Dec. 1686 (S.W. Singer (ed.), *The correspondence of Henry Hyde, earl of Clarendon* (2 vols, London, 1828) ii, 121–2). The dying judge was Samuel Gorges.
81 Warrant to Tyrconnell, 9 Mar. 1687 (C.S.P.D., 1686–7, p. 385); F.E. Ball, *The Judges in Ireland, 1121–1921* (2 vols, New York, 1927), i, 304–10, 364.

of the Restoration land settlement and followed this a year later by securing permission to propose a legislative alteration of that settlement. The Catholic 'new interest' were now faced with a paradoxical problem. A Catholic king and Catholic viceroy meant that there was no bulwark against revocation, partial or otherwise, of the land settlement that provided the legal foundation for the ownership of their land. The rear-guard action that the new interest had fought, in an attempt to preserve the land settlement, relied upon a viceroy who supported their position. Faced with no alternative, it would appear that the 'new interest' changed tack and negotiated with Tyrconnell to mitigate the effect of his proposals. Tyrconnell sent two bills relating to the land settlement to James II in March 1688; the legislation he favoured allowed the 'new interest' to retain half of their estates, with remuneration for any improvements made on land otherwise repossessed by the crown.[82]

William of Orange's invasion of England in November 1688 and James II's decision to flee to France before arriving in Ireland in March 1689 changed everything. The decision of the deposed monarch to summon an Irish parliament when war was inevitable has been roundly criticised, both by contemporaries and modern scholars.[83] Such criticisms ignore the exigencies that forced James's hand, primarily his lack of money. The later enactment of the penal laws during the 1690s has been linked to the decision of the 1689 Irish parliament to pass the controversial acts of repeal and attainder, with ultimate responsibility for the acts assigned to James II.[84] This lays an undue portion of blame at James II's feet and ignores the fact that two bills for repealing the land settlement were introduced to the Irish parliament in May 1689.[85] The compromise bill of repeal favoured by Tyrconnell, drafted in consultation with the 'new interest'

---

[82] For a detailed analysis of the Catholic 'new interest' during the reign of James II, see Eoin Kinsella, '"Dividing the bear's skin before she is taken": Irish Catholics and land in the late Stuart monarchy, 1683–91' in Dennehy (ed.), *Restoration Ireland*, pp 161–75. For James II's reign in Ireland, the standard and as yet unsurpassed account is J.G. Simms, *Jacobite Ireland, 1685–91* (London, 1969, repr. 2000). See also Miller, 'Tyrconnel and James II's Irish policy'; James McGuire, 'James II and Ireland, 1685–1690' in W.A. Maguire (ed.), *Kings in conflict: the revolutionary war in Ireland and its aftermath, 1689–1750* (Belfast, 1990), pp 45–57; Hayton, *Ruling Ireland*, pp 8–34 (a revised version of idem, 'The Williamite revolution in Ireland, 1688–1691' in J.I. Israel (ed.), *The Anglo-Dutch moment: essays on the Glorious Revolution and its world impact* (Cambridge, 1991), pp 185–213).

[83] For contemporary criticism, see Charles O'Kelly, *Macariae excidium; or, the destruction of Cyprus*, ed. J.C. O'Callaghan (Dublin, 1853) pp 34–6; [Nicholas Plunkett], *A Jacobite narrative of the war in Ireland, 1688–91*, ed. J.T. Gilbert (Dublin, 1892, repr. 1971), pp 69–70.

[84] John Morrill, 'The causes of the Popery laws: paradoxes and inevitabilities' in John Bergin, Eoin Magennis, Lesa Ní Mhunghaile & Patrick Walsh (eds), *New perspectives on the penal laws* (*E.C.I.* special issue no. 1, Dublin, 2010), pp 72–3.

[85] Little is known of the extent to which James was either inclined or able to manage the introduction of bills to parliament. See Bergin and Lyall (eds), *The acts of James II's Irish parliament*, introduction; Hayton, *Ruling Ireland*, pp 20–1.

between August 1687 (when Tyrconnell received permission to repeal the settlement) and March 1688, was rejected by the Irish house of commons in favour of a much more radical version. As passed by the Irish parliament, over the fervent objections of James II, the 'new interest', and the few Protestants present in both houses, the act of repeal restored the Catholic landowners who had been dispossessed as a result of the Confederate wars of the 1640s *in toto*. The 'new interest' were to be compensated with confiscated Protestant lands.[86] By threatening to reject a money bill unless this radical version of the repeal passed all stages in parliament, the majority in the 1689 house of commons had, in fact, pre-empted the tactic famously used by its Protestant successor in 1692. If James II erred in calling parliament, it was by not ensuring beforehand that consideration of the land issue was postponed until after his intended restoration to the throne. But his pressing need for money to finance the coming war left him at the mercy of parliament, and the majority of MPs expected the land settlement to be altered.

Given the size of his estate, John Browne had the means and influence to secure a seat in parliament, yet he was not among the MPs elected. He had in fact travelled to England early in 1689, thereby missing the elections and the opening of parliament on 7 May.[87] Ostensibly in England to manage his commercial interests, Browne's decision to leave Ireland with war imminent was reckless and costly.[88] It not only allowed the Jacobite authorities to confiscate his goods and stocks of iron on the grounds that the trip was unlicensed, but also ensured that Browne's voice would not be heard in parliamentary debates on the repeal of the Restoration land settlement. A telling indication of Browne's poor standing with the Jacobite administration in mid-1689 was his omission from the list of collectors appointed by the 'Act of supply for his majesty for the support of his army'. The act levied a land tax on each county, to be raised every month for thirteen months. County Mayo was to contribute £518.11s.5d. monthly. Seventeen men were appointed as collectors in Mayo, six of whom were kinsmen or close acquaintances of Browne: Garrett Moore; George Browne (either John Browne's brother or nephew); Henry Dillon; Colonel Walter Bourke; John Bermingham; and Michael Cormick. In every other county most of the leading men, including peers, were appointed.[89]

---

[86] The forfeiture of Protestant estates was achieved through the enactment of the controversial act of attainder. See Bergin and Lyall (eds), *The acts of James II's Irish parliament*, pp xlii–l, 88–167; Simms, *Jacobite Ireland*, pp 74–94; idem, 'The Jacobite parliament of 1689' (Dundalk, 1966, repr. in idem, *War and politics*, pp 65–90); Thomas Davis, *The Patriot Parliament of 1689*, ed. C. Gavan Duffy (2nd ed., London, 1893).

[87] Browne was in Bristol in April (N.L.I., Ms 40,899/1/13; *A true account of the whole proceedings of the parliament in Ireland*, p. 19 [recte, p. 13]).

[88] See below, pp 147–51.

[89] 5 James II, c. 2 (Bergin & Lyall (eds), *The acts of James II's Irish parliament*, p. 16). Col. John

35

Perhaps Browne anticipated that his election to parliament would be blocked by supporters of the repeal of the land settlement. Garrett Dillon, James II's prime serjeant and Browne's nephew and business partner, failed to be elected as a burgess of Dublin City 'because he had purchased a considerable estate under the Act of Settlement, and they feared lest this might engage him to defend it'.[90] Dillon managed to bypass this opposition by securing election in the borough of Mullingar, while other Connacht-based members of the 'new interest' sat in parliament and opposed the act of repeal.[91] Browne would certainly have been among the opposition's ranks had he been present.

Browne was due to suffer more than most by the act of repeal. He petitioned against the loss of his estate in the house of commons on 1 June; it was one of the few petitions seeking a proviso in the act to receive a favourable ruling. Indeed, Browne was one of only two men who was not a peer or member of either house of parliament to secure a proviso exempting all or part their estates.[92] It was, however, a limited victory. In an uncanny foreshadowing of article 13 of the articles of Limerick, it began: 'Provided always, that John Browne, esq., and his heirs and assigns, shall in trust for his creditors ...'. The proviso was limited to Browne's ironworks, 'which are of public advantage to your majesty'. Browne was to retain ownership of the ironworks and any associated buildings and improvements he had made on the adjoining land, which were for the specific use of the ironworks and his workmen. The commissioners appointed to put the act into effect were to survey the lands claimed by Browne under the proviso, to ascertain their 'quantity and rates ... to order and appoint such rents to be paid yearly to the said ancient proprietors'.[93]

The 'new interest' organised stiff resistance to this more radical version of the repeal. A lengthy petition presented to the house of lords outlined their legal arguments. It also issued a stark warning:

Browne is mistakenly listed as a commissioner in an abstract of this act made by Walter Harris (N.L.I., Ms 10, f. 166). D'Alton cites Harris as his source when naming Browne as a commissioner (John D'Alton, *Illustrations, historical and genealogical of King James's Irish army list (1689)* (Dublin, 1855; reprinted, Limerick, 1997), p. 37). As a result, Browne has occasionally been named as one of the commissioners for Mayo in modern accounts.

90 King, *State of the Protestants*, p. 171.
91 Kinsella, 'Dividing the bear's skin', pp 174–5; Sheila Mulloy, 'The transfer of power: Galway 1642–1702' in Gerard Moran (ed.), *Galway: history and society* (Dublin, 1996), p. 224; eadem, 'Galway in the Jacobite war' in *Journal of the Galway Archaeological and Historical Society*, xl (1985–6), p. 4.
92 The other was Martin Supple (5 James II, c. 4, ss 52–3 (Bergin & Lyall (eds), *The acts of James II's Irish parliament*, pp 46–7)). For a discussion of the enactment of the act of repeal, see ibid., pp l–liv.
93 5 James II, c. 4, s. 51 (Bergin & Lyall (eds), *The acts of James II's Irish parliament*, pp 45–6).

It's said, that this [bill] will unite your Majesty's subjects in this kingdom: That is too gross to pass. Since the first mention hereof, hath it not made a division and a breach betwixt them? Nay, where there was none before? And doth it not grow daily wider? It was never heard, that accommodations, where all in contest was given to one of the parties, made a union and friendship. It is so far the contrary, that where nothing is awarded to one of the parties, it makes the whole award void and of none effect … If the design be what is pretended, to restore this kingdom to peace and plenty … to unite your Majesty's subjects … this can never be affected, except all pretenders recede in some degree from the full of their pretensions.

An implicit threat of desertion from the Jacobite cause followed: 'Suffer me to make one step more, and query: Whether the Catholic Purchasers now to be turned out of possession, will join heartily with those that enter upon them'?[94] The appeal was in vain and within weeks of the prorogation of parliament the process of dispossessing the 'new interest' had begun. War was looming, yet the attention of the Jacobites was diverted by a fresh scramble for estates.

The extent to which the act was enforced has remained obscure, with Thomas Davis convinced that even partial redistribution of 'new interest' estates to their old proprietors was improbable. Davis believed that there simply wasn't time: parliament was not prorogued until mid-June; the act prescribed a lengthy legal process before repossession was allowed; and Frederick Schomberg, duke of Schomberg, landed in Ireland at the head of a Williamite invasion force on 13 August. The act, which received the royal assent on 22 June, required at least three men to be appointed as commissioners to determine the claims of the old proprietors, with power to call witnesses.[95] Shortly after parliament was prorogued, a proclamation was issued stating that no court of claims was planned for the immediate future, to prevent army officers and officials endangering the public safety by 'attending their private concerns'.[96] William King, whose account of the period was written from the Protestant perspective and hostile to the Jacobite administration, accused Catholics of dispossessing Protestant landlords without recourse to the commission, which he claimed never sat.[97] After Williamite forces occupied Dublin in 1690, a grand jury assembled to indict Jacobites for treason voted to include any 'Old Proprietor that entered into possession by virtue of the late Acts [of repeal and attainder]'.[98] Using records subsequently destroyed in 1922, however, Davis was

---

[94] N.L.I., Ms 20,665. William King reprinted this petition in its entirety. The quoted passage is found at King, *State of the Protestants*, pp 398–9.
[95] 5 James II, c. 4, ss 6–7 (Bergin & Lyall (eds), *The acts of James II's Irish parliament*, pp 24–5).
[96] Proclamation, 30 July 1689 (Kelly & Lyons (eds), *Proclamations of Ireland*, ii, 113).
[97] King, *State of the Protestants*, p. 182. Naturally preoccupied with the wrongs done to Protestants, King made no mention of the impact of the act on the Catholic 'new interest'.
[98] Charles Leslie, *An answer to a book, intituled, The State of the Protestants in Ireland under the late King James's government* (London, 1692), Appendix, p. 27.

unable to discover any proof that the act was implemented and dismissed King's evidence to the contrary as unpersuasive and perhaps forged.[99]

Yet it is no surprise to find evidence of preparations by the old proprietors for the implementation of the act.[100] In February 1690 John Browne was given permission to lease the estates of Sir Oliver St George, Sir Edward Crofton and three other forfeiting Protestants from the crown, 'pursuant to such instructions as you [the commissioners of the treasury] have for setting leases to reprisable persons'.[101]

At least part of the estate Browne had built over the preceding twenty years had been taken from him as a result of the act of repeal, while preliminary work for the implementation of the act had clearly been undertaken. In a reversal of the policy announced in July 1689, James II issued a proclamation on 18 February 1690 announcing that three commissioners of the revenue were to tour

> Waterford, Wexford, Kilkenny, Tipperary, Cork, Limerick, Kerry, Clare, Sligo, King's County, Galway, Mayo, Roscommon, Longford and Leitrim … to make diligent enquiry after such lands and tenements as are forfeited to or vested in us … and to set the same during our will and pleasure … wherein they are to give the preference to such reprisable persons as have lost their late estates by the late statute of repeal.[102]

Two months later James and his government realised the folly of attempting to implement the act while at war. The commissioners were instructed to cease letting forfeited estates, due to the number of officers leaving their troops to pursue leases.[103] Yet the damage to the 'new interest' was done. The extent of

---

[99] Thomas Davis, 'Retrospect of the parliament of 1689, and its acts' in *The Dublin Magazine and Citizen* (April, 1843), p. 197. This section of Davis's original articles was not reproduced in the collection of his essays on the 1689 parliament, edited by Charles Gavan Duffy and published after Davis's death. For King's evidence, see *State of the Protestants*, pp 411–12.

[100] Christopher Peppard loaned £30 in May 1689 to Robert Sarsfield of Sarsfieldstown, County Meath, to assist him 'recover his ancient estate as intended by this present parliament for the restoration of the Old and Ancient Proprietors' (N.L.I., D 16,250).

[101] N.L.I., Ms 40,899/4/17.

[102] Proclamation, 18 Feb. 1690 (Kelly & Lyons (eds), *Proclamations of Ireland*, ii, 154–6).

[103] Proclamation, 25 Apr. 1690 (Kelly & Lyons (eds), *Proclamations of Ireland*, ii, 167). The commissioners of the treasury as of 31 December 1690 were Sir Patrick Trant, Sir William Ellis, John Trinder, Richard Collins, Francis Plowden, Sir Toby Butler ('Calendar of patent rolls, 1685–8' (N.A.I., 2/446/37 (2), f. 71)), with Charles Playdell serving as secretary, Nicholas Fitzgerald as solicitor, Robert Longford as clerk of quit-rents and forfeited estates and Sir Henry Bond and Lewis Doe as surveyors general. This John Trinder may have been the John Trinder, of St Martin's in the Fields, appointed in 1687 to a commission to enquire into money levied from recusants and dissenters in the city of London. He was appointed to the Irish treasury in July 1688 on a salary of £1,000, and as a commissioner of the mint in June 1689 (C.T.B., 1685–9, pp 1695, 2019). Playdell was in receipt of a pension of £60 per annum on the Irish establishment (ibid., pp

the reclamation of estates by the pre-1641 Catholic proprietors at the expense of their fellow Catholics will probably never be fully known. Browne was one who suffered at their hands. There were others. Sir Patrick Bellew leased lands from the Jacobite commissioners of the treasury having

> had taken from him by the late act of repeal in the year '89 every effect of his estate, yet so contested with the then government that he kept his estate from the old proprietors till the year '90 at which time he was turned out by special orders.[104]

The Protestant neighbours of James Plunkett of Castleplunkett, County Roscommon, wrote in 1693 in support of his application for a pardon from William, noting that he had lost his estate by the act of repeal, 'only now restored by their Majesties' laws made in England'.[105] Almost twenty years after the 1689 parliament sat, the scholar Roderick O'Flaherty recalled that in the days before the Battle of Aughrim, in July 1691, 'a swarm of bees not known from whence fell down from the sky and lodged in an old wall next my house at Moycullin then newly recovered by virtue of K. James's act'. The family turned out of O'Flaherty's house were Catholic transplanters.[106] Sir Walter Blake, MP for the county of Galway in the 1689 parliament, took advantage of the act to recover an ancestral estate. His father-in-law, Sir John Kirwan (MP for the town of Galway in 1689), was dispossessed of the land 'he had purchased under the said Acts of Settlement'. Some £260 remained outstanding from the portion due to Blake after his marriage to Kirwan's daughter, which, according to Kirwan, Blake remitted in consideration of 'the hard circumstances [Kirwan] was under by the loss of his said estate'. Blake later refused to acknowledge any remittance, and by the mid 1690s the two were in dispute in relation to the marriage portion.[107] There can be little doubt that the act was at least partially implemented, with dispossessions receiving sanction from the Jacobite administration.

1288, 2019). Bond and Doe were appointed receivers of the revenue on 6 June 1688, replacing John Price (ibid., pp 1930–1). See also 'Calendar of Patent Rolls, 1685–8', ff 29, 55, 57, 64, 68, 71.
[104] 'Sir Patrick Bellew's instructions for a bill', c.1692 (Barmeath Castle, Bellew of Barmeath papers, L/3).
[105] T.N.A., SP 63/360, ff 56–8. For the English parliament's formal annulment of the acts of the 1689 parliament see Bergin & Lyall (eds), *The acts of James II's Irish parliament*, pp liv–lvii.
[106] Roderick O'Flaherty to Samuel Molyneux, 9 April 1708, in Richard Sharpe (ed.), *Roderick O'Flaherty's letters to William Molyneux, Edward Lhwyd, and Samuel Molyneux, 1696–1709* (Dublin, 2013), pp 28–9, 333.
[107] *John Kirwan, esq; commonly called Sir John Kirwan, knt. Appellant. Sir Walter Blake, bart. Respondent. The appellant's case* [London, 1721]; *John Kirwane, esq; commonly called Sir John Kirwane, Knight. Appellant. Sir Walter Blake, Baronet. Respondent. The respondent's case* [London, 1721]. I am indebted to Dr Coleman Dennehy for providing me with the respondent's case.

V

The accession of James II to the thrones of the three kingdoms in 1685 initially brought with it positive signs for the continued prosperity of the 'new interest', as Catholics were readmitted to corporations and appointed to the judiciary and to the privy council. James II chose a Protestant viceroy in 1685 and also issued a declaration promising to preserve the integrity of the land settlement. The 1689 parliament's decision to repeal the settlement, in a manner that was far more wide reaching than even Tyrconnell had initially envisaged, was a particularly painful blow to the 'new interest'. Most of these men had carved their estates out of the confusion and financial distress created for other Catholic landowners by the Restoration land settlement, and were acutely aware of the uncertainty that accompanied ownership of previously forfeited lands. The estates of the 'new interest' rested upon the legitimacy of the Restoration land settlement, which underpinned a huge variety of land transactions completed after 1660.

Tyrconnell's success in undermining Clarendon and his determination to at least partially revoke the Restoration land settlement soon altered the political landscape, and brought the 'new interest' into conflict with the majority of the Catholic population. The 'Glorious Revolution' set in train a series of events that were potentially ruinous for the 'new interest', culminating in the act of repeal. The timing of the act was baffling for a variety of reasons, not least of which was its impact on a substantial number of Catholic landowners, who were expected to raise troops and expend their financial and material resources to support the Jacobite army. For John Browne the act was a miserable end to a difficult decade, which saw his stunning rise to prominence among Connacht landowners undermined by a financially ruinous attempt to establish himself as an ironmaster. At the end of 1689 the loyalty of the 'new interest' hung in the balance. Sir Patrick Bellew's vigorous attempt to oppose the loss of his estate hints at their frustration. By the time Schomberg arrived in Ireland in August 1689 with the first wave of the Williamite army, some of the 'new interest' had already been stripped of their estates. Their loyalty to the Jacobite cause was now in doubt, at a time when James II needed their support more than ever before.

2

'You must engage your plate, your credit and all is at stake': Jacobite colonel, ironmaster and negotiator, 1689–91[1]

The 1689 parliament and its legislative achievements represented the high point of the brief Catholic resurgence of James II's reign. The time and space necessary to implement the new Catholic polity's programme of reform could only be afforded by the restoration of James II to the throne. Following William and Mary's coronation in London as king and queen of England, Scotland and Ireland in April 1689, it became increasingly clear that an invasion of Ireland was imminent. Much to the frustration of Irish Protestants sheltering in England, preparations for that invasion took longer than anticipated and it was not until August 1689 that Williamite forces landed at Bangor Bay, under the command of the duke of Schomberg. The war of the two kings had commenced, and the future of the Catholic counter-revolution hung in the balance.

This chapter provides a fresh analysis of the Jacobite war effort up to and including the negotiation of the articles of Limerick, the terms of surrender signed in October 1691 that brought the war to an end. As the owner of substantial ironworks in the west of Ireland, John Browne became increasingly important as a supplier of raw iron, tools and weaponry to the Jacobite army. Though relations between the Jacobite administration and Browne were strained throughout 1690, his importance to the war effort and his legal expertise led to his inclusion in the commission appointed to negotiate a Jacobite surrender in September 1691. Conscious of his still dire financial position, Browne took full advantage of the negotiations to spread liability for his personal debts to every Catholic landowner in Ireland.

I

Irish Jacobite preparations for a possible invasion from England began in earnest in December 1688, when Tyrconnell issued commissions for raising 50,000 men. Tyrconnell's aims were overly ambitious on several fronts, not

[1] The quotation is taken from Lieut. Col. George Browne to Col. John Browne, [Aug./Sept.] 1689 (N.L.I., Ms 40,899/2/3).

least of which was the near impossibility of moulding such a large body of inexperienced men, for the most part commanded by wholly unqualified officers, into a functioning, disciplined army. Realising the logistical challenges that his actions had presented, Tyrconnell sought to reduce the Jacobite army to more manageable proportions throughout the first months of 1689, causing friction with the newly commissioned officers.[2] His intention to amalgamate newly raised troops with the more experienced members of the standing army proved just as contentious, and was strongly resisted by officers who feared a diminution of their authority and, it seems, prestige. Lieutenant Colonel George Browne informed his uncle, John Browne, that Tyrconnell viewed the new recruits as 'a mighty hindrance to the recruits of the old army'. Colonel Charles O'Kelly was instructed to consult with the new Connacht colonels and to persuade them to send their companies to Dublin to be mixed with the standing army, presumably for training purposes. O'Kelly was to assure the colonels that the men would be returned to their command. The odds against the return of the men were given as ten to one by George Browne, while Sir Ulick Bourke, eldest son of the earl of Clanricarde, simply refused to countenance the idea.[3]

Equally problematic for Tyrconnell were the practicalities of supplying and equipping such a large force. Contracts for providing bread and hay to the army were awarded in 1689 and 1690, but neither appears to have been particularly well administered. The resulting shortage of provisions, a problem shared with the Williamite army, forced soldiers on both sides to pillage localities in which they were stationed.[4] Throughout the war the Jacobites were hampered by a major dearth of weaponry, especially guns. Before the war began Tyrconnell reputedly distributed 20,000 guns confiscated from Protestants to Jacobite soldiers, but 'not above one thousand … were found afterwards to be of any use'.[5] One report from April 1689 noted that there were only '878 muskets serviceable, 895 muskets unserviceable, 1,152 pistols in pairs' to be found in

[2] Simms, *Jacobite Ireland*, pp 69–73; John Childs, *The Williamite wars in Ireland, 1688–91* (London, 2007), pp 25–6.

[3] Lieut. Col. George Browne to Col. Browne, [Aug./Sept.] 1689 (N.L.I., Ms 40,899/2/3). Col. Charles O'Kelly later wrote an account of the Williamite war that was highly critical of the 'new interest' and the Jacobite military leadership (*Macariae excidium; or, the destruction of Cyprus*, ed. J.C. O'Callaghan (Dublin, 1853)).

[4] Simms, *Jacobite Ireland*, pp 187–8; Childs, *Williamite wars in Ireland*, pp 15–32; Diarmuid Murtagh and Harman Murtagh, 'The Irish Jacobite army, 1689–91' in *Irish Sword*, xviii (1990–2), p. 33.

[5] J.S. Clarke (ed.), *The life of James the Second* (2 vols, London, 1816), ii, 328; Simms, *Jacobite Ireland*, pp 70–3; Alan J. Guy, 'The Irish military establishment, 1669–1776' in Thomas Bartlett and Keith Jeffery (eds), *A military history of Ireland* (Cambridge, 1996), p. 213; Childs, *Williamite wars in Ireland*, pp 21–2.

the Jacobite stores.[6] By the end of 1689 the French had delivered 1,000 pairs of pistols, 1,500 muskets and carbines and 19,000 swords to the Jacobite army.[7] These were significant additions to the existing stock but nowhere near what the Irish army needed, while Louis XIV's ambassador to the Jacobite court in Ireland, Jean-Antoine de Mesmes, Comte d'Avaux, was highly critical of the quality of the French weapons.[8] Cannons and other supplies were purchased from Lisbon merchants using French money and cash raised from jewellery sold by James II's wife, Queen Mary.[9]

As deputy lord lieutenant of Mayo, John Browne was expected to play his part in securing food for the army.[10] In the autumn of 1690, as the Jacobites prepared for the expected fall of Limerick, Tyrconnell ordered Browne and Athenry to gather over 2,000 head of livestock for the anticipated retreat to Galway. Labourers were also required to strengthen the town's fortifications.[11] The spirited defence of Limerick caused a rethink in strategy; the Jacobites now busied themselves preparing for the winter and campaigning season to come. Tyrconnell's departure for France left the Jacobite commissariat under the direction of James FitzJames, duke of Berwick, illegitimate son of James II. Berwick issued a string of instructions to the County Mayo authorities in late 1690, requesting provisions for the Boffin and Sligo garrisons totalling over 1,000 barrels of meal, in addition to weavers for manufacturing army uniforms to be sent to Galway.

The army's strength stood at approximately 35,000 men in the winter of 1689–90 and the provision of arms remained a high priority. Tyrconnell wrote to Queen Mary of the need for raw materials: 'I pray, Madam, let 50 tons of copper be sent us (besides the 40 now coming) before the end of March … for we are undone whenever that metal fails us … and 10 tons of steel, for we begin now to make firearms here, without which we cannot work'.[12] John Browne's real value to the Jacobites lay in his ironworks, recognised by the Irish parliament as a potentially vital source for equipping the Jacobite army. It was

6   James Macpherson (ed.), *Original papers, containing the secret history of Great Britain* (2 vols, London, 1775), i, 178.

7   Sheila Mulloy (ed.), *Franco-Irish correspondence: December 1688–February 1692* (3 vols, Dublin, 1983–4), i, xlii.

8   James Hogan (ed.), *Négociations de M. le comte d'Avaux en Irlande, 1689–90* (Dublin, 1934), pp 232, 253.

9   Hogan (ed.), *Négociations*, pp 296–311; Clarke (ed.), *Life of James the Second*, ii, 391.

10 Browne was appointed deputy lord lieutenant of Mayo in October 1689, probably on the interest of his son-in-law Lord Athenry, who had been appointed lord lieutenant for the county (N.L.I., Ms 10, ff 90–1; microfilm pos. 940; King, *State of the Protestants*, p. 321).

11 Orders from Tyrconnell to Athenry and Browne, 16 Aug. 1690 (N.L.I., Ms 40,899/3/13–14).

12 Tyrconnell to Queen Mary, 22 Dec. 1689 (James Hogan & Lilian Tate (eds), 'Letter-book of Richard Talbot' in *Analecta Hibernica*, 4 (1932), p. 108). The copper was necessary for minting coins.

realising this potential that prompted Tyrconnell's request for French steel. As the war progressed, however, the ironworks both proved to be a valuable asset to Browne, and a source of immense frustration.

II

The first year of the Williamite war was not a happy one for Browne. Before turning his hand to the production of materiel at his ironworks, Browne took out his commission in the Jacobite army as colonel. He first raised a regiment of his own, then entered into a contract to raise a second regiment for Colonel Robert Feilding, which was completed by mid-September 1689. Feilding suspected that the regiment would not be well equipped and asked Browne to arm the men with a pike or skean at the minimum. A dispute arose over the cost of outfitting and paying this regiment, necessitating the arbitration of William Herbert, duke of Powis, in December. Relations between Browne and Feilding were further strained when James II decreed that their two regiments were to be merged, placed under Feilding's command and sent to France with Justin MacCarthy, Viscount Mountcashel.[13] George Browne wrote to his uncle in late 1689, asking Browne to ensure that he 'take care not to leave in Colonel Feilding's power to order me to march as early as he wishes to Sir Richard Nagle', and to procure him four horses, 'if we really be designed for the French service'. An earlier letter from George hinted that bribery might be used to prevent the amalgamation or deployment of the regiment to France: 'If we fail of money, you must engage your plate, your credit and all is at stake, and without money I tell you it will all be lost. Pray contrive and order a constant post twice a week'.[14]

Browne fought against deployment to France and the loss of his colonelcy on two fronts. The first was a tactical delay in obeying orders to march his troops to Munster for embarkation. Feilding berated Browne for his prevarication, complaining that

> it would be ridiculous to expect the pay of the regiment at Limerick when the men are commanded to march directly to Cork where the French treasurer is, who already has orders ... to pay them, so that all objections being answered I leave you, who are a man [of] sense, to imagine what must be the issue of these matters if a fourth time the king's commands, and which I have already given in orders, be disobeyed.

[13] N.L.I., Ms 40,899/2/4–5, 8–9. Born in England, Feilding converted to Catholicism after the accession of James II and followed him to Ireland. He sat in the 1689 parliament for Gowran, Co. Kilkenny, later leaving Ireland with Mountcashel to serve in the French army. He returned to England in 1692 to lead a life of some notoriety as a bigamist and 'stallion' to wealthy mistresses (*Oxford Dictionary of National Biography*).

[14] Lieut. Col. George Browne to Col. Browne, [Aug./Sept.] 1689 (N.L.I., Ms 40,899/2/3, 14). Mountcashel did not leave for France until April 1690 (Simms, *Jacobite Ireland*, p. 72).

Warning Browne that he was suspected of 'evasion', Feilding invited him to 'imagine of [what] fatal consequence it may prove to all those your relations you have employed whose blood is like to answer such disobedience, when once they shall be found guilty of it by a court martial'.[15] Nor was the threat an idle one; in March 1690 Feilding ordered the arrest of Captain William Jordan, whose men had been transferred from Browne's regiment to Feilding's, for his failure to march his troops to Cork in preparation for embarkation to France.[16]

Browne's second ploy was to petition the king.[17] Complaining of the high cost of subsisting both his own and Feilding's regiments, Browne offered to raise 'four men for one' for James's army if he was not sent to France. The appeal was successful, as Browne did not embark at Cork with his troops. Having just signed a major contract with the Ordnance Office, it may be assumed that his services were recognised as of greater value if he remained in Ireland.

Browne received orders from James II in October 1689 to 'employ men in making of firelocks, matchlocks, cannon and other balls for ordnance, grenado shells, spades, shovels and pickaxes'.[18] This order was put on a more official footing in December, when Browne signed the contract with the Ordnance Office to manufacture tools, muskets and other implements of war. The contract gave detailed instructions regarding the design of the muskets:

> 3½ [feet] in length of the barrel, English bore to be provided with ten bullets in the pound; stocked, socked and well fixed according to the pattern, with IR and Crown graved on the lock and stamped upon each barrel.[19]

The type of musket expected was the flintlock, colloquially known as the 'firelock', a more reliable and efficient musket than the matchlock.[20] Browne appears to have later become the main contractor for Irish muskets; in 1690 he was reported to be supervising the production of musket-barrels in Dublin with a work-force of 150 men, mostly Protestants.[21] As was the case with many pamphlets published in London during the war relaying news from Ireland, this intelligence was not wholly accurate. It was, in any case, an arrangement that could not have continued following the Jacobite defeat at the Boyne, with

15 Col. Robert Feilding to Col. Browne, 26 Feb. 1690 (N.L.I., Ms 40,899/2/15).
16 Warrant from Col. Robert Feilding to all military and civil officers, 5 Mar. 1690 (N.L.I., Ms 40,900/2/1). See also Ms 40,899/4/10 for Feilding's warrant for the arrest of Capt. Francis Cormick for his failure to march his troops to Limerick.
17 Petition of Col. Browne to James II, 10 Feb. 1690 (N.L.I., Ms 40,899/4/18).
18 N.L.I., Ms 40,899/4/5.
19 N.L.I., Ms 40,899/4/20. 'IR' presumably symbolised 'Iacobus Rex'.
20 Childs, *Williamite wars in Ireland*, pp 28–9.
21 *An account of the present state Ireland is in, under King James: and the deplorable condition of the Protestants* (London, 1690); Simms, *Jacobite Ireland*, p. 133; Murtagh & Murtagh, 'Irish Jacobite army', p. 39.

William's troops entering Dublin for the first time on 3 July 1690. It is also unlikely that Browne ever produced a large quantity of muskets; by May 1690 perhaps a handful had been made, with 200 promised by June.

Most of the information about the running of his ironworks during the war is provided in an *apologia* composed by Browne in or around May 1690, probably just before or during his brief incarceration for failing to fulfil the terms of his contract with the Ordnance Office.[22] It gives no indication that Browne ever used Dublin for manufacturing muskets, though he did take Dublin gunsmiths to Mayo in January 1690. Based at his Mayo ironworks from at least January 1690, Browne's productivity was hampered on several fronts. For a start, the tools required for musket manufacture were not available in Mayo and were not brought by the Dublin workmen, necessitating their manufacture on-site.

Browne also had a tendency to overstretch the resources available to him. A separate contract to manufacture carbines was signed with Henry Jermyn, earl of Dover, one of the commissioners of the treasury, obliging Browne to send his chief gunsmith back to Dublin in February 1690 to fulfil the commission. The gunsmith, Thomas Fitzpatrick, failed to report for duty in Dublin and never returned to Browne's ironworks in Mayo. Adam Colclough, secretary to the treasury, rebuked Browne in April:

> I have twice written to you of late about my Lord Dover's carbines and have had no answer, so that I have no reason to suppose that this will succeed better. However I will venture once more to tell you that my Lord Dover is much astonished at your giving him no account of any progress you have made in order to furnish him according to your promise ... I should for your own sake, if there were no other argument, be glad to hear you are in a likely way to comply with what is reasonably expected from you.[23]

The loss of Fitzpatrick was exacerbated by the lack of skill in firelock manufacture and low morale among Browne's remaining Dublin forgers. Only two men, John Johnson and Robert Symms, specialised in the forging of musket barrels. Johnson deserted the ironworks almost immediately while Symms proved more reliable, but not before he 'spoiled a great number of barrel skelps'.[24] Marcus Loghra, another of the Dublin workmen, was ill for several weeks. Other factors were outside Browne's control. Though he had already raised two regiments by the end of 1689, he was ordered by James to raise more troops to

---

[22] 'An account of Col. John Browne's proceedings in relation to his articles with the Office of his Majesty's Ordnance', [May 1690] (N.L.I., Ms 40,899/5/9).

[23] Adam Colclough to Col. Browne, 1 Apr. 1690 (N.L.I., Ms 40,899/2/19). For Colclough's career, see John Bergin, 'Irish Catholic interest', pp 37–48. For his representation of the articlemen in 1691 and 1692, see pp 89–90, 100, 104–6 below.

[24] A skelp was a flat strip of steel, tempered and wrought into a gun barrel.

augment Feilding's regiment, for transport to France with Mountcashel.[25] Not only did this involve additional expense for subsisting the troops mustered, Browne also learned by 'dear experience that his personal attendance at the works was necessary, as well to bring in and settle the country gunsmiths and other workmen, as to govern them that were there, being a quarrelsome unruly generation'.[26]

Defending the slow pace of production at his ironworks during the early part of 1690, Browne pointed to the need to accompany the newly raised troops to Cork. He returned on 15 March to find his Dublin gunsmiths had deserted the ironworks. In his absence they had fought with local workers and cut the nose off one tenant, causing them to flee for fear of their lives. Browne was not alone in having problems with his gunsmiths. Most members of this trade in Ireland were Protestant, and were reported as 'going unwillingly about their business' for the Jacobites.[27] D'Avaux repeatedly requested French gunsmiths, stressing that the Jacobites were almost completely ignorant of the trade. French gunsmiths were finally sent in 1691, though by that time it was too late.[28] Browne's *apologia* ended by noting that the payments he received from the Ordnance Office allowed no room for profit, while £700 of his own money had been invested in equipping the ironworks and paying the workers, without any charge to the treasury, not to mention the great cost of raising the equivalent of three regiments.[29]

The difficulties Browne experienced in fulfilling his contract highlight the immense problems the Jacobite administration faced in equipping its army. Tyrconnell's letters to Queen Mary in early 1690 regularly entreated her to use her 'wit and credit upon furnishing us with arms and ammunitions, for where at least 20,000 firearms were wanting what is 3,000 able to do'. A lack of gunpowder was also crippling the army's effectiveness: 'our common soldiers know not yet what it is to fire for the want of [it]'.[30] Tyrconnell was prone to

---

[25] Feilding's regiment embarked with Mountcashel in April 1690 (D'Avaux to Tyrconnell, 28 Mar. 1690 in Marquis MacSwiney of Mashanaglass, 'Some unpublished letters of the Count d'Avaux in the National Library of Ireland' in *P.R.I.A.*, 40C (1931–2), p. 303.) These troops were to become part of the famous regiment of Mountcashel, which served under various names in the French army until the French Revolution (David Murphy, *The Irish brigades, 1685–2006* (Dublin, 2007), pp 10–23; Nathalie Genet-Rouffiac, 'The Wild Geese in France: a French perspective' in idem and David Murphy (eds), *Franco-Irish military connections, 1590–1945* (Dublin, 2009), pp 34–6).

[26] 'An account of Col. John Browne's proceedings in relation to his articles with the Office of his Majesty's Ordnance', [May 1690] (N.L.I., Ms 40,899/5/9).

[27] Macpherson (ed.), *Original papers*, p. 179.

[28] Hogan (ed.), *Négociations*, pp 34, 79, 322, 334, 504, 524.

[29] 'An account of Col. John Browne's proceedings in relation to his articles with the Office of his Majesty's Ordnance', [May 1690] (N.L.I., Ms 40,899/5/9).

[30] Tyrconnell to Queen Mary, 29 Mar. 1690 (Hogan & Tate (eds), 'Letter book of Richard Talbot',

overstating the weakness of the Jacobite position in an attempt to solicit more supplies, but there is no doubt that the Jacobite forces were gravely under-equipped. The Ordnance Office and army officers made frequent demands of Browne. Throughout 1690 various urgent requests were issued for musket barrels and tools to be sent to Kinsale; workmen to be sent to Carlow, Sligo and Galway; 150 muskets to be made for Tyrconnell; cannonballs for Galway, Athlone and Sligo; tools for workmen at Sligo, Galway and Limerick; steel and building tools for the fortification of Sligo.[31] Under immense pressure, Browne's ironworks struggled to keep pace. In May 1690 the Ordnance Office lost patience with Browne's persistent failure to deliver, and ordered an investigation. Browne was somewhat exonerated by the investigation's conclusion that his ironworks were largely hampered by a lack of steel, but was nonetheless sentenced to imprisonment for ten weeks.[32]

As a spirited defence of his conduct and reputation, and possibly written in prison, Browne's *apologia* needs to be treated with caution. It does, however, reveal some weaknesses in Browne's managerial acumen. By agreeing a contract with Dover, above and beyond his contract with the Ordnance Office, he ensured his resources were spread too thinly. While the lack of steel was a factor in the slow production from the ironworks, Browne's mismanagement of a recalcitrant work force also played a part. His absence from the works in early 1690 while raising troops for James, though enforced, was a major setback. His complaint that constant attendance at the works was necessary indicates a lack of a competent overseer, emphasising the folly of his contract with Dover, which forced Browne to send Thomas Fitzpatrick back to Dublin. It also carries echoes of Sir William Petty's observation on his own ironworks: 'I vehemently fear that an Irish estate cannot subsist without the owner's daily presence and inspection.'[33] In addition, Browne's ironworks were not set up for the production of weaponry, nor were his regular workmen trained in their manufacture. Irish ironworks in the seventeenth century concentrated on the production of pig and bar iron for the Irish and, occasionally, English markets.[34] Browne needed time to adapt his ironworks, a luxury that neither he nor the

---

p. 116). See N.L.I., Ms 40,899/5/15 for complaints of Connacht-based officers about the lack of muskets available to them in September 1689.

[31] N.L.I., Mss 40,899/3/3, 6–12, 14; 40,899/4/5; 40,899/5/1, 3–4, 6, 10–14; 40,900/1/7, 11–13; 40,900/2/3.

[32] N.L.I., Ms 40,899/5/7–8. The investigation was led by Col. Barker of the Ordnance Office, probably Lieut. Col. William Maunsell Barker (John D'Alton, *Illustrations, historical and genealogical of King James's Irish army list (1689)* (Dublin, 1855; reprinted, Limerick, 1997), pp 414, 420. It is unlikely that Browne served the full ten weeks in prison.

[33] Quoted in T.C. Barnard, 'Sir William Petty as Kerry ironmaster' in *P.R.I.A.*, 82C (1982), p. 23.

[34] Andrews, 'Notes on the historical geography of the Irish iron industry' in *Irish Geography*, iii (1956), pp 139–49.

Jacobite administration had. Even so, Browne still managed to produce several hundred tons of iron and steel, as well as numerous horseshoes, pickaxes, shovels and other tools. How this compared with other ironworks in Ireland is impossible to gauge without surviving records. Some ironworks, including those at Enniscorthy and Kilkenny, would not have remained in Jacobite hands following retreat west of the Shannon after defeat at the Boyne.[35] Other works were destroyed during the war, including those of Sir Francis Brewster in County Kerry, and Sir James Caldwell in County Fermanagh, who were both Protestant and Williamites.[36]

Indecision on the part of the Jacobite army also inhibited the manufacture of guns. Patrick Sarsfield issued an order in July 1690 for all gunsmiths and blade-makers at Westport to be escorted under armed guard to Galway, where there may have been another ironworks operational, though it's more likely they were destined to be sent to France as the Jacobites contemplated withdrawing from Ireland after the Boyne.[37] But the war continued into 1691 and Browne's ironworks, situated in western Connacht, were safe from Williamite forces until July 1691. Their importance was emphasised in Williamite intelligence sent to London in October 1690. The only Jacobite ironworks in operation at that time was John Browne's, near 'The Owls' (Burrishoole, County Mayo). Browne was supplied with iron from the mines of Sir Henry Waddington at Scariff, County Clare.[38] It is difficult to see how the Jacobites could have operated any other ironworks for the remainder of the war.

One of the more notable aspects of Browne's activities during the war is the extent to which he continued to negotiate and conclude land deals. Browne may have been preparing for a Jacobite victory, beginning the process of carving out a new estate. It is, however, more feasible to regard Browne's land sales and conveyances in 1690 and 1691 as an attempt to acquire money for the operation of his ironworks. Even this strategy was probably compromised by the lack of good coin. Commodities became the currency of necessity. Two deals concluded in March and April 1690 saw Bryan Geraghty, John McHubert Stanton and Edmond McThomas Stanton release their interest in various lands in the baronies of Burrishoole and Carra (County Mayo) for a combined total of £5, five cows, two bushels and a barrel of meal. In May, Richard Gibbon conveyed

---

[35] J.G. Simms, 'Kilkenny in the Jacobite war, 1689–91' in idem, *War and politics in Ireland, 1649–1730*, eds. D.W. Hayton & Gerard O'Brien (London, 1986), p. 152; T.C. Barnard, 'An Anglo-Irish industrial enterprise: iron-making at Enniscorthy, Co. Wexford, 1657–92' in *P.R.I.A.*, 85C (1985) pp 101–44. There is some doubt as to whether the works at Enniscorthy were in operation during the war (p. 136).

[36] *C.S.P.D., 1693*, pp 221–2; *C.S.P.D., 1695 & Addenda*, pp 136–7; *C.S.P.D., 1698*, pp 293–4; *Calendar of Treasury Papers, 1556–1696*, pp 473–4.

[37] N.L.I., Ms 40,899/3/3.

[38] *C.S.P.D., 1695 and Addenda*, p. 158.

his lands in the baronies of Tirawley (County Mayo) and Burrishoole to Browne for £10, two milch cows, six sheep and a quantity of oatmeal.[39] A bill of exchange from Browne to Sir Abel Ram, drawn up while Browne was in Bristol, suggests that attempts were made to adhere to the agreement made with his creditors in November 1688.[40] Yet more evidence points to continued pressure on Browne in the courts through 1689 and 1690, this time from Catholic creditors.[41]

The fact that Browne's ironworks were specifically excluded from the provisions of the act of repeal indicates their importance to the Jacobite war effort. Their continued operation was crucial to Browne, both during and after the war.[42] Browne's unlicensed trip to England in April and May 1689 was overlooked by the Jacobite administration on the understanding that he would apply his ironworks to the Jacobites' needs.[43] The dependence of the Irish army on the ironworks later allowed him to bargain with the administration; continued output was made contingent on his continuance as lessee of certain crown lands. Others were instructed to applot their lands to supply the ironworks with more fuel for the furnaces and forges.[44]

The year 1689 and the first half of 1690 were, it seems, quite miserable for Browne. His trip to England in April and May 1689 was foolhardy in the extreme given the political climate, though it appears to have been motivated by business concerns rather than wavering loyalty. The 1689 parliament then stripped him of his estate and decreed that the ironworks, which remained in his possession, should pay rents to the 'ancient proprietors'. Browne's efforts to raise regiments for James II caused yet more heartache at the hands of Colonel Feilding. Even the boon to his business provided by the Ordnance Office contract proved to be a double-edged sword; imprisonment and the chaotic work environment that prevailed at Westport were surely uncomfortable experiences. His imprisonment in the spring of 1690 had, he said, caused rumour to spread that he had betrayed James II – without a sign of the king's favour, Browne declared himself 'unfit to live among men'.[45] Nonetheless, Browne's dedication to the Jacobite cause seems to have been total. In spite of his many early troubles, Browne's importance to the Jacobite war effort from the second half of 1690 became more and more obvious. A silver candlestick with

---

[39] N.L.I., Mss 40,899/1/2, 4; 40,889/24/2.

[40] See above, pp 29–31.

[41] N.L.I., Mss 40,899/1/13, 17; 40,893/2/15–16; 40,897/1/4.

[42] N.L.I., Mss 40,889/24/1.

[43] N.L.I., Ms 40,899/4/14–16.

[44] N.L.I., Mss 40,900/1/14; 40,900/2/6. Applotment was a tax raised on property, in this case applied specifically for running Browne's ironworks.

[45] 'An account of Col. John Browne's proceedings in relation to his articles with the Office of his Majesty's Ordnance', [May 1690] (N.L.I., Ms 40,899/5/9).

an inscription from Patrick Sarsfield made for a handsome gift in wartime.[46] By April, with his troops embarked for France with Feilding, Browne was relieved of the burden of command yet retained the honorific of colonel. The tone of his communications with the Jacobite administration, particularly the Ordnance Office, was greatly improved in 1691.[47]

III

Browne's *apologia* referred to overtures made to him by the Williamites while he was in England in April and May 1689 but he does not appear to have communicated with them after the outbreak of hostilities in Ireland. The same cannot be said of some of his 'new interest' contemporaries, still bitter from the loss of their estates by virtue of the act of repeal and eager to exploit any chance to regain their land. Referring to the 'new interest', Ignatius White, marquis d'Albeville, noted that 'gold and silver is become their only God'.[48] Colonel Charles O'Kelly, a Jacobite officer who wrote a scathing indictment of the army's military leadership after the war, shrewdly observed that

> there wanted not even some of the Irish Catholics, who coveted nothing more than to submit to William III. These were men of New Interest, so called because they purchased from usurpers the inheritance of their own countrymen ... and these lands being all restored to the ancient proprietors by a late decree of the [1689 parliament] ... the coveting purchasers, preferring their private gain before the general interest of religion and country, were for submitting to a government, which they very well knew could never allow that decree.[49]

During the war the 'new interest' appear to have been somewhat powerless until the aftermath of the successful defence of Limerick in August 1690, a victory for the Jacobites that came against the expectation of Tyrconnell and the French commander, the Comte de Lauzun, both of whom had taken up residence at Galway in anticipation of defeat and a swift evacuation.[50] Connacht was well populated with 'new interest' landowners and many were no doubt in Galway, where they would have been aware of Tyrconnell's inclination at that time to explore terms of surrender. Prior to the successful defence of Limerick,

---

46 The candlestick carried the inscription 'Ye gift of Coll. Patrick Sarsfield, Earl of Lucan, to Coll. Jn Browne, of Kinturk and Cahernamart', and is currently on display in Westport House, Co. Mayo. It dates from the first half of 1691. See below, p. 56.

47 N.L.I., Mss 40,900/1/11–14; 40,900/2/3–6.

48 Marquis d'Albeville to Tyrconnell, 6 Nov. 1690 (H.M.C., *Finch Mss*, ii, 475–8).

49 O'Kelly, *Macariae Excidium*, p. 71.

50 O'Kelly, *Macariae Excidium*, pp 57–8; *A Jacobite Narrative of the War in Ireland*, ed. J.T. Gilbert (2nd edition, Shannon, 1971), pp 110–11; Simms, *Jacobite Ireland*, p. 159.

tentative steps had been taken to learn what those terms might be.[51] Repelling the Williamites at Limerick strengthened the hand of those who favoured a negotiated settlement for, in the absence of a resolution before the spring of 1691, William would be forced to commit his troops to Ireland for another year. With William and his advisers eager to conclude the war as swiftly as possible, the chance to gain a negotiated settlement, in which their estates could be guaranteed, was too good for the 'new interest' group to miss. Yet the defence of Limerick had also strengthened the resolve of those who were committed to continuing the war and reinstalling James II to the throne. During the winter of 1690–91, the resistance faction remained in the ascendancy, necessitating secret communications between the Williamites and the 'new interest'.

Tyrconnell departed for France in September 1690, returning the following January. A commission of twelve men governed Jacobite territory in his absence, known as the lords commissioners for civil affairs. Among the members were Clanricarde, the Marquis d'Albeville, Jenico Preston, Viscount Gormanston, and Thomas Nugent, Baron Riverston.[52] The Williamite lords justices, Henry, Viscount Sydney, and Thomas Coningsby, wrote to Nottingham in October 1690 enclosing some intelligence on the composition of the Irish government. Their information indicated that, in addition to the above men, Judges Peter Martin and Henry Lynch were also commissioners, as were Sarsfield, Sir Michael Creagh and 'John Brown, a lawyer'.[53] With the Jacobites largely confined west of the Shannon at this point, Browne's status as Connacht's greatest landowner made him an ideal candidate to serve on the temporary governing commission.

In Tyrconnell's absence the lords commissioners were riven with tensions, centring around different factions within the army's leadership.[54] Conflict over whether to sue for peace with William III, or to continue the war, also consumed much of their time. The peace party were led by the 'new interest' with Riverston particularly prominent, ably supported by Judge Denis Daly. Soon after Tyrconnell's departure, the lords commissioners were presented with tempting terms of surrender. Tentative negotiations with the Williamites had previously begun in July 1690, shortly after the Battle of the Boyne and before the Williamites were repulsed at the first siege of Limerick. Counsellor John Grady was sent, with Tyrconnell's blessing, to William's camp to assess the

---

[51] H.M.C., *Finch Mss*, ii, p. 478; O'Kelly, *Macariae Excidium*, pp 60–6; *A Jacobite Narrative of the War in Ireland*, ed. Gilbert, pp 110–11; J.G. Simms, 'Williamite peace tactics, 1690–1' in *I.H.S.*, viii (1952–3), p. 309.

[52] Order from the lords commissioners for civil affairs to Athenry and Browne, 15 Sept. 1690 (N.L.I., Ms 40,899/4/11).

[53] Sydney and Coningsby to Nottingham, 5 Oct. 1690 (SP 63/352, ff 49–51; *C.S.P.D., 1695 & Addenda*, pp 156–9).

[54] Simms, *Jacobite Ireland*, pp 185–93.

terms that might be on offer.[55] Grady was slow to return to the Jacobite camp, arriving in Galway in October with terms that were very acceptable to the peace faction, including a promise that those who held estates in 1684 would be restored to their land, with some exceptions.[56] With Tyrconnell absent, Grady returned to the Williamites with a power of attorney from nine of the twelve lords commissioners for civil affairs, with the promise that if French aid did not arrive soon, they would surrender on condition that they retain their estates and were allowed the 'exercise of their religion as in King Charles' time'.[57] Yet the Williamite administration's decision to send Grady to London shortly thereafter robbed the initiative (and the Jacobite peace party) of crucial momentum and allowed the Jacobite resistance faction, led by Sarsfield, to regroup.[58]

On 10 January, with Grady yet to return, Sarsfield ordered the arrest and imprisonment of Denis Daly, while Colonel Alexander MacDonnell and Riverston were dismissed from their posts as, respectively, governor of Galway and secretary of war. Sarsfield had received word from Dublin that these three men were in secret negotiations with William, corroborated by intelligence sent from London to James II in France.[59] By the time of Grady's return to Ireland later that month, Jacobite morale had been stiffened and Grady advised Godard van Reede Ginkel, the Williamite commanding officer in Ireland, that he was no longer able to travel into Jacobite territory for fear of his life.[60] Tyrconnell returned to Ireland on 14 January and immediately released Daly from prison, but does not appear to have resumed negotiations with the Williamites.[61] His return also relieved the twelve lords commissioners for civil affairs, including John Browne, of control of the civil government. The identity of the nine commissioners who declared in October that they were ready to surrender is unknown, but John Browne was almost certainly one.

It was not until July 1691, on the back of two successive military defeats, that a Jacobite surrender once more became a real prospect. Retreat from the garrison at Athlone on 30 June was quickly followed by the disastrous defeat at Aughrim, decisively turning the tide of the war in favour of the Williamites.

---

[55] Grady's family were from Derrimore, Co. Clare, and were closely connected with the family of Sir Toby Butler. Grady was admitted to Inner Temple on 25 Nov. 1680 (Maynard, 'Irish membership of the English inns of court', pp 101, 288, 400).

[56] Hogan (ed.), *Négociations*, pp 738–9. The exceptions were Lords Clancarty and Antrim. For a precise chronology of negotiations between the Jacobites and Williamites, see Simms, 'Williamite peace tactics'.

[57] Duke of Württemberg to Christian V, 29 Oct. 1690 (K. Danaher & J.G. Simms (eds), *The Danish Force in Ireland* (Dublin, 1962), pp 90–1).

[58] Duke of Württemberg to Christian V, 29 Oct. 1690 (ibid., pp 91–2).

[59] Sarsfield to Mountcashel, 24 Feb. 1691 (Mulloy (ed.), *Franco-Irish correspondence*, ii, 230).

[60] Ginkel to Coningsby, 13 Jan. 1691 (H.M.C., *Fourth report*, p. 318).

[61] O'Kelly, *Macariae excidium*, p. 106.

When coupled with Ginkel's publication of a proclamation on 7 July promising restoration of estates to those who submitted to him within three weeks, the 'new interest' was presented with compelling arguments for surrender.[62] Clandestine negotiations for surrender had continued throughout the first half of 1691, with Denis Daly taking the lead on the Jacobite side.[63] According to George Story, chaplain to the Williamite army, Daly and 'some others of the Irish had kept a correspondence with our government for several months past, and had proposed the surrendering of Galway, and some other things, which was the occasion of a part of our armies marching to the Shannon the winter before'.[64]

Open communication with the Williamites, however, remained dangerous. As Ginkel advanced on Galway in the aftermath of the Battle of Aughrim, Daly requested the general to arrange a kidnapping of sorts to allow the two to consult directly.[65] Sir John Kirwan was imprisoned in Galway town for corresponding with Ginkel; Kirwan's information was said to have helped to persuade Ginkel he had no need to wait for his heavy cannon before advancing on Galway.[66] Arthur French, mayor of Galway, arranged for Robert Shaw, one of the Protestants then in town, to be smuggled out by sea to rendezvous with Ginkel at Athenry. According to French, a 'strong party' organised by the resistance faction within Galway narrowly missed intercepting Shaw, 'and if they had taken him this deponent believes they would have put him to death'. Shaw sent letters from Ginkel and copies of the 7 July proclamation to French from Athenry, through the services of a Catholic priest who concealed the papers in his stocking. Distributing copies of the proclamation within Galway led to death threats against French.[67] Fearing for his own life, Kirwan, a merchant with ships at his disposal, received permission from Ginkel to sail for France until the war was ended.[68]

Whether Ginkel played along with Daly's proposed ruse is unclear, though Daly reportedly travelled from Athenry to Galway with the Williamite force.[69]

---

[62] Simms, 'Williamite peace tactics', pp 313–15.

[63] Duke of Württemberg to Christian V, 7 Jan. & 14 Feb. 1691 (Danaher & Simms (eds), *The Danish force in Ireland*, pp 94–9). In the letter of 14 February, Württemberg refers to correspondence with a Col. Butler, whom he had previously met in Hungary.

[64] George Story, *A Continuation of the Impartial History of the Wars in Ireland* (London, 1693), p. 159.

[65] Ibid.

[66] 'Copy of Sir Richard Cox's speech at the adjudication of the men of Gallway', 1699 (B.L., Add. Ms. 38,153, f. 18r).

[67] Deposition of Arthur French, 16 Aug. 1707 (B.L., Add. Ms. 61,633, f. 17); O'Kelly, *Macariae excidium*, pp 137–8. Shaw was later appointed town clerk of Galway (N.L.I., Annesley Mss, xxiii, ff 102–3).

[68] 'Copy of Sir Richard Cox's speech at the adjudication of the men of Gallway', f. 19v; C.S.P.D., 1691–2, p. 134; C.S.P.D., 1696, pp 57–8; C.T.B., x, 1693–6, pp 1,327–9.

[69] N.L.I., Annesley Ms xxiii, fols 102–3; xxvii, fol. 155; H.M.C., *Fourth Report*, appendix, p. 322.

A second report places Daly within the town walls as the Williamite army approached, taking advantage of the panic to urge the governor to capitulate.[70] Ginkel's forces arrived at Galway on 19 July and negotiations for surrender were concluded on 21 July, with Daly likely to have taken a leading role on the Jacobite side. In his despatches to the lords justices Ginkel noted that 'Judge Daly has done good service'.[71] The 'new interest' were duly granted their wish under the articles of Galway, which guaranteed not only the preservation of their estates, but also the freedom to continue in their legal practices. In return for his services Daly, along with the other beneficiaries of the articles, received a general pardon from all crimes committed since the beginning of the reign of James II, as well as a personal guarantee from Ginkel that his estate would be free from the threat of forfeiture.[72]

IV

John Browne was in Galway at the time of its surrender, though it's not known if he played a role in negotiations. He did, however, assist negotiations at Inis Boffin (surrendered on 19 August), after which he travelled to Limerick. There he was appointed to the most important Jacobite commission of the war: that which negotiated the articles of Limerick. It was a position he used to his personal advantage, at the expense of his fellow Catholic landowners, by negotiating an article that imposed on them a special levy to assist in the payment of his creditors.[73] Though its appearance has long been recognised by modern scholars as somewhat mystifying, no convincing explanation for this last-minute addition to the terms of surrender has yet been offered.

Coming so soon after Aughrim, the surrender of Galway was a crushing blow to the morale of the Jacobite forces. By the time Ginkel's army arrived before Limerick at the end of August, the appetite among the Jacobites for continued resistance was waning. Negotiation of the articles of Limerick took place between 26 September and 2 October. The initial Jacobite proposals, delivered on 27 September, sought full indemnity from prosecution, the restoration of all Catholics to their estates, freedom to worship publicly, eligibility for all manner of civil, military and professional employment, as well as freedom to live and trade within all towns and to be members of corporations.[74]

70 Danaher and Simms (eds), *The Danish force in Ireland*, pp. 124–5.
71 Ginkel to Coningsby, 21 July 1691 (P.R.O.N.I., De Ros Mss, D/638/12/47); H.M.C., *Fourth report, Appendix*, p. 322; N.L.I., Annesley Mss, xxvii, fol. 155.
72 TCD, Ms 744, f. 191; N.L.I., Annesley Mss xxvii, f. 155; Simms, 'Irish Jacobites', p. 133; H.M.C., *House of Lords Mss*, n.s., vol. 4 (1699–1702), p. 30.
73 For a full analysis of the impact of article 13 of Limerick, see Part III below.
74 Story, *Continuation*, p. 230; Simms, *Jacobite Ireland*, p. 251.

Plate 2: A silver chamber candlestick presented to Colonel John Browne by
Patrick Sarsfield, earl of Lucan, in 1691. The underside of the candlestick
has the following engraving: 'Ye gift of Coll. Patrick Sarsfield, Earl of Lucan,
to Coll. Jn Browne, of Kinturk and Cahernamart'. Currently on display in
Westport House. Reproduced by kind permission of Westport House.

Ginkel refused to accede to these proposals, which went well beyond what
he was authorised to allow, choosing instead to send into Limerick twelve
articles that were, according to Story, 'much the same in substance with those
afterwards agreed upon'.[75] Ginkel lent force to his proposals by ordering a
new battery of artillery to be raised, in readiness for a potential breakdown in
negotiations.

On 28 September, Colonel John Browne and his nephew Colonel Garrett
Dillon joined Sarsfield, Sir Toby Butler and eight other Jacobite officers and
Catholic bishops in Ginkel's quarters for more intense discussions. The articles
sent into Limerick by Ginkel, complete with the amendments made by the
Jacobite negotiators, survive in the papers of George Clarke, William's secretary
at war in Ireland.[76] By 29 September the first twelve articles of the final text

[75] Story, *Continuation*, p. 231.
[76] 'Articles for the capitulation of Limerick', [Sept. 1691] (B.L., Eg. Ms 2618, ff 161–3), edited by
J.G. Simms in 'The original draft of the civil articles of Limerick, 1691' in *I.H.S.*, viii (1952–3),
pp 37–44.

had been agreed. The Jacobites insisted on some changes to Ginkel's proposals, including the addition of an article indemnifying merchants who were abroad on business. Discussions between the Williamite and Jacobite negotiators were then suspended for three days in anticipation of the arrival of the Williamite lords justices, Sir Charles Porter and Thomas Coningsby. On 2–3 October a further conference took place, with the lords justices present, between 3pm and 12am. At that point, the articles were ordered to be engrossed in preparation for signing later that day. The status of the rapparees – irregular soldiers who fought in support of the Jacobite army – appears to have been the main point of discussion on 2 October, with no mention in any of the sources of Browne's article.[77]

Of the additions made to the articles originally sent into Limerick by Ginkel, the article in favour of merchants abroad (article 3) was evidently discussed and agreed in principle on 28 September.[78] Article 13 came as a surprise to many who played no active part in the negotiations. It was the only substantive change made to the articles once the initial conference concluded on 29 September. Carl Rudolf, duke of Württemberg, was not alone in believing that negotiations were effectively concluded that day.[79] Browne was presumably present at the conference with the lords justices on 2 October, and it is possible the article was added then. That sequence of events is, however, difficult to reconcile with the opening sentence of article 12, which begins: 'Lastly, the lords justices and general do undertake …'. Had article 13 been negotiated by 2 October, article 12 would hardly have begun with the word 'lastly'. This very point was made in a petition listing objections to article 13, presented to the lords justices and Ginkel in late 1691, a document that throws new light on the negotiation of the articles from the Jacobite perspective.[80] On the available evidence, it seems that article 13 was added just before the official signing of the articles, on the afternoon of 3 October.

To understand the circumstances that allowed article 13 to be added at such a late stage, it is necessary to understand Browne's relationship with the other Jacobites involved in the negotiations. Twelve men were appointed to discuss

---

[77] Story, *Continuation*, pp 230–2, 237–8; *A diary of the siege and surrender of Lymerick: with the articles at large, both civil and military* (London, 1692), pp 16–17. Rapparees were irregular soldiers who often supported the Jacobite army, though were outside of its authority.

[78] 'Articles for the capitulation of Limerick', [Sept. 1691] (B.L., Eg. Ms 2618, f. 162); Simms, 'Original draft', pp 40, 44, n. 19. Simms remarks in his final footnote that 'the document contains nothing corresponding to the final clause relating to the debts of Colonel John Browne'.

[79] Württemberg to Christian V, 29 Sep. 1691 (Danaher & Simms (eds), *Danish force in Ireland*, pp 135–6).

[80] 'The examination of Col. John Browne's clause in the articles of Limerick', [1691] (S.R.O., D641/2/K/2/3/1). For a full discussion of the petition, see below, pp 147–53. I am indebted to John Bergin for providing me with all of the material cited in this book from the S.R.O.

terms of surrender with the Williamites, with the stipulation that the articles were to be approved by the Jacobite lords justices and an appointed army council.

Eight of the commissioners can be identified with reasonable certainty: Sarsfield; Sir Toby Butler; Major General John Wauchope; Colonel Nicholas Purcell (sometimes referred to as Baron Purcell of Loughmoe); Colonel Garrett Dillon; Colonel John Browne; John Brenan, archbishop of Cashel; and Dominic Maguire, archbishop of Armagh. Piers Butler, Viscount Galmoy, attended at least one conference with the Williamites and was a signatory to the articles, as was Colonel Nicholas Cusack, marking these two as likely commissioners. The remaining two came from the following six Jacobites: Thomas Nugent, earl of Westmeath; Henry Dillon, Viscount Dillon of Costello-Gallen; Matthias Barnewall, Baron Trimlestown; Oliver Plunkett, Baron Louth; Brian Magennis, Viscount Iveagh; and Lieutenant-General Dominic Sheldon. Westmeath, Iveagh, Trimleston and Louth served as hostages during the negotiations, leaving Dillon and Sheldon as the most probable candidates. A Major Cordon is mentioned in one source, but this name does not appear in the surviving Jacobite army lists. There was, rather pointedly, no Frenchman chosen as commissioner.

The Jacobite lords justices, appointed following the death of Tyrconnell on 14 August, were Sir Richard Nagle, James II's secretary of war in Ireland, lord chancellor Alexander Fitton and Francis Plowden, a revenue commissioner.[81] That these lords justices did not personally engage with the negotiations is not surprising. Irish Jacobites resented Fitton's and Plowden's appointments on the basis of their nationality.[82] More pertinently, the exclusion of the Jacobite lords justices from negotiations ensured that the Williamite authorities gave no official recognition to any person acting under James II's authority.[83] Without Nagle's participation the Jacobites were denied considerable legal expertise and experience, but the commissioners selected by the Jacobite lords justices made up for Nagle's absence by including at least three seasoned lawyers in Sir Toby Butler (James II's solicitor general), Garrett Dillon (former king's counsel and prime serjeant) and John Browne.

The commissioners fulfilled their duty by reporting back to the Irish government during negotiations, with the last report probably delivered very early in the morning of 3 October. At this meeting, the first twelve articles were shown to the Jacobite lords justices and later read to a council of army officers in Sarsfield's presence, 'and not a word therein mentioned of Colonel John

[81] Sir Richard Nagle to Viscount Merrion, 14 Aug. 1691 (T.C.D., Ms 749/10/1017).
[82] Simms, *Jacobite Ireland*, p. 242.
[83] I am grateful to Prof. James McGuire for bringing this point to my attention.

Browne's clause or proviso'. The accusation was later made that Browne, Garrett Dillon and Sarsfield acted independently by negotiating article 13 without the knowledge or consent of the other commissioners or the Irish lords justices:

> It is apparent King James's lords justices and the major part of the commissioners (for none of them owns to have consented to it but the Lord Lucan and Col. Garret Dillon who is the said John Browne's nephew and bound for most of his debts) never knew or saw the said Col. John Browne's clause until after the articles were signed.[84]

While it is conceivable that the Jacobite lords justices were kept in the dark, it is not credible that the other commissioners were similarly ignorant of the negotiations for Browne's article. It is possible that article 13 was negotiated on 2 October and its existence kept from the Jacobite lords justices and army council, for fear of provoking opposition if word of its existence leaked. The more likely scenario is that Browne prevailed upon the Irish negotiators to press for the inclusion of his article during the early morning of 3 October, later convincing the Williamite lords justices to amend the engrossed articles prior to signing. Porter recalled, in 1697, that after he and Coningsby arrived on 2 October, they were unhappy with the untidy state of the draft of the articles presented to them and stayed up all night to draft a clean copy.[85] This presents the possibility of a message from Browne to the Williamite lords justices in the very early morning of 3 October, requesting the inclusion of article 13. Contemporary accounts do not, however, support Porter's sequence of events. A large party of Jacobites arrived in the Williamite camp on 3 October, where, after dining with Württemberg, 'they went all afterwards to the General's tent, where the ... articles were interchangeably signed'.[86] There could have been no further additions to the articles after this point. The question then, is how was Browne was able to convince his fellow commissioners to agree to the article?

Garrett Dillon, one of Browne's nephews, would have served as a natural and willing ally. The affairs of the two men were closely connected from the time Dillon followed his uncle in attending Gray's Inn.[87] As Browne's financial

---

84 'The examination of Col. John Browne's clause in the articles of Limerick', [1691] (S.R.O., D641/2/K/2/3/1).

85 C.S.P.D., 1697, pp 269–70; James McGuire, 'The Treaty of Limerick' in Bernadette Whelan (ed.), The last of the great wars: essays on the war of the three kings in Ireland (Limerick, 1990), p. 131.

86 Story, Continuation, p. 238.

87 Col. Browne to Lucas Dillon, 25 Aug. 1669 (N.L.I., Ms 40,893/4/13–14). Browne first entered Gray's Inn on 17 April 1662 and was admitted to the King's Inns on 5 February 1669, with Garrett admitted to Gray's Inn on 16 February 1669. He was admitted to the King's Inns on 16 November 1674 (K.I.A.P., pp 57, 132). However, Browne was back in London later in 1669. While they may not have attended Gray's Inn at the same time, their close connection appears in such details as the fact that they shared the same London tailor.

woes had worsened during the 1680s, Garrett became intimately involved with his business affairs – an involvement that included assuming trustee status for Browne's debts and entailments, as well as entering into several joint bonds.[88] Another commissioner, Henry, Viscount Dillon, who succeeded to the peerage on the death of his father at the battle of Aughrim, had prior connections with Garrett Dillon and Browne. The Dillons of Costello-Gallen retained the services of both men as legal advisers in the 1670s and 1680s.[89] Garrett secured the post of surveyor general for another of Browne's nephews, Christopher Malone, in July 1689, at the request of the Duchess of Tyrconnell; the fees and profits of the position were due to be paid to the Duchess's daughter, Frances, wife of Henry Dillon.[90] In the mid-1680s, the Dillons entangled their own financial affairs with those of Browne. Theobald, Viscount Dillon, Henry's father, was personally indebted to Roger Moore, one of Browne's Protestant creditors. Several of the Dillon estates, leased to Browne, were also used as security for a sum of £4,000 owed to Moore, thus drawing the Dillons into the web of debts covered by article 13.[91]

Sarsfield's support for the article was probably due to his desire to rid himself of responsibility for the repayment of Browne's debts, and he may have felt an obligation to Browne following the Jacobite army's requisitioning of his goods. The acquiescence of the other commissioners is more difficult to explain. The remaining army officers were probably swayed by Sarsfield, their *de facto* commander. This is particularly true of Wauchope and Sheldon, a Scot and Englishman respectively, who held no Irish land and had no intention of remaining in Ireland. Colonel Nicholas Cusack (a nephew of Tyrconnell) followed Sarsfield to France, as did Viscount Galmoy, both men forfeiting their estates and, in the process, any charge for Browne's debt.[92] As landowners, Colonel Nicholas Purcell and Sir Toby Butler probably opposed the article. The attitude of archbishops Brenan and Maguire is more difficult to gauge. However, the majority of the commissioners are likely to have supported article 13, or at least to have had few personal reasons to oppose it. It is also possible that Sarsfield placated opponents by promising to undervalue the debt owed to Browne, thus limiting the exposure of Catholic landowners. Pressure is also sure

---

[88] N.L.I., Mss 40,889/21/3–4; 40,889/22/1–3; 40,889/23/1–3; 40,894/17–19; 40,895/1/13; 40,897/4/1–21; 40,898/1/3; 40,898/6/13; 40,900/4/10.

[89] N.L.I., Mss 40,894/3/2, 4; 40,894/5/1; 40,895/1/11; 40,896/3/21. Thomas, 3rd Viscount Dillon, was a signatory of the 'Remonstrance of the Roman Catholic nobility and gentry' in 1669 (*Calendar of State Papers Ireland, 1669–70 & Addenda*, p. 562).

[90] N.L.I., Ms 40,899/1/1; King, *State of the Protestants*, p. 331. Christopher was almost certainly the younger brother of the lawyer Edmund Malone, whose mother, and Garrett Dillon's, was a sister of John Browne.

[91] N.L.I., Ms 40,897/2/10.

[92] John D'Alton, *King James's Irish army list*, pp 85–8, 96–105.

to have been applied from the Williamite camp. Browne's debt was hardly part of the agenda of either Ginkel or the lords justices at the outset of negotiations but, once the extent of the money owed to Protestants was brought to light, their support was surely guaranteed. Browne was indebted to several influential and wealthy Irish Protestants, including the Dublin-based goldsmith and former lord mayor Sir Abel Ram (himself no stranger to large debts), Sir John Topham, Robert Dillon, earl of Roscommon, and William Blayney, Baron Monaghan.[93]

One further consideration points to the addition of article 13 on 3 October, perhaps even as the articles were being signed. The confusion that last-minute negotiations and additions to the articles would have caused may go some way towards explaining the notorious lapse on the part of the Irish signatories, whereby they signed an incorrect or 'foul' draft of the articles. The notorious 'missing clause' had originally been added on the back of Butler's protestations and Sarsfield's famous declaration that he would 'lay his bones in these old walls rather than not take care of those who had stuck by them all along'.[94] The civil articles were not a lengthy document, and when one considers that the clause omitted from the signed copy had been declared crucial by Sarsfield and Butler for the continuation of the negotiations, this lapse is made less inexplicable if amendments were being made up to the last minute.[95]

V

Colonel John Browne's importance to the Jacobite war effort had been made clear by the 1689 act of repeal, which highlighted the potential value of his ironworks. Realising the full depth of that potential during the war had, however, proved beyond Browne. Relations with the Jacobite administration were initially strained as the Jacobites suffered a series of setbacks in early 1690 and Browne proved unable to fulfil the terms of various contracts for steel and weapons. By the time the Jacobites repelled the Williamite forces during the first siege of Limerick in the late summer of 1690, however, Browne had restored himself to the administration's good graces. His appointment as one

93 N.L.I., Ms 40,889/24/4. On his death in 1692, Ram had debts of more than £20,000. See *The case of the creditors of Sir Abel Ram, Kt, deceased, humbly presented to the honourable, the knights, citizens and burgesses in parliament assembled* ([Dublin, 1695]).

94 Sarsfield's statement was made on 28 September. See H.M.C., *Leyborne-Popham Mss*, p. 280; Simms, *The Treaty of Limerick* (Irish History Series, no. 2, Dundalk, 1965), p. 10; idem., *Jacobite Ireland*, p. 252; idem, *Williamite confiscation*, p. 56.

95 For a comprehensive analysis of the issue of the 'missing clause', see Simms, *Williamite confiscation*, pp 55–65. For contemporary accounts of the efforts of the articlemen to have the omission rectified, see B.L., Eg. Ms, 2618, ff 168–9; N.L.I., Annesley Mss, xxiii, f. 95; H.M.C., *Leyborne-Popham Mss*, pp 280–1.

of the lords commissioners of civil affairs during Tyrconnell's absence in France was an important moment, prefacing his later presence on the team of Jacobite negotiators for the surrender of Limerick. It was an opportunity that he was able to exploit to the fullest.

The articles of Limerick brought to an end two years of sporadically intense warfare in Ireland. The cost to Catholic landowners of fighting for James II had been high, and many were now left with estates that had been repeatedly plundered by both armies and by irregular troops. Some followed James II to France in anticipation of another attempt to restore their king to the throne. For many of the 'new interest', however, their primary aim, of surrender terms in which they retained their estates, had been achieved. These terms were subject to ratification by William and Mary and by parliament, and to the inclination of the Irish government to ensure their implementation. The challenge that now faced Browne, along with other Catholic landowners who remained in Ireland, was to ensure that the articles of surrender were fully implemented by the new Williamite government.

Part II

The Articles of Surrender

THE
CASE
OF

All Perfons comprized in the Articles or Capitulations of the City of *Waterford*, Fort and Caftle of *Bophin*, and the Towns of *Sligo* and *Drogheda* in the Kingdom of *Ireland*, humbly offered to the Confideration of the Honourable the Knights Citizens and Burgeffes in Parliament affembled.

THe Capitulations of *W A T E R F O R D*, whereby all Perfons comprized therein, are to enjoy their Eftates, were made with, and figned by, his Majefty in Perfon in the fecond Year of his Reign, at his Royal Camp near *C A R R I C K*. And his Majefty being refolved, that the faid Articles, fo given and agreed to by himfelf, fhould be punctually kept and performed, and all the Security poffible given to the Perfons concerned, was gracioufly pleafed to order that the faid Articles fhould be ratified under the great Seal of *E N G L A N D*, which was accordinly done, and all the Perfons entitled to the Benefit of the fame, continued and protected ever fince, in the Poffeffion of their Eftates and Properties.

But now fo it is, That by a Bill depending before the Honourable the Houfe of Commons, for applying all the forfeited Eftates and Interefts in *I R E L A N D*, and all Grants thereof, and all the Rents and Revenues belonging to the Crown within that Kingdom, fince the 13th Day of *February* 1688, to the Ufe of the Publick, the Adjudications of thofe comprized in the Articles of *L I M E R I C K*, and *G A L W A T* are to be comfirmed; and no mention of, nor Provifion whatfoever made for, the faid Capitulations of *W A T E R F O R D*, to the great Surprize of thofe included in the fame; who always took themfelves to be upon as fecure a bottom, as any other articled Men in *I R E L A N D*, and their faid Capitulations every way as binding, and as Authentick as theirs.

There is no Provifion neither made in the faid Bill for the Articles of *B O P H I N*, which are confirmed alfo under the Great Seal of *E N G L A N D*, nor no Saving for the Articles of *S L I G O*, or *D R O G H E D A* which was the firft Town that fubmitted to their Majefty upon the Security of Publick Faith; both which laft recited Articles, are by the Law of Nations, as obligatory and as binding as any of the reft, although the Perfons concerned, confiding very much in the publick Faith giving them as aforefaid, and being for the moft part indigent, and not in a Condition to be at the neceffary Expence, made no Application to have their faid Capitulations ratified under the great Seal of *E N G L A N D*. Which Ommiffion in the faid Bill, if not remedied, or redreffed by the Honourable the Houfe of Commons, may be of the laft ill Confequence to a great many Perfons, comprized in the faid feveral Articles, confidering that there is a latitude given in the faid Bill, to Profecute on ftill for high Treafon, any Perfon or Perfons, concerned in the late War in *I R E L A N D*, againft the prefent Government, to which Profecution feveral of the faid articled Men apprehend themfelves to be liable, if not protected by their faid Capitulations, and provided for in the faid Bill.

It is therefore humbly hoped, that the Honourable the Houfe of Commons, will take the Cafe of all the Perfons concerned in the faid Capitulations into Confideration, and make fuch a Provifion for them in the faid Bill, as they may hereafter have the Benefit of their faid refpective Articles.

Plate 3: *The case of all persons comprized in the articles or capitulations of the city of Waterford … Bophin, and the towns of Sligo and Drogheda …* [London, 1700]. Though this appeal is dated to 1692 by the English Short Title Catalogue, it was in fact printed in 1700 for distribution to members of the English parliament. By permission of the Royal Irish Academy © RIA.

3

'They were drawn by some furious lawyer': Implementing the minor articles of surrender, 1691–1704[1]

Following the surrender of Limerick, for many Catholics the choice was stark: to endure exile on the continent, or to remain in Ireland under the government of a victorious yet resentful Protestant minority. Perhaps 12,000 members of the Jacobite army left for France, determined to return and restore their king to the throne. Thousands more snubbed the Jacobite cause and sought to enlist with William's allies in Europe.[2] Some were simply unable to leave, hampered by familial ties or a lack of money. Others firmly resisted the temptation to flee, preferring to retain possession of their land and to enjoy the rights promised to them by the articles of surrender. These were the articlemen, the 'dastard gentry' of Catholic Ireland.[3]

The historiography of Catholic Ireland in the 1690s has been dominated by the articles of Limerick; understandably so given their status as the end point of the Williamite war, and the various controversies surrounding their confirmation by the Irish parliament. One of the results of this focus has been to overshadow the importance of the other articles of surrender to the Williamite settlement in Ireland. Articles of surrender were also signed at Drogheda, Waterford, Galway, Inis Boffin and Sligo. The principal advantage of the articles was protection from forfeiture of the estates of those who claimed under them. Claimants to the articles of Galway and Limerick were required to prove their eligibility in specially established courts of claims, which sat in 1692, 1694 and from 1697 to 1699.

The articles of Drogheda, Waterford, Inis Boffin and Sligo are referred to here as minor articles, due to the low numbers known to have received their benefit, relative to Galway and Limerick. The Irish and English governments also devoted a much smaller degree of attention to their interpretation and

[1] The quotation is taken from D. Campbell to Sir Arthur Rawdon, 24 July 1690 (Edward Berwick (ed.), *The Rawdon papers* (London, 1819), p. 326). Part II of this book considerably expands upon Eoin Kinsella, 'In pursuit of a positive construction: Irish Catholics and the Williamite articles of surrender, 1690–1701' in *E.C.I.*, 24 (2009), pp 11–35.
[2] C.I. McGrath, *Ireland and empire, 1692–1770* (London, 2012), pp 20, 145.
[3] One of the derogatory names applied to them by the exiles. See J.M. Flood, *The life of Chevalier Charles Wogan: an Irish soldier of fortune* (Dublin, 1922), p. 138.

implementation. These articles were, however, of great importance to the men who claimed their benefit, as each surrender was adjudged to protect the real estates of its claimants. Yet proving eligibility to the articles was merely the first step for the articlemen in ensuring that they received their benefit. Acts of the Irish and English parliaments were required to enshrine the articles in legislation. With three exceptions, these acts were not passed with the intention of confirming the articles.[4] One of the ironies of the Williamite era is that most of the legislative protection for the articlemen was actually inserted as saving clauses in the earliest laws restricting Catholic rights – the penal laws. Without intensive lobbying of the Irish and English governments by the articlemen, such protection may not have been implemented. Even so, the articles of Galway and Limerick were eventually almost completely undone by acts of the Irish and English parliaments.[5]

This chapter analyses the circumstances in which the minor articles were signed, and the attitude of the Irish government to their implementation. The minor articles were beyond the remit of the courts of claims, forcing the articlemen to solicit William III for royal pardons. Section III also examines the fate of the 'protectees' – Catholic men and women who had individually surrendered to the Williamite authorities during the war, relying on various promises of leniency published in proclamations. Ineligible to claim under the articles of surrender, the protectees were in a substantially weaker position than the articlemen. In the decade after Limerick the articlemen and the 'protectees' maintained a constant dialogue with William III and his courts in Dublin and London. It was far from a dialogue between equals, yet Catholics could at least point to the articles of surrender and the proclamations as the foundation for their attempts to preserve their economic and social standing within the kingdom.

I

One month to the day after the signing of the articles of Limerick, the articlemen of Waterford petitioned the king, asking him to prevent the loss of their estates. Though the petition was referred to the Irish lords justices (Sir Charles Porter and Thomas Coningsby), no report appears to have been made.[6] Resubmitted in March 1692, the petition was probably revived at this time

---

[4] The exceptions are the act for confirming the articles of Limerick (see below, pp 119–20), and the private acts passed for Col. John Browne (see chapters 6, 7 and 8).
[5] See table 2 for details of the use of legislation to confirm or abrogate the articles of surrender. Private acts to extend the benefit of the articles to individuals (as with Lord Bophin, discussed in chapter 5) were a rarity. The most notable exception was article 13 of Limerick, discussed in chapters 6 and 7.
[6] C.S.P.D., 1691–2, p. 3.

because of William's ratification of the articles of Galway and Limerick.[7] On 15 March the English privy council once again referred to the Irish lords justices the Waterford articlemen's petition, along with another from the articlemen of Boffin. Both petitions requested ratification of their respective articles under the great seal of England, the restoration of the articlemen to their estates and a guarantee against future forfeiture.[8] The two petitions met with very different responses.

The Jacobite-held town of Waterford had found itself in a precarious position at the end of July 1690. Defeat at the Boyne on 1 July led to the haphazard retreat of Jacobite forces, with little leadership or organisation evident. The majority of the retreating forces made their way to Limerick, ensuring that Waterford was poorly defended and ill equipped to withstand a siege. A desire for a negotiated settlement at this time was prevalent among the Jacobite leadership, helped in no small measure by James II's reported parting speech to his privy council in the early morning of 2 July: '[I] do now resolve to shift for myself and so, gentlemen, must you'.[9] Jacobite losses at the Boyne were in fact relatively small.[10] However, the abiding impression in both the Williamite and Jacobite camps was that a fatal blow had been dealt to the Catholic cause, leading William to issue a proclamation at Finglas on 7 July that gave the Jacobite leaders little hope for lenient treatment.[11] It was in the context of this uncompromising Williamite attitude that the garrison at Drogheda capitulated on what have been described as poor terms.[12] When the Williamite forces reached Waterford three weeks later little had changed and the garrison surrendered on the same terms as those signed at Drogheda.

Before the war had even finished the Waterford articlemen had begun planning their efforts to lobby for the implementation of the articles, specifically the protection of their estates. By the first week of August 1691, John Fitzgerald, resident in London, had been empowered to act on their behalf.

---

7   T.N.A., SP 63/354, ff 15, 21–2; C.S.P.D., 1691–2, p. 111.

8   H.M.C., *Finch Mss*, iv, 29–30; C.S.P.D., 1691–2, p. 180.

9   *Villare Hibernicum* (London, 1690), p. 24; George Story, *An impartial history of the wars in Ireland* (London, 1693), p. 89.

10   It is generally agreed that approximately 1,000 Jacobite soldiers were killed. Lenihan calculates that 2,000 Jacobite soldiers, including injured and deserters, were lost at the battle, out of a total of about 25,000 (Pádraig Lenihan, *1690: Battle of the Boyne* (Stroud, 2003), pp 178–9; Simms, *Jacobite Ireland*, pp 151–2).

11   See Appendix C for the text of this proclamation and Section III of this chapter for a discussion of how it affected the 'protectees'. William was principally advised in this matter by Irish Protestants, who were anxious that as few Catholics as possible should retain their estates (N.L.I., Ms 13,653, ff 1–4, 12–16, 19–20; J.G. Simms, 'Williamite peace tactics, 1690–1' in *I.H.S.*, viii (1952–3).

12   Lenihan, *Battle of the Boyne*, p. 176.

Thomas Porter was to provide assistance if necessary. Fitzgerald and Porter were instructed to

> petition and solicit to their Majesties for the benefit of the articles of surrender or capitulation upon the rendition of Waterford, and particularly to procure such clause in the act, which is to be passed relating to the forfeited lands of Ireland or some other effectual order whereby we might enjoy our real estates pursuant to the extent and signification of the word Properties which are granted to us by the said articles.

The proposed method of doing so was to make an agreement with 'some courtier or favourite' to act as an intermediary with the king to ensure the retention of the articlemen's estates. Fitzgerald and Porter were authorised to offer up to £500 to the intermediary 'in consideration of his trouble therein'. Six Waterford articlemen signed a bond making their estates liable for payment of this gratuity, should the articlemen retain their estates: former mayors Thomas Wyse and Richard Fitzgerald (father of the articlemen's agent, John), Edward Browne, Peter Cranisbrough, John Porter and Matthew Porter.[13]

Neither the identity of the intermediary nor the cost of his services are known, but the articlemen's petition was presented in London and referred to the Irish lords justices on 3 November. The petition rested on article 3 of the surrender, worded as follows: 'The Roman Catholic dwellers of the city shall not be molested in their properties.'[14] Compared with similar articles subsequently negotiated it is poorly worded, reflecting the pressure that the Waterford negotiators were under. The protection offered was vague at best, leaving scope for varied interpretation. The articlemen claimed that article 3 protected their estates both real and personal, while their March 1692 petition also requested permission to practise their professions. On 21 March, William Blathwayt, acting secretary of state, notified the earl of Nottingham that the king had no objections to the ratification of the articles of Waterford, Boffin, or Sligo.[15]

The Waterford petition ran into difficulty, however, as the Irish government prepared their report. Nottingham informed Blathwayt that there was 'a difficulty made about the import of the word "properties", which his Majesty by those articles promised to secure to them, whether it meant of their real

---

[13] Bond of the Waterford articlemen, 8 August 1691 (Medieval Museum of Waterford, display item). John Porter represented the city of Waterford in the 1689 parliament. I am indebted to John Bergin for bringing this document to my attention, and to Julian Walton for providing a transcript.
[14] See Appendix A.
[15] William Blathwayt to Daniel Finch, earl of Nottingham, 21 Mar. 1692 (H.M.C., *Finch Mss*, iv, 35–6). Nottingham was secretary of state for the southern department, which included responsibility for Ireland.

estates, that is estates for life or inheritance, as well as personal'. Nottingham noted that the affair depended upon William's judgment as to what he had intended by the term 'properties' at the time the articles were signed. The word, he wrote, 'is certainly in common speech equally applicable to real as personal estates'.[16] William's ruling was swift and disappointing for the articlemen. 'Properties' was to apply only to personal estates, not to estates of life or inheritance.[17]

Fortunately for the articlemen, this was not William's final ruling on the matter. In March 1693 (the reason for the delay is not apparent) ratification of the articles of Waterford was ordered.[18] Opposition to a construction of the word 'properties' favourable to the articlemen seems once more to have been raised, for ten days later William wrote to Henry, Viscount Sydney to reverse the ruling made a year earlier. He explained:

> The word property ought, according to the true meaning and signification thereof, to be construed to extend to both real and personal estates. Roman Catholics are therefore to enjoy the full benefit of the said article according to our said declaration; and you are to give order accordingly.[19]

The reason for William's *volte face* is unclear. Perhaps his presence in England in 1693 allowed the articlemen greater scope for more effective lobbying.

Having arrived in Ireland as lord lieutenant in August 1692, Sydney's response to this change of policy was dilatory. In a lengthy letter to Nottingham, he outlined the reasons for his opposition to the broad construction of the word 'properties' now ordered. The value of the estates in question, according to Sydney, was between £1,500 and £2,000 per annum.[20] According to witnesses present at the signing of the articles of Waterford, the initial terms proposed to Waterford were returned by the garrison, with the request that the real estate of the inhabitants be explicitly protected:

> We yesterday summoned Waterford; the answer sent the king was, that … securing them in their lives and properties, exercise of their religion, 15 days time for absentees to claim the like benefit, and the mayor and sheriff of their own choosing, they upon these terms will surrender, and be good boys. The king laughed at it, saying, he believed they were drawn by some furious lawyer.[21]

---

16 Nottingham to Blathwayt, 15 July 1692 (ibid., p. 315).
17 Blathwayt to Nottingham, 21 July 1692 (ibid., p. 329).
18 C.S.P.D., 1693, p. 62.
19 William III to Sydney, 23 Mar. 1692 (T.N.A., SP 67/1, f. 177; C.S.P.D., 1693, pp 81–2).
20 C.S.P.D., 1693, pp 157–8.
21 D. Campbell to Sir Arthur Rawdon, 24 July 1690 (Berwick, The Rawdon papers, p. 326).

Following William's threat to lay siege to the city, the original draft was signed.[22] Nottingham responded two weeks later, on 10 June 1693, stating that the king had, with the privy council of England, given full consideration to the issue. He had thought it best 'not to restrain that word to a narrower construction than the just and legal import of it'. The decision of March 1693 was to stand.[23]

William's reversal of his own decree of the previous year amounted to a substantial victory for the Waterford articlemen. Despite the ambiguous wording of article 3, with its potential for an unfavourable construction, their estates were now protected from forfeiture. The Waterford petition also requested freedom for the articlemen to practise their professions, probably referring to the lawyers present in the city. This was an ambitious claim, for the articles contained no provision for professions, and it may have been inspired by the success of the Galway and Limerick negotiators in securing such protection. It is no surprise that this request was not entertained. In spite of this rebuff the articles of Waterford, by a strict interpretation of their wording, were fully implemented by June 1693.[24]

The articlemen of Boffin also petitioned William III in March 1692. The surrender of Inis Boffin had been relatively straightforward and came three weeks after the fall of Galway. There was little chance that the Jacobite garrison on the island could hold out much longer after Galway's surrender, despite its impressive Cromwellian-era fort.[25] From a strategic standpoint, the capture of Inis Boffin came to be viewed by some Williamites as essential 'so long as we have war with France, for their privateers might shelter themselves very well in Boffin harbour'.[26] After some initial anxiety caused by a delayed response from

---

[22] B.L., Add. Ms 38,146, ff 194–5. For supporting contemporary accounts see Kevin Danaher and J.G. Simms (eds), *The Danish force in Ireland, 1690–1691* (Dublin, 1962), p. 65; *A letter from an English officer ... with what passed at the surrender of Waterford and Duncannon* (London, 1690); George Story, *A true and impartial history of the most material occurrences in the kingdom of Ireland during the last two years* (London, 1691); *London Gazette*, 28–31 July 1691.

[23] Nottingham to Sydney, 10 June 1693 (T.N.A., SP 67/1, f. 233; *C.S.P.D.*, 1693, pp 176–7).

[24] Reference has been made to letters patent issued in 1693 that pardoned all of the citizens who were within the walls of Waterford when it was surrendered (Harman Murtagh, 'Waterford and the Jacobite war, 1689–1691' in *Decies: Journal of the Waterford Archaeological and Historical Society*, 8 (1978), p. 6). Presumably this refers to the ratification of article 3, which was not an actual general pardon for the articlemen.

[25] Sheila Mulloy, 'Inisbofin – the ultimate stronghold' in *Irish Sword*, xvii (1987–8), pp 105–15; eadem, 'Military history of the western islands (with special reference to Inishbofin)' in *Cathair na Mart*, 9 (1989), pp 101–19.

[26] Sir Henry Bellasis to Ginkel, 20 Aug. 1691 (T.C.D., Clarke Correspondence, Ms 749/10/1036). Bellasis had originally advised Ginkel that the fort should be destroyed once captured, 'being 20 leagues off on an [in]significant island' (same to same, 2 Aug. 1691 (T.C.D, Clarke Correspondence, Ms 749/10/956)).

Colonel Timothy Riordan, the Jacobite commanding officer at Boffin, articles of surrender were signed on 19 August.[27]

The terms drew heavily on the articles of Galway, with specific provisions for the inhabitants of Boffin and members of the garrison. Unlike the other articles of surrender under review here, there were no face-to-face negotiations for the surrender of Boffin; terms were agreed via messengers sent between Riordan on Boffin and Sir Henry Bellasis in Galway town. It can be assumed that Colonel John Browne, who was present in Galway at the time of its surrender and afterwards travelled to Inis Boffin, probably assisted the garrison during negotiations and he was personally named within the articles. Inis Boffin was leased by the earl of Clanricarde to Browne, which may go some way to explaining why he went first to Inis Boffin rather than to Limerick. Article 3 protected the estates of the inhabitants from forfeiture, free from any quit- or crown-rents, while article 4 promised a general pardon. In addition to specifying that the governor (Riordan) and officers of the garrison were to retain their estates, article 3 named Edward, Lord Athenry, and Colonel John Kelly as beneficiaries. Colonel John Browne's presence at Inis Boffin was not to debar him from the benefit of the articles of Galway and he was also given liberty to travel to Limerick.[28] Article 10 gave an assurance that the articles would be ratified in the same manner as the articles of Galway.[29]

William ordered the ratification of the articles of Boffin in April 1692.[30] They explicitly protected real estate, avoiding the objections made in the case of the Waterford articles. However, it was not until 1697 that Athenry and Kelly, the two sole claimants, pressed to have the benefit of these articles. In July of that year a draft Irish bill to confirm outlawries and attainders arising from the Williamite war was transmitted to England. The bill went through several further drafting stages before receiving the approval of the Irish parliament as 'An act to hinder the reversal of several outlawries and attainders, and to prevent the return of subjects of this kingdom who have gone into the dominions of the French King in Europe'.[31] The initial draft of the bill was sent to London on 12 July. The Irish government's explanatory letter noted that 'the articles of Galway and Limerick only are mentioned, the others being looked

[27] Bellasis to Ginkel, 4 Aug. 1691; Porter to [?], 19. Aug. 1691 (T.C.D., Clarke Correspondence, Ms 749/10/970, 1031).

[28] Col. John Browne was actually entitled to claim the benefit of the articles of Galway, Boffin and Limerick. He was present at the surrender of all three garrisons. George Story took note of this anomaly and posed the following question: 'Whether it be conform [sic] to the laws of war, that one and the same person should be included in articles of surrender of three distinct places, as was Col. J. Browne.' (Story, A continuation of the impartial history of the wars of Ireland, p. 253).

[29] See Appendix A for the articles in full.

[30] C.S.P.D., 1691–2, p. 247.

[31] 9 William III, c.5. See Bergin, 'Irish legislative procedure', ii, 81–6, 164–6.

upon as military articles, relating solely to the surrender of particular places'. This interpretation did not prevent the inclusion of a proviso in the draft for Colonel Kelly and Lord Athenry, 'who are included by name in the articles granted at the surrender of Boffin'.[32] In spite of the extensive alterations made to this draft, Athenry's and Kelly's proviso was included in the approved bill. The proviso reversed their outlawries and attainders, subject to confirmation by William.[33]

The king's confirmation was duly granted in July 1698 in the form of a royal pardon.[34] At this point, Colonel Kelly's son, also named John, appeared on behalf of his father, who evidently had died between the passing of the above act and the granting of William's pardon. At no stage during the 1690s were Athenry and Kelly dispossessed of their estates. They received a pardon from William and the articles of Boffin were ratified under the great seal of England. There does not appear to have been any other claimant under these articles. However, article 8 dealt exclusively with the right of Captains Michael Cormick and Dominick Browne to 'enjoy their stock, corn and other goods under safe protection, with their servants and families'. They were given permission either to remain on Inis Boffin or to travel to Mayo 'where their concerns are, and there remain'.[35] That neither man is mentioned as having an estate suggests that both were landless but hopeful of settling in Mayo after the war, possibly as tenants or purchasers.[36] The fact that an article was negotiated solely for these men suggests that they had no interest in furthering their military careers on the continent in the event of the Jacobite army's surrender. Dominick Browne later claimed and received the benefit of the articles of Galway.[37]

Cormick's conduct immediately after the surrender of Boffin was not entirely honourable. On 30 August, Sir Henry Bellasis reported that Cormick had taken possession of Boffin fort, boasting that he would hold it for King James. His bravado was short-lived, with the appearance of part of the English navy off the coast of Boffin prompting Cormick to abandon the fort.[38] He later joined the Jacobite garrison at Limerick – a decision possibly influenced by a desire to remain close to Colonel Browne, for whom he acted as a land agent – and

[32] Irish lords justices and privy council to the lords justices of England, 12 July 1697 (T.N.A., SP 63/359, ff 66–8; C.S.P.D., 1697, pp 243–6). I have changed the spelling of Boffin here from the original to conform to the convention used in this chapter.
[33] 9 Will. III, c. 5, s. 23.
[34] N.L.I., Ms 40,901/6/2, 6; C.S.P.D., 1698, p. 348.
[35] See Appendix A.
[36] See below, pp 203, 208–9, for the connection between Michael Cormick and Col. John Browne, including Cormick's purchase of more than 1,000 acres of the Browne estate in 1700.
[37] Simms, 'Irish Jacobites', p. 107.
[38] Bellasis to Ginkel, 30 Aug. 1691 (Utrecht Archive, Huis Amerongen, no. 3220).

was adjudicated within the articles of Limerick.[39] Athenry and Kelly were landowners and probably were not present in either Galway or Limerick when those garrisons surrendered, forcing them to pursue implementation of the articles of Boffin. As neither man had been dispossessed of their estate during the war there were no Protestants in possession to raise objections.

II

The draft bill of July 1697 for confirming outlawries and attainders was also proposed as the mechanism for implementing the articles of Drogheda and Sligo. The articles of Drogheda were the first to be signed during the war and were identical to those of Waterford. The letter accompanying the draft bill made mention of the articles of Drogheda, specifically article 3. The lords justices wrote that it

> provides that the Roman Catholic dwellers in the town should not be molested in their property. They have not hitherto been molested in the enjoyment of their real estates, although several of them have been outlawed. These outlawries will be confirmed by this bill, unless they are specified in the saving clause.[40]

This was not the first time the Irish privy council had considered the articles of Drogheda. In January 1692 the council had put a stay on dispossession of the Drogheda articlemen, pending a report by the prime serjeant and an indication from William as to his preferred 'construction' of article 3 of Drogheda.[41] The privy council's actions were prompted by a petition submitted on behalf of Thomas Peppard, senior; Luke Conolly; John Bath; Ignatius Fleming; Thomas Delahide; Bartholomew Hamlin; Patrick Plunket; John Evers; James Bird; Peter Wotton; 'and other Roman Catholic dwellers in the town of Drogheda, praying the benefit of the capitulation made with the town'.[42] The names of two further claimants to the articles of Drogheda appear from later records: Nicholas Peppard and Michael Moore.[43]

No report from the prime serjeant survives, nor is there any indication of a royal decree on the interpretation of article 3. No attempt was made by the Drogheda articlemen to have the articles ratified under the great seal of England,

[39] Simms, 'Irish Jacobites', p. 109.
[40] Irish lords justices and privy council to the lords justices of England, 12 July 1697 (T.N.A., SP 63/359, ff 66–8; C.S.P.D., 1697, p. 244).
[41] 'Copy of the lords justices and Council's order', 20 Jan. 1692 (N.L.I., D 16,251).
[42] The petition is no longer extant, but the names of the petitioners are provided in the privy council's order (ibid.).
[43] N.L.I., D 16,255; C.J., xii, 144 (5 Mar. 1698).

with the expense associated with the maintenance of agents in London and assorted fees said to be beyond their means.[44] This may have actually been to their benefit. As discussed above, it was not until the Waterford articlemen pressed for ratification that they encountered opposition. The Waterford attempt was based on an article that was an exact copy of article 3 of Drogheda, and William had initially ruled that the formula of words used at Waterford did not protect real estate. Yet this ruling seems to have had no detrimental effect on the Drogheda articlemen and all of the petitioners of 1692 appear to have retained their estates. At least eight of the named articlemen – and possibly all ten – were never indicted for treason during the war. The names Thomas Peppard and Patrick Plunkett appear on the indictment lists for County Louth and Drogheda town, but it is unlikely that these are the same men. There were, however, other claimants to the articles who had been indicted but who nevertheless retained their estates, probably on the basis of the privy council's order of 1692. It is worth noting that, in a legal opinion offered in 1692 on the general interpretation of the articles of surrender, Sir Richard Cox specifically referred to the terms agreed at Drogheda as illustrative of a surrender that did *not* protect the estates of the men within the town.[45] Cox's assessment probably influenced William's initial judgment on the articles of Waterford in 1692; the alternative interpretation of the articles of Drogheda held by the lords justices in 1697 was in turn informed by William's reversal of his Waterford decision in 1693.

Following receipt of the draft bill confirming outlawries and attainders, the lords justices and privy council of England inspected the correspondence held between the garrison of Drogheda and the Williamite forces during negotiations on 22 July.[46] No proviso for the Drogheda articlemen was forthcoming, with the reasoning behind this decision unknown. A further complication arose when the English parliament turned its attention to the Irish forfeitures in 1698. A proposal that all grants in Ireland should be resumed (thus revoking grants of Irish land made by William after the war) caused widespread consternation.[47] In response, Irish Catholics and Protestants besieged the English parliament with petitions seeking saving clauses in any resulting bill. Michael Moore petitioned 'in behalf of himself, and others comprised within the articles made upon the surrender of Drogheda'. Moore declared that, notwithstanding their outlawries, the articlemen of Drogheda had managed to retain their estates,

---

[44] *The case of all persons comprized in the articles or capitulations of the city of Waterford … and Drogheda … in parliament assembled* ([London, 1700]).

[45] See pp 90–2, 100–1 below for a more detailed discussion of Cox's legal opinion.

[46] *C.S.P.D., 1697*, p. 262.

[47] For further discussion of these proceedings, see below, pp 93–4. See also Simms, *Williamite confiscation*, pp 110–62; Patrick Walsh, *The making of the Irish Protestant Ascendancy: the life of William Conolly, 1662–1729* (Woodbridge, 2010), pp 44–60; Hayton, *Ruling Ireland*, pp 71–84.

which he claimed were worth no more than £300 per annum. A saving clause in any bill that resulted from parliament's investigations into Irish forfeitures was requested in order to honour the articles.[48] When the bill of resumption finally came before the English parliament in 1700, the proposed clause for confirming the articles of Drogheda, Waterford, Boffin and Sligo was rejected.[49]

No record has been found of anyone seeking a pardon under the articles of Drogheda. In spite of their failure to secure saving clauses in either the 1697 attainders act or the act of resumption, the articlemen of Drogheda do not appear to have suffered any ill consequences and there is no record of any having been prosecuted on the basis of outlawry. Since no Drogheda articleman suffered confiscation of his estate by the Williamites during or after the war, it is not surprising that the records of the Irish forfeiture inquiry commissioners, compiled in 1699, make no reference to any estate having been restored under the articles of Drogheda. Thus, whether by default or design, those articles were fully implemented.

A more complicated situation was created by the handling of the articles of Sligo, both by the Irish government and the sole claimant under the articles, Sir Henry Crofton. The surrender of Sligo town had been a protracted affair, stretching out over four weeks. The most recent and comprehensive study attributes this to a combination of the incompetency of Colonel John Michelburne, the Williamite commander, and clever delaying tactics from Sir Teague O'Regan, his Jacobite counterpart. The same account also refers to the surrender of Sligo as 'the banalities of the small war', a description that does not convey the intensity of feeling on both sides of the conflict.[50] Though the war in Ireland may well have been decided at Athlone, Aughrim, Galway and Limerick, and the Jacobite garrison at Sligo relatively small in number, the surrender of Sligo was treated with great urgency by O'Regan and Michelburne. Indeed, Michelburne faced a court-martial for his alleged mismanagement of the affair.[51] The seriousness with which both parties approached the surrender reflected the fact that the town was of 'strategic significance as the key to Connacht' from

48 C.J., xii, 144 (5 Mar. 1698). It is not clear whether Moore meant that the value of all the estates covered by the articles of Drogheda was no more than £300, or that no individual articleman possessed an estate of greater value.

49 C.J., xiii, 292 (21 Mar. 1700); Simms, Williamite confiscation, p. 116.

50 John Childs, The Williamite wars in Ireland, 1688–1691 (London, 2007), pp 347–64.

51 Michelburne was acquitted. See [John Michelburne], An account of the transactions in the north of Ireland, Anno Domini, 1691 (London, 1692), pp 97–115. This account, published to vindicate Michelburne's conduct at Sligo, is a particularly valuable source for the surrender of Sligo. Correspondence between Michelburne and O'Regan are reprinted, along with several other related letters. Much of this correspondence is not otherwise extant, though some survive among the Ginkel papers at Utrecht Archive.

Ulster.[52] That significance may have waned with the fall of Galway, but Sligo's surrender remained a priority for the Williamites. The siege of Sligo was begun in the first days of August, a little over two weeks after the surrender of Galway. Negotiations between O'Regan and Michelburne quickly followed, resulting in articles signed on 6 August. Ginkel and Sarsfield both gave their blessing to the terms.[53] Yet Williamite forces did not occupy Sligo until 14 September, by which time (in a circumstance unique among the Jacobite surrenders) a number of further articles were agreed. Michelburne had unwisely agreed to a clause in article 5 that put off the date of occupation until 15 August 'in case relief do not come by that time'. The arrival of a troop of men in the vicinity of Sligo, under the command of the maverick Jacobite Hugh 'Balldearg' O'Donnell, allowed O'Regan to claim that relief had arrived and he duly reneged on the articles.[54] Respite for the garrison was brief. O'Donnell made little real effort to repel the Williamite forces and soon sought to make terms for himself. There was no hope of further reinforcements for the Jacobites, forcing O'Regan to bow to the inevitable and re-open negotiations on 11 September.[55] Ginkel was so enraged by O'Regan's conduct that he wrote to Michelburne to express his hope that he could be excluded from any terms: 'However, I would not have you stand so much upon that as to lose the town.'[56]

This second round of negotiations added eleven articles to the sixteen originally agreed. Michelburne remarked that the additional articles were simply for the 'reinforcements they had taken into the fort, to be included in the [original] articles'; this fact, and the omission from Michelburne's account of the text of the additional terms, is probably the reason the articles of 14 September have not been noticed in modern historical accounts.[57] In the additional articles Captains Owen O'Neill, Edmund McSweeney, Denis McSweeney and Henry Crofton were named as entitled to the terms of the surrender of 6 August, as were Lieutenant Colonel John McDonnogh, Major Terence McSweeney, Kean

[52] J.G. Simms, 'Sligo in the Jacobite war, 1689–91' in *Irish Sword*, vii (1965), p. 125.

[53] See Appendix A for the articles agreed; Simms, 'Sligo in the Jacobite war', p. 176; [Michelburne], *An account of the transactions in the north of Ireland*, p. 40.

[54] For O'Donnell, see Simms, *Jacobite Ireland*; D.I.B. O'Regan's initial negotiations do not appear to have been undertaken in good faith. In a letter to Patrick Sarsfield, dated 13 August, one of O'Regan's officers wrote: '[Michelburne] sent us a letter from General Ginkel, with some proposals, and money for surrendering this place, which we refused to do; but three or four days after we agreed to surrender, if we were not relieved in ten days, which was only a project to save about 5,000 cows we had about the fort, and thereby got an opportunity to send to O'Donnell' ([Michelburne], *An account of the transactions in the north of Ireland*, pp 65–6).

[55] Simms, 'Sligo in the Jacobite war', pp 176–9; Childs, *Williamite wars in Ireland*, pp 362–4.

[56] Ginkel to Michelburne, 7 Sept. 1691 ([Michelburne], *An account of the transactions in the north of Ireland*, p. 96).

[57] [Michelburne], *An account of the transactions in the north of Ireland*, p. 92. See also Simms, 'Sligo in the Jacobite war', p. 178; Childs, *Williamite wars in Ireland*, p. 363.

O'Hara and Henry Crofton's son Edward. In addition, the Jacobite garrisons at Bellaghy (County Sligo), Newtown and Castle Bourke (County Mayo) were also to be entitled to the articles. As a Protestant, Kean O'Hara's inclusion in the articles is noteworthy and perhaps was prompted by his acceptance of an appointment as a burgess of Sligo town under the charter granted by James II.[58]

Commenting on the original terms, Sir Charles Porter observed that 'the articles are very large, especially the last; but I think the king's affairs will be abundantly recompensed by that surrender'.[59] The article referred to read: 'That the said governor, officers and soldiers, garrison town and county of Sligo, shall have the benefit of all and singular other advantageous articles that Galway or any other got, in case it was surrendered', though Ginkel insisted that this was to apply only to those who were in Sligo at the time it was surrendered.[60] The Sligo articles were already quite comprehensive and this last article represented a prudent piece of negotiation, as the articles gave no firm guarantee protecting the inhabitants of Sligo from forfeiture. Article 9 merely promised that they 'shall be protected in their bodies, liberties and goods'. Though 'goods' could be construed to extend to estates real and personal, a favourable construction of the term for any claimant was by no means certain. Despite the king's willingness, the articles were not ratified – as had been the case with Drogheda, the expense proved beyond the sole claimant.[61] However, the supplemental articles appear to have been honoured; Major Terence McSweeney was later adjudicated within the articles of Limerick.[62] Of the other named beneficiaries of Sligo, O'Regan left for France at the war's end, while Kean O'Hara remained in Ireland in possession of his estate.[63] There is no record of the remainder claiming entitlement to articles, suggesting that they had no need to claim their benefit or that they followed O'Regan's example. The exception was Sir Henry Crofton, born to a Protestant father but raised as a Catholic by his mother, a

---

[58] O'Hara's loyalties during the war were not certain and accusations of conversion to Catholicism and of commanding troops in the Jacobite army were levelled at the war's end. O'Hara thus followed the pattern established by Irish Catholics of procuring statements from Protestant neighbours attesting to his good behaviour during the war. Unlike his Catholic counterparts, O'Hara did not use these to seek a pardon from the king, and they may never have actually been presented to the Irish government. His estate was never forfeited (Thomas Bartlett, 'The O'Haras of Annaghmore c.1600–c.1800: survival and revival' in *Irish Economic and Social History*, ix (1982), pp 38–40). For the testimonials to O'Hara's good behaviour, see N.L.I., Ms 36,386/5.

[59] Sir Charles Porter to George Clarke, 10 Aug. 1691 (T.C.D., Clarke correspondence, Ms 749/10/1005).

[60] [Michelburne], *An account of the transactions in the north of Ireland*, p. 40; W.G. Wood-Martin, *Sligo and the Enniskilleners, from 1688–1691* (Dublin, 1882), p. 181.

[61] *The case of all persons comprized in the articles or capitulations of the city of Waterford … in parliament assembled.*

[62] Simms, 'Irish Jacobites', p. 119.

[63] N.L.I., Ms 20,386.

daughter of the O'Conor Don.[64] Present at the surrender of Galway, Crofton preferred to rendezvous with O'Regan in Sligo, where his estate lay, rather than marching to Limerick. He was named in article 11 of the supplemental articles of Sligo, yet appeared before the court of claims on 8 July 1692 to seek the benefit of the articles of Galway. His application was rejected.[65] Nothing further is heard of Crofton's case until a supplementary letter was sent by the lords justices relating to the 1697 bill for confirming outlawries and attainders. Crofton presumably petitioned the lords justices for redress, who obliged by requesting the insertion of a saving clause in his name. Crofton was said to be entitled to the benefit of the articles of Sligo, 'under which no other person claims anything'.[66]

A saving clause for Crofton was duly included in the act to hinder the reversal of outlawries and he received a royal pardon in July 1698. According to the warrant for pardon, Crofton was entitled to claim under the articles of Galway because of his posting as a captain of foot in the earl of Clanricarde's regiment and because of his presence in Galway during the negotiations. When the court of claims sat in 1692, the Sligo articles were not within its remit, leading Crofton to claim under the articles of Galway. The king's counsel, however, produced a witness to state that Crofton was a prisoner of war at the time, making him ineligible for the articles and leading the court to dismiss his appeal.[67] Crofton's status as the sole claimant to the Sligo agreement must have hampered any effort to have those articles ever considered by the various courts of claims. Once this anomaly was brought to light, his case was favourably received by the Irish and English privy councils in 1697 and no opposition was raised in the Irish parliament to his proviso. Crofton's estate was listed by the inquiry commissioners as consisting of almost 1,200 profitable acres.[68] Almost seven years after they were signed, the articles of Sligo were fully honoured by the Irish government.

Table 1 shows the date of signing for each set of articles and the numbers of successful claimants and estates restored by articles. The number of estates restored shown in the table is liable to give a misleading picture of the real importance of the articles to Catholic landownership in the 1690s. Many Catholic estates, particularly in the west and south-west of the country, were

---

[64] H.T. Crofton, *Crofton memoirs* (York, 1911), pp 134–6; Mary O'Dowd, *Power, politics and land: early modern Sligo, 1568–1688* (Belfast, 1991), p. 139; Simms, *Williamite confiscation*, p. 79.

[65] T.C.D., Ms 744, f. 106.

[66] Irish lords justices and privy council to the lords justices of England, 22 July 1697 (*C.S.P.D., 1697*, p. 263).

[67] *C.S.P.D., 1698*, pp 347–8. The accusation that Crofton was a prisoner of war was almost certainly fabricated.

[68] T.C.D., Ms 744, ff 77–100.

Table 1: Numbers of Successful Claimants to Articles and Estates Restored by Articles.

	Date of Signature	No. of Successful Claimants, 1692–4	No. of Successful Claimants, 1697–9	No. of Estates Restored Under*
Drogheda	2 July 1690	None	None	None
Waterford	25 July 1690	None	None	2
Galway	21 July 1691	2	74	3
Boffin	19 Aug. 1691	None	None	2
Sligo	14 Sept. 1691†	None	None	1
Limerick	3 Oct. 1691	481	709	156

* See discussion below for the distinction between numbers of estates restored and numbers of successful claimants.

† The Articles of Sligo were originally signed on 6 August 1691, before being repudiated by the Jacobites and then signed a second time, with additional concessions for the garrison, on 14 September 1691.

never confiscated by the Williamites (since articles of surrender had been signed before William's forces took possession of these areas). The question of restoring these estates never arose as their Catholic proprietors remained in possession. In addition, many Catholics were not outlawed, or never had their outlawries prosecuted, which meant that it was not necessary for them to submit their claim to articles for adjudication.[69] These two considerations account for the fact that the number of estates restored, relative to the number of successful claims to articles, is quite low.

In reality, many more Irish Catholics retained their estates by virtue of the articles but left little or no record of their ownership. An examination of the figures for the articles of Galway amply demonstrates the point. To date, 124 beneficiaries of these articles have been identified.[70] Almost two fifths of these men were never declared within articles in the courts of claims, yet assumed their protection. It is more difficult to provide definite numbers for the articles of Drogheda, Waterford, Boffin and Sligo. In the case of Waterford six claimants can be identified, but there were certainly more. Five of these men were never indicted or outlawed and probably remained in possession of their estates. Two were explicitly restored to their estates by the articles of Waterford: former

69 Simms, *Williamite confiscation*, pp 21–44.

70 The number accepted previously was 78. Simms's calculations were based on the records of the forfeiture inquiry commission of 1699 (*Williamite confiscation*, p. 72). Using the same source, I have identified 76. An additional 47 individuals have been identified through the Galway articlemen's quit rent petition of June 1693, while the addition of Lord Bophin brings the total to 124. See below, p. 134 for the quit-rent petition, and pp 135–42 for a discussion of Bophin and the articles of Galway.

mayor of Waterford Thomas Wyse and John Porter.[71] The articles of Boffin and Sligo (in addition to Athenry, Kelly and Crofton) name several men who do not appear in the records of forfeited estates. At least twelve men claimed the benefit of the articles of Drogheda yet, again, there were certainly more. The estates of the articlemen of Drogheda, Waterford, Sligo and Boffin so far identified were never confiscated and the majority of the claimants never appeared before the courts of claims. In terms of the numbers of successful claimants and of estates preserved or restored by virtue of the articles, Drogheda, Waterford, Boffin and Sligo were not of major significance. On the other hand, the terms of these surrenders allowed each garrison to rejoin the Jacobite army. Many of them, such as Captain Michael Cormick and Major Terence McSweeney, travelled to Limerick where they were included in its articles of surrender. At least twenty-five men with addresses in Waterford claimed the benefit of the articles of Limerick.

The only major garrison not permitted to rejoin the Jacobite army was Cork, which surrendered to John Churchill, earl of Marlborough, on 28 September 1690.[72] The articles signed at Cork were drafted in the spirit of William's proclamation at Finglas on 7 July 1690 and were purely military in nature; the only concession to leniency for the garrison was Marlborough's promise to endeavour to obtain the king's clemency on their behalf.[73] There was no mention of retaining estates or even personal property. The ordinary soldiers of the garrison were treated deplorably and died in 'large numbers'.[74] The fate of the members of the nobility and army officers garrisoned at Cork starkly demonstrates the importance of the articles of surrender, for Marlborough does not appear to have kept his promise. Colonel Roger MacElligott, the Jacobite commander, was imprisoned in the Tower of London until the Treaty of Ryswick was signed in 1697. Donough MacCarthy, earl of Clancarty (nephew of Justin MacCarthy, Viscount Mountcashel), and Richard Power, earl of Tyrone, were also imprisoned in the Tower. Tyrone died less than a month after his imprisonment. Clancarty would probably have shared MacElligott's fate had he not escaped to France in late 1694 or early 1695. The estates of all three were forfeited.[75] Clancarty's estate, the largest

---

[71] See above, p. 68, for the names of the Waterford articlemen. The only man outlawed was Richard Fitzgerald, while the two men listed in the 1699 inquiry commission records as restored to their estates by virtue of the articles of Waterford were Thomas Wyse and John Porter (T.C.D., Ms 744, f. 91).

[72] For an account of the military aspects of the surrender of Cork, see J.G. Simms, 'Marlborough's siege of Cork, 1690' in Irish Sword, ix (1969), pp 113–23.

[73] A full and true relation of the taking Cork, by the right honorable the earl of Marlborough, Lieut. Gen. of their Majesties forces: together with the articles of their surrender ([London?], 1690).

[74] Simms, 'Marlborough's siege of Cork', p. 122.

[75] MacElligott had sat in the Irish parliament of 1689 for the borough of Ardfert, County Kerry.

Jacobite estate forfeited, was granted away by William III and later sold by the forfeiture trustees in 1703.[76] Tyrone's family recovered his estate by obtaining a posthumous reversal of his outlawry, no doubt aided by his son John's early support for William.[77] Had the Williamite army succeeded in taking Limerick in the autumn of 1690, similar terms would probably have been forced on all Jacobites, with potentially devastating consequences for the Catholic landowning class in Ireland.

The articles of Waterford and Boffin were fully implemented by the Williamite government in Ireland. Though not ratified under the great seal of England, the same may be said of Drogheda and Sligo. The attempt by the Waterford articlemen to secure freedom to practise their professions constituted a *post facto* effort to append additional concessions to the original agreement. Their failure was consistent with William's intention to treat the articlemen 'with justice but not favour'.[78] The achievement of the claimants under the minor articles is all the more impressive when contrasted with the Irish government's partial and begrudging implementation of the Limerick and Galway articles. The terms agreed at Limerick and Galway were, however, of fundamental importance to the Williamite settlement and subjected to more intense scrutiny by the Irish and English governments.

III

The Jacobite negotiators of the articles of Limerick made every effort to extend protection to each remaining Jacobite garrison that had not yet surrendered to the Williamite army. In the face of concerted opposition from the Williamite negotiators, the articles neglected to protect the estates and property of those who had previously availed of periodic proclamations offering incentives to Jacobite officers and civilians who personally surrendered to the Williamite authorities. Such men and women had technically taken protection from the king and came to be known as 'protectees'. Throughout the 1690s, until the passage of the act of resumption in 1700 and its immediate aftermath, the protectees lobbied the Dublin and London administrations in an attempt to

For the cost of his imprisonment and his attempts to secure a release, see B.L., Add. Ms 34,195, ff 119–22; C.S.P.D., *1695 & Addenda*, p. 67; C.S.P.D., *1696*, pp 226, 360. The date of Clancarty's escape has been given as April 1694 (*D.I.B.*). However, this is contradicted by the presentation of a letter, signed by Clancarty, to the chief governor of the Tower of London (Robert, Lord Lucas) in August 1694 (*Calendar of Treasury Papers, 1556–1696*, p. 402).

76 For the disposal of Clancarty's estate, see Simms, *Williamite confiscation*, pp 87, 149–52

77 Simms, *Williamite confiscation*, p. 76. John Power was said to have fought against the Jacobites at the siege of Derry in 1689.

78 T.N.A., SP 63/354, f. 43; C.S.P.D., *1691–2*, p. 169.

receive the full benefit of the proclamations and to protect their estates from forfeiture. Like the articlemen, the protectees occasionally formed a distinct lobby group but found greater success with individual appeals than joint efforts. They met official hostility, arising from a widespread suspicion that many who took protection later reneged on their commitment to 'live peaceably' and actively communicated with or assisted the Jacobite forces. Indeed, claimants to articles during the 1690s were occasionally refused their benefit if it could be proved that they had taken protection during the war.

Proclamations offering leniency to rebels were a common tactic from both sides before and during the war. Tyrconnell issued one days before James II's arrival in Ireland, directed at the Protestant associations formed to resist the deposed monarch in Ulster and Sligo.[79] William and Mary likewise issued a proclamation promising leniency to their Irish subjects, should they lay down their arms by 10 April 1689.[80] A full enjoyment of estates was among the offers extended. However, the defeat of the Jacobite army at the Boyne in July 1690 hardened William's resolve and led to the ill-advised proclamation issued at Finglas on 7 July, which encouraged only rank and file soldiers to surrender and made no mention of the retention of estates.[81] The subsequent setback for the Williamite army at Limerick in September 1690 and the worsening military situation on the continent forced William into a grudging acceptance of the need to offer greater concessions to the Jacobites. The result was a proclamation issued exactly one year later, on 7 July 1691 – the first since February 1689 to promise to preserve the estates of those who surrendered.[82] This proclamation

---

[79] Proclamation, 7 Mar. 1689 (Kelly & Lyons (eds), *Proclamations of Ireland*, ii, 83–4).

[80] Proclamation, 22 Feb. 1689 (Kelly & Lyons (eds), *Proclamations of Ireland*, ii, 187–8).

[81] The licence issued to those who submitted to the Williamites following the extension on 1 August of the offer of 7 July 1690 read: 'Whereas his Majesty by his second gracious declaration of 1 August 1690, hath ordered that such of his subjects as desired particular protections might have the same, provided they remain steadfast in their obedience, and have neither since 7 July last past, plundered his Protestant subjects, nor concealed the arms or goods of his Majesty's enemies, or if they have so plundered or concealed, have made restitution to the right owners, and discovered such concealment to some justice of the peace. And whereas A.B. of C. in the county of D. affirms that he is qualified according to the conditions aforementioned, and is content to stand accountable if it shall otherwise appear, and prays to be protected in his person, goods and stocks. These are therefore in his Majesty's name, and in virtue of his said Royal Declaration, to require all officers civil and military, and all other his good subjects whatsoever; that until due proof shall be made before some justice of the peace that the said A.B. is defective or criminal as to the qualifications aforesaid, that they presume not to do him any violence or injury, in person, goods or stock, as they will answer the contrary to his Majesty, at their utmost perils' (N.L.I., Ms 13,653/13).

[82] Proclamations issued between 7 July 1690 and 7 July 1691 occasionally offered incentives (or coercive measures) to Jacobites to surrender, but lacked guarantees regarding estates. The proclamation of 7 July 1690 was reissued on 1 August 1690, extending the time allowed for submission to 25 August (see Appendix C for the text of these proclamations). On 19 November, protection was rescinded from those whose sons remained in the Jacobite quarters. For a detailed analysis of

was significant as it not only provided the Jacobite peace party with compelling arguments in favour of surrender, but also served as the template for the articles of Galway and Limerick.

Article 2 of the articles of Limerick, the legal foundation upon which the vast majority of Catholic-owned estates were retained, excluded from the benefit of the articles all those who were prisoners of war or had taken protection, a stipulation generally credited to Sir Richard Cox.[83] Prior to the accession of James II to the throne, Cox rose to prominence in County Cork following his call to the Irish bar in 1673, earning the patronage of the powerful Boyle and Southwell families. His experience as a Williamite judge during the war led Cox to conclude that many of the murders and other crimes committed in the Williamite quarters were done with the assistance of the protectees. In a memorandum composed in 1690 for the king, Cox observed that 'it is a great oversight to receive the Irish into protection till they are subdued because not one of them is converted to your interest, but in the contrary comes up to eat your victuals, and be spies upon you'.[84] At the time of the negotiation of the articles of Limerick, Cox warned the lords justices that many of the protectees had gone to Limerick in the hope of making themselves eligible to claim under the articles, leading the lords justices to insist on their exclusion.[85] Cox may indeed have been the inspiration for this proviso, though the lords justices hardly needed reminding of the suspected duplicity of many of the protectees. Several proclamations issued between July 1690 and the end of the war referred to their treacherous behaviour. On 18 September 1690, the lords justices issued a proclamation restricting the movement of Catholics within Williamite territory in consequence of their having

> most ungratefully relapsed into their former rebellious courses and whilst they feignedly pretended to pay allegiance to their majesties have most treacherously aided and assisted their majesties' enemies not only by giving them intelligence but also by assembling themselves in great numbers to terrify, plunder and destroy their majesties' good Protestant subjects … notwithstanding the grace and favour extended to them by their majesties' gracious declaration and the protection they enjoyed under their government.

Just eight days later two further proclamations were issued to forbid protectees from 'privately and perfidiously [giving] their utmost assistance to their majesties'

Williamite peace tactics from July 1690 to October 1691, including a comprehensive account of the drafting of the proclamation of 7 July 1691, see Simms, 'Williamite peace tactics'.
83 Simms, *Williamite confiscation*, pp 47–8. See Appendix A for the text of the article.
84 'Several things offered by Mr Cox in relation to the reduction of Ireland', 1690 (R.I.A., Ms 24 G 1).
85 *The whole works of Sir James Ware concerning Ireland, revised and improved*, ed. Walter Harris (2 vols, Dublin, 1764), ii, 210–13.

enemies', and forbidding them from living within ten miles of the frontier garrisons on account of the 'constant correspondence, commerce, and inter-course, that is between the rebels, and several Papists pretending to live under their majesties protection'.[86]

On 19 November 1690, the lords justices went so far as to declare that the Protestant population suffered more 'from those Irish Papists that pretend to submit, than from those that are in open rebellion against them'.[87] The patience of the lords justices was finally sapped by March 1691, when a proclamation was issued threatening to withdraw the benefit of protections from Catholics who did not assist the Williamite authorities in apprehending the perpetrators of murders of soldiers committed within their neighbourhoods.[88] It is thus not surprising that the Williamites insisted the protectees should be excluded from the benefit of the articles of Limerick, despite their recognition that some had observed the terms of their submission.[89] The attitude of the Jacobite negoti-ators towards the protectees is unknown; perhaps their early abandonment of the Jacobite banner caused some resentment. Sarsfield certainly made a point during negotiations of insisting on looking after those who had 'stuck by them all along'.[90]

Simms' analysis of the Irish forfeitures has demonstrated the lengths to which the Irish government went in seeking to prove that some claimants to the articles of Limerick had taken protection before 3 October 1691, thereby disqualifying themselves.[91] Several claims were rejected on these grounds. In one instance, James Magrath of Limerick was originally declared within articles but the judgment was later rescinded and his case reopened to give the king's counsel 'time to prove him in protection'.[92] Similar annotations appear beside the names of sixteen claimants to the articles of Limerick in 1694; the only year for which there are extant lists of pending claims, with annotations as to the outcome. Some protectees, probably aware that they had no chance of success at the courts of claims, found alternative methods of retaining their estates – principally through lobbying for the king's pardon. Simms suggests that the majority of these successes were gained in an 'arbitrary

---

86 Proclamation, 26 Sept. 1690 (Kelly & Lyons (eds), *Proclamations of Ireland*, ii, 212–13).

87 Proclamation, 19 Nov. 1690 (Kelly & Lyons (eds), *Proclamations of Ireland*, ii, 217–19).

88 Proclamation, 26 Mar. 1691. A similar threat was made in a proclamation of 14 May 1691 (Kelly & Lyons (eds), *Proclamations of Ireland*, ii, 238–9; 244–5).

89 See proclamations of 1 Aug., 8 Dec. 1690, 17 Jan., 21, 24 Feb., 14 May 1691 (Kelly & Lyons (eds), *Proclamations of Ireland*, ii, 204–5, 222–3, 226–7, 231–3, 244–5).

90 H.M.C., *Leyborne-Popham* Mss, p. 280.

91 Simms, *Williamite confiscation*, pp 47–50, 52–3, 80–1. See also the annotations to scheduled claims to the articles in Appendix B.

92 See Appendix B, claims scheduled for 29 Nov. and 10 Dec. 1694.

manner'.[93] However, the issue was considerably more complex than Simms' analysis allows.

The key to success was, as with the articlemen, effective lobbying and sufficient money to employ agents in Dublin and London. Testaments from Irish Protestants confirming the good behaviour of their Catholic neighbours accompanied Catholic petitions in almost every case – echoing the requirement that claimants under the articles of Galway and Limerick should produce Protestant witnesses. Most importantly, early submission to the Williamite authorities allowed many of the protectees to appear before the courts in Dublin during the war and halt their outlawry proceedings. By doing so they theoretically secured for themselves the greatest benefit of the articles of surrender – retention of their estates. In the absence of a verdict of outlawry, their estates were not legally forfeited. However, it appears that very few of the protectees' outlawry cases actually proceeded to trial. Appearance before the courts to answer the *capias* or *exigent* (thus preventing automatic outlawry) in most cases did not lead immediately to hearings.[94] One factor that complicated matters was that many Catholics were outlawed in several counties and thus not all proceedings were stopped, leading to outlawry *in absentia*.[95] Even in those cases where all outlawry proceedings had been stopped, the legal interpretation applied by the Williamite government, during and after the war, was that the *accusation* of treason was sufficient for forfeiture until the trials were completed and innocence proven. In this interpretation, emphasis was placed on one of two competing legal realities. Without a conviction for treason, the protectees should have been left in possession of their estates. However, the proclamations under which the protectees submitted implicitly reserved their real property to the king, allowing the Williamite government to find the protectees' estates forfeit.

Legal advice given to some protectees while the war was still in progress recommended seeking a royal pardon as a prudent precaution while they awaited trial.[96] It proved to be prescient advice, for only those who were

---

[93] Simms, *Williamite confiscation*, pp 73–81 (quote on p. 74).

[94] Simms provides a concise account of the process of outlawry: 'Such process began with the finding of a bill of indictment by a jury and the issue of a writ of "capias", or warrant, by the sheriff. If the accused was produced he was either bound over for further appearance or put on trial before a judge and jury. If after two writs of "capias" the sheriff returned "non est inventus", a writ of "exigent" was issued which directed the sheriff to have name of the accused called out on five successive court-days, charging him to appear on pain of outlawry. If he did not appear by the last time of calling, he was said to be "quinquies exactus" and was declared an outlaw' (Simms, *Williamite confiscation*, p. 30). See the petition of Oliver Grace in May 1691 for an example of a protectee stopping outlawry proceedings against him (*C.S.P.D.*, *1690–1*, pp 372–3).

[95] Simms, *Williamite confiscation*, pp 34–5.

[96] *C.S.P.D.*, *1690–1*, pp 360–1

pardoned were able to recover their estates. Some, such as Oliver Grace, could rely on support from well-placed and influential figures within the Irish administration. Formerly an apprentice in the office of the chief remembrancer in Ireland to Francis Godolphin and Richard Aldworth, Grace assumed the office outright in the reign of James II and sat in the Irish parliament of 1689 for the borough of Ballinakill, Queen's County. Grace submitted to the Williamites immediately after the Battle of the Boyne and appeared before the courts to put a stop to his outlawry. Lord Chief Justice Sir Richard Pyne 'and several other gentlemen' provided the necessary testaments and in 1696 Grace received the king's pardon.[97] Others secured theirs through bribery.[98] In total, twenty-three pardons granted to protectees have been identified, including one Irish Protestant.[99] Two of these were granted to Edmund Malone and John Galwey, who acted as lobbyists for the Limerick articlemen during the 1690s.[100] Malone's father, John, also received a pardon as a result of his taking protection after the Battle of the Boyne.[101] Dame Ellen Aylmer (widow of Sir Fitzgerald Aylmer, baronet) procured a pardon for herself and her two sons based on her submission to the Williamites before her departure for England in the aftermath of the Boyne.[102]

Only two cases have been identified where protectees who petitioned for a pardon were unsuccessful. Francis Leigh of Rathbride, County Kildare, was able to put a stop to outlawry proceedings against him in 1690 and petitioned the following year for a pardon. By March 1692 Leigh had obviously had little

---

[97] C.S.P.D., 1694–5, pp 406–7; C.S.P.D., 1696, pp 40, 159 (Simms' discussion of Grace includes a misprint in the relevant footnote, referring to C.S.P.D., 1698, p. 40). See C.S.P.D., 1690–1, p. 221, for a petition of James MacCartney in January 1691 for a grant of Grace's interest in the chief remembrancer's office on account of his alleged forfeiture.

[98] Simms, Williamite confiscation, pp 78–9.

[99] The successful Catholic claimants were Edmund Malone; John Malone; Oliver Grace; Edward Geoghegan; Charles White; Richard Talbot; Sir John Morris; Marcus Shee (procured after his death by his son, Richard); James Power, earl of Tyrone; John Galwey; Ignatius Purcell; Matthew Hore; Robert Longfield; Theobald Butler, Baron Cahir; Richard Martin; John Kerdiffe; Robert Porter; Francis Forster; Thomas Cowdall; Dame Ellen Aylmer and her sons, Luke Aylmer and Sir Justin Aylmer, baronet. The Protestant was George Crofts, of Churchtown, County Cork. Crofts applied for and received protection from Sir Robert Southwell during the first siege of Limerick. However, prior to his application he had served under the Jacobite high sheriff in order to protect himself and his Protestant neighbours. Elected to the 1692 Irish parliament for Charleville, Crofts received his pardon on 22 September 1692 but was investigated by parliament for his activities during the war and expelled from the commons on 11 October (C.S.P.D., 1691–2, pp 334, 458; H.I.P., iii, 542).

[100] C.S.P.D., 1691–2, pp 177, 311. See p. 104 for Galwey and Malone's agency on behalf of the Limerick articlemen, and Part III for Malone's work on behalf of his uncle, Col. John Browne.

[101] C.S.P.D., 1693, pp 281–2.

[102] C.S.P.D., 1691–2, pp 189–90, 336, 401.

success and his estate was granted to lord lieutenant Sydney.[103] In May 1694 the Irish lords justices professed ignorance of Leigh's case:

> As regards your directions for an enquiry into the case of Mr Francis Leigh, of Rathbride, we have not, till now, heard of this Mr Leigh, and there is no petition of his brought or sent referred that may bring it regularly before us. If, therefore, his agent, who solicits his business at Whitehall, be still there, it would do very well if he were directed to take care that one of them were forthwith done.[104]

This appears to have been the last time the Irish government considered Leigh's case and his failure may be attributed jointly to the incompetence of his agent and the confusion created by the change of government in 1693. The other unsuccessful claimant was Owen Carroll, who later appeared as a named party on a petition to the English parliament relating to the act of resumption.[105]

There were, however, far more than twenty-five claimants to the benefit of protections. Protectees who had never been outlawed presumably felt they had no need to seek a royal pardon, which explains in part the relatively low number sought. The prohibitive cost was also likely to have hindered some.[106] A list of persons who had appeared before the courts and answered the charge of treason, thereby putting a stop to their prosecutions, was sent to London by the Irish government in December 1697. It included those outlawed for domestic as well as foreign treason and named ninety-two men and five women. All were Catholic with the exception of John Dalton. Four of those listed had already received pardons from William III: Oliver Grace, Dame Ellen Aylmer and her two sons. Two others were subsequently adjudicated within the articles of Galway or Limerick.[107] Of the remaining ninety-one, not all submitted during the war, though the vast majority probably did. Nor can they all be presumed to have been landowners. The available evidence indicates that at least one hundred men and women can be classed as protectees. Just over one fifth received royal pardons on the basis of their early submission during the war, while the majority appear to have been able to halt outlawry proceedings taken against them. Presumed guilty until proven otherwise, the failure of the Irish government to bring them to trial prevented the protectees from reclaiming whatever goods and lands had been forfeited during the war.

---

[103] *C.S.P.D., 1690–1*, pp 360–1; *C.S.P.D., 1691–2*, p. 165; *C.S.P.D., 1693*, pp 2–3.

[104] Irish lords justices and privy council to Sir John Trenchard, 7 May 1694 (*C.S.P.D., 1694–5*, p. 125).

[105] *C.S.P.D., 1695 & Addenda*, p. 104.

[106] The cost of procuring a pardon c.1698 seems to have been well over £100. £100 appears to have represented the average sum paid to various officers and courtiers in London, while counsel also had to be employed in London. See below, pp 212–16.

[107] Thomas Bourke and Thady Quin (for whom see Simms, *Williamite confiscation*, pp 40, 51–2).

In general, the Irish government treated the protectees in the same manner as the articlemen. The proclamations they submitted under were strictly interpreted and any attempts to expand upon their terms were rebuffed. Those who submitted following the proclamations issued in July and August 1690 were at a distinct disadvantage. Though article 2 of Limerick might seem to indicate an administration hostile to the protectees, there was never any real intent, at least by the executive branch of government, to deny them their rights. The difficulty for the protectees of 1690 was that there were very few rights granted by those proclamations. On the other hand, those who submitted under the terms of the proclamation of 7 July 1691 were promised retention of their estates. Some members of the Irish Protestant polity regarded the exclusion of the 1690 protectees from the benefit of the articles, and particularly from possession of their estates, as a potentially destabilising development. Contrasting their situation with the articlemen, James Bonnell expressed his concern that

> others that have submitted at the Boyne and have continued peaceable ever since, are outlawed and lose their estates. This is such a wondrous inequality that it can hardly be that even a settlement should be founded on it. If the Irish were so clamorous against the former Act of Settlement which took away their estates for their notorious rebellion in 1641, what will these men hereafter say for losing their estates now for adhering to King James while he was among them and submitting to King William as soon as King James left them, when yet they see so many others enjoy their estates who stood out above a year longer. How will it look hereafter that Lord Gilmoy [Galmoy] should flourish in his estate and sit in parliament while Mr Talbot of Malahide should go begging.

Bonnell's reservations were based upon fears for the future stability of Irish affairs rather than upon any perceived injustice.[108] The Irish government held a different view. Instructions issued to Sydney in March 1692, before his departure for Ireland, directed that no attempt to prosecute the outlawries of protectees should be undertaken, provided that the protectee in question had not violated the terms of his submission.[109] Sydney had not yet left for Ireland, leading the Irish government to write to Nottingham in April requesting further instructions relating to the protectees. It was anticipated that during the next term the court of king's bench would be inundated with applications from protectees who had 'appeared upon the capias and exigent, and so prevented their being outlawed', yet had nevertheless had their estates confiscated. The protectees were naturally anxious to have their cases heard and their estates restored.

[108] James Bonnell to Robert Harley, 3 Nov. 1691 (H.M.C., *Portland Mss*, iii, 480); Simms, *Williamite confiscation*, pp 73–4. For more on Bonnell see his *D.I.B.* entry.
[109] Additional instructions to Viscount Sydney, 3 Mar. 1692 (*C.S.P.D., 1691–2*, p. 169).

The Irish government warned that, unless instructions were given to the king's counsel to conduct the prosecutions, the protectees' estates had to be restored.[110]

No instructions appear to have been sent until August 1692, when Nottingham informed Sydney that a clause should be added to a proposed bill of indemnity 'for pardoning … all such as have submitted pursuant to his majesty's proclamations and declarations, or any others issued by his majesty's directions or have taken protections'. It was again emphasised that this was to apply only to those who had lived peaceably since submitting. These instructions were complied with, though the bill, following modification by the English privy council in November 1691, made no mention of the protectees.[111] In spite of the warning issued by the Irish government in April 1692, the majority of the protectees had still not had their cases heard before the courts and were still without possession of their estates, real and personal, even after the passage of the act of resumption in 1700. The majority of the protectees were thus never brought to trial.[112]

The nature of the protectees' cases meant that most of their lobbying was done individually. Occasionally, however, circumstances dictated a joint effort, as in 1692, 1698 and 1701. Unfortunately, little can be said of the promoters or subscribers of these joint petitions, or the agents employed. In only one instance is an agent known: Adam Colclough argued the case of the protectees who found themselves within the Jacobite quarters at the end of the war and were thus excluded from the articles of Limerick. Colclough petitioned the English government in late spring or early summer 1692, on behalf of the protectees and the articlemen of Limerick and Galway, indicating his status as one of the most important lobbyists for Irish Catholics in the aftermath of the war. Referring to the protectees, Colclough argued that the exclusionary clause of article 2 of Limerick applied only to officers of the army and that the interpretation applied by the court of claims was a 'strained construction'. The relevant passage of the article excluding certain people from its benefit read: ' … all the commissioned officers in their Majesties' quarters that belonged to the Irish regiments then in being, that were treated with, and were not prisoners of war, or have taken protection'.[113] Colclough's representation produced an extraordinary

---

[110] Irish lords justices and privy council to Nottingham, 21 Apr. 1692 (C.S.P.D., 1695 & Addenda, pp 184–5).
[111] Nottingham to Sydney, 25 Aug. 1692 (T.N.A., SP 67/1, f. 172; C.S.P.D., 1691–2, p. 421); Sydney and Irish privy council to Nottingham, 28 Sept. 1692 (T.N.A., SP 63/354, f. 155; C.S.P.D., 1695 & Addenda, p. 205). See below, pp 111–15 for a detailed analysis of the drafting of this bill.
[112] Irish lords justices to Edward Villiers, earl of Jersey, 16 Mar. 1700 (T.N.A., SP 63/360, ff 233–4; C.S.P.D., 1699–1700, p. 402); Simms, Williamite confiscation, pp 36–7.
[113] See Appendix A for the article in full.

judgment that prioritised domestic security over the law to deny the validity of the protectees' case.[114]

Acknowledging the controversy surrounding the protectees, Sir Richard Cox resolved to give a thorough reasoning for their exclusion from the articles. Though Colclough advocated on behalf of only those who had taken protection and subsequently found themselves within Jacobite quarters at the conclusion of the war, Cox's opinion encompassed all protectees, whom he divided into four categories: (1) those who took protection in the summer of 1690 and remained within Williamite territory for the duration of the war; (2) those who took protection and afterwards remained in Jacobite territory and claimed the articles of Limerick; (3) those who took protection but were left outside Williamite territory after the first siege of Limerick following the withdrawal of the Williamite army; (4) those who lived on the outskirts of Limerick and were surrounded by the Williamite army during the second siege and were thus obliged to live under protection.

The latter three categories were dismissed with the following arguments. Addressing Colclough's contention that the wording of article 2 applied only to army officers, Cox was dismissive: 'If it be English, it is impossible to have such a construction, for the exception comes after all the particular enumerations'. Having already accused the articlemen of altering the text of the articles of Limerick before their ratification by William in March 1692, Cox further argued that, this alteration having been allowed, 'it is unquestionably reasonable that those that treated for his Majesty should be allowed to add what was intended if omitted'.[115] In dealing with categories (2) and (3), Cox used an example to make his case.[116] Referring to 'Mr [James] Fitzgerald's case, the lawyer', Cox used Fitzgerald's failure to travel to Williamite territory after a proclamation defining the territory within which protections were valid as sufficient evidence that Fitzgerald had forfeited his rights. Fitzgerald's claim that the Williamite army had plundered his goods in spite of his protected status, leading him to seek refuge with the Jacobites, was contrasted with the burning of his house by the

---

[114] All quotations in the following paragraphs are taken from 'A copy of and answers to several complaints made by the Irish by their agent Mr Cockly against judgements given by the Justices and Council in several cases relating to the Articles of Limerick and Galway, together with the case of the protected Irish that came in upon the two first declarations after the Battle of the Boyne' [1692]. See Appendix C for the document in full along with a discussion of its provenance. For Adam Colclough's role as agent for the articlemen, see below, pp 104–6, 113, 157; Bergin, 'Irish Catholic interest', pp 36–48.

[115] See below, pp 100–2 for a discussion of this judgment as it relates to the articles of Galway and Limerick. Cox's contention that the articles were altered was wrong.

[116] The benefit of protection was withdrawn from those who resided beyond Williamite territory in a proclamation dated 21 Feb. 1691. The proclamation delineated the territory, roughly corresponding to the course of the Shannon, Williamite territory extending to within ten miles of the river (Kelly & Lyons (eds), *Proclamations of Ireland*, ii, 231–3).

Jacobite army to prevent its use as an enemy garrison during the second siege of Limerick. Had Fitzgerald been genuine in his submission, Cox argued, he would have taken refuge with the Williamites when they surrounded the city in 1691, rather than within the walls of Limerick. Fitzgerald was held as an exemplar of all protectees who did not remain within Williamite territory, whatever the reason.[117]

Cox turned the wording of article 2 against the protectees to exclude from the articles those in category (4). Noting that the article expressly covered only those who were in Jacobite quarters or under the army's protection in the named counties (Kerry, Cork, Clare and Mayo), Cox argued that it was implicit that those who were not within Jacobite territory so defined could make no claim to articles, as they were within Williamite quarters. These men

> did no service upon their surrender and therefore ought to have no benefit by it, it being at the opening of the treaty proposed by the [lords] justices that nobody should be treated with, but such who were at that time without our lines or protection, it being never our intention to give such advantageous terms to any who had not the power to pretend to them.

Cox devoted most of his opinion to category (1), judging them to be ineligible to the articles and their estates under three criteria: they had no right to their estates; their continuance within Williamite territory while behaving subversively disqualified them; and restoring their estates was a security risk. Under the first criterion, Cox's argument referred to the wording of the proclamations of 7 July and 1 August 1690. Those proclamations promised a pardon from the king of all crimes committed during the war and to secure those who submitted 'in their goods, their stocks of cattle, and all their chattels personal whatsoever'. As Cox pointed, out the intention was clear: 'To those of the first rank, nothing is granted but their lives'. The proclamations implicitly reserved the disposal of their estates to the king. Cox also rejected the argument – advanced by James Bonnell (and quoted above) – that it was illogical to withhold the estates of those who submitted early, while rewarding others who had held out to the last:

> That because others who held out longer have their estates must not be a reason why [the protectees] should not have theirs, because they delivered up the kingdom, and these gentlemen did not deliver up themselves, only as the country was conquered and brought under their Majesties' obedience by force of arms.

The distinction made here displayed some elements of sophistry, for the articles of surrender must surely be defined as capitulations gained through force of

---

[117] See Appendix C, n. 5 for James Fitzgerald.

arms. However, Cox went on to reveal the Irish government's predominant rationale, encompassing the second and third criteria:

> It is opposite to the interest of England to restore them. The greatest part of the forfeitures would be remitted by so doing. The estates of the forfeiting persons under this qualification lie near the metropolis of this kingdom, which should be altogether Protestant if possible, and if this opportunity be lost, it will be impracticable to make it so, for Papist landlords will have Papist tenants, which will neither answer to the present intention either of security or improvement.

Cox underpinned the force of this argument by echoing proclamations issued during the war accusing the protectees of seditious activity. A note of vengeance was also struck in the assertion that several category (1) protectees had occupied positions within the Jacobite administration and could be considered responsible for the 1689 parliament's act of attainder. Cox's opinion essentially rested on the fact that submission under the proclamations of 1690 did not qualify the protectees for restoration to their estates. The best they could hope for was to maintain their 'chattels personal' – legally defined as goods moveable, such as jewellery, furniture, livestock and harvested crops. Estates of inheritance and freehold were not classed as chattels. Land held by lease was defined as 'chattels real', thus also beyond the protection offered by the proclamations.[118]

Rebuffed by the Irish government in 1692, the protectees joined with the articlemen in 1693 to complain to the government following the imprisonment of over 200 former Jacobite officers in December 1692. More pertinently, the protectees complained that those who had managed to obtain a royal pardon had been prevented from taking out their warrants.[119] No restitution appears to have been forthcoming for their imprisonment.

As mentioned above (in the analysis of the articles of Drogheda), the English parliament began proceedings to resume the king's grants of Irish forfeited lands in 1698. A petition from the protectees seeking the insertion of a clause in their favour in the anticipated bill was presented to the house of commons on 5 March (naming Thomas Lacy, Patrick Sarsfield and William Galwey). This petition differed somewhat from the other Irish petitions presented on this subject, in that it did not seek a clause saving lands, but rather one to reverse their outlawries.[120] An eloquent reiteration of the protectees' arguments, rejected by Cox in

---

[118] Giles Jacob, *A new law dictionary* (London, 1729), p. 121.

[119] For the list of officers arrested, see *C.S.P.D., 1693*, pp 13–15. The joint articlemen–protectees petition was presented between January 1693 and the recall of Sydney in May 1693, but is calendared for December 1693 (ibid., pp 443–5). Warrants for royal pardons were, for a brief period, not accepted by the Irish government as a result of the presentation of a list of grievances from members of the Irish parliament to the English parliament (Simms, *Williamite confiscation*, p. 79).

[120] *C.J.*, xii, 144 (5 Mar. 1698).

1692, was printed in 1700. Arguing that those who supported King James had 'all the fundamental laws in force then … to fortify, back, second and guide them through that war', and that it would be 'unparalleled hardship to take away the subjects lives, liberties and estates, for acting in their own defence', the protectees lamented the favour shown to the articlemen:

> This is an odd distinction, that the same Public Faith given to the Protectees, for their security, and protection, shall be violated; and of the other hand, the same shall be performed to the Articlemen. Now, with submission, it should seem that the Protectees are preferable to King William, and Queen Mary's Public Faith, before the Articlemen (not to have the latter excluded by any means) for the Protectees had so much confidence in the great security, and pledges, tendered unto, and by them accepted of, that they have immediately submitted themselves to King William … That clause in the bill of resumption, which directs the protectees to be proceeded against … carries so much destruction along with it, that 'tis as killing as the war itself was, because nothing can be termed more destructive, than to revive old rancour, and malice, by laying open those old wounds healed up.[121]

As might have been expected, the protectees had no more success with this attempt. Following their failure to secure a clause in the Act of Resumption, several protectees again petitioned parliament on 19 May 1701.[122] On this occasion, Owen Carroll, Richard Barnwall and Walter Pritchet were the named parties.[123] Seeking to bring to parliament's attention the effect of the act of resumption on their livelihoods, the protectees' noted that their personal estates had largely been lost during the war through plundering (by both armies), while their real estates had been vested in the king. To maintain their families, new leases and farms had been taken out and improvements made. The forfeiture trustees, on the grounds of their outlawries, had now resumed the protectees' new leaseholds: these protectees had effectively suffered forfeiture twice in ten

---

[121] *A short memorial humbly offered in behalf of the Old English of Ireland* (London, 1700).

[122] C.J., xiii, 557 (19 May 1701). In 1699 a lengthy treatise putting forward the case of the protectees was presented to the English parliament: *The case of several of his majesties subjects in Ireland, commonly called Protectees, most humbly offered to the consideration of both houses of parliament* ([London, 1699]).

[123] In the case of the two petitions, the journals of the house of commons appear to have printed just the first three named petitioners, followed by 'etc.'. Those named should thus not necessarily be regarded as leaders of the protectees, especially in light of the fact that Patrick Sarsfield senior (father of the more famous earl of Lucan) had been dead for eight years. In a long-running case involving the granddaughter of Patrick Sarsfield senior, Charlotte Vesey (née Sarsfield), the reversal of his outlawry was necessary to allow her to come into possession of the estate. Sarsfield had died in 1690, and his name was probably included in the 1698 petition at the behest of the Vesey's agent in London, Edmund Malone, on account of their failure to reverse the outlawry by that date. The outlawry was reversed the following month. See below, pp 216–19, for a more detailed examination of Malone's agency on behalf of the Veseys. For Charlotte Sarsfield's case see Simms, *Williamite confiscation*, pp 80, 144–5.

years. In asking parliament to remedy this situation, the protectees argued that the 1699 inquiry commissioners had excluded these leases from their report as too insignificant to make any difference in the revenue that might be raised. The report of the trustees on the petition was evasive and noted that Carroll's status as a protectee was under investigation.[124] Once again the protectees' claims were rejected.

An appeal to the English parliament for private acts relieving petitioners from the provisions of the act of resumption was, essentially, the last hope for the protectees. None of the protectees secured an act. Their failure to obtain redress contributed greatly to the decline in Catholic landownership in Leinster, where up to half of Catholic-owned land was lost in Counties Meath, Westmeath, Wicklow and Kilkenny in the decade after the surrender of Limerick.[125] Only those who had received a royal pardon were able to prevent forfeiture.

IV

The Irish government generally applied the terms of the minor articles and the protection proclamations 'with justice but not favour'. There were no instances in which the government or courts flagrantly ignored the guarantees written into the articles of Drogheda, Waterford, Boffin or Sligo. Yet Sir Richard Cox's 1692 legal opinion on the case of the protectees gave a clear indication of the attitude that successive Irish administrations would adopt both towards the protectees and the articlemen for the remainder of William's reign, and beyond. If at any time the implementation of the various terms of surrender was found to be 'opposite to the interest of England', the Irish government (with some honourable individual exceptions) would not hesitate to interpret those terms in a manner that best protected the Protestant interest, even when that interpretation was unlawful. The protectees were presumed guilty of treason until proven innocent, but successive Irish and English administrations lacked the will or desire to bring them to trial. The evidence points to the failure of the majority to retain their estates beyond the end of the seventeenth century. It was against this backdrop of strict interpretation, allied with a willingness to ignore the terms of surrender if they were found to be in conflict with the Protestant interest, that the articlemen of Limerick and Galway sought the implementation of their terms of surrender.

---

[124] *The true and deplorable case of those called Protectees in Ireland, who stand outlawed and are not within articles* ([London, 1701]). This was an abstract, probably intended for distribution to members of parliament. The full text of the petition, with the trustees' report, is in N.L.I., Annesley Mss, xx, ff 150–2.
[125] Simms, *Williamite confiscation*, p. 198.

4

'With justice but not favour': Implementing the articles of Limerick, 1691–1704[1]

The articles of Galway and Limerick were considerably more complex than the surrenders previously negotiated and, owing to the number of Catholics expected to claim their benefit, were much more important to the Williamite settlement in Ireland. As a consequence both sets of articles – particularly the articles of Limerick – were subjected to intense scrutiny by the Irish and English administrations. Moreover, the greater number of claimants to the articles of Limerick allowed the articlemen to fund and direct a lobbying effort more concentrated in nature than that of the minor articlemen. Throughout the 1690s, the interpretation and implementation of the articles of Galway and Limerick provoked controversy. This chapter examines the articles of Limerick, with a particular focus on their early interpretation by the Irish and English governments. The articles of Limerick were viewed with deep suspicion and hostility by Irish Protestants, who feared a repeat of the Catholic resurgence of the 1680s. The Irish government came under intense pressure, both from the articlemen and the Protestant polity, to interpret the articles in different ways. Protestants argued for as narrow an interpretation as possible, while the articlemen naturally pressed the opposite case.

Section II identifies the leading Catholic lobbyists in London and analyses the inconsistent attitude adopted by the Irish government to the implementation of the articles. The king's official attitude to the articles of surrender during the 1690s was that they should be interpreted with 'justice but not favour'.[2] Justice was, however, a fluid concept and the Irish and English administrations sought ways to exploit the weaknesses of the articles. The potential for instability in Ireland was enormous, and the Williamite authorities were mindful that to revoke the articles entirely was potentially catastrophic. They were required to tread a fine line between pandering to Protestant hostility to

---

[1]   The quotation is taken from 'Queries from Mr Solicitor of Ireland', 2 Mar. 1692 (T.N.A., SP 63/354, ff 43–5).
[2]   'Queries from Mr Solicitor of Ireland', 2 Mar. 1692 (T.N.A., SP 63/354, f. 43); 'Additional instructions to Viscount Sydney', 3 Mar. 1692 (C.S.P.D., 1691–2, p. 169); 'Instructions for the Irish lords justices', 26 June 1693 (C.S.P.D., 1693, p. 196); 'Instructions for lord deputy Capel', 5 May 1695 (C.S.P.D., 1694–5, p. 459); Instructions for the Irish lords justices, 10 July 1696 (C.S.P.D., 1696, p. 265).

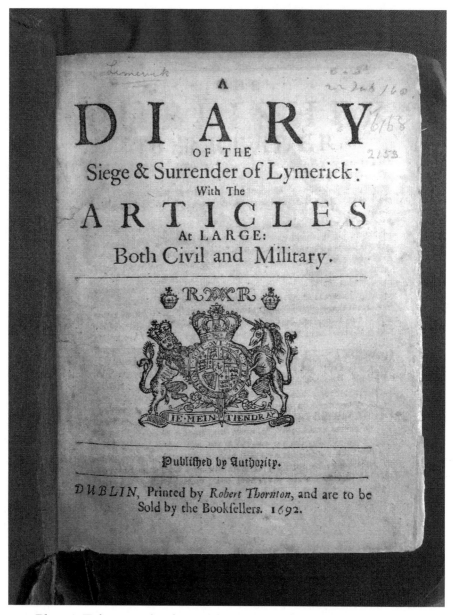

Plate 4: Title page of A *diary of the siege & surrender of Lymerick: with the articles at large: both civil and military* (Dublin, 1692). Reproduced by permission of the National Library of Ireland.

the articles, and appearing overly sympathetic to the recently defeated Jacobite rebels. Section III addresses attempts in 1692 to give legislative protection to the articles of Limerick through a proposed bill of indemnity, while Section IV provides an overview of continued hostility to the articles among Protestant politicians, up to the passing of the act confirming an abridged version of the articles of Limerick in 1697 and the opening of the third and final court of claims.

The articlemen were far from passive during the 1690s. As has been shown in chapter 3, the minor articlemen moved swiftly to protect their interests, even before the surrender of the Jacobite army in October 1691. This chapter, along with chapter 5, further illustrates the remarkable speed and organisational capacity shown by Irish Catholics as they transferred their energies and money from the military to the political arena. Lobbyists arguing the case of the Limerick articlemen were active in Dublin and London within weeks of the end of the war. Over the next decade, their powers of persuasion and legal acumen would be strenuously tested.

I

The Irish government began to consider how best to implement the articles of Limerick earlier than has previously been appreciated.[3] Lobbying by the articlemen commenced within weeks, possibly days, of the surrender of Limerick. Less than a month after the articles were signed, the lords justices instructed the prime serjeant, John Osborne, to gather all king's counsel then present in Dublin to discuss the best method of restoring the articlemen to their estates. Counsellor Alan Brodrick suspected the lords justices of seeking to deflect responsibility for the proper interpretation of the articles onto the king's counsel:

> If I understand the thing right, the Justices have a mind to pull the thorn out of their own foot and put it into ours; that is if there be any thing in the articles which relates to the giving possessions not consistent with our laws, that the blame shall be laid at our doors if they are not fully executed, by reason that we give our opinions they cannot be restored by law to their possessions in such manner as the articles require; if we shall advise their being put into possession in as large, speedy and beneficial manner as the articles seem to promise, then we are accountable for any illegal methods that shall be used in execution or pursuance of our advice.[4]

---

[3] Simms believed that the earliest consideration given to the articles by the Irish and English governments was in January 1692 (*Williamite confiscation*, p. 46).
[4] Alan Brodrick to St John Brodrick, 11 Nov. 1691 (S.H.C., Midleton papers, Ms 1248/1, ff 255–6); cf. Hayton, *Ruling Ireland*, p. 41. The king's counsel who attended were John Osborne,

The lords justices also sent a draft order for restoring the articlemen to their estates for the opinion of the counsellors. Their response may have been an attempt to stall the implementation of the articles, or perhaps may simply have been a detailed legal brief, warning of the different formalities to be observed before the articlemen could be restored. Some counsellors can be identified as strongly anti-Catholic, including Brodrick and Osborne. On the other hand, Sir John Meade had sat in the 1689 parliament and was married to a Catholic.[5]

There were two categories of articlemen identified by the king's counsel – those who were never indicted or indicted but not yet prosecuted, and those outlawed for high treason.[6] The king's counsel approved the use of the draft order only for those whose estates had been seized by the Williamite authorities, but were either never indicted or had yet to have their outlawries prosecuted. Such estates had 'never been legally vested in their Majesties'.[7] The lords justices were to instruct the commissioners of the revenue to write to any tenants then in possession of the estates instructing them to vacate the premises, but allowing them to reap any crops sown. An important proviso was added: no creditor was to be ejected from the land of an articleman, if the creditor was in possession by virtue of a defaulted mortgage. For those outlawed, however, counsel advised that 'there can be no legal order framed or conceived by your Lordships for dispossessing the Crown of the estates of the persons so outlawed or putting the former owners into the possession thereof'. The outlawries first had to be reversed, a procedure that required a pardon from William and Mary. Brodrick and Meade proposed granting custodiams to associates of outlawed articlemen, but were dissuaded by their fellow counsel.[8]

Armed with this advice, the lords justices were faced with two difficult tasks: determining which claimant had not yet been outlawed, and adjudicating on some of the finer points raised by the wording of the articles. A delicate balancing act was required as Irish Protestant opinion was relentlessly hostile to the articles of Limerick, yet the king's honour (the 'public faith') was at stake and Catholic landowners expected quick restoration to their estates. Some

Sir John Meade, Alan Brodrick, Nehemiah Donnellan, Thomas Pakenham, Robert Dixon and Thomas Coote.

[5] Sydney described Meade as 'a man of excellent parts; all the exception that can be made against him is that his wife is a papist' (quoted in A.R. Hart, *A history of the king's serjeants at law in Ireland: honour rather than advantage?* (Dublin, 2000), pp 70–1). I am indebted to Hazel Maynard for bringing this reference to my attention.

[6] For the process of indictment and outlawry, see Simms, *Williamite confiscation*, pp 30–44. For lists of indictments and outlawries, see Simms, 'Irish Jacobites'.

[7] This interpretation was in direct contrast with that applied to the estates of the protectees who had not been brought to trial. Their estates were deemed to be in the possession of the king by virtue of proclamations.

[8] Alan Brodrick to St John Brodrick, 11 Nov. 1691 (S.H.C., Midleton Papers, 1248/1, ff 255–6).

measure of revenge for Catholic actions during the war was also expected. Shortly after the war's conclusion Francis Aungier, earl of Longford, evicted Mark Baggott from a farm leased from the duke of Ormond for arrears of rent. The eviction was somewhat premature, for the lords justices had issued a proclamation in mid October suspending the dispossession of any Catholic who intended to claim the benefit of the articles of surrender. Longford dismissed any chance of Baggott successfully appealing the eviction:

> It will be an hardship upon the lords justices to deny him the benefit of the articles of Limerick. But since he betrayed his trust to my lord duke and was the single man entrusted by him, who undertook the management of his estate in the county of Carlow, to gratify my Lord Tyrconnell's malice to the family of Ormond, I will put all the difficulties in his way I can.[9]

Longford was assured by Coningsby that though the government was obliged to restore the articlemen, this applied only to real estate and not to chattels (which included leasehold land). This opinion was surely a shock to the articlemen, for it went directly against the wording of article 2 of Limerick, prompting a hearing before the lords justices on the issue just days later. As reported by Longford, the hearing lasted two hours, with the articlemen represented by 'Mr Whitehead' and 'Mr Handcock' – probably Thomas Whitshed and William Handcock, Jr, two Irish Protestants.[10] Several of the king's counsel, including Osborne, argued against the articlemen.

---

9   Francis Aungier, earl of Longford, to John Ellis, 21 Nov. 1691 (Patrick Melvin, 'Letters of Lord Longford and others on Irish affairs, 1689–1702' in *Analecta Hibernica*, 32 (1985), pp 80–1). Longford was one of the commissioners appointed to manage the duke of Ormond's Irish estates, while Ellis was Ormond's secretary. For Baggot, see Appendix C, n. 4, and Patrick Walsh, *The making of the Irish Protestant Ascendancy: the life of William Conolly, 1662–1729* (Woodbridge, 2010), pp 28–9.
10   Thomas Whitshed was admitted to Lincoln's Inn 18 Aug. 1666 and called to the Irish bar as Thomas Whitehed, Easter Term 1672. Whitshed sat as MP for Carysfort in the 1692 parliament (*H.I.P.*, vi, 538). 'Mr Handcock' was either Thomas or, more probably, William (first and second sons of William Handcock of Athlone, County Westmeath), admitted to Middle Temple on 5 Dec. 1673 and 30 Jul. 1674 respectively. There is no record of either Handcock having been called to the Irish bar, though records for admissions are missing for the early 1680s. Thomas Whitshed and William Handcock both remained in Ireland during the war and their names appeared on chancery bills between 1689 and 1691, while there is no indication that Thomas Handcock ever pursued a career in the law – in keeping with the custom that eldest sons who stood to inherit land were educated at the inns of court but rarely practised (I am indebted to Hazel Maynard for sharing her knowledge of Thomas Whitshed and William Handcock Jr. with me). All three Handcocks sat in the 1692 Irish parliament. Thomas Handcock voted for the impeachment of lord chancellor Sir Charles Porter in 1695, while William Jr. voted against (*H.I.P.*, iv, 358–9). William Jr. also continued to appear in Chancery during the 1690s. For the admission of Whitshed and the two younger Handcocks to the inns of court, see Maynard, 'Irish membership of the English inns of court', pp 386, 396. See also *K.I.A.P.*, p. 510.

The articlemen lost their appeal, apparently on the basis of the king's counsel's argument that chattels real were not mentioned in the articles. Longford welcomed the judgment:

> By this explanation of the articles their lordships have not only freed themselves from the endless trouble of the Irish importunities but the king has also gained considerable profit by the beneficial forfeited leases which will thereby accrue to him.[11]

Longford may have been misinformed as to the reason for denying the articlemen their right to retain leasehold estates. Article 2 of Limerick included a clause explicitly preserving chattels real to the articlemen. Though no other evidence relating to this hearing survives, the reasoning behind the decision of the Irish government appears in the legal opinion offered by Sir Richard Cox on a variety of issues relating to the surrender of the Jacobites, delivered in 1692.[12]

Responding to lobbying in London by Adam Colclough, agent to the articlemen, Cox came to the paradoxical conclusion that article 2 in fact attempted to protect too many distinct definitions of property:

> That the first part of the second article provides only for their estates of inheritance and [was] never intended to meddle with any chattel real or personal needs not other argument to prove, than there being a subsequent part of the second article which relates wholly to them, and says they shall only be restored to such as are in their own possession, or in the possession of any one in trust for them and the complainants themselves saying, that if the second clause be left out, and a favourable construction made of the words 'right, title and interest' in the former part of the second article, it might very well be supposed it was intended to restore them to their chattels real.

Cox's opinion appears to have been influenced by a belief that the articlemen's agents somehow managed to amend the letters patent issued by the English privy council for ratifying the articles of Limerick (issued on 25 January 1692) by adding an 's' to each word in the phrase 'rights, titles and interests'. Cox incorrectly claimed that the phrase in the signed articles was 'right, title and interest' and that by adding each 's' the articlemen were able to make article 2 'much more favourable to their demands than before it was'.[13]

Lastly, Cox rejected the argument that the articlemen's entitlement to a general pardon, which legally removed any penalty of forfeiture and restored them to their landowning status before the outbreak of the war, meant that denial of their leasehold interests was a 'strained construction' of the article:

[11]   Longford to Ellis, 24 Nov. & 30 Nov. 1691 (Melvin, 'Letters of Lord Longford', pp 81–3).
[12]   See Appendix C for the full text of Cox's opinion.
[13]   The evidence contradicts Cox's implausible assertion: the original draft of the articles of 28 Sept. 1691 contained the phrase 'rights, titles and interests' (B.L., Eg. Ms. 2618, f. 161; J.G. Simms, 'The original draft of the articles of Limerick, 1691' in *I.H.S.*, viii (1952–3), p. 41).

> It is true that had that been the first and only article for them, as Sir Stephen Rice the most cunning man of their party said, if he had been concerned in the treaty he would not have asked for, nor taken more, their reasoning had been just, but since in the body of the articles there are several things to be performed on their part to the king and his Protestant subjects, it is reasonable that they should give security for doing the same before their outlawries are reversed, or otherwise both will be at their mercies afterwards.[14]

The implication was that forfeiture of their chattels real was a form of condign punishment to secure the future good behaviour of the Limerick articlemen, holding out the possibility of future restoration to their chattels. Cox echoed Longford's assessment when he noted that the judgment would be advantageous to the king, 'especially in the estates of the Dukes of York and Ormond'. The legal ground for the judgment of the Irish government seems unconvincing and was, in effect, an abrogation of the articles of Limerick.[15] On the other hand, it is doubtful whether this interpretation of article 2 endured; Colonel John Browne's estate included large areas of leasehold land, none of which was vested in the king.

The rationale for Cox's narrow interpretation of the benefit of the articles was his belief that the articles were not intended to have the same effect as a law of restitution, to be 'construed in favour of the persons restored'. Rather, they were to be seen as a bargain between rebellious subjects and their king. Thus William was obliged only to honour the 'plain words' of the surrender terms. The corollary interpretation, Cox argued, was that

> If any part of it be dubious, and will bear two constructions, it ought to be made in favour of the crown rather than of such subjects who by such means came to it, unless it is believed that the Irish want encouragement to rebel which nobody that is acquainted with that country even in its present circumstances can imagine.

The context in which the Irish government made their judgment in November 1691 was one of deeply felt hostility among the Protestant polity to the articles of Limerick. Strong undercurrents of opposition to the articles sporadically erupted in public anger. Anthony Dopping, bishop of Meath, denounced the terms of surrender from the pulpit in Christ Church Cathedral on 26 November.[16]

---

[14] See Appendix C. For Browne's debts to Sir Stephen Rice, see chapters 1 and 6.

[15] The judgment dealt exclusively with the articles of Limerick and it is not clear whether a similar judgment was made in respect of the articles of Galway. Article 9 of Galway (which protected the articlemen's estates) made no mention of chattels. Whether this prevented an interpretation of that article in the same manner as Cox interpreted article 2 of Limerick is unclear.

[16] Anthony Dopping, 'Sermon on the day of Thanksgiving for the reduction of the kingdom of Ireland', 26 Nov. 1691 (T.C.D, Ms 1688/2, ff 77–140). My thanks to Suzanne Forbes for providing me with the text of this sermon.

His sermon, the lords justices reported to London, 'so wonderfully dissatisfied the Irish gentlemen who are now in town in order to be restored according to the articles, that we are humbly of opinion it is necessary for his majesty to show some mark of his displeasure against him'. Dopping was removed from the privy council the following month.[17] Cooler heads argued for a more practical view of the articles. James Bonnell, former accountant-general in Ireland, urged the English 'country' MP Robert Harley that it was

> vain to find fault with the Articles of Limerick, as I conceive; the enquiry must now be how to make the best of them and provide against the inconveniences of them, without enquiry whether these inconveniences happened out of necessity or design.[18]

Dopping's sermon may be seen as an attempt to apply pressure on the Irish government to interpret the articles as narrowly as possible, in response to widely held fears about the administration's intentions.[19] It was no doubt well known that the government had sought the advice of the king's counsel, while the appearance of the articlemen before the government so soon after the surrender of Limerick was surely disquieting. In an apposite illustration of the fine line trodden by the Irish government at this time, the lords justices requested the removal of Dopping from the privy council on the day they ruled that the articlemen were to be denied their chattels real.

II

The articlemen had lost no time in transferring their energies from negotiating the terms that ended the war to negotiating the implementation of those terms. There was a certain amount of impatience in their demands for restoration to their estates so soon after the surrender of Limerick for, as the Irish government

---

[17] Irish lords justices to [Nottingham], 30 Nov. 1691 (H.M.C., *Finch Mss*, iii, 304); Nottingham to the Irish lords justices, 8 Dec. 1691 (*C.S.P.D.*, *1691–2*, p. 27); Simms, *Williamite confiscation*, p. 29; idem, *Jacobite Ireland*, p. 258. Dopping was replaced by William Moreton, bishop of Kildare, but readmitted to the council in September 1692. It has been suggested that Dopping was restored to the privy council much earlier (Felix Waldman, 'Anthony Dopping's restoration to the Irish privy council: a correction' in *Notes and Queries*, no. 255 (2010), pp 69–70). However, that contention is founded upon a misreading of the evidence. The date on which William III *decided* to restore Dopping is irrelevant. Previous accounts have also assumed that Dopping was readmitted to the council in August 1692. However, Nottingham's letter of 1 Sep. 1692 (*C.S.P.D.*, *1691–2*, p. 430) makes it clear that September was the earliest month that Dopping could have been readmitted to the council.

[18] James Bonnell to Robert Harley, 3 Nov. 1691 (H.M.C., *Portland Mss*, iii, 479–81). See also James McGuire, 'The Treaty of Limerick' in Bernadette Whelan (ed.), *The last of the great wars: essays on the war of the three kings in Ireland* (Limerick, 1990), p. 134.

[19] Hayton, *Ruling Ireland*, p. 42.

were advised by the king's counsel, several legal formalities required the attention of the English government. Nor were the lords justices the only targets of the articlemen's lobbying. In an undated petition to William's commanding officer in Ireland, Godard van Reede van Ginkel, the articlemen of Limerick complained that no method of implementing the articles had yet been established.[20] They also objected to the lords justices' decree that a recognisance was necessary before restoration to their estates, 'which is not conformable to the articles'. The vexed issue of the 'missing clause' was also raised. The articlemen noted that no reply had been received to the letter sent by the lords justices and Ginkel to England explaining that the clause had been omitted by mistake.[21] They requested that a second letter be entrusted to Colonel Henry Luttrell for delivery to London. Ginkel and the lords justices were also encouraged to draft a letter urging the English parliament to confirm the articles. In addition, the articlemen asked Ginkel to ensure that the articles were published, and to allow their agents to inspect the general pardon that was to be given to them before it was engrossed, 'and that it may be done without delay, the rather for that your petitioners are not entitled to the benefit of the law, or any privilege of a subject, till the said pardon be passed or outlawries reversed'. The petition closed with an appeal for a general order allowing the articlemen the freedom to practise both their professions and their faith.[22] In what may have been a response to this petition, the lords justices issued a proclamation on 14 October declaring that any person who took the oath of allegiance to William and Mary before any justice of the peace (the oath specified in the articles of Limerick as acceptable to the articlemen) was entitled to the full benefit of the law.[23] A month later the lords justices instructed all justices of the peace to ensure that the articlemen and protectees were not disturbed in their persons or property.[24]

The identity of the agent(s) employed by the articlemen to present the petition to Ginkel is unknown, and it was almost certainly submitted to him before his departure for England on 5 December.[25] By the end of 1691 there were several agents acting on behalf of the articlemen in England. These agents constituted a small yet vocal lobby group in London, sharing a common goal,

---

[20] 'A memorial to his excellency the Baron of Ginkle general of their majesties army in Ireland, etc', [1691] (Utrecht Archive, Huis Amerongen, no. 3221). The petition was probably composed very soon after the surrender of Limerick.

[21] The letter had actually been lost in London (Nottingham to Porter, 24 Oct. 1691 (*C.S.P.D., 1690–1*, p. 551); Simms, *Williamite confiscation*, p. 59).

[22] 'A memorial to his excellency the Baron of Ginkle' (Utrecht Archive, Huis Amerongen, no. 3221).

[23] Proclamation, 14 Oct. 1691 (Kelly & Lyons (eds), *Proclamations of Ireland*, ii, 270–1); H.M.C., *Finch Mss*, iii, 306; McGuire, 'Treaty of Limerick', p. 133.

[24] Irish lords justices to the sheriffs [of Ireland], 19 Nov. 1691 (H.M.C., *Finch Mss*, iii, 305).

[25] H.M.C., *Leyborne-Popham Mss*, p. 281.

though they do not seem to have co-operated to any great degree. Indeed, there was probably a degree of animosity or, at the least, competition between representatives of the articlemen who actually lobbied *against* the implementation of article 13 of Limerick, and those employed by Colonel John Browne to argue its merits.[26] The articlemen of Boffin and Waterford certainly employed lobbyists in London in late 1691 and early 1692. Their efforts were probably not on the scale of the articlemen of Limerick, who from November 1691 employed several agents in London. Similarly, the articlemen of Galway sent Denis Daly and Arthur French (among others) to London at various times during the 1690s.[27] The evidence that survives suggests the formation of *ad hoc* committees of articlemen of Limerick and Galway to instruct their agents. When viewed alongside the Limerick articlemen's petition to Ginkel and the hearings before the Irish lords justices in November 1691, the articlemen's activities in London indicate how rapidly Catholic energies and organisation were deployed from the military to the political arena in the aftermath of defeat.

Such speed was necessary. While the Irish government began to rule on the interpretation of the articles of Limerick in Dublin, the Irish lord chief justice Sir Richard Reynell and the law officers of Ireland and England assembled in London to 'consider of the capitulation [of Limerick]'.[28] The English parliament was also in the final days of its consideration of a bill to exclude Catholics from the practice of the law in Ireland, despite the protection promised in the articles of surrender.[29] Recognising the necessity of maintaining agents in Dublin and in London, the articlemen moved swiftly to protect their interests.

On 16 November, William Talbot, earl of Tyrconnell, wrote from London to Adam Colclough (probably also then in London) to inform him that 'the gentry of Ireland … have fixed upon you as one of their agents to represent their grievances to their majesties'.[30] A month later a second summons was sent, again from London but on this occasion signed by John Galwey and Edmund Malone (Colonel John Browne's nephew). Colclough was notified that he, Colonel Henry Luttrell and Sir Toby Butler were empowered 'to act for them as well such as are under the benefit of articles as all those under protections'.[31]

---

[26] Article 13 of Limerick imposed a special levy on all Catholic-owned estates in Ireland, to help pay Col. John Browne's debts. See Chapter 5 for opposition to article 13 of Limerick by the articlemen of Galway, and Chapter 6 for Col. John Browne's efforts to ensure its implementation in 1692.

[27] For lobbying by French and Daly see below, pp 121, 127–33, 136–7.

[28] Nottingham to the Irish lords justices, 1 Dec. 1691 (*C.S.P.D., 1691–2*, p. 21).

[29] Enacted as 3 William & Mary, c. 2 [Eng.].

[30] William Talbot, earl of Tyrconnell, to Adam Colclough, 16 Nov. 1691 (S.R.O., D641/2/K/2/4/J). William Talbot was nephew to James II's Irish lord deputy, Richard Talbot, duke of Tyrconnell.

[31] Edmund Malone and John Galwey to Adam Colclough, 15 Dec. 1691 (S.R.O., D641/2/ K/2/4/K). This is the only extant evidence that suggests an initial attempt to organise cooperative

Colclough responded to this second call. Sir Richard Cox's opinion of early 1692 was made in response to 'several complaints made by the Irish by their agent Mr Cockly'. The question of payment for these agents arose in November 1692 during correspondence with a committee of articlemen. Several of the committee's members signed a letter sent to Colclough that month: Sir Stephen Rice; Colonel Nicholas Purcell; Sir James Cotter; George Aylmer; Colonel Walter Butler; Henry Oxburgh; Sir Toby Butler; and John Rice.[32] All were in Dublin, perhaps to monitor the proceedings of the Irish parliament. Colclough was almost certainly one of the Irish agents soliciting at this time to view an indemnity bill affecting the articlemen, and a bill relating to Colonel John Browne, which were both under consideration at the English privy council.

Each of the signatories to this letter were important articlemen and most had held prominent positions in the civil administration or army of James II. Colonel Nicholas Purcell and Sir Toby Butler had been among the Jacobite negotiators and signatories at Limerick and Butler had served as James II's solicitor general. Sir Stephen Rice had been appointed chief baron of the exchequer and had been entrusted with the delivery to James in March 1688 of bills for modifying the Restoration land settlement.[33] Colonel Walter Butler was a cousin of the duke of Ormond, while Sir James Cotter had been appointed commander of the Jacobite forces in west Munster in 1691.[34] Henry Oxburgh had sat in the 1689 parliament and later participated in the Jacobite rising of 1715. He was hanged, drawn and quartered for his role.[35] With the exception of Sir Stephen and John Rice, all had sat in the 1689 Irish parliament as MPs (Sir Stephen Rice's status as a member of the judiciary meant that he sat in the lords in an advisory capacity; John Rice was not elected to parliament).

As for the articlemen's agents, Colclough had been appointed as secretary to the Jacobite treasury commissioners in 1689 and also participated in the

---

lobbying between all the articlemen and the protectees. Sir Richard Cox's judgment (discussed above and in chapter 3) related to the articlemen of Limerick and Galway and the protectees and was in response to Colclough's representations on behalf of all of them.

[32] Col. Nicholas Purcell *et al* to Adam Colclough, 19 Nov. 1692 (S.R.O., D641/2/K/2/4/L). This committee does not appear to have been one of fixed membership, but rather an ad hoc gathering of the 'chief of the parties concerned ... to that purpose as many of them as I could conveniently see this night have subscribed hereunder'.

[33] Simms, *Jacobite Ireland*, p. 40.

[34] For Cotter generally, see his *D.I.B.* entry. For his disputed claim to the articles of Limerick, see Simms, *Williamite confiscation*, pp 49–50. For attempts by Ormond to extend his patronage to his cousin Walter during the 1700s, see Thomas Doyle, 'Jacobitism, Catholicism and the Irish Protestant elite, 1700–1710' in *E.C.I.*, 12 (1997), pp 37–9.

[35] Oxburgh sat for either King's County or the borough of Philipstown, and was said to have attempted to raise forces for service with William or his allies during the 1690s. See his *D.I.B.* entry.

1715 rising, as banker to the 'king's friends'.[36] Colclough did not sit in the 1689 parliament, though his cousin Patrick represented the county of Wexford. Luttrell represented County Carlow in James' parliament and after the surrender of Limerick was said to have persuaded several thousand Jacobite soldiers not to travel with Sarsfield to France. His reward was a commission from William to raise a troop of 1,500 men for employment in the Venetian army. The troops seem to have departed, though Luttrell did not accompany them. He did, however, receive a pension of £500 on the English establishment and travelled to Holland to wait on King William on several occasions during the 1690s.[37] Edmund Malone (agent for the articlemen of Limerick, alongside John Galwey, in London at the end of 1691) sat in the 1689 parliament for the borough of Athlone. Malone and Galwey both obtained a pardon from William in 1692.

It is doubtful that these agents had any influence on the consideration of the articles of surrender by the Irish and English law officers at the beginning of December 1691. Early indications from London certainly were not promising for the articlemen. Sydney wrote to the Irish lords justices to explain that William was reluctant to rescind his grant of forfeited lands to Sydney, now threatened by the potential restoration of the articlemen's estates:

> His Majesty was thereupon pleased to tell me that he thinks fit to ratify and confirm the several articles of capitulation as far as it is in his power, yet further than that, it could not be intended; nor does he think himself obliged to do it … he thinks it a thing out of his power to maintain the said articles, and intends that I should still keep possession of [the estates] according to his grant and promise.

The lords justices were instructed to reject the affected articlemen's claims.[38] William's reticence in this case was an early indication of his aversion to the 'resumption' of his gifts to favoured courtiers. That William considered himself under no obligation to honour the articles when they stipulated the restoration of land to the articlemen was, however, extraordinary. If that interpretation had formed the basis of official policy, it would have had a gravely destabilising effect on Ireland. Surely aware of this fact, William's advisers prevailed with the king and Sydney surrendered the lands in question, in return for fresh grants.[39]

---

[36] Bergin, 'Irish Catholic interest', p. 45. See above, p. 46, for Colclough's correspondence with Col. John Browne when secretary to the treasury commissioners.

[37] T.C.D., Clarke correspondence, Ms 749/10/1031–2; T.N.A., SP 63/353, ff 201, 206; B.L., Add. Ms 21,136, ff 59–60; B.L., Add. Ms 35,838, f. 323; C.S.P.D., 1691–2, pp 41, 196; C.S.P.D., 1693, pp 19, 90, 104–5, 192; C.S.P.D., 1694–5, p. 404; C.S.P.D., 1698, p. 439; George Story, A continuation of the impartial history of the wars in Ireland (London, 1693), pp 188-9 [recte 182–3].

[38] Sydney to the Irish lords justices, 12 Dec. 1691 (C.S.P.D., 1690–1, pp 30–1).

[39] Warrant for letters patent, 2 Mar. 1692, (ibid., p. 165).

Instructions for drawing up a bill for confirming 'so much of the articles of Limerick as we have promised to use our utmost endeavours [...] shall be confirmed by parliament' were sent from London to the Irish lords justices in late December 1691.[40] These instructions contained the first formal indication that William intended to exploit the ambiguity of article 12 of Limerick, which merely committed Coningsby, Porter and Ginkel to 'use their utmost endeavours, that the [articles] shall be ratified and confirmed in parliament', thus allowing William's evasive order.[41] That policy was made formal with the ratification and publication of the articles under the great seal of England in March 1692.[42] The Irish and English administrations had, by the end of 1691, accepted that wholesale denial of the right of the articlemen to the restoration of their estates was impractical and a threat to the stability of the kingdom. Yet they were alert to the weaknesses of the articles of surrender and, over the next decade, did not hesitate to exploit these weaknesses.

At the beginning of 1692 the pressure on the Irish government was immense. Not only were they pressed by the articlemen and opponents of the articles, they were expected to maintain law and order in a country only recently fully restored to their control and filled with potential tories (the Irish bandits, rather than the English politicians). Concerted pressure from the articlemen led the lords justices to ignore some of the advice they received from the king's counsel in November 1691. Though no indicted articlemen had yet to reverse their outlawry, at least sixty were restored to their estates by virtue of the draft order approved by the king's counsel, which was intended only for those who had not been indicted. Sir Patrick Bellew of Barmeath, County Louth, was given possession of his estate in December 1691 after lodging a recognisance for £1,000 in chancery.[43] In early January the lords justices informed Nottingham that 'if it shall appear that any of those are not justly entitled to the benefit of the articles, we can soon remove them, they still continuing outlawed for treason, and having only a bare possession without a title from the crown'.[44]

---

[40] [Nottingham?] to [the Irish lords justices?], [29 Dec. 1691?] (T.N.A., SP 63/353, f. 207; C.S.P.D., 1691–2, p. 44). This document appears to be an early draft of the letter sent on 29 December, but the letter sent has not been located. There is no mention in the draft of the method for hearing claims, but later correspondence clearly states that a letter of 29 December contained these instructions.

[41] The instructions were issued following the approval of a declaration for confirming the articles of Limerick at the English privy council on 21 December 1691 (T.N.A., PC 2/74, f. 296).

[42] McGuire, 'Treaty of Limerick', p. 133. McGuire's point was made in respect of the published ratification of March 1692. As is clear from the above, that policy had been decided by December 1691.

[43] Bellew of Barmeath papers, M/1/8. Bellew was restored to land in counties Louth, Galway and Dublin.

[44] Irish lords justices to Nottingham, 8 Jan. 1692 (T.N.A., SP 63/354, ff 3–4; C.S.P.D., 1695 & Addenda, pp 174–5); Simms, Williamite confiscation, p. 46; idem, 'Treaty of Limerick', p. 13.

This was followed by a proclamation instructing all those who claimed the benefit of the articles of Limerick to lodge their claim with the privy council not later than 20 February 1692, a time limit subsequently extended to 15 April 1692. The articlemen of Galway were also instructed to submit their claims, with the privy council and lords justices to preside over the court.[45]

III

Sydney's appointment as lord lieutenant in early March 1692 was accompanied by official instructions that addressed the implementation of the articles in cursory fashion.[46] Four months after the king's counsel had advised the Irish government on some of the finer points of restoring the articlemen to their estates, and just weeks before hearings on claims to the articles of Limerick and Galway were scheduled to begin, many issues of interpretation and implementation remained outstanding.

Twenty-six questions, raising outstanding issues arising from the war in Ireland, were submitted to the English government in early March 1692 by Sir Richard Levinge, solicitor general for Ireland. The majority sought clarity on the interpretation to be applied to the articles, though only six appear to have been answered in any fashion.[47] Perhaps the most important reply was given to the most general query:

'In what manner would his Majesty have the Articles to be construed; according to a common and reasonable intendment, or most amply and beneficially to the capitulators? ... *With justice but not favour.*'[48]

Responses were also forthcoming on other vexed topics. The elaborate nature of encumbrances on land was acknowledged by Levinge's observation that no forfeited estate in Ireland was likely to be without an equitable interest

---

The order restoring Bellew to his estate was dated 7 December 1691; the lords justices' letter to Nottingham of 8 January 1692 enclosed a different version of this order, stipulating a recognisance of £500.

[45] Proclamations, 11 Jan., 18 Feb. & 23 Mar. 1692 (Kelly & Lyons (eds), *Proclamations of Ireland*, ii, pp 280, 284, 293–4); [Nottingham?] to [the Irish lords justices?], [29 Dec. 1691?] (T.N.A., SP 63/353, f. 207; C.S.P.D., 1691–2, p. 44).

[46] C.S.P.D., 1691–2, p. 169.

[47] 'Queries from Mr Solicitor of Ireland', 2 Mar. 1692 (T.N.A., SP 63/354, ff 43–5). These queries were presumably submitted to Nottingham. The 'answers' quoted below were in the form of marginal annotations to Levinge's queries. No formal reply has been located and it is unclear whether any was actually sent.

[48] Emphasis added to indicate the marginal annotation, or 'answer', to the query. Sydney's instructions were issued on 3 March, before Levinge's queries could have reached London.

– whether in the form of a lease or loan secured on land – held by an innocent third party. All forfeited lands were vested in the king's hands and, as it was not possible to sue the king in a court of equity, an innocent person's interest in forfeited land could not be legally recovered. Whether or not such persons were to receive compensation was to be dealt with on an individual basis through appeals to the king.[49] The outlawry of Jacobites after their death proved a contentious topic after the war, and Levinge requested clarity on 'what shall be done for the son where the father or next ancestor died before he was outlawed'. These posthumous outlawries were acknowledged as 'illegal' and 'unjust'. In such cases, however, official policy was shaped not by justice but by political considerations. Because it was thought probable that the Irish parliament would insist that estates affected by such outlawries should be forfeited, regardless of the law, 'such reversals may be delayed as much as may be'.[50]

A host of other queries, which appear to have gone unanswered, indicate the complexity of the issues associated with the articles of surrender. Some were relatively minor: were prosecutions of those who served in James II's civil administration to be conducted in the same fashion as those who served in the Jacobite army? Others were of potentially enormous significance: what liberty was to be given to Catholics to exercise their religion until parliament decided the issue? To what extent should the government interfere in the prosecution of civil law suits arising from the war? Where indictments were issued against any person claiming the articles of Limerick or Galway, how were they to be treated until their trial at the court of claims? The latter two queries were of paramount importance. The process of adjudicating eligibility to articles took another seven years, effectively leaving hundreds of claimants to the articles in legal limbo. Though no formal policy appears to have been formulated, the evidence suggests that those who claimed the benefit of the articles were, for the most part, left in possession of their estates until the conclusion of their trials at the courts of claims.

The first court of claims began hearings in April 1692 with the first adjudications under the articles of Limerick delivered on 20 April.[51] Claimants were expected to produce three supporting witnesses, one of whom was to be a

---

[49] This issue was addressed in controversial fashion by the passage of the act of resumption in 1700, and the attendant work of the Forfeiture Trustees between 1700 and 1703. See Simms, *Williamite confiscation*, pp 110–57; Hayton, *Ruling Ireland*, pp 71–84; Walsh, *Making of the Irish Protestant ascendancy*, pp 43–60.

[50] This issue was eventually decided by the 1697 act for hindering the reversal of outlawries and attainders (9 Will. III, c.5, s.2). All Catholics who were found to have died in rebellion were attainted of high treason and their estates forfeited. Individual petitions to the king saved a handful of estates from forfeiture in this manner. See Simms, *Williamite confiscation*, pp 43–4, 114.

[51] Simms, *Williamite confiscation*, pp 46–7.

Protestant.[52] A total of 246 men and four women were adjudicated within the articles of Limerick and two men within the articles of Galway during 1692, with just five claims rejected.[53] Colonel John Browne's application was as certain of success as any could be; his status as signatory alone would probably have sufficed. He was well known to the lords justices, who presided over the court. His creditors would also have had a keen interest in a successful claim; if Browne's estate was forfeited it would have become vested in the king, an outcome that could have had serious repercussions for the recovery of debts.[54]

Lord Athenry urged Browne, his father-in-law, to take on clients at the court of claims, claiming it to be 'the best course you can take to get money'.[55] The courts certainly proved lucrative to the legal profession and placed a strain on the Irish government's finances. Sydney claimed that counsel employed to argue for the government in 1692 had yet to be paid a year later, which was a factor in the court's failure to sit in 1693. An additional £500 was required for counsel's fees and accommodation for government witnesses, over and above the £3,000 already allocated. Sydney also provides some clues as to the government's management of the hearings, particularly in relation to the strategy employed to discover false claims and protectees. A manager (presumably one of the king's counsel) was appointed for each province, whose job was to find evidence and witnesses against claimants.[56] Claimants also had to fee counsel to prepare their petitions and to argue their cases at the court, while also agreeing to two separate recognisances of £1,000 and £1,200 before repossession of their estates was permitted.

Sir Patrick Bellew of Barmeath was one of the first articlemen to appear before the court and was adjudged on 6 May 1692 to be within the articles of Limerick.[57] His brief for counsel listed six potential witnesses to support his claim (including Sir Toby Butler), all of whom appear to have been Catholic. Among the materials Bellew supplied his counsel were a letter of recommendation from General Ginkel dated 5 October 1691 and a manuscript copy of the articles of Limerick, which Bellew had 'demanded' from Butler as soon as the articles were

---

[52] Proclamation, 23 Mar. 1692 (Kelly & Lyons (eds), *Proclamations of Ireland*, ii, 293–4).

[53] T.C.D., Ms 744, ff 77–118; Simms, 'Irish Jacobites', pp 89–104. The women adjudicated within the articles of Limerick were the wives of Capt. Derby Long, Capt. Nicholas Harrold, Sir Oliver Bourke and Lt. Col. Daniel MacCarty (Elizabeth, Lady Cahir). The claims rejected were from Capt. Jasper Grant, John Baggot (father of Mark Baggot, discussed above), James Fitzgerald, Nicholas Adams, and Henry Crofton (see above, p. 78). The successful claimants to the articles of Galway are discussed below, p. 127.

[54] Browne's certificate of adjudication is extant. It is signed by the lords justices and seven members of the privy council and is one of the few original certificates still extant (N.L.I., Ms 40,900/3/9–10).

[55] Lord Athenry to Col. Browne, 8 Feb. 1692 (N.L.I., Ms 40,900/6/2).

[56] Sydney and the privy council to Nottingham, 15 May 1693 (*C.S.P.D., 1695 & Addenda*, pp 226–7). £500 was duly added (*C.S.P.D., 1693*, p. 179).

[57] Simms, 'Irish Jacobites', p. 90.

signed. The brief ended with an important note: 'Remember in particular that the reversing of one outlawry may serve for all, he being, as he is informed, nine times indicted.' Neither the identity of Bellew's counsel, or his fees, are apparent.[58]

As an experienced and well-regarded lawyer, in different circumstances Browne might well have made a tidy sum at the courts of claims. The competition for clients was lessened by the fact that the king's counsel directed prosecutions against claimants: 'If you remember that we could not be for the claimants that were to have the benefit of the Limerick articles (from whom the money was to be got) and that our allowance from the king on those claims is hardly any of it paid.'[59] It is, however, unlikely that Browne acted as counsel to any of the articlemen. All successful claimants were required to enter into a bond to pay the equivalent of one year's quit-rent to fulfil the obligations imposed by article 13 of Limerick; an imposition they bitterly resented.[60] The prudent course would have been to maintain a discreet distance from the court, unless an appearance was unavoidable.

The Irish government initially ignored the instructions it had received in late 1691 to prepare a bill for confirming the articles of Limerick. Following intervention from the English administration these instructions were eventually obeyed – a point which has largely been missed in modern accounts of the fate of the articles of Limerick.[61] Though hardly any Irish Protestants favoured even a limited parliamentary ratification of the articles of Limerick and Galway, the English government recognised their importance to post-war stability and sought to cajole their Irish counterpart into presenting the necessary bills to the Irish parliament. As a result, a confirmation of some of the articles of Limerick and Galway appeared in a bill prepared by the Irish privy council in August 1692. The bill promised indemnity for Jacobites and Williamites from private lawsuits, a key protection for the articlemen that was designed to prevent Protestants from suing Catholics for crimes allegedly committed during the war.[62] If left to its own devices, however, the Irish government would have legislated for indemnity only for Irish Protestants.

The Irish government initially sent an indemnity bill to London on 6 February 1692. The lords justices explained that it was necessary to 'quiet the minds' of

---

[58] Sir Patrick actually appears to have never been indicted. The letter of recommendation does not survive among the Barmeath papers, though the manuscript copy of the articles of Limerick does. It is one of very few surviving contemporary copies of the articles, and the only one so far located among the papers of an articleman (Bellew of Barmeath papers, M/1/8).

[59] Alan Brodrick to Thomas Brodrick, 11 Oct. 1700 (S.H.C., Midleton papers, 1248/2, ff 11–12).

[60] C.S.P.D., 1693, p. 444.

[61] The exception is Wouter Troost, 'William III and religious tolerance' in Whelan (ed.), *The last of the great wars*, pp 49–50. That account does not draw on all of the available material.

[62] Indemnity for the articlemen of Galway was stipulated in article 8, and for the Limerick articlemen in articles 5 and 6 (see Appendix A).

the population, to 'indemnify all that have acted for their majesties' service …
and to put the British into an equal condition with the Irish that have submitted
upon articles'.[63] The bill was intended to extend indemnity only to Protestants,
not the articlemen, who were protected only by lord chancellor Porter's refusal
to hear private law suits against claimants to the articles.[64] Instructions to
redraft the bill as one of 'indemnity against private suits' were sent to Dublin by
Nottingham on 2 April: it was probably one of the bills returned to London and
referred to the English attorney general on 20 July for a report.[65] By late July the
alterations to the indemnity bill envisaged by the English privy council encompassed several outstanding issues relating to the articles of surrender, including a
proviso allowing the Galway lawyers to resume their practices.[66] When the bill
was returned to the Irish government on 25 August the accompanying instructions specified that clauses pardoning all those who claimed the benefit of the
articles of surrender, and those who had taken protection, should be added to
the bill. All Jacobites still abroad were to be excluded.[67]

Sydney's response was cautious and he warned that if parliament considered
the indemnity bill to be too favourable to Irish Catholics, it would be rejected.[68]
Soon afterwards Sydney complained that redrafting the bill was proving
problematic, 'so great a resentment does the Protestant party here still retain
of the injuries and oppression they suffered from the papists during the late
rebellion'.[69] On 28 September the redrafted bill was transmitted to London,
accompanied by a lengthy explanatory letter. Noting that the bill comprehensively answered the instructions of 25 August, Sydney admitted that

---

[63] Irish lords justices to Nottingham, 6 Feb. 1692 (T.N.A., SP 32/4, f. 18). For a discussion of this
bill's importance in the evolution of Poynings' law procedure, see Kelly, *Poynings' law*, pp 55–8.

[64] Porter informed James Vernon (under secretary to the duke of Shrewsbury, then secretary of
state for the southern department) in August 1695 that directions relating to confirming article 6
of Limerick were necessary as he had, to that point, 'hitherto stayed such suits by injunction, but
if there be no bill sent over for confirming that part, I must then dissolve those already granted,
and hinder none from proceeding as they can at law for the future' (Porter to Vernon, 6 Aug. 1695
(*C.S.P.D., 1695 & Addenda*, p. 36)).

[65] Nottingham to the Irish lords justices, 2 Apr. 1692 (T.N.A., SP 67/1, f. 159); Nottingham to
John Somers, 20 Jul. 1692 (T.N.A., SP 44/98, f. 510). The exact chronology for the transmission
of this bill from Dublin and its consideration at the English privy council is unclear, due to
Nottingham's occasional failure to specify the nature of the bills he refers to in correspondence.

[66] Nottingham to the Irish lords justices, 30 Jul. 1692 (T.N.A., SP 67/1, f. 171; *C.S.P.D., 1691–2*,
p. 391). See below, pp 128–34 for a discussion of the exclusion of Galway lawyers from practising
the law.

[67] Nottingham to Sydney, 25 Aug. 1692 (T.N.A., SP 67/1, f. 172; *C.S.P.D., 1691–2*, p. 421).

[68] Sydney to Nottingham, 3 Sept. 1692 (T.N.A., SP 63/354, f. 131; *C.S.P.D., 1695 & Addenda*,
p. 199).

[69] Sydney to Nottingham, 9 Sept. 1692 (*C.S.P.D., 1695 & Addenda*, pp 200–1). To make the
new bill more palatable to parliament, additional clauses confirming the attainder of those who
had died during the war were also added (Bergin, 'Irish legislative procedure', ii, 23).

the new draft actually went 'beyond her Majesty's intentions' by attainting all Irish Jacobites who remained abroad, rather than simply excluding them from indemnity. It was hoped that the inclusion of attainder clauses within the indemnity bill would make it more acceptable to parliament. Yet another thorny issue, sidestepped by the bill, was the date from which any indemnity was to begin. Protestants favoured the later date of 14 August 1689 (the day after Schomberg's arrival in Ireland, mistakenly stated in the explanatory letter as the day of arrival), while Catholics argued that the war had properly begun with the disturbances in Ulster and Bandon in January and February. Sydney explained that 10 April 1689 seemed an acceptable compromise, as it was the date named in William and Mary's February 1689 declaration by which Jacobites were to lay down their arms. The final decision was to be left to the king and queen.[70]

At the English privy council the bill was fraught with difficulties. Irish Catholic lobbyists (unnamed, but probably including Adam Colclough, Henry Luttrell and John Galwey) sought a copy, and were required to submit their objections to the bill.[71] This does not mean that Catholics were, as has been suggested, the bill's 'sharpest critics'.[72] Their efforts seem to have concentrated largely on procuring saving clauses for fifteen individual Irish Catholics.[73] On 10 October the Irish and English attorneys general were instructed to examine the petitions to establish if a general order could be drafted for insertion in the bill, to preserve the 'estates and honours' of the petitioners.[74]

Catholic lobbyists did, however, petition against some of the indemnity bill's clauses. One of the objections raised was to a provision that all remainders to forfeited estates were to be cut off, presumably even those of persons who were not attainted. The wide scope of the attainder provisions also appears to have been disliked.[75] Informed by Nottingham in mid-October that the bill was still under consideration, Sydney responded that if it was returned with amendments

---

[70] Sydney and the Irish privy council to Nottingham, 28 Sept. 1692 (T.N.A., SP 63/354, f. 155; C.S.P.D., 1695 & Addenda, pp 205–7).

[71] T.N.A. PC 2/75, ff 6, 8, 10–12 (7, 10 Oct. 1692).

[72] Kelly, Poynings' law, p. 56; cf. Wouter Troost, 'William III and religious tolerance', pp 49–50.

[73] The petitioners were 1) Elizabeth, countess Clancarty; 2) Francis Taaffe, earl of Carlingford; 3) Col. Richard Butler (uncle to the duke of Ormond); 4) Col. Thomas Dongan on behalf of the earl of Limerick and his wife Mary; 5) Jane Knight on behalf of Baron Trimleston; 6) Theobald, Baron Cahir, Christopher Fagan, Matthew Bellew and John Galwey on behalf of themselves and 'others'; 7) John Hussey; 8) Sir Robert Southwell on behalf of Margaret, countess of Fingal and Peter, earl of Fingal; 9) Col. Thomas Bourke on behalf of his wife Helena Bourke, countess dowager of Clanricarde; 10) John, Lord Bellew; 11) Lady Bellew; 12) Viscount Iveagh; 13) Agnes Bourke on behalf of herself and her grandson John Bourke, and Giles Bourke on behalf of herself and her grandson Richard; 14) Sir John Eustace and Sir Maurice Eustace; 15) James, Viscount Lanesborough.

[74] T.N.A., PC 2/75, ff 10–12.

[75] Robert Yard to Sir Joseph Williamson, 11 Oct. 1692 (T.N.A., SP 32/4, f. 151; C.S.P.D., 1691–2, p. 478).

in favour of Catholics beyond those in the Irish government's draft, the bill would fall in parliament.[76]

To overcome these difficulties the privy council ordered the English law officers, with the assistance of the Irish attorney general, to redraft the bill as a 'confirmation of the capitulations of Limerick and Galway and a discharge of all actions and suits … against any person or persons comprised within those articles'.[77] In effect the English privy council had taken the remarkable decision to ignore the Irish government's advice and entirely redraft an Irish bill. Nottingham somewhat disingenuously informed Sydney that the new bill was to be sent *in lieu* of the indemnity bill, which was unlikely to be ready in time for presentation to parliament.[78]

Bafflingly, the redrafted bill returned to the English privy council on 3 November actually contradicted the privy council's instructions. In its new form the bill indemnified only the Limerick articlemen from private lawsuits. The Galway articlemen and the protectees were omitted entirely, nor was there any mention of a general pardon for any Irish Jacobite. As finally approved, the bill's title was amended with the addition of the words 'for certain persons named therein'.[79] The text of the bill was completely redrafted:

> Whereas by the articles made upon the surrender of the city of Limerick to their majesties bearing date 3 October 1691, it was agreed that the persons comprised within the said articles should not be sued or impleaded by any person whatsoever for any the causes therein mentioned, and that the said articles touching the discharge of suits and actions should be mutual and reciprocal, Be it therefore [enacted that all] persons comprised within the said articles shall be, and are hereby freed of and from all actions and suits of what nature soever from which by the true intent and meaning of the said articles they were to be discharged. And be it further enacted, that no person comprised within the said articles, and hereby freed and discharged from the said actions and suits, shall bring or prosecute against any other person whatsoever any action or suit for such or the like causes as are mentioned in the said articles.[80]

There is no explanation as to why the final draft explicitly ignored the privy council's earlier instructions that the bill should also include the Galway articles and protectees, or why these omissions were neither mentioned or rectified.

---

[76] Nottingham to Sydney, 14 Oct. 1692 (T.N.A., SP 67/1, f. 219); Sydney to Nottingham, 22 Oct. 1692 (T.N.A., SP 63/354, ff 183–4; *C.S.P.D., 1695 & Addenda*, pp 214–5).

[77] T.N.A., PC 2/75, f. 22 (27 Oct. 1692). The Irish attorney general was Sir John Temple.

[78] Nottingham to Sydney, 2 Nov. 1692 (T.N.A., SP 67/1, f. 219; *C.S.P.D., 1691–2*, p. 492); Kelly, *Poynings' law*, p. 58.

[79] The full title of the bill does not appear in any of the sources.

[80] T.N.A., PC 2/75, f. 23 (3 Nov. 1692). This is one of the rare occasions in which the entire text of a bill, amended at the privy council, is in the privy council register. No copy of the indemnity bill transmitted from Dublin on 28 September survives, making a direct comparison with that measure impossible.

Nottingham returned the bill to Sydney on 9 November, explaining that it was now 'a very short one, being only to pardon and discharge all suits against those of Limerick'.[81] The Irish parliament had, however, been prorogued on 3 November and the first Irish parliament of the post war era failed to enact any legislation protecting the articles of surrender. Even if parliament had been in session and had considered the indemnity bill, Sir Charles Porter noted that it would not have answered what was required, as William had not specified a date from which the war was to be officially said to have begun.[82]

IV

Continued opposition from MPs to Sydney's government, inflamed by the lord lieutenant's heavy-handed treatment of the opposition, led to the dissolution of the 1692 parliament in June 1693, with no indication as to the date of a new election.[83] The parliamentary row over the right to initiate money bills had provided Sydney with a pretext to prorogue the 1692 parliament after just a few weeks' sitting. Much more pressing, for Sydney at least, was the commons' pending report into the mismanagement of forfeited estates, with accompanying accusations of corruption within the government.[84] Prorogation of the Irish parliament led to the presentation of a set of 'grievances' to the English parliament by several Irish Protestant politicians in February and March 1693.[85]

Sydney's government was the main target of the opposition's ire, but there remained deep Protestant hostility towards the articles of Limerick. Indemnity for crimes allegedly committed by Catholics against Protestants during the war continued to be a contentious issue. Among the many accusations levelled at Sydney's government was that of giving undue protection to Catholics from prosecutions for alleged offences, particularly those who were not entitled to the benefit of the articles.[86] Here, the articles merely formed a minor part of the wider scope of complaints presented to the English parliament, with Irish

---

[81] Nottingham to Sydney, 9 Nov. 1692 (T.N.A., SP 67/1, f. 220; C.S.P.D., 1691–2, p. 497).

[82] Porter to Coningsby, 18 Nov. 1692 (P.R.O.N.I., De Ros Mss, D/638/18/2).

[83] Sydney to Nottingham, 29 Jan. 1693 (C.S.P.D., 1693, p. 22); C.I. McGrath, *The making of the eighteenth-century Irish constitution: government, parliament and the revenue 1692–1714* (Dublin, 2000), pp 91–2; James McGuire, 'The Irish parliament of 1692' in Thomas Bartlett and D.W. Hayton (eds), *Penal era and golden age: essays in Irish history* (Belfast, 1979), pp 26–7.

[84] *An account of the sessions of parliament in Ireland, 1692* (London, 1693), p. 24; McGuire, 'Irish parliament of 1692', pp 21–2; McGrath, *Eighteenth-century Irish constitution*, pp 87–8.

[85] C.J., x, 826–34 (24 Feb. 1693); 842–3 (4 Mar.); L.J., xv, 253 (28 Feb. 1693), 255 (1 Mar.), 256–71 (2 Mar.), 273–5 (4 Mar.).

[86] C.J., x, 827 (24 Feb. 1693). Article 6 of the articles of Limerick protected the articlemen of Limerick from private actions 'for any trespasses by them committed, or for any arms, horses, money, goods, chattels, merchandises or provisions, whatsoever, by them seized or taken, during

115

Protestants articulating fears about the interpretation of the articles, rather than their wording.[87]

The resulting addresses from the English houses of lords and commons to William 'concerning the state of Ireland' complained of Catholics not entitled to the articles of Limerick having their outlawries reversed and enjoying protection from private suits, while 'poor Protestants were left to be prosecuted by the Irish'.[88] The addresses also queried the 'missing clause' of article 2, ratified by William in February 1692. The commons requested that

> the articles of Limerick, with the said addition, may be laid before your commons in parliament, that the manner of obtaining the same may be inquired into; to the end it may appear by what means the said articles were so enlarged; and to what value the estates thereby claimed do amount.

Complaints regarding granting of protections from lawsuits were somewhat premature. Hearings to determine eligibility to the articles had only just begun; those who claimed the benefit, but had yet to have their cases heard, were exposed to prosecution without such protection. Sydney's lengthy response noted that he was unaware of

> any instance wherein the Irish or papists have had any encouragement at all or any favour shown them other than that to which they were entitled by articles and the protections given by the government; and there has never been any instance in which the protestants were sued by the Irish, whilst the Irish were protected.[89]

The adjudications of Daniel Magennis, Phelim Magennis and Cormac O'Neill within the articles of Limerick had caused some disquiet, but the complaints to parliament contained nothing more tangible than insinuation and these three men appear to have been a random selection.[90] In the case of Alexander MacDonnell, earl of Antrim, and Robert Longfield, the complainants' cases may have been more substantive.[91]

Buried within the plethora of objections to Sydney's government was another, more serious challenge to royal authority. James Sloane, MP for Killyleagh, County Down, questioned the right of the Irish privy council to adjudicate on claims to articles and to restore Irish Catholics to their estates:

the time of the war'. The article was reciprocal, thus prohibiting the articlemen from suing any Williamite.

[87] Hayton, *Ruling Ireland*, p. 42.
[88] *L.J.*, xv, 275 (4 Mar. 1693).
[89] Sydney to Nottingham, 30 June 1693 (*C.S.P.D.*, 1693, p. 204).
[90] *C.J.*, x, 828–31 (24 Feb. 1693).
[91] Ibid. For Antrim and Longfield, see Simms, 'Irish Jacobites', p. 131 and idem, *Williamite confiscation*, p. 50.

[The forfeited estates] have been much lessened by the articles of Limerick and Galway, and by the judgments made at council board since that time, determining who are, and who are not, within the articles: how they came so far to intermeddle, I know not; but it seemed the stranger to me, for that I remember this honourable house had, in some measure, laid their hands on those forfeitures; and a bill now depending for disposing thereof; and therein a clause to avoid (as I remember) all such judgments as should be given relating thereto, save such as were pursuant to that intended act.[92]

Sloane's implicit challenge to William's authority fell on deaf ears. The king's response to parliament was brief and vague to the point of evasion: 'You may be sure, that whatever may have been amiss, all possible care shall be taken to remedy it.'[93]

Between 1694 and 1697 soundings were made by the English government as to the possibility of a bill devoted solely to providing a parliamentary confirmation of the articles of Limerick.[94] Mindful of the pressing need to hold a new parliament in Ireland, and of the difficulties of the session of 1692, Henry, Lord Capell, one of the lords justices, advised Shrewsbury in 1694 that a bill for confirming the articles was unwise: 'I find the first and sixth articles [of Limerick] may meet with some opposition.'[95] Appointed lord deputy in May 1695, Capell used his position to obstruct the drafting of a bill for confirming the articles, declaring his belief that without a specific application from the articlemen for such an act the government was under no obligation to initiate one. Capell's contention that no such application had ever come from the articlemen was disingenuous.[96] His opinion may have been relayed to the articlemen, for Colonels Henry Luttrell and Nicholas Purcell petitioned the English privy council requesting a bill confirming the articles of Limerick on 31 October 1695.[97] Lord chancellor Porter also pressed strongly for a confirmatory bill, but despite an instruction from London to legislate for the articles of Limerick the Irish privy council declined to act, citing fears of a renewal of the concerted opposition of 1692 to the government's legislative programme.[98] The decision was influenced in part by the hostility towards Porter among the Protestant polity, largely as a result of his perceived liberal interpretation of

[92] C.J., x, 830 (24 Feb. 1693).
[93] L.J., xv, 283 (10 Mar. 1693). A similarly worded response was given to the commons the same day (C.J., x, 848).
[94] Shrewsbury to Capell, 14 Jun. 1694 (H.M.C., Buccleuch Mss, ii, 81–2).
[95] Capell to Shrewsbury, 14 Jul. 1694 (ibid., pp 100–1). Article 1 related to freedom of religious practice, while article 6 concerned indemnity from law suits arising from the war.
[96] Capell to Shrewsbury, 18 Jun. 1695 (ibid., pp 193–4).
[97] H.M.C., Downshire Mss, i, 574.
[98] Porter to Vernon, 6 Aug. 1695; Shrewsbury to Porter, 29 Aug. 1695 (C.S.P.D., 1695 & Addenda, pp 36, 54); Capell to Shrewsbury, 15 Aug. 1695; Shrewsbury to Capell, 29 Aug. 1695 (H.M.C., Buccleuch Mss, ii, 215–16, 220); McGuire, 'Treaty of Limerick', pp 134–5; Troost, 'William III and religious tolerance', pp 51–2.

the articles of Limerick.[99] Capell wrote some months later that the chief source of animosity towards Porter was his protection of the articlemen from private lawsuits.[100]

Table 2: Methods of Implementing the Articles

	Ratification under the great seal of England	Confirmed by Act of Parliament*	Abrogated by an Act of Parliament	Terms of Articles Fully Implemented (pre–1704)[101]
Drogheda	No	No	2 Anne, c.6;[102] 8 Anne, c.3[103]	Yes
Waterford	Yes	No	2 Anne, c.6; 8 Anne, c.3	Yes
Galway	Yes	7 William III, c.5;[104] 9 William III, c.5[105]	3 William & Mary, c.2[106] [Eng.]; 2 Anne, c.6; 8 Anne, c.3	No
Boffin	Yes	9 William III, c.5	2 Anne, c.6; 8 Anne, c.3	Yes
Sligo	No	9 William III, c.5	2 Anne, c.6; 8 Anne, c.3	Yes
Limerick	Yes	3 William & Mary, c.2 [Eng.]; 7 William III, c.5; 9 William III, c.5	9 William III, c.2;[107] 2 Anne, c.6; 8 Anne, c.3	No

* Shading in grey indicates that the articles were only confirmed in part by these acts.

[99] McGrath, *Eighteenth-century Irish constitution*, pp 121–2; cf. Hayton, *Ruling Ireland*, pp 56–9.

[100] Capell to John Somers, lord keeper of the great seal of England, 7 Oct. 1695 (S.H.C., Somers-Cocks papers, 371/14/F/13).

[101] The articles of Galway and Limerick both included provisions relating to the freedom of Catholics to practise their religion. No attempt has been made here to discuss this issue. These articles were open to various interpretations, while the imposition of penal legislation directed against the Catholic clergy and hierarchy in the 1690s further complicates the issue.

[102] An act to prevent the further growth of popery (1704).

[103] An act for explaining and amending an act, entitled, an act to prevent the further growth of popery (1709).

[104] An act for the better securing the government, by disarming papists (1695); saving clause for the articlemen of Galway and Limerick at s. 4.

[105] An act to hinder the reversal of several outlawries and attainders, and to prevent the return of subjects of this kingdom who have gone into the dominions of the French King in Europe (1697); saving clauses for the articlemen of Galway and Limerick at s. 1, and for the articlemen of Boffin and Sligo at s. 18 and s. 23 respectively.

[106] An act for the abrogating the oath of supremacy in Ireland and appointing new oaths ([Eng.], 1691); saving clause for the articlemen of Limerick at s. 9; abrogation of the articles of Galway by the omission of a saving clause for lawyers.

[107] An Act for the confirmation of articles, made at the surrender of the city of Limerick (1697); abrogated primarily by the omission of article 1, the 'missing clause' of article 2 and article 9.

Table 2 shows how the articles of surrender were confirmed or abrogated by various acts of parliament during the 1690s, in 1704 and in 1709. As can be seen, parliamentary confirmation of some of the articles of Limerick and Galway was, for the most part, ironically achieved through penal legislation enacted in 1695 and 1697 and the private acts for Colonel John Browne of 1695 and 1705.[108] The 1704 'Act to prevent the further growth of Popery' and its explanatory act of 1709 abrogated all of the articles of surrender, particularly Galway and Limerick. A column for ratification under the great seal of England has been included, though the legal implications of ratification are unclear. This is amply illustrated by the ratification under the great seal of England and publication of the complete articles both of Limerick and Galway in March 1692, despite the abrogation of the latter by the 1691 Oaths Act. The disparity between the text of the articles of Limerick ratified in 1692 and the version later approved by the Irish parliament is even starker. It is also important to note that though some of the articles of Limerick were confirmed by legislation in 1697, this confirmation was almost entirely undone in the reign of Anne by the Popery Acts of 1704 and 1709.

An act for confirming the articles of Limerick was finally passed by the Irish parliament in September 1697.[109] However, its adherence to the terms signed in 1691 was accurately summed up by fourteen members of the house of lords who objected that 'not one of the said Articles is therein, as we conceive, fully confirmed'.[110] Most controversially, the 'missing clause' and article 1, which promised freedom of conscience, were omitted. Also missing was article 9, which specified that the only oath to be required of Irish Catholics was the oath of allegiance. The way was thus clear for the imposition of the oath of abjuration on all Irish Catholics in 1709. Article 6 was included, with the date of the war's beginning fixed at 10 April 1689. This was a disappointment to Catholics and the act allowed one year for the prosecution of lawsuits arising from the period of November 1688 to April 1689.[111] The impact of the omission of article 1 needs no elaboration; the 'missing clause' proved to be less important than might have been suspected. The act, and negotiations between the Irish and English administrations about its provisions, have been thoroughly examined.[112] For the articlemen, its most important provision was the establishment of a third and final court of claims, which sat between October 1697 and September

---

108 For Browne's private acts, see Part III.

109 An act for the confirmation of the articles made at the surrender of the city of Limerick (9 Will. III, c. 2).

110 A collection of the protests of the lords of Ireland, 1634–1771 (Dublin, 1772), p. 20.

111 Simms, The Treaty of Limerick (Irish History Series, no. 2, Dundalk, 1965), pp 13–14.

112 Simms, Williamite confiscation, pp 50–65; idem, Treaty of Limerick, pp 12–17; McGuire, 'Treaty of Limerick', pp 133–8; Troost, 'William and religious tolerance', pp 52–4; McGrath, Eighteenth-century Irish constitution, pp 129–30; Kelly, Poynings' law, pp 80–91.

1699. It heard 783 claims in total (709 under Limerick, 74 under Galway), with just 8 rejected.[113]

There is, however, some doubt as to whether all claimants to articles were heard by the courts of claims. John Pulteney, clerk of the privy council, petitioned for payment for having copied 1,150 claims and 440 related orders by April 1697.[114] The third and final court of claims, which considered just under 800 cases, did not begin to adjudicate until October 1697. Claims were clearly lodged at the privy council even when the court was not in session and at least 2,000 claims were made in total. Some of these were undoubtedly repeat submissions from those who had yet to be heard in court, but almost every person for whom a record of adjudication is extant would have had to claim twice for the figure of 2,000 to be reached. J.G. Simms speculated that this discrepancy can be explained by the 'missing clause'. He hypothesised that articlemen whose claims rested on having been within the territory covered by this clause simply never appeared before the court, but retained their estates.[115] That may well have been the case, though the forfeiture inquiry commissioners appointed by the English parliament in 1699 would surely have noticed and commented upon such a large discrepancy between adjudications and estates held by Catholics. Simms' own calculations of acreage held by Catholics in 1703, which rested on the findings of the inquiry commissioners and their successors, the trustees appointed to oversee the resumption and sale of forfei-tures, rules out this possibility. The lists of claims scheduled for 1694 shows that many of the claimants failed to appear at their hearings, or were put off to a later date.[116] It is perhaps more plausible to suggest that the delay between the hearings of 1694 and the re-opening of the court of claims in October 1697 caused problems for many prospective claimants.

The intervening period may have seen some encounter financial diffi-culties that prevented them from appearing before the court. For others, the costs may always have been too high. Article 5 of Limerick stipulated that all beneficiaries to the articles were to have their outlawries reversed free of charge, with the exception of writing clerks' fees. Yet an investigation into Irish forfeitures concluded that the fees associated with the three courts of claims were 'extravagant' and accused several clerks of extortion, particularly William Palmer, registrar to the courts of claims and deputy clerk of the privy council.

---

[113] This is a slight revision of Simms' calculations of 793 in total (715 and 78 claims). Simms, *Williamite confiscation*, pp 51–2; idem, *Treaty of Limerick*, p. 14. The second court of claims had sat in 1694 (and was in reality a second session of the 1692 court), hearing only claims to the articles of Limerick.

[114] C.T.B., 1697, p. 111.

[115] Simms, *Williamite confiscation*, p. 64.

[116] See Appendix B.

Luke Dillon of Clonbrock, County Galway, paid at least £168 in fees to Palmer and other clerks of the court to secure his father Robert's adjudication within articles.[117] Catholics were also willing to bribe officials or to pay 'managers' who sold their influence and contacts. Mrs Margaret Uniack reportedly received at least £600 to use her influence with former lord lieutenant Sydney to obtain pardons, while John Bellew, Baron Bellew of Duleek, paid almost £3,000 for his pardon to Sydney and Thomas Wentworth, Baron Raby.[118]

Nor were the expenses of the articlemen limited to the courts of claims. As will be discussed in chapter 5, Lord Bophin's expense in recovering his estate and receiving a pardon ran to at least £9,000. Though his case was complex and the associated costs untypical, proving eligibility to the articles, procuring pardons and preserving the possession of estates was an expensive business. Several commissions were appointed to manage the Jacobite forfeitures between 1692 and 1697, necessitating the vigilance of the articlemen to ensure their estates were unmolested.[119] The exact remit of these commissions and the extent of their jurisdiction was unclear, even to those appointed as commissioners.[120] Their ineffectiveness led to accusations of mismanagement of the forfeitures. Catholics occasionally received no advance warning of the appearance of commissioners in their locality, forcing them to rely on their own information networks. In one instance, articlemen with estates in County Roscommon believed they were protected from forfeiture commissioners appearing in the county in August 1696, only to belatedly discover that the inquiry had received separate instructions from the courts of exchequer and chancery. Exemptions for twenty articlemen, including Colonel John Browne, Lord Bophin and Robert Dillon of Clonbrock and which 'cost a great deal of money', had been sanctioned by the Irish government following petitions from Browne and Arthur French. But these exemptions only applied to the commission issued by the court of exchequer, with Browne and French unaware of the chancery proceedings. Protection from chancery's investigation was quickly obtained, though at considerable extra cost.[121]

---

[117] N.L.I., Annesley Mss, xii, ff 6, 10–11, 118; xxvii, ff 7, 8, 30, 41, 104; *Report of the commissioners appointed by parliament to inquire into the Irish forfeitures* (London, 1700), pp 9–10. Robert Dillon was adjudicated within the articles of Galway on 2 May 1699 (Simms, 'Irish Jacobites', p. 110).

[118] N.L.I., Annesley Ms xxiii, ff 26, 29, 47, 55–6, 100; *Report of the commissioners appointed by parliament to inquire into the Irish forfeitures*, pp 12–13.

[119] These commissions were periodically appointed by the Irish government as it sought to establish the extent of the land forfeitures arising from the Williamite war. They were not well managed, and failed to produce any substantive reports.

[120] C.S.P.D., 1693, pp 284, 301–6; B.L., Add. Ms 38,153, f. 14.

[121] Luke Dillon to Robert Dillon, 21 Aug. 1696 (N.L.I., *Reports on private collections*, i, no. 4, pp 34–6).

V

The 1697 act that confirmed a mutilated version of the articles of Limerick continued a trend that had become apparent as early as November 1691. As outlined by Sir Richard Cox, protecting and preserving the Protestant interest was the foremost objective of the Irish government, which in 1692 showed an unwillingness or inability to secure support for the articles within the Irish parliament. Following the appointment of Henry Capell as lord deputy, both the legislative and executive branches of government were inclined to obstruct the implementation of the articles whenever possible. The English government, however, showed – at least until 1697 – what Simms termed a 'commendable' intent to have the articles implemented.[122] Together with the Irish government's practical realisation that to deny the articlemen restoration to their estates would have dangerously destabilised the kingdom, this was sufficient to have the most important of the guarantees within the articles honoured. The articlemen received even-handed and arguably generous hearings at the courts of claims, which allowed for the retention of at least half of the land held by Catholics in 1689. William's repeated instructions that the articles be interpreted 'with justice but not favour' were in this respect followed. However, the failure of the Irish government to draft a bill for confirming the articles of Limerick between September 1692 and April 1697, despite repeated instructions from London, illustrates the limits of William's power in governing Ireland. The burgeoning role of the Irish parliament in initiating Irish legislation throughout the 1690s ensured that the English privy council's instructions to the Irish government were not as effective as previously. The delay also highlights the contentious nature of the articles and the hostility to them among the Protestant polity. The articlemen were occasionally able to rely on the honour of the signatories to the articles. As lord chancellor, Porter proved to be an important ally. His position allowed him to put a stop to all private actions taken against articlemen and protectees in the court of chancery; his reward was impeachment proceedings in the Irish parliament. Yet as a lord justice in 1691, even he had denied the articlemen their chattels real. He was thus party to the first abrogation of the articles of Limerick, neatly illustrating the inconsistent attitude adopted by the Irish government to the articles throughout the 1690s.

[122] Simms, *Williamite confiscation*, p. 46.

5

'The same was refused to the Galway men': Implementing the articles of Galway, 1691–1704[1]

Coming so soon after the defeat at Aughrim, the surrender of Galway in July 1691 was a crushing blow to the Jacobite army. Galway was long recognised as a weak point in Jacobite resistance and several of the town's inhabitants, including the Jacobite judge, Denis Daly, had maintained contact with the Williamite forces from late 1690. Others, such as Sir John Kirwan (a former mayor), Arthur French (mayor in 1691) and Oliver Martin were instrumental in convincing Ginkel to approach the town in July 1691 without waiting for his artillery. Their motivation was the retention of their estates in return for the surrender of the town without a siege.[2] The articles of Galway were significantly more comprehensive than previous terms of surrender, indicating the importance of Galway to the Jacobite war effort, the pressure on Ginkel to conclude the war that year and the presence of skilled lawyers on the Irish side. The agreed terms related only to the residents and officials of Galway and the soldiers garrisoned there. Throughout the 1690s the Galway articlemen doggedly pursued the rights promised them by the articles. On several occasions their efforts led to the creation of an informal lobby group or committee, which met with qualified success. Concurrently, individual claimants petitioned for their rights under the articles. Their efforts were concentrated on the four principal articles: 8, 9, 12 and 13.

The articlemen of Galway, no less than those of Limerick, lobbied throughout the decade to ensure that the terms signed in July 1691 were honoured. Two separate bills were drafted by the Irish government in 1692 in an attempt to implement in part the articles of Galway. Of these, the indemnity bill has already been discussed in chapter 4. Section I of this chapter discusses the second bill, which related to the right of lawyers claiming the articles of Galway

---

1 The quotation is taken from James Vernon to Sir Joseph Williamson, 15 Oct. 1697 (T.N.A., SP 32/8, f. 100r).

2 Simms, *Jacobite Ireland*, pp 230–6; idem, *Williamite confiscation*, pp 66–72; John Childs, *The Williamite wars in Ireland, 1689–1691* (London, 2007), pp 340–3; Eoin Kinsella, '"Dividing the bear's skin before she is taken": Irish Catholics and land in the late Stuart monarchy, 1683–91' in Coleman A. Dennehy (ed.), *Restoration Ireland: always settling and never settled* (Aldershot, 2008), pp 176–7.

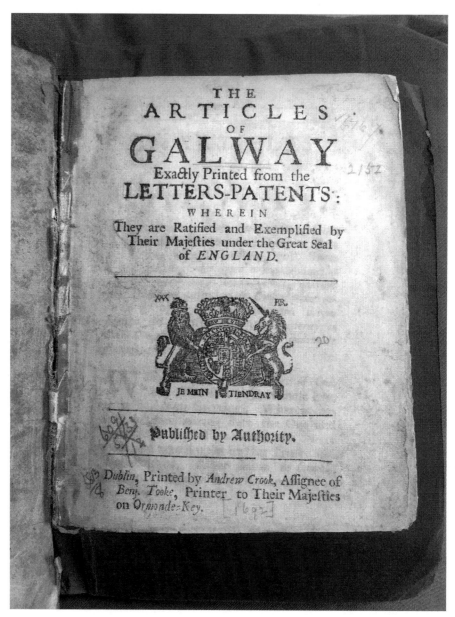

Plate 5: Title page of *The articles of Galway exactly printed from the letters-patents: wherein they are ratified and exemplified by their Majesties under the great seal of England* (Dublin, 1692). Reproduced by permission of the National Library of Ireland.

to continue practising after the war, alongside the reaction of the Galway articlemen to article 13 of Limerick. Several other issues arose in the 1690s that required the close attention of the Irish and English governments. Three men played prominent roles as lobbyists and advocates for the articles of Galway: Arthur French, Denis Daly and John Bourke, Baron Bophin and future earl of Clanricarde. French and Daly were instrumental in the negotiation of the articles, while article 13 of Galway was designed with Lord Bophin in mind. Bophin's case, which set a precedent for other Galway articlemen and later inspired the introduction of the discoverer clause in the 1709 Popery Act, is examined in section II.

I

Negotiations for the surrender of Galway were swiftly concluded, allowing Nottingham to enclose a copy in a letter to Sydney on 28 July 1691, with the observation: 'Perhaps your lordship will think they are very large concessions and they are censured here [in London] as such, especially by the gentlemen of Ireland.'[3] The terms agreed certainly went beyond those contemplated by the Irish government, as the proclamation of 7 July 1691 promised liberty of conscience, a free pardon and retention of estates, but made no mention of lawyers or the right of Catholics to bear arms.[4]

Viscount Henry Dillon, governor of Galway, signed the articles on behalf of the garrison on 21 July, but scrupled as to some of the clauses to the last minute. His chief concern was to ensure that those who wished would have safe conduct to Limerick. He also professed distaste for article 2, which required the Jacobites to hand over all Williamite deserters in the town. Referring to it as a 'thing so inconsistent with our honour', Dillon requested that it be removed. In this he failed, as the articles had already been signed by Ginkel and sent into Galway for signature, not renegotiation.[5] Two days later came an early indication that the articlemen intended to extract every concession possible from the surrender. Dillon again wrote to Ginkel, informing him that goods belonging to several merchants in the town had been confiscated by the Jacobite authorities for use in reinforcing the town's defences. The Williamite army officers then monitoring the handover of Galway refused to return the goods until Ginkel's orders were known. Dillon requested a letter from Ginkel informing the officers that it was 'no breach of capitulation' to return the goods.[6]

3   Nottingham to Sydney, 28 July 1691 (H.M.C., *Finch Mss*, iii, 180).
4   See Appendix C for the text of the proclamation; Simms, *Jacobite Ireland*, p. 234.
5   Viscount Dillon to Ginkel, 21 July 1691 (Utrecht Archive, Huis Amerongen, no. 3219).
6   Viscount Dillon to Ginkel, 23 July 1691 (Utrecht Archive, Huis Amerongen, no. 3219).

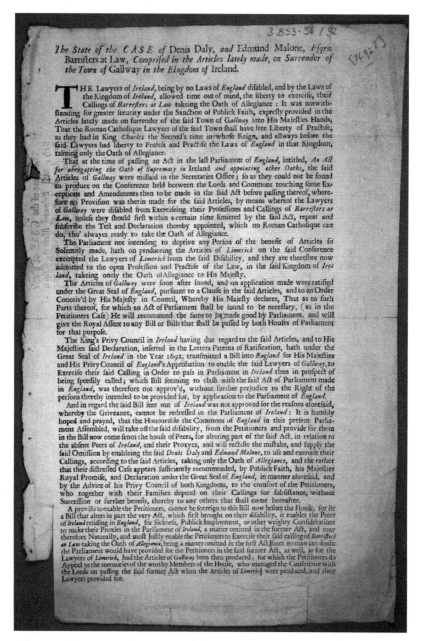

Plate 6: *The state of the case of Denis Daly, and Edmund Malone, Esqrs;
barristers at law, comprised in the articles lately made, on surrender of the town
of Gallway in the kingdom of Ireland* [London, 1696]. This case was printed in
London by Denis Daly and Edmund Malone, for distribution to the members
of the English parliament in 1696, as they sought the full implementation of
the articles of Galway. By permission of the Royal Irish Academy © RIA.

Article 8 secured a general pardon for the governor and the various office holders of Galway corporation, the freemen, natives and the inhabitants of the town.[7] Article 9 protected from forfeiture the estates of the persons just mentioned, as well as the officers of the Irish army then in Galway town. Article 12 promised the Catholic lawyers present the freedom to practise their profession as they had done in the reign of Charles II. Article 13 was designed to provide the protection of article 9 to any officer of a regiment garrisoned in the town at the time of negotiation, even if he had not been within the town walls.[8] Article 9 gave protection of personal and real estates vastly superior to article 3 of the previously negotiated surrenders at Waterford and Drogheda, while article 12 secured the protection for lawyers that had eluded the negotiators at Waterford.

Articles 8 and 9 were implemented through the courts of claims of 1692 and 1697–9. At the latter court, 74 men were admitted to the benefit of the articles.[9] In 1692, only three men claimed the benefit of the articles of Galway, with one rejected.[10] A dispute arose in 1692 regarding the interpretation of articles 8 and 9 of Galway (discussed below), ensuring that no Galway articlemen were heard when the court of claims sat in 1694.[11]

The earliest instance of lobbying so far discovered in relation to the articles of Galway was undertaken as the war was still under way, when Arthur French called upon Ginkel at his camp at Limerick, to inquire as to the status of several prisoners of war for whom article 13 had been drafted.[12] On 10 November, Francis Galway wrote to Ginkel, requesting that the general use his influence with the lords justices to expedite the restoration of Galway's personal estate – effectively seeking the implementation of articles 8 and 9.[13] The articlemen

---

[7] Crucially, those who held office under the new charter issued by James II in 1688 were specifically covered by article 8. For the *quo warranto* proceedings and reissuing of borough charters in Ireland under James II, see Simms, *Jacobite Ireland*, pp 34–5; James McGuire, 'A lawyer in politics: the career of Sir Richard Nagle, c.1636–1699' in Howard Clarke & Judith Devlin (eds) *European encounters: essays in memory of Albert Lovett* (Dublin, 2003), pp 124–5; Hayton, *Ruling Ireland*, pp 14–15.

[8] See Appendix A for the articles in full.

[9] See Table 1 above, p. 79.

[10] The successful claimants were Denis Daly and Patrick French (T.C.D., Ms 744, ff 108–9); Simms, 'Irish Jacobites', pp 94–5. The rejected claim was from Henry Crofton, who later successfully claimed the benefit of the articles of Sligo.

[11] This is a revision of Simms, who noted that two claims to the articles of Galway were heard in 1694, with one rejected (*Williamite confiscation*, p. 47). This is apparently a misreading of the manuscript lists of hearings scheduled for 1694, the only year for which such lists are extant. Thady Concannon's claim, scheduled for 15 June, was not heard and was annotated 'claims the articles of Galway'. Similarly, John Crelly's claim, scheduled for 12 and 16 November, was annotated 'to be heard among the claimants of the Galway articles' (see Appendix B).

[12] Deposition of Arthur French, [1701] (Bodl., Carte Ms 113, ff 368, 370–1).

[13] Francis Galway to Ginkel, 10 Nov. 1691 (Utrecht Archive, Huis Amerongen, no. 3220).

of Galway also appeared before the Irish lords justices on 30 November 1691, with the articlemen of Limerick, seeking restoration to remainders on estates of outlawed persons who had died during the war. In keeping with the rest of the lords justices' judgment, the appeal was denied.[14]

The strength of article 12 was immediately put to the test by the passage of the 1691 Oaths Act by the English parliament.[15] The act does not refer to the articles of Galway, nor do they appear to ever have featured in the debates on the bill in parliament. According to a later petition, the reason for this omission was the simple mislaying of the copy of the articles then held in the office of the secretary of state.[16] Richard Levinge's contribution to the debates on the act suggests that, even if a copy of the articles were available, the Galway articlemen may have been excluded. Commenting on the proviso for the articlemen of Limerick that allowed them to practise the law, Levinge noted that 'the words of the article qualify all those then treated with, not persons before the treaty'.[17] The introduction of this bill to parliament, in addition to the Galway articlemen's opposition to article 13 of Limerick and desire to see the articles ratified under the great seal, prompted the despatch of Denis Daly to London as the Galway articlemen's agent in December 1691.[18]

Daly had played a pivotal role in the surrender of Galway and was an ideal representative for the articlemen. Sir Charles Porter described him as 'always inclinable to the English interest, and to dispose the Irish to submit to their majesties' obedience'.[19] A memorandum submitted to the Irish government in late 1691 recommended a pension of £250 for Daly on the Irish establishment,

---

[14] Though this judgment does not feature in his discussion, see Simms, *Williamite confiscation*, pp 43–4, for the controversial question of the attainder of those who died in rebellion.

[15] An act for abrogating the oath of supremacy in Ireland and appointing new oaths (3 William & Mary, c. 2 [Eng.]).

[16] *The state of the case of Denis Daly, and Edmund Malone, Esqrs; and of a few other lawyers, of the town of Gallway, in the Kingdom of Ireland* (Dublin, 1696); *C.S.P.D., 1695 & Addenda*, p. 190; Colum Kenny, 'The exclusion of Catholics from the legal profession in Ireland' in *I.H.S.*, xxv (1986–7), p. 351.

[17] Anchitell Grey, *Grey's debates in the house of commons* (10 vols, London, 1769), x, 201 (5 Dec. 1691). Grey attributes the comment to the solicitor general for Ireland, whom he names as Sir William Leman – almost certainly an error for Sir Richard Levinge.

[18] Denis Daly (c.1638–1721) of Carrownakelly, Co. Galway, was a justice of the common pleas during James II's reign. He was a controversial figure in the Jacobite parliament of 1689, where as a leader of the Catholic 'new interest' he was a vocal opponent of the act of repeal. During the war, he corresponded with the Williamite forces and was arrested by Sarsfield in January 1691. However, he was released soon after on Tyrconnell's orders and played a prominent role in the surrender of Galway, leading Ginkel to write to the lords justices that 'Judge Daly has done good service' (H.M.C., *Fourth report*, appendix, p. 322; Kinsella, 'Dividing the bear's skin', p. 177).

[19] Porter to [Nottingham], 6 Dec. 1691 (*C.S.P.D., 1691–2*, p. 25). The calendar of state papers infers that Porter's letter was addressed to Viscount Sydney, but later correspondence suggests that Nottingham was the intended recipient.

describing him as 'a prudent and moderate man of more good effects and good interest among the natives than any of them, for they do all depend upon his advice, both in matters of law and policy'.[20] This recommendation was repeated in 1693.[21]

Daly almost certainly arrived in London too late to put the case of the Galway articlemen to the English parliament. His letter of introduction to the English government from Porter is dated 6 December. Even if he had embarked for England on that day, he could have done nothing to alter the oaths act before it was approved by parliament on 10 December.[22] The articles of Galway were thus abrogated by the English parliament. In response the Galway articlemen lobbied for an Irish act of parliament to remedy the situation. A petition presented to the lords justices and privy council of Ireland by the claimants stated that it was to the 'utter ruin of themselves and their families' that they were excluded from the benefit of the articles.[23] Transmitted to Nottingham with a positive recommendation from the Irish government in mid 1692, Daly once more managed the articlemen's affairs in London.[24]

Nottingham proposed that the issue be addressed in the bill of indemnity.[25] Within a matter of weeks, however, the Galway articlemen's attempts to have article 12 implemented had become entangled with the implementation of article 13 of Limerick. One of the most controversial aspects of the Williamite settlement of Ireland, article 13 imposed a special levy on all Catholic landowners for the payment of debts owed to Colonel John Browne by the Jacobite administration. Browne was in turn to use this levy to pay substantial debts he owed to his Protestant creditors.[26] In August 1692 a bill for 'enabling persons comprehended in the articles of Galway to use certain professions and callings and for the better securing the Protestant creditors of Colonel John Browne', was transmitted from Dublin to London (hereafter referred to as the

---

20 'Bishop M's paper', [1691] (T.N.A., SP 63/353, f. 210; C.S.P.D., 1691–2, pp 55–6). 'Bishop M' was probably William Moreton, bishop of Kildare, rather than Narcissus Marsh, archbishop of Cashel. The memorandum was likely submitted after Moreton's appointment to the Irish privy council in December 1691.

21 'Colonel Fitzpatrick's paper', 22 Apr. 1693 (T.N.A., SP 63/355, f. 82; C.S.P.D., 1693, p. 106).

22 The earl of Clanricarde entered into a bond with Daly for £40 in December 1691 'towards the ratification of Galway Articles' (N.L.I., Ms 47,873/1).

23 'The humble petition of the lawyers and physicians of Galway', [July] 1692 (T.N.A., SP 63/354, ff 98–9; C.S.P.D., 1695 & Addenda, p. 190).

24 Irish lords justices and privy council to Nottingham, 18 July 1692 (T.N.A., SP 63/354, f. 97; C.S.P.D., 1695 & Addenda, p. 190).

25 Nottingham to the Irish lords justices, 30 July 1692 (C.S.P.D., 1691–2, p. 391).

26 See Part III below for a full discussion of article 13. Technically the beneficiaries of all the articles negotiated before 3 October were under Williamite rather than Jacobite authority. It is thus arguable that the Jacobite negotiators at Limerick, who assumed the power to negotiate for the Jacobite interest at large in article 13, were acting *ultra vires*.

dual-purpose bill).[27] It has previously been assumed that the intention of the lords justices to reinstate the Galway lawyers, coupled with the drafting and transmission of this bill, meant that the Galway lawyers were immediately relieved.[28] The dual-purpose bill was not, however, returned to the Irish privy council because its section dealing with the Galway lawyers was 'a contradiction to the act made here, and would overrule it, which would have been of ill consequence and therefore this must be endeavoured to be remedied here for it is very just to be done'.[29]

The Irish and English governments clearly recognised that the articles of Galway had been abrogated and were content to restore the Galway articlemen to their practices if possible. Yet though the section of the rejected dual-purpose bill dealing with Colonel John Browne's debt (article 13 of Limerick) was swiftly sent to London in a new bill, the Irish government's hands were now tied with respect to article 12 of Galway. Any legislation they proposed to rectify the issue would fall foul of the English government's determination to ensure that no act passed by the Irish parliament could overturn English legislation. Only an act of the English parliament could restore the Galway lawyers to their profession. The Irish government refused to re-engage with the issue before the Irish parliament was prorogued in November 1692, leaving the Galway lawyers in limbo. It was a further three years before another opportunity arose to press their case.

By 1695 the fate of the Galway lawyers remained entwined with article 13 of Limerick. There is no doubt that the Galway articlemen (and indeed all other articlemen and protectees) were deeply unhappy with article 13, which was agreed without their input or consent. Several Galway articlemen opposed a bill sent to England in October 1695 to authorise collection of the money owed by Catholic landowners to Browne's Protestant creditors. In a counter-petition presented to Capell, the Protestant creditors reminded the Lord Deputy of the 'many debates and hearings' held before the Irish lords justices in the summer of 1692, at which Catholic agents finally conceded that article 13 applied not just to the articlemen of Limerick, but to all articlemen.[30] The agreement reached at the privy council at that time provided for a special levy of one year's quit-rent from each Catholic-owned estate, for distribution to Browne's Protestant creditors.

[27] T.N.A., SP 66/B/13, f. 9; C.S.P.D., 1695 & Addenda, p. 195.

[28] Kenny, 'The exclusion of Catholics from the legal profession in Ireland', p. 351, n. 85. Kenny's footnote contains a minor typographical error in referring to pp 190 and 195 in C.S.P.D., 1697, where C.S.P.D., 1695 & Addenda is meant.

[29] Nottingham to Sydney, 13 Sept. 1692 (C.S.P.D., 1691–2, p. 447). Nottingham was referring to the 1691 oaths act.

[30] 'Petition of the Protestant creditors of Colonel John Browne', [Oct. 1695] (T.N.A., SP 63/357, ff 151–2).

A bill to give effect to this agreement on article 13 was sent to England for approval in October 1695. On 31 October the English privy council received two petitions against the bill. There were two distinct groups of Catholic lobbyists; one representing the 'articled men of Ireland' and a separate group solely representing Galway articlemen.[31] On 7 November the petitions were referred to the attorney and solicitor general. The focal point of the objections put forward by the two groups of petitioners was a certificate, signed by Ginkel on 10 February 1692, which stated:

> Whereas in the Articles of Limerick there is a provision made for a sum of money to be secured to Colonel John Browne and his creditors as by the said articles bearing date the third day of October last may appear, I do declare that the said sum was to be secured on the estates of those managers of the Irish that were party to the said articles of Limerick only and not on any other person whatsoever.[32]

Sir Charles Porter, a former lord justice and Williamite signatory to the articles of Limerick, cast doubt upon the accuracy of Ginkel's recollection:

> There is some obstruction as I understand it on the behalf of Galway against Colonel John Browne's creditors' bill and this upon the mistake of a certificate made by General Ginkel. This is a popular bill for the Protestant creditors of Mr Browne, and I do assure your lordship this unhappy mistake of my Lord Athlone [Ginkel] if it should hinder the passing of Mr Browne's bill may prevent the passing of his lordship's bill. And you cannot do anything more grateful than to assist the passing of this bill.[33]

The petition presented to Capell by the Protestant creditors alleged that Ginkel's certificate was either forged or 'had by surprise'.[34] Ginkel himself had no memory of the certificate, which had been given to Denis Daly.[35] A lengthy report was sent to London from the Irish privy council, leading to the rejection of the articlemen's petitions:

> Upon hearing their Majesties' counsel, the counsel for the creditors of Colonel John Browne, and counsel for the claimants of the Galway articles, on 17 June 1692, in relation to the said Colonel John Browne's clause, it was settled by consent of most of the persons claiming under the articles of Galway that they should give the same

---

31 H.M.C., *Downshire Mss*, i, 574; T.N.A., PC 2/76, ff 208–9.

32 T.N.A., SP 63/357, f. 152.

33 Porter to Coningsby, 13 Nov. 1695 (P.R.O.N.I., De Ros Mss, D/638/18/58). 'His lordship's bill' was a bill to secure grants of lands to Ginkel in Ireland, which was before the English privy council in November 1695. It received the royal assent in Ireland on 7 December 1695 (7 Will. III, c. 3 (private)).

34 'Petition of the Protestant creditors of Colonel John Browne', (T.N.A., SP 63/357, ff. 151–2).

35 Bartholomew van Homrigh to Ginkel, 6 Jan. 1696 (Wouter Troost, 'Letters from Bartholomew van Homrigh to General Ginkel, earl of Athlone, 1692 to 1700' in *Analecta Hibernica*, 33 (1986), p. 109).

security as the claimants of Limerick did ... for satisfaction of Colonel John Browne's debt, and in pursuance thereof, as appears by several affidavits, the most considerable persons claiming under the articles of Galway signed an instrument to that purpose.[36]

Appended to the report were two supporting affidavits, from Arthur French and Martin Blake, both Galway articlemen.[37] These affidavits imply division among the Galway articlemen as to whether to oppose the passage of this bill. The key phrase in the above report is that which refers to *most* of the Galway articlemen agreeing to the payment. There were certainly some who opposed the bill. However, the support offered by a separate group to the Protestant creditors' petition and the Irish privy council's report is compelling evidence for a split. French's and Blake's affidavits are almost identical in wording and were delivered on the same day, suggesting co-ordination. The evidence they presented stated that about three years previously (i.e. sometime in 1692) several men of 'good estates' signed and sent an instruction to Denis Daly, then acting as agent for the Galway articlemen in London. Daly was informed that the articlemen consented to payment of their proportion of Browne's debt and he was ordered not to contest article 13 of Limerick.[38]

The dual purpose bill of 1692, which was intended to restore the Galway lawyers to their practises, has some relevance to this carefully choreographed display of Catholic support for article 13, and co-operation with the Irish government. It can hardly have been a coincidence that the dual-purpose bill combined relief for the Galway lawyers with a guarantee for Browne's Protestant creditors. It is likely that the Irish government combined the two in order to prevent the Galway articlemen lobbying in London against article 13, for fear of jeopardising their own provision. Though the 1692 bill ultimately failed, the 1695 initiative overcame the objections of the articlemen, was returned to the Irish parliament and received the royal assent on 7 December.[39]

The reference made by French and Martin to instructions issued by men of 'good estates' to Daly in London in 1692 indicates that the Galway articlemen had formed an ad hoc committee to manage their opposition to article 13 of Limerick. The signatories to the instruction included the earl of Clanricarde; Viscount Dillon; Sir Walter Blake; Colonel Dominick Browne; Lord Athenry; Robert French; Patrick French and Richard Martin. Athenry's appearance

---

[36] Capell and the Irish privy council to Shrewsbury, 15 Nov. 1695 (T.N.A., SP 63/357, ff 149–50; C.S.P.D., 1695 & Addenda, pp 101–2).

[37] For their adjudications, see T.C.D., Ms 744, ff 122, 129.

[38] Depositions of Arthur French and Martin Blake, 14 Nov. 1695 (T.N.A., SP 63/357, f. 154; C.S.P.D., 1695 & Addenda, p. 102).

[39] 'An act for securing the debts owing to the Protestant creditors of Colonel John Browne' (7 Will. III, c. 2 (private)). See chapter 6 for discussion of this act.

as signatory to the instruction indicates that the minor articlemen were also involved in these negotiations with the Irish government.[40]

The 1695 Browne bill did not have a clause providing relief for the lawyers of Galway, which could have cleared the way for all of the Galway articlemen to renege on their promise and actively oppose the bill. The affidavits of French and Blake make it clear that this course was not pursued by all articlemen. Indeed, the Irish house of commons extended a protection to French and Colonel Garrett Moore to 'attend the passing of Colonel Browne's Bill'.[41] Once again, the position of the Galway lawyers appears to have forced the hands of the articlemen. On 24 November 1695 Denis Daly and Edmund Malone petitioned the English privy council, requesting freedom for the Galway articlemen to practice the law.[42] The Galway claimants perhaps feared that antagonising the authorities would undermine these petitions. French and Blake's affidavits can be seen as an attempt to curry favour with the Irish and English administrations, while it is conceivable that the timing of the petitions of Daly and Malone was planned to coincide with the arrival of the affidavits.

Daly's and Malone's decision to appeal to the English privy council and parliament reflected the reality that, with the Whig and staunchly anti-Catholic Capell as lord deputy, there was little hope of the Irish government supporting an initiative to confirm an article of surrender (with the notable exception of article 13 of Limerick). These petitions were the forerunners of legislation considered by the English parliament in 1696 for relief of the Galway lawyers. In January of that year Daly, Malone and several (unnamed) others presented a petition to the English parliament, setting forth much the same claim as the previous petition of 1692 and Daly and Malone's petitions of November 1695.[43] Malone's petition demonstrates the resourceful and, strictly speaking, extra-legal processes some claimants embarked upon in order to attain the benefit of the articles. Malone, who acted as agent for the articlemen of Limerick, had left Ireland in 1690 in order to avoid any association with the Jacobite forces, moving with his family to Wales, where he lived until at least March 1692. He successfully petitioned for a free pardon and the reversal of his outlawry, which had been prosecuted in his absence.[44] The pardon alone would not, however, have been sufficient to allow him to continue to practise the law.

---

[40] Athenry was a beneficiary of the articles of Boffin. He was also Col. John Browne's son-in-law and his initial opposition to article 13 illustrates how deeply Catholic landowners resented the article.

[41] C.J.I., ii, 131 (5 Dec. 1695).

[42] T.N.A., PC 2/76, f. 213.

[43] C.J., xi, pp 392–3 (16 Jan. 1696); *The state of the case of Denis Daly and Edmund Malone, Esqrs.*

[44] C.S.P.D., 1691–2, pp 10–11, 162, 177; H.M.C., *House of Lords Mss*, new series, iv (1699–1703), p. 28.

The commons submitted the Galway lawyers' case to a committee already considering legislation designed to modify the 1691 Oaths Act. A counter-petition was subsequently presented by Robert Johnson, 'on behalf of himself and the Protestants of Ireland', in an effort to undermine the Galway articlemen's efforts. Johnson alleged that the true intent of the Daly–Malone petition was 'to introduce great numbers of Irish papists into the free practise of the law in Ireland, and to repeal a statute made to prevent the dangers that might arise from such encouragement'. On 10 February, the committee reported that prior to Johnson's petition they had agreed a clause to provide relief to the articlemen. Johnson's representation caused them to reconsider and they requested more time to review the evidence. The entire bill, including the articlemen's saving clause, was subsequently dropped.[45] There does not appear to have been any further effort to reverse the provisions of the 1691 Oaths Act as they related to the Galway articlemen. Lawyers from Connacht who had been prominent in chancery prior to 1689 did not appear at the court after 1691.[46]

A more successful petition was presented to the Irish government by the Galway articlemen in June 1693. Article 9 of Galway stipulated that all estates preserved or restored by virtue of the articles should be exempt from all crown- and quit-rents payable for the duration of the war.[47] The petition complained that the commissioners of the revenue had presented the claimants (69 of whom are named by the petition) with a demand for four and half years' quit-rent. Stating that such payment would 'render your petitioners' estates waste', it asked that the demand be reduced to just one year's quit-rent.[48] The petition was referred to a committee of the privy council who found in favour of the petitioners.[49] The articlemen's offer to pay one year's rent arose from the fact that the revenue commissioners' demand covered 1689–1693, the latter two years of which the articles did not include. The articlemen successfully argued that they had been denied the profits of their estates for another year due to the depredations of the English army. Nonetheless, in March 1695 the Galway articlemen were obliged to raise the issue again when the commissioners of the revenue once more sought quit-rent arrears dating back to the war. Their petition to the English privy council was referred to the lords of the treasury and in turn to the Irish lords justices, but the outcome is uncertain.[50]

---

45 C.J., xi, pp 417, 437 (28 Jan., 10 Feb. 1696); H.M.C., *House of Lords Mss*, new series, ii, 123. It is possible that this was the same Robert Johnson later appointed as a baron of the court of exchequer (see below, p. 204).

46 Maynard, 'Irish membership of the English inns of court', pp 293–4.

47 See Appendix A.

48 N.A.I., Wyche papers, 2/119, ff 1–2.

49 N.A.I., Wyche papers, 2/119, ff 2–3. The committee members were Sir Charles Porter, Richard Coote, Sir John Hely and John Jeffreyson.

50 T.N.A., PC 2/76, f. 96; C.T.B., x, 1693–6, pp 983–1000.

II

John Bourke, the second son of William, earl of Clanricarde, was called to sit in the Irish parliament of 1689 as Baron Bourke of Bophin.[51] He was colonel of a regiment of foot during the war and taken prisoner at the Battle of Aughrim in July 1691.[52] This capture was to prove a considerable inconvenience to Bophin for the following decade. It meant that during the time of the negotiations for the surrender of Galway, he was imprisoned in Dublin Castle.[53] However article 13 of Galway, which extended the protection of the articles to all officers whose regiment was in Galway at the time of the negotiations, covered Lord Bophin. According to witnesses and letters from Ginkel himself, the general explicitly guaranteed Bophin's eligibility to the articles. Article 13 of Galway stipulated that all regimental officers were to submit to the governor of the town within three weeks, a proviso that appears to have been predicated on Ginkel's belief that Bophin would quickly be released following the signing of the articles. Despite the apparent foresight on the part of the Jacobite team of negotiators, Bophin's continued imprisonment prevented him making his submission to the governor of Galway within the specified time limit.[54]

Bophin's subsequent efforts to receive the benefits of the articles of Galway became intimately entwined with a wider campaign by the Galway articlemen. A dispute arose in 1692 regarding the interpretation of articles 8 & 9 of Galway. Many of the claimants to the Galway articles were not actually within the town at the time of the negotiations.[55] The wording of the articles did not require them to have been present if they were members of Galway corporation, yet the clamour raised by Protestants against such judgments caused the suspension of hearings in 1692.[56] There was certainly some merit to these complaints. Arthur French, mayor of Galway prior to its surrender, admitted using his position to improperly insert the names of two men in the list of freemen of Galway in order to have them qualify under the articles.[57]

---

[51] H.M.C., *Stuart Mss*, i, 39; G.E. Cokayne, *The complete peerage*, ed. Vicary Gibbs (14 vols, London, 1913), iii, 234. This is one of the few instances of the creation of a peerage by virtue of a summons to parliament.

[52] F.G. James contends that Bophin went into exile with James II after the war, returning later in the decade (*Lords of the ascendancy: the Irish house of lords and its members, 1600–1800* (Dublin, 1995), p. 53). The account given here suggests that this was not the case.

[53] C.S.P.D., 1693, p. 231.

[54] C.T.B., 1698–9, pp 336–7; *The case of John Burke…humbly offered to the consideration of the Honourable the House of Commons* (London, 1701).

[55] N.L.I., Annesley Mss, xxiii, ff 100–115.

[56] The suspension of hearings in 1692 helps to explain why only two claims to the articles of Galway were admitted by the court of claims that year.

[57] Deposition of Arthur French, 15 Sept. 1699 (N.L.I., Annesley Mss, xxiii, ff 102–3, 112).

It was not until April 1697 that the controversy was addressed by the king. Following consultation with the English privy council, an order was made to the effect that the articles were to apply only to those who were in the town of Galway at the time of the negotiations.[58] William's decision marked a distinct shift from his earlier policy of encouraging a construction of the articles within the boundaries of the law. There was no stipulation within articles 8 or 9 that the parties protected by those articles were required to be within the town during the negotiations. The declaration also nullified article 13, specifically negotiated to include military officers of the garrison who were not present within the town.

Alarmed by the decision, the Galway articlemen raised a fund to send agents seeking a reversal of the decision.[59] Denis Daly lobbied in London, while Arthur French was sent to the continent to solicit the king to rescind his declaration. French was present in London from July to September 1697, petitioning for a grant of lands to his son-in-law, James Farrell. In September, French received permission to travel to Holland, presumably in order to seek an audience with William.[60] While on the continent, French also sought the assistance of Ginkel, who seemed well disposed to such requests.[61] London was awash with Irish agents at this time, actively lobbying against the passage of several Irish bills then under consideration, including one to confirm a mutilated version of the articles of Limerick, one for the banishment of Catholic bishops and regular clergy and another to prevent Protestants intermarrying with Catholics.[62] The Williamite authorities intercepted the correspondence of Daly and French, revealing the dual purpose of their presence in London. Remarkably, this does not seem to have adversely affected the personal petitions both men were pressing at Whitehall or to have led to restrictions on their movement. In French's case it merely led the lords justices of England to observe that his efforts to undermine the decisions of the government to which he was appealing 'did not much recommend one who had private business of his own depending'.[63]

Their efforts were unsuccessful. William does not appear to have formally rescinded his declaration, which helps to explain the relatively low number

[58] T.N.A., PC 2/76, f. 623 (23 Apr. 1697 – this entry seems to have been added at a later date, in a different hand); N.L.I., Annesley Mss, xxvii, f. 159; John Methuen to John Somers, lord keeper of the great seal of England, 26 June 1697 (S.H.C., Somers-Cocks papers, 371/14/F/2); C.S.P.D., 1697, pp 144, 197.

[59] Earl of Galway to Shrewsbury, 29 June 1697 (H.M.C., Buccleuch, ii, 485).

[60] C.S.P.D., 1697, pp. 265, 270, 357.

[61] Ginkel was always ready to intercede with William on behalf of claimants to the articles of Galway, particularly those with whom he had met before and during the negotiations (C.S.P.D., 1697, pp 265, 269–71, 341–2, 355, 357, 392); Simms, Williamite confiscation, p. 68.

[62] C.S.P.D., 1697, pp 220–400, passim.

[63] Ibid., pp 392, 460.

of successful claims under the Galway articles in the third court of claims. Yet individual petitions to William seeking pardons, by men who would ordinarily have claimed the benefit of the articles of Galway, were granted in 1698 and afterwards. Protestant support was paramount.[64] Lord Bophin was a prominent example.

Following his capture at the battle of Aughrim in July 1691, Bophin remained in captivity for approximately six months. In the weeks after the surrender of Galway, Arthur French travelled to Ginkel's camp at Limerick to investigate why Bophin, along with the others for whom article 13 had been negotiated, had not yet been released. Article 13 specified that each officer was to submit to the governor of Galway by the middle of August 1691. The matter had been taken out of Ginkel's hands, as he had received orders to transport the prisoners to London. He did, however, promise to pursue their release as vigorously as possible.[65] French travelled to England early in 1692 and met with Bophin twice. At their first meeting in Chester, Bophin was still in custody. By the time of their second meeting, in London, Ginkel had secured Bophin's freedom.[66] Following his release Bophin took the oath of allegiance and returned to his estate where he joined his wife and nine children.[67]

The re-opening of the court of claims in October 1697 forced Bophin to pursue his claim for the legal title to his estate. The provisions of the act establishing the court confirmed the pardons and titles of those whose claims, under the respective articles agreed in 1691, had been passed by 2 September 1699.[68] Bophin had never previously pursued his adjudication under the articles. As a result, he was forced to bring his case before the judges. They in turn declared that, in the light of William's April 1697 declaration limiting the benefit of the articles to those who were actually within the town, Bophin was not eligible to the articles of Galway.[69] There is no record of Bophin's appearance before the court of claims, which provides some grounds for supposing that there were many more claimants to articles than surviving records indicate. Later testimony from Bophin stated that 'it was given out that it was the opinion of the commissioners for hearing claims that the words of the said articles were

64   B.L., Add. Ms 21,136, f. 5; C.S.P.D., 1698, pp 176–7, 345–6, 347–8, 358, 363; C.S.P.D., 1699, pp 103, 197; C.S.P.D., 1700–2, p. 31.

65   Affidavit of Arthur French, [1701] (Bodl., Carte Ms 113, f. 368). It is not well known that, apart from the famous 13 'civil' articles of Limerick, the terms of surrender also included a set of military articles. Article 17 of the military articles stipulated that all prisoners of war were to be released immediately, but this article was not implemented.

66   Deposition of Arthur French, [1701] (Bodl., Carte Ms 113, f. 368); N.L.I., Annesley Mss, xx, f. 2; Nottingham to Sir John Morgan, 4 Feb. 1692 (C.S.P.D., 1691–2, p. 126).

67   Bodl., Carte Ms 113, ff. 373–4; N.L.I., Annesley Mss, xx, f. 2.

68   9 Will. III, c. 2, s. 9.

69   N.L.I., Annesley Mss, xx, f. 2; The case of John Burke.

not sufficient'.[70] The implication is that this was private advice from the judges. Bophin possessed the resources to pursue the matter in Dublin, London and on the continent and to employ a team of agents, which would not have been the case for other claimants who encountered similar difficulties.

Bophin next applied to William for a special pardon. His case was complicated by a previous grant of his lands to Joost van Keppel, earl of Albemarle, a favoured courtier.[71] Accordingly, Bophin entered into negotiations with Albemarle to be restored to his estates. It was at this time that the Catholic network based in Galway again came to the fore.

In January 1698 Bophin met Albemarle in London, where it was agreed that in return for £7,500 Albemarle would use his influence with the king to have him send a letter to the lords justices instructing that Bophin be adjudged within articles. Bophin simultaneously sought a letter from Ginkel to reinforce his claim. Letters from the general and king to this effect were procured.[72] Alan Brodrick, solicitor general for Ireland, argued that this was still insufficient to make Bophin eligible to the articles.[73] John Methuen, lord chancellor of Ireland, informed Bophin that he had little chance of succeeding in his claim with letters alone and advised him to seek a private bill in the Irish parliament.[74] Two obstacles had hindered Bophin's case up to this point. The first was William's 1697 declaration limiting the scope of the articles. The second was his own inability to produce a certificate of submission to the governor of Galway within three weeks of 26 July 1691.[75] Though Bophin succeeded in securing a private bill, transmitted to England by the Irish privy council and returned from London with minor amendments, it was rejected by the house of commons on 17 January 1699.[76]

In spite of this setback, Bophin resorted to the ultimate authority in Irish affairs, seeking and receiving a private act for reversing his outlawry in the English parliament in 1702.[77] His estate was placed in the hands of trustees for the benefit of his children, who were to be raised as Protestants, a stipulation he had already agreed to during his negotiations with Albemarle.[78] Bophin's estate

---

[70] N.L.I., Annesley Mss, xx, f. 2.

[71] Simms, *Williamite confiscation*, p. 70.

[72] London Metropolitan Archives, MJ/SP/XX/515, f. 6v; N.L.I., Annesley Mss, xx, f. 2; Annesley Mss, xxvii, ff 161–3; Bodl., Carte Ms 113, ff 373–4; C.S.P.D., 1698, pp 176–7. I am grateful to John Bergin for providing me with the reference in the London Metropolitan Archives.

[73] N.L.I., Annesley Mss, xxiii, f. 139; Simms, *Williamite confiscation*, p. 70.

[74] N.L.I., Annesley Mss, xxiii, f. 145.

[75] Bodl., Carte Ms 113, ff 382–3, 394. Galway was invested by the Williamite forces on 26 July.

[76] B.L., Add. Ms 9715, f. 28; T.N.A., PC 2/77, ff 279, 282; C.J.I., ii, 298 (17 Jan. 1699).

[77] An act for the making provision for the Protestant children of the Earl of Clanricarde and the Lord Bophin (1 Anne, c. 39 [Eng] (private)).

[78] B.L., Add. Ms. 4761, f. 64; Simms, *Williamite confiscation*, p. 71.

was also charged with a 'fine' of £25,000, payable to the exchequer by 25 March 1703, a mere nine months after the act received the royal assent. According to the records of the forfeiture inquiry commissioners, Bophin's estate consisted of more than 45,000 acres across Counties Galway, Mayo and Roscommon, with a yearly value of almost £8,500.[79]

The act of 1702 restoring Bophin to his estate subsequently became known as the 'Bophin Act'.[80] This private act and two subsequent explanatory acts were more important than is generally recognised. The first of the explanatory acts was passed in 1703 and was a broad measure covering certain administrative issues that arose from the proceedings of the forfeiture trustees. Throughout 1701 the English parliament had passed several private acts (and one public) providing relief for Irish Catholics and Protestants from the act of resumption.[81] The majority of these acts included a clause restricting Catholics from inheriting, purchasing or leasing any of the lands saved. However, some of the acts neglected to include this proviso, leading the English parliament to use the first Bophin explanatory act to clarify that the disposal of all such lands was restricted in this manner. Any purchase or lease held on these lands in trust for Catholics was declared void.[82] The provision for Bophin extended the time limit for payment of the £25,000 to 1 June 1704, payable in three instalments.[83] The private acts passed by the English parliament in 1701 and the Bophin explanatory act of 1703 were the first pieces of legislation that restricted Catholic landowners in Ireland from disposing of their land as they pleased, foreshadowing the provisions of the Popery Act of 1704.

It is not well known that the discoverer clause in the Popery Act of 1709 arose from the second explanatory act, also passed in 1709, which allowed further time for Bophin (now earl of Clanricarde) to pay the 'fine' on his estate.[84]

---

[79] T.C.D., Ms 744, ff 93–5. The estate was comprehensively mapped as part of a survey made by the forfeiture trustees of forfeited estates in Ireland (B.L., Add. Ms 13,956). The maps of forfeited Galway estates are one of the few surviving from this survey, the majority of which were destroyed in 1922 (Simms, *Williamite confiscation*, p. 134).

[80] G.E. Howard, *Several special cases on the laws against the further growth of popery in Ireland* (Dublin, 1775), pp 27–30; C.W. Russell and J.P. Prendergast, *The Carte manuscripts in the Bodleian library, Oxford* (London, 1871), pp 100–02.

[81] Transcripts of these private acts are found in N.L.I., Annesley Mss xxii. The public act was An act for the relief of the Protestant purchasers of the forfeited estates in Ireland (1 Anne, c. 26 [Eng]).

[82] An act for advancing the sale of the forfeited estates in Ireland and for vesting such as remain unsold by the present trustees in her majesty, her heirs, and successors, for such uses as the same were before vested in the said trustees and for the more effectual selling and setting the said estates to Protestants and for explaining several acts relating to the Lord Bophin and Sir Redmond Everard (1 Anne, sess. 2, c. 18, ss 6, 9).

[83] *The statutes of the realm*, viii, 206.

[84] An act for the relief of the Earl of Clanricarde (lately called Lord Bophin) of the kingdom of

Whereas the Bophin Act had simply declared any lease made to a Catholic void, the second explanatory act provided that any person who informed the government of any parcel land on the Clanricarde estate leased to a Catholic was to be entitled to his share, thus introducing the discoverer to Ireland.[85]

Bophin's attempts to secure his estate from forfeiture, a process that took more than a decade, were not typical of the average Galway articleman. However, his case was of importance in that his circumstances in July 1691 were influential in both the negotiation and interpretation of the articles. He and Colonel Walter Burke were the inspiration for article 13, while the reopening of the court of claims for the articlemen in 1697 forced Bophin to lobby hard for William's declaration on the articles of Galway of that year to be ignored.

The evidence that survives from Bophin's case also offers insight into the activities of a Catholic elite following defeat in the Williamite war and the importance attached by both sides to the articles of Galway. Denis Daly and Arthur French, both beneficiaries of the articles, were instrumental in securing Bophin's estate. From the time of the surrender negotiations until the passage of the private act, French consistently brought Bophin's case to the attention of the Dublin and London administrations. Daly was no less important to Bophin's cause, representing him in negotiations with Albemarle's agent, Thomas Brodrick. In the course of his agency on behalf of Bophin, Daly adroitly enlisted the assistance of John Methuen, Thomas Coote, a justice of the common pleas, William Conolly and Thomas Brodrick.[86]

The appearance of prominent Protestant politicians as advisors to or supporters of Bophin's efforts serves as a useful reminder of the generally inconsistent attitude of Irish Protestants towards the articlemen during the 1690s. For most of the decade the prevailing inclination of the Protestant polity was one of opposition to the articles of surrender. The 1695 Irish parliament was a trenchantly anti-Catholic body and legislated to that effect.[87] Privately, however, Irish Protestants supported individual Catholics in their attempts to escape the disaster of forfeiture, signing affidavits attesting to their good behaviour during the war or assisting in the preparation of lobbying efforts in London. John Methuen, an Englishman who had little experience with Irish affairs prior to his appointment as lord chancellor in 1697, wrote soon after his arrival

Ireland, in relation to his estate; and for the more effectual selling or setting the estate of the said earl to Protestants (7 Anne, c. 29 [Eng.] (private)).

85 Russell & Prendergast, *The Carte manuscripts in the Bodleian library*, p. 102.

86 Daly also employed his son James, a student at Gray's Inn, when he was absent from London (N.L.I., Annesley Mss, xxiii., ff 14, 39, 144–8).

87 C.I. McGrath, 'Securing the Protestant interest: the origins and purpose of the penal laws of 1695' in *I.H.S.*, xxx (1996–7), pp 25–46; idem, *The making of the eighteenth-century Irish constitution: government, parliament and the revenue, 1692–1714* (Dublin, 2000), pp 73–117; Hayton, *Ruling Ireland*, pp 52–62.

that Irish politicians seemed 'earnest against the Papists upon account of the English interest, but often proposing to themselves other matters'.[88] Catholics regarded Methuen as a 'virulent promoter' of anti-Catholic legislation in the Irish parliament, yet even he acclimatised to Irish politics and provided assistance to Bophin.[89]

As Methuen discovered, even in the aftermath of the Williamite war Irish society remained closely interlinked on a far more intense level than its English counterpart, with Protestant families often tied to Catholics through marriage.[90] These links were strengthened by the role of the professional classes in the period following the Restoration through the formation of business relationships and alliances. No less a figure than archbishop William King wrote in support of a Catholic friend, decrying the use of religion and faction to the disadvantage of a man of 'good integrity and honour'.[91] Sir Richard Cox, author of the 1692 legal opinion that interpreted the articles of surrender in as narrow a fashion as possible, declared in 1699 that 'there are not in Europe any Papists better affected to the English interest than the inhabitants of Galway'.[92] This remarkable statement was part of a longer speech made when he passed judgment in favour of six men seeking the benefit of the Galway articles. His perception of the Catholics of Galway was probably coloured by the considerable peace faction present in the county during the war, which had been responsible for the swift surrender of the town. A large number of the Galway claimants had belonged to this party, and their adherence to legal avenues to pursue their claims probably improved official perceptions of their cause.

There were two further important considerations. Large sums of money smoothed the way for Bophin. Payments made by Bophin, along with questions about who received it, came under considerable scrutiny from the forfeiture inquiry commissioners in 1699.[93] In their report to the English parliament the commissioners included details of the deals that Bophin struck with the earl of Albemarle and his agents, totalling £9,000. This, they concluded, was the primary consideration that prompted the Irish house of commons to reject Bophin's private bill.[94] Alan Brodrick later cautioned his brother Thomas to be

---

[88] John Methuen to Robert Harley, 27 Sept. 1697 (H.M.C., *Portland Mss*, iii, 588–9).

[89] Cathaldus Giblin, 'Catalogue of material of Irish interest in the collection Nunziatura di Fiandra, Vatican Archives', in *Collectanea Hibernica*, iv (1961), p. 73.

[90] Thomas Doyle, 'Jacobitism, Catholicism and the Irish Protestant elite, 1700–1710' in *E.C.I.*, 12 (1997), pp 28–59.

[91] T.C.D., Ms 1489/1, f. 55; Doyle, 'Jacobitism, Catholicism and the Irish Protestant elite', p. 40.

[92] B.L., Add. Ms 38,153, f. 21.

[93] N.L.I., Annesley Mss, xxiii, ff 3, 6–7, 9–10, 13, 39, 47, 65, 109–10, 114, 137, 139, 145–8.

[94] *The report of the commissioners appointed by parliament to enquire into the Irish forfeitures, delivered to the honourable House of Commons the 15th of December, 1699* (London, 1700), pp 13–14.

wary of Sir Richard Levinge: 'Retain always in your thoughts his management during the last session, his personal hatred to you and endeavours to expose you in the matter of the Bophin bill.'[95]

Equally important was Bophin's consent to educate his two eldest sons as Protestants, ensuring that his extensive estates passed into Protestant hands. His sons were duly enrolled at Eton.[96] By doing so Bophin was taking heed of Protestant fears of a vibrant landowning Catholic class remaining in Ireland after Limerick. Catholics were of course also banned from almost all official employment and military careers. As such, Bophin's decision reflected a pragmatic attempt to ensure that his estates would remain within his immediate family, while also providing career opportunities for his eldest sons and the possibility of supplementary income for the family. Conformity did not always lead to total abandonment of fellow Catholics. There is evidence to suggest that Bophin and his eldest son Michael, Lord Dunkellin and future earl of Clanricarde, leased their estates to Catholics during the 1700s on terms contrary to the provisions of the existing penal laws and of Bophin's private act.[97] Bophin's management of his affairs in the decade after the surrender of Limerick displayed a willingness to embrace emerging political and social realities, reflecting a personal and social progression that was typical of the articlemen. He adapted his personal principles to ensure the survival of his family as a social force into the eighteenth century through the abandonment of both Jacobitism and Catholicism. Bophin's willingness to educate his sons as Protestants was crucial in garnering Protestant political support for his cause. With the backing of these politicians, and Ginkel's continued assistance, the likelihood of Bophin's restoration to his estate was greatly enhanced. The successful outcome of this case was a testament to the perseverance and skilful handling of a complicated legal process by Daly, French and Bophin.

III

The articles of surrender which concluded the Williamite war in Ireland had a turbulent history in the 1690s, especially the articles of Galway and Limerick.

---

[95] Alan Brodrick to [Thomas Brodrick], 17 Mar. 1700 (S.H.C., Midleton papers, 1248/1, ff 313–14).

[96] Bodl., Carte Ms 113, ff 363, 373–4, 385, 390, 397; N.L.I., Annesley Mss, xx, ff 3, 10, 14; C.T.B., 1699–1700, pp 343, 375; C.T.B., 1700–1, p. 405. In his correspondence with Edward Lhwyd, the scholar Roderick O'Flaherty inquired in July 1704 after Bophin's eldest son Michael's education at Oxford: 'I pray let me know, how does my Lord of Boffin's son there Michael student in Oxford' (Richard Sharpe (ed.), *Roderick O'Flaherty's letters to William Molyneux, Edward Lhwyd, and Samuel Molyneux, 1696–1709* (Dublin, 2013), p. 244.

[97] Josiah Browne, *Reports of cases, upon appeals and writs of error, in the High Court of Parliament, from the year 1701 to the year 1779* (7 vols, London, 1779–83), ii, 588.

The minor articles of Drogheda, Waterford, Sligo and Boffin were generally treated 'with justice but not favour'. Due to their less controversial wording, the articles of Galway never enjoyed the dubious distinction of a parliamentary confirmation; article 16 stated 'as to such parts for which an act of parliament shall be found to be necessary we [William and Mary] shall recommend the same to be made good by parliament'. Though their right to bear arms received parliamentary confirmation, misfortune initially denied the Galway articlemen their right to continue to practise the law, with the Irish government's initial attempt to rectify this error thwarted by the English privy council in 1692. The articles of Drogheda, Waterford, Sligo and Boffin were never seriously considered as candidates for parliamentary approval and the articlemen had no need to press for one.

In the pursuit of their goal, the articlemen proved to be adept at the art of political lobbying. Agents for each of the agreements were employed in Dublin and London to press for the implementation of specific articles, or to secure a favourable construction of their wording. Protestant gentry and politicians were enlisted to plead on behalf of the articlemen in parliament, before the Irish and English privy councils and at the court of William III. While some may have been motivated by personal connections to assist their Catholic neighbours, others were handsomely paid for their services. Each of these factors were also prominent in Colonel John Browne's success in securing legislation for article 13 of Limerick.

The efforts of the articlemen to ensure that the articles were honoured by the Williamite authorities did not end with the winding-up of the third court of claims in September 1699. The passage through the English parliament of the act of resumption in 1700 forced the articlemen once more to employ lobbyists and agents in London, while the growing corpus of penal legislation passed by the Irish parliament from 1695 onwards ensured that they maintained a vigilant eye on developments in both parliaments.[98] The pursuit of the articles provided the Catholic elite in Ireland with a focus that far outweighed any thoughts of adherence to Jacobitism.

The 1690s and early eighteenth century witnessed Catholic agents – in Dublin, London and on the continent – actively seeking to influence or reverse the Irish government's policy, not to usurp its authority. Small victories were

---

98 *An impartial relation of the several arguments of Sir Stephen Rice, Sir Theobald Butler and Councillor Malone* (Dublin, 1704); Gregory Nolan to Col. Browne, 16 Jan. & 3 Feb. 1700 (N.L.I., Ms 40,902/6/11–12); *The case of all persons comprized in the articles or capitulations of the city of Waterford, fort and castle of Bophin, and the towns of Sligo and Drogheda in the kingdom of Ireland* ([London, 1700]). The English Short Title Catalogue dates this latter printed appeal to 1691/2. This is certainly wrong. In his letter of 3 February Gregory Nolan refers to a joint appeal between the agents for the articlemen of Waterford and Boffin.

often won on behalf of individuals or small groups. The importance of these victories should not be underestimated. They provided initial grounds for optimism that Irish Catholics could continue to prosper in the eighteenth century, as they had done during the reign of Charles II. However, from 1695 the Irish parliament began to enact penal legislation that increasingly restricted the rights of the Catholic population as a whole, demonstrating the limits of the articlemen's success, and conferring on them a unique status in Irish society. The penal laws made conformity to the Church of Ireland a pressing concern for Catholics in the eighteenth century. While some articlemen conformed, it was their children that did so in large numbers to secure their families' lands or to pursue political and legal careers. The articlemen stood alone as possessors of immunities from several legal restrictions on Catholics, immunities that could not be bestowed upon their heirs and would expire with their generation. As late as December 1748 the obituary of Thady Dunne described him as a 'most upright and eminent agent and solicitor in chancery, a sincere friend, and endued with every virtue; he retained his memory and his senses to the last. [He] was one of the persons included in the Articles of Limerick, which benefit he enjoyed during his life.'[99] By 1748 those benefits were somewhat meagre.

---

[99] John Brady, *Catholics and Catholicism in the eighteenth-century press* (Maynooth, 1965), p. 77. The Irish house of commons passed a resolution in 1707 that 'Thady Dunn, Popish solicitor, being employed as agent on the behalf of the children of Sir James Cotter, hath been instrumental in their being brought up in the Popish religion' (C.J.I., ii, 526 (7 Aug. 1707)).

Part III

Article 13 of Limerick

6

'*This clause was surreptitiously obtained*': Implementing article 13 of Limerick, 1691–8[1]

One of the most controversial aspects of the articles of Limerick was the protection, enshrined in article 13, for the payment of debts owed by John Browne to his Protestant creditors and which *predated* the outbreak of the war. The article stated that the assets Browne had put aside to pay his debts had been commandeered by Tyrconnell and Sarsfield, and put to use supplying the Irish army. Browne had been promised compensation, but this was an undertaking that obviously could not be fulfilled following the defeat of the Jacobites. Article 13 transferred responsibility for the Jacobite administration's debt to Browne to all estates held by Irish Catholics after the war, by virtue of 'articles and capitulations'. Sarsfield was required to certify the amount of money owed to Browne by the Jacobite government within twenty-one days of the signing of the articles.[2] By 1692 the majority of the articlemen had reluctantly agreed to honour the terms of article 13 through the payment of a special levy, equivalent to one year's quit-rent. The intended beneficiaries were, uniquely under the articles of surrender, mostly Protestant. Browne too stood to gain by staving off financial ruin, but article 13 was, in theory and eventual implementation, punitive to his fellow Catholic landowners.

As a result, the usual pattern of Catholic lobbying in relation to the articles of surrender was reversed. Article 13 created an anomalous situation where articlemen actually sought to prevent the implementation of one of the articles of Limerick. The quit-rent levy imposed by the article was, however, vital to John Browne's efforts to repay his debts and he pursued its implementation vigorously. Between 1692 and 1705, Browne joined forces with his creditors to lobby for legislation to implement the article and to thwart any opposition. Browne and his creditors employed agents in Dublin and London to argue their case, where they were opposed by the articlemen. Rather than lobbying

---

[1] The quotation is taken from 'The examination of Col. John Browne's clause in the articles of Limerick' [1691], (S.R.O., D641/2/K/2/3/1). This is the only copy known. It is unsigned and there is no evidence as to who composed the petition. It is addressed to Porter, Coningsby and 'Lieutenant General Ginkel', which suggests a date before the latter's naturalisation as 'Baron de Ginkel' on 24 Feb. 1692 and certainly before his elevation to the peerage as earl of Athlone on 4 Mar. 1692 (G.E.C., *Complete peerage*, i, 300).

[2] The full text of the article is contained in Appendix A.

for as broad an interpretation as possible, as they had done with the remaining articles, the articlemen sought to restrict the scope of article 13 as narrowly as possible.

The articlemen and protectees argued against article 13 before the Irish and English privy councils. They were in fraught territory. Objections had to be carefully worded so as not to appear to question the legality or binding nature of the articles as a whole. To do so might have cleared the way for the Irish parliament or administration to declare the articles in their entirety invalid, making the already difficult position of Irish Catholics untenable. If the goal of the articlemen's lobbying during the 1690s was to hold the Williamite authorities to their word, convincing them to do just the opposite for article 13 was a difficult task. The Irish and English governments paid little heed to the articlemen's objections. Article 13 of Limerick was the only one of the articles that the Irish government specifically legislated for; the other rights conferred on the articlemen by the articles of surrender were enshrined as saving clauses exempting the articlemen from legal restrictions imposed on the general Catholic population by the penal laws.

The substance of the articlemen's arguments against article 13 is found in a petition presented to the Irish government in late 1691. Section I of this chapter analyses this petition, which lays out a comprehensive series of objections that illustrate the frustrations of Catholic landowners at the prospect of a levy on their lands to help pay John Browne's debts. The petition failed to gain traction, and section II traces the attempts in 1692 of the Irish government, working in tandem with John Browne and his creditors, to legislate for article 13. Their endeavours were inadvertently thwarted by the 1691 Oaths Act, and later by the quarrelsome nature of the 1692 Irish parliament. Tensions among the Irish Protestant polity and between the Irish government and advocates of the Irish parliament's sole right to raise revenue for the crown prevented the recall of the Irish parliament until 1695. Section III surveys the impact of this delay on John Browne's financial situation, which worsened as interest on his debts continued to accrue. When parliament finally reconvened in August 1695, one of its first orders of business was to draft a private act for the implementation of article 13 and the sale of Browne's estate to meet his debts. While the special levy on Catholic landowners required by article 13 was collected with relative speed, the sale of Browne's estate did not begin until the end of 1698. The delay prompted Browne and his creditors to seek a second private act of parliament during its 1698–9 session. Section IV discusses this attempt as well as two separate, serious allegations in 1697 and 1698 that Browne and other prominent articlemen were engaged in Jacobite plots to restore James II. These allegations highlight the precarious position of Irish Catholics in the 1690s. The presence of the Jacobite army on the continental mainland fed regular fears of an imminent invasion, prompting intermittent arrests of prominent Catholic landowners throughout the decade.

I

Article 13 required Ginkel and the lords justices to 'intercede with the king and parliament' to charge each Catholic-owned estate in Ireland, protected by the articles of surrender and proclamations, with their share of the special levy. The articlemen lost no time in mobilising to prevent the implementation of article 13. A petition arguing the injustice of the article, titled 'The examination of Col. John Browne's clause in the articles of Limerick', was presented to Porter, Coningsby and Ginkel in late 1691 or early 1692. A copy of 'The examination' survives among the papers of Adam Colclough, who acted as agent in London to different groups of articlemen and the protectees.[3] Whether or not Colclough was arguing for or against article 13 is not clear.

'The examination' sought to persuade the three Williamite signatories that Browne and Sarsfield had acted in bad faith, misleading both the Williamite and Jacobite authorities. Five objections were raised. First, 'The examination' claimed the article was 'surreptitiously obtained' and inserted without the consent of the Jacobite lords justices, or the army council appointed to approve the articles of Limerick. Second, it was impossible for Sarsfield to know the extent of Browne's debts, since the relevant records were in Dublin and thus beyond the reach of the Catholic negotiators in September 1691. Third, when Sarsfield certified the amount due to Browne from the Jacobite administration, he failed to take account of various payments made to Browne in return for materiel supplied during the war. Fourth, preventing Browne's financial ruin was not the concern of king and parliament when Browne had been so handsomely paid for his services. Fifth, and finally, Browne's creditors were already well protected by the value of his estate and ironworks, which could be sold to pay his debts, and therefore had no need for further financial protection.[4]

The first two objections were easily the weakest. Whether or not the rest of the Irish garrison at Limerick knew of Browne's article before 3 October was irrelevant. The fact remained that the commissioners appointed by the Jacobite administration had signed the articles. To suggest that *sub rosa* negotiations invalidated a single article risked undoing the terms in their entirety. If they expected the Williamites to keep faith with the articles as signed, the articlemen

---

3   See above, pp 89–90, 104–6 for Colclough's lobbying on behalf of the articlemen and the protectees.
4   'The examination of Col. John Browne's clause in the articles of Limerick', [1691] (S.R.O., D641/2/K/2/3/1).

could hardly hope to be allowed to cherry-pick the articles to which they wished to adhere. It may have been 'surreptitiously obtained', but article 13 was now fixed in place. As to the extent of the Jacobite administration's knowledge of Browne's debt, 'The examination' was misinformed. Browne's goods were first commandeered in early 1689, with both Tyrconnell and Sarsfield well aware of the extent of his debts and to whom they were owed.[5]

As required by article 13, Sarsfield certified that £13,000 was owed to Browne.[6] 'The examination' claimed the true sum was closer to £2,500, citing several payments made to Browne by the Jacobite treasury during the war. The total of these payments was, however, unspecified and the argument was slightly disingenuous. Browne could not have been expected to keep workmen at his various ironworks without providing pay. By his own account, he paid out £1,055 in wages between November 1689 and May 1690.[7] The total laid out over the entire war in pay alone might have been double or triple that figure. Browne was still supplying horseshoes and cannonballs to the Irish army in June 1691, around which time his ironworks were probably shut down as the Williamites advanced into Connacht.[8] 'The examination' underplayed the burden Browne faced in paying his workmen, arguing that

> for the payment of some of his workmen he would have some brass money, for which he was to apply himself to the then lords of the treasury appointed by King James, who from time to time furnished the said Col. Browne with several sums of brass money in part satisfaction of the goods delivered by him to the use of King James's army, and what was due over and above was to be applied to the debts due from the said Col. Browne to his Protestant creditors, which he believed then to be forfeited to King James.

At least one payment of £500 was made to Browne by the treasury, and in February 1690 he was permitted to lease the estates of several forfeiting Protestants. These leases were, however, made in compensation for the loss of his estate, rather than payment for supplying the Irish army.[9] Pointing to the alleged treasury payments, 'The examination' claimed that Sarsfield was

> as ignorant thereof as he is to this day of what sums were paid the said Col. John Browne or what agreements were then and afterwards made by the government with the said John Browne.

---

5   N.L.I., Mss 40,899/4/13–16, 18–20; Ms 40,899/5/7–8.
6   N.L.I., Ms 40,889/24/4.
7   N.L.I., Ms 40,899/5/5. Browne operated ironworks at Gortnagare, Co. Mayo (three fineries), Westport (a finery and chaffery), Knappagh [either Co. Mayo or Co. Sligo], Kellicoore [possibly Kilcar, Co. Roscommon], Bellass (Foxford), Co. Mayo and Feagh, Co. Galway.
8   N.L.I., Ms 40,900/1/7.
9   N.L.I., Ms 40,899/4/17, 20. See above, pp 35–6 for the effect of the 1689 act of repeal on Browne's estate.

Any additional payments to Browne are likely to have been for the materiel supplied to the Jacobite army. 'The examination' offered a price list for the equipment manufactured by Browne, including £1 for every sword; 10s. per bayonet; 7s. per pickaxe or shovel; £120 per ton of cannonball and £112 per ton of iron. Applying these rates to goods Browne is known to have supplied would mean that by May 1689 he was in fact owed at least £29,000 by the Jacobite administration. But the actual rates Browne contracted for in December 1689 were nowhere near as generous as 'The examination' alleged. Under these terms, Browne was to be paid £18 per ton of iron ball; 1s.6d per shovel and bayonet; 6s. per sword and £5 per firelock musket. King James had also decreed in May 1689 that Browne was to be paid £50 per ton of iron already supplied, giving a figure of £12,900 before the war had even started.[10] There is no doubt Browne provided the Jacobite army with far in excess of £13,000 worth of materiel.

The final value of this materiel is impossible to quantify, but possibly lies somewhere between £20,000 and £30,000. The Jacobite mints at Dublin and Limerick (which ceased operations in July and October 1690 respectively) coined approximately £1,100,000 during the Jacobite war. It is conceivable that the Jacobite administration paid Browne sizeable amounts during the war, but it is worth bearing in mind that the brass money of James II's time in Ireland was rendered practically worthless by William's proclamation after the Battle of the Boyne 'crying down' its value, a move cemented by his victory in 1691.[11] Without detailed accounts it is impossible to calculate the total value of Browne's supplies to the Jacobites. The debt owed to Browne by the end of the war is, however, known. Sarsfield's figure of £13,000 was deliberately under-valued; the true sum owed was £18,173.0s.8d.[12] How 'The examination' arrived at the sum of £2,500 is unclear, but its calculations wildly underestimated the sum owed to Browne.

The fourth objection contained in 'The examination' suggested that, in the light of the qualifications already offered, Browne's financial ruin was not a business fit for consideration by William or his parliament. However, the Jacobites themselves had insisted on parliamentary ratification of the articles during the negotiations. It was the fifth and final objection that carried most force:

---

[10] N.L.I., Ms 40,899/4/13. Browne's iron had actually been confiscated in May 1689 due to his unlicensed trip to England, with the payment of £50 per ton applied following a petition from Browne to James II.

[11] Proclamation, 10 July 1690 (Kelly & Lyons (eds), *Proclamations of Ireland*, ii, 197); Michael Dolley, 'The Irish coinage, 1534–1691' in T.W. Moody, F.X Martin & F.J. Byrne (eds), *A new history of Ireland*, iii: *early modern Ireland, 1534–1691* (Oxford, 1976), pp 418–20.

[12] T.N.A., SP 66/B/13, f. 9; N.L.I., Ms 40,889/24/4.

Another motive is for the satisfaction of the said John Browne's creditors. This (with submission) is as frivolous as the former for his creditors are sufficiently secured upon the great estate of £4,000 per annum purchased by him, and upon the ironworks for which he [be]came thus indebted, and it is more reasonable and just the said Col. Browne should pay his just debts out of the said estate, valued in the year 1684 at £4,000 per annum, and out of the ironworks, the produce whereof yields or may yield him £3,000 per annum more, than the persons no way concerned should pay his debts and he go with the said estate and ironworks free.

The author(s) of 'The examination' had precedent on their side. Browne had previously secured the consent of fifteen creditors in November 1688 to have the rents from his estate and the profits from his ironworks assigned to a receiver, who would then regulate their repayment.[13] As 'The examination' stated, Browne's estate was then valued at £4,000 per annum, with 'two furnaces for iron and eight fineries and two chafferies in good order'.[14] No mention was made in this agreement of projected annual profits from the ironworks but they are not likely to have even approached £3,000.[15]

When the objections in 'The examination' are distilled, they amount to a complaint about the injustice of burdening Catholic landowners with a debt incurred by Browne through the mismanagement of his business interests. Lacking a detailed list of the payments made to Browne during the war, its author(s) had no firm basis for their argument that these were sufficient to cover his outlay for the Irish army. Browne was in fact owed a substantial amount by the Jacobite administration at the end of the war, which was now all but irrecoverable. His great success with article 13 was to assign liability for this debt to his fellow Catholics. In truth, article 13 constituted a beguiling piece of chicanery on Browne's part. The Jacobite administration may have owed Browne a considerable sum of money, but this was a situation that pertained to many Irish Catholics at the war's end. Article 13 essentially imposed a levy on Catholic landowners in order to pay Browne's business debts, owed mostly to Protestants, and which *predated* the war. It is easy to see why article 13 aroused opposition from the articlemen. There is, however, no evidence that the promoters of 'The examination' met with any success, and their appeal is unlikely to have been seriously entertained so soon after the signing of the articles. The simple truth remained that Browne had secured, within the instrument partly designed to

[13] See above, p. 29.
[14] N.L.I., Ms 40,898/2/11; Eileen McCracken, 'Charcoal-burning ironworks in seventeenth and eighteenth century Ireland' in *Ulster Journal of Archaeology*, 3rd series, xx (1957), pp 123–38; eadem, 'Supplementary list of Irish charcoal-burning ironworks' in *Ulster Journal of Archaeology*, 3rd series, xxviii (1965), pp 132–6. McCracken notes that the ironworks at Foxford were still in operation in 1760, under the ownership of William Rutledge (p. 135).
[15] See above, pp 24–7.

safeguard their economic futures, the financial assistance of Irish Catholics in the payment of his personal debts.

II

Browne's debt was now an issue of national concern, destined for scrutiny and further objections during preparations for the next sitting of the Irish parliament. However, those preparations did not begin in earnest until January 1692 and a legislative programme was still not finalised when parliament sat in October of that year.[16] The uncertainty about the fate of the articles of Limerick, particularly regarding the Irish government's plan for the implementation of article 13, may have allowed Browne some respite from his creditors. The market for land acquisition largely lay dormant until the Williamite court of claims began sitting in April 1692. Deals could hardly have been concluded when ownership of over a quarter of Irish land remained uncertain. Browne's *modus operandi* in dealing with his debt had, up to this point, revolved around various agreements of lease, mortgage and rental assignment with certain creditors. In the three months between the signing of the articles of Limerick and the turn of the year, there are no records of such transactions. However, the success of any appearance by Browne in the court of claims was a near certainty, once its sitting and procedures had been confirmed in February 1692. For Browne at least, the market had resumed by March 1692, and he became exposed to his creditors' demands.

Some pursued Browne through the traditional avenue of the courts.[17] Others took matters into their own hands: John Bingham, a recent creditor, used his position as sheriff of County Mayo to seize iron and livestock owned by Browne, claiming they were forfeited.[18] Thomas Scurlocke showed some sympathy for Browne's plight by agreeing to suspend interest payments on his debt for four years due to 'the late wars and of great waste in land'.[19] Acts of kindness such as this were, however, in short supply. Browne's most important creditor was

---

16 Tentative steps for drafting legislation necessary for Ireland were first taken by several bishops of the Church of Ireland in September 1691, followed by Sir Richard Reynell's trip to London in November carrying drafts of several bills (Bergin, 'Irish legislative procedure', i, pp 239–50; James McGuire, 'The Irish parliament of 1692' in Thomas Bartlett & D.W. Hayton (eds), *Penal era and golden age: essays in Irish history* (Belfast, 1979), pp 5–6; Hayton, *Ruling Ireland*, pp 40–8).

17 See for example Jacob Peppard's suit in the court of king's bench during 1692 (N.L.I., Ms 40,900/3/12–15).

18 N.L.I., Mss 40,896/1/1–2, 11; 40,898/4/10; 40,900/3/3–8. The goods were eventually returned to Browne and given to Lord Athenry in part payment of a dowry; see below, p. 221 for Athenry's marriage to John Browne's daughter Bridget.

19 N.L.I., Ms 40,900/2/10.

Sir Stephen Rice, the former Jacobite privy councillor and chief baron of the exchequer and, of course, actually a Catholic. Not only was Browne's largest debt owed to Rice, the majority of Browne's estate was heavily mortgaged to him for the sum of £7,200. Several years' worth of arrears meant that Rice had some measure of control over the estate.[20] Several portions of the estate were leased by Rice to Richard Thompson in March 1692. Browne's consent was necessary, with the transaction representing the resumption of his land deals after a six-month hiatus. The lease was for twenty-one years, with rent set at £500 the first year, £600 the second, and £700 for every year thereafter, payable to Rice. Though already heavily indebted to the former chief baron, Browne also took a further loan of £1,000 from Rice. Thompson instructed Robert Mason, Browne's estate manager, to use his 'skill and power [to] buy £1,500 sterling out of the rents of the said estate and pay the same to me', which would then be used to make the annual payments to Rice, with a further £300 to be paid to other creditors. Any profits from the ironworks were to be split between continuing their operation and repaying creditors:

> It being hereby intended that the said John Browne's creditors shall have all his effects applied to answer them from time to time as far as they can go until the security intended them by the Articles of Limerick shall be answered.[21]

The respite afforded to Browne in the aftermath of the war was clearly a brief one. Sir Stephen Rice proved to be the first creditor to resume pursuit of his debt, which stood well above £10,000. It is tempting to view Rice's haste as a consequence of article 13, with perhaps an element of spite present. In pushing Browne hard so soon after the war, Rice may have been influenced by the fact that, as both Catholic landowner and creditor, he faced the ludicrous prospect of paying a special levy to fund debt repayments to himself.

Due to article 13 of Limerick, the repayment of Browne's debts was a task that extended beyond the offices of court clerks and conveyancers. Porter, Coningsby, Sydney and the rest of the Irish privy council also became important figures. They were to sit as the court of claims and adjudicate in June 1692 on Browne's claim to the articles of Limerick. The same men also decided the method whereby Catholic landowners would pay the levy imposed by article 13. As a direct consequence, Browne was drawn into the hapless confusion surrounding preparations for the Irish parliament. It was against this backdrop

---

[20] Browne's business relationship with Rice dated back to 1678. By the end of 1684 Browne had mortgaged large swathes of his estate to Rice for the total of £7,200. Interest repayments alone would have come to £720 per annum (N.L.I., Mss 40,889/16/4–6; 40,889/19/1, 4–5; 40,900/5/11–12).

[21] N.L.I., Ms 40,889/24/3.

that Browne moved to secure the implementation of article 13, first defending the imposition of payments on Catholic landowners and then attempting to procure an act of parliament to protect his creditors. The first challenge to article 13 had failed entirely. More concerted opposition was raised in late June 1692, spearheaded by the articlemen of Galway. Several conferences were held between the lords justices, counsel for Browne and counsel for the articlemen of Galway, who initially disputed the imposition of Browne's debt on their estates before agreeing to each pay the equivalent of a year's quit-rent. A charge of one year's quit-rent was eventually imposed on every Catholic-owned estate to meet the requirements of article 13. An undated petition, probably from mid-1692, of several articlemen of Limerick to the lords justices sheds further light on the bond required from each successful claimant under the articles of Limerick and Galway. Payment was to be made in two instalments, over two years, to Sir John Topham in trust for the Protestant creditors. The petition requested that the sum owed by each claimant be speedily calculated and deducted from the recognisances already paid to the court of claims.[22]

It seems likely that the lords justices applied pressure to the Galway articlemen by informing them that the legislation being prepared to allow eligible claimants to resume practising the law was to be combined with the protection for Browne's creditors within one bill. This dual-purpose bill was sent to England from the Irish privy council on 1 August, Sydney later writing to Nottingham to impress upon him that the bill contained a clause for Browne's creditors and asking him to 'move her majesty upon it'.[23] The bill was rejected and Nottingham urged caution before any other attempt to legislate for article 13 was retransmitted to London:

> The clause relating to Mr Browne's creditors may be inserted in some other act, as you shall judge proper; but you will do well to cause that matter to be thoroughly examined, for it has been represented to the Queen as if, in truth, there were no just grounds for Mr Brown's pretensions, at least not for so great a sum as is demanded. If, however, there is, and it be due to Protestants, as it was reasonable they should be satisfied, the papists cannot complain, it being one of the articles made by themselves at Limerick.[24]

Catholic lobbyists were clearly active in London, intent on stalling or defeating any legislative provision for article 13. Porter warned Coningsby that 'some of the Irish will endeavour to obstruct it'.[25] The evidence suggests that the

---

[22] T.N.A., SP 63/357, f. 153; C.S.P.D., 1695 & Addenda, pp 101–2.
[23] T.N.A., SP 63/357, ff 112, 130–1.
[24] Nottingham to Sydney, 13 Sept. 1692 (C.S.P.D., 1691–2, p. 447). See above, pp 129–32, for a discussion of this bill as it relates to the Galway articlemen.
[25] Porter to Coningsby, 28 Nov. 1692 (P.R.O.N.I., De Ros Mss, D638/18/4).

majority of the articlemen of Limerick and Galway had, by the middle of 1692, resigned themselves to the burden. Agents for the articlemen of Waterford and Boffin were not as vulnerable to the tactics of the lords justices.

The dual-purpose bill was certainly drafted in consultation with Browne and his creditors, and sheds some light on Browne's position. The bill confirmed that Sarsfield deliberately undervalued the debt owed to Browne by the Jacobite administration, 'out of his regard to the condition and circumstances of the persons that by the articles are to pay the said monies'. The sum of £18,127.8s. was claimed as the correct figure, rather than the £13,000 certified by Sarsfield, 'after deductions for all payments and allowances' received by Browne. He offered to sell whatever portion of his estate was necessary to meet any debts that remained after collection of the levy. His overall debt stood at approximately £30,000. Negotiations between Browne and his creditors on the method of repaying his debts had produced an agreement, formalised in indenture drawn up on 19 July 1692, appointing Sir Richard Reynell, Sir John Topham, Henry Monck, James Grace and Edmund Reynell as trustees for the sale and disposal of Browne's estate. The dual-purpose bill was intended to give legislative force to the indenture, as well as to empower the lord lieutenant and privy council to determine the sum to be paid by each Catholic landowner and to levy the same. The trustees were to be given power to enter the homes of recalcitrant articlemen and force the sale of whatever goods met the value of one year's quit-rent.[26] At the English privy council the bill was laid aside because the clause dealing with the articlemen of Galway contradicted the 1691 Oaths Act of the English parliament.

The Irish government reacted swiftly to the news of the bill's failure, transmitting another bill solely concerned with Browne's creditors on 29 September.[27] The speed of this bill's transmission suggests that no material changes had been made, other than to remove any reference to the Galway articlemen. Sydney again recommended the creditors' case to Nottingham, informing him that

> a considerable number of the Protestants of this kingdom, who are concerned therein, apprehending lest none of those bills, in which the said clause is, should pass, have been very earnest with the council that this bill might be transmitted, and therefore it is hoped her majesty will consent to the passing thereof.

Referred to the English law officers on 4 October, the bill was returned and read at the privy council a week later. In the meantime, the 'Roman Catholics of Ireland' petitioned the privy council to be allowed a copy of two bills, including

[26] T.N.A., SP 66/B/13, f. 9. The indenture does not survive. If it followed the form of the 1695 indenture (see p. 160 below), it was probably invalidated by the failure to secure an act of parliament for the creditors within six months.
[27] Sydney to Nottingham, 29 Sept. 1692 (T.N.A., SP 63/354, ff 157–8; C.S.P.D., 1695 & Addenda, pp 207–8).

Browne's, 'that they may be heard to the same before her majesty's ratification of them in council'. Sir John Somers, the attorney general, was ordered to allow them to read the bill in his presence, but not to have a copy. The articlemen's agents again requested copies of the bills a week later, and to have their counsel allowed time to examine them and to make observations. They had more success on this occasion, accounting for the temporary suspension of discussion of Browne's bill. Any observations the agents had on Browne's bill are not recorded.[28]

The identity of the Catholic lobbyists is not certain, though it is known that Adam Colclough, Henry Luttrell and probably John Galwey were lobbying in London at that time on behalf of the articlemen of Limerick. Several Limerick articlemen wrote to Colclough on 19 October to inform him that they had shown 'what relates to our common interest to the chief of the parties concerned'. Among those who signed the letter were Sir Toby Butler and Nicholas Purcell, signatories of the Limerick articles.[29] The main focus of the petitioners appears to have been the bill of indemnity then under consideration at the privy council. If Colclough, Luttrell and Galwey led the petitioners, it is probable that they had no objections to Browne's legislation. Queen Mary approved the bill in council with a single minor amendment on 27 October and it was returned to the Irish government on 2 November.[30] It was too late; Sydney prorogued the fractious Irish parliament on 3 November.[31] Even so, that was not quite the end of Browne's efforts.

With no hope of the Irish parliament sitting again soon, Browne and his creditors contemplated seeking an act of the English parliament. Porter wrote of this attempt to Coningsby three weeks later:

[28] Nottingham to Sir John Somers, 4 Oct. 1692 (T.N.A., SP 44/98; T.N.A., PC 2/75, ff 3–4; C.S.P.D., 1691–2, p. 470); Nottingham to Sydney, 4 Oct. 1692 (T.N.A., SP 67/1, f. 217; C.S.P.D., 1691–2, p. 471); same to same, 11 Oct. 1692 (T.N.A., SP 67/1, f. 219; C.S.P.D., 1691–2, pp 477–8); Robert Yard to Sir Joseph Williamson, 11 Oct. 1692 (T.N.A., SP 32/4, f. 151; C.S.P.D., 1691–2, p. 478); T.N.A., PC 2/75, ff 6–7, 8–9.
[29] Sir Toby Butler, Nicholas Purcell et al to Adam Colclough, 19 Oct. 1692 (S.R.O., D641/2/K/2/4L); Bergin, 'Irish Catholic interest', p. 40.
[30] T.N.A., PC 2/75, ff 20–1; Nottingham to Sydney, 2 Nov. 1692 (SP 67/1, ff 219–29; C.S.P.D., 1691–2, pp 492–3). It has been argued that the return of Browne's bill from the English privy council in November 1692 represented a 'dramatic change in fortune' for the measure (James Kelly, Poynings' law and the making of law in Ireland, 1660–1800 (Dublin, 2007), p. 58). This overstates the case. The reason for the failure of the original transmission was the combination of the clause for Browne's creditors with that for the Galway lawyers. Though Nottingham urged caution with regard to Browne's clause, the dual-purpose bill fell as a result of a conflict with the 1691 oaths act, not opposition to Browne's clause.
[31] McGuire, '1692 parliament', p. 21; C.I. McGrath, The making of the eighteenth-century Irish constitution: government, parliament and the revenue, 1692–1714 (Dublin, 2000), p. 87; David Hayton, 'Introduction: the long apprenticeship' in idem (ed.), The Irish parliament in the eighteenth century: the long apprenticeship (Edinburgh, 2001), p. 23.

The creditors of Mr John Browne as well as himself have combined to try if they can get the same bill which should have passed here to be enacted in the parliament in England. And for that purpose have sent over Mr Malone to follow it; but he is instructed to attend you and not to stir in it if you think it will not pass, but rather to wait till the parliament meets here.

Porter warned that obstructionist tactics from Catholics were likely:

How far they may prevail your lordship upon the place will be best able to judge. But I think that interest could not obstruct it here. If it should be baffled there I doubt it would hinder its being transmitted hither again from the council if that should be thought necessary (which yet I think is not). If you shall be of opinion to try to pass it there then Mr Malone will deliver a letter which I have writ to my lord treasurer for his assistance as a matter very advantageous to many English protestants. But if you are of a contrary opinion there he is not to deliver it.[32]

Nothing further seems to have been done, however, and an English act was not pursued. Efforts to obtain legislative protection for Browne's creditors fell into abeyance for the time being. Even so, at the close of 1692, relief for Browne and his creditors seemed a little closer to hand than it had been when the articles of Limerick were signed. The form of the Catholic levy had been decided and, though it was not yet enshrined in legislation, those Catholics whose claims under the articles had been allowed were now bound for payment in a court of record.

III

The breakdown in relations between the executive and legislative branches of the Irish government in 1692 had repercussions that extended beyond the concerns of the Protestant polity. For John Browne it meant that legislation for implementing article 13 of Limerick fell not just into abeyance, but limbo, as the Irish parliament did not sit again for almost three years. This ensured an uneasy period between 1692 and 1695 as the interest on Browne's various debts continued to accrue. His predicament was exacerbated by a stagnation of trade in Connacht in the years immediately after the war. Browne maintained an income through rents and the produce of his ironworks, but the war had left

---

[32] Porter to Coningsby, 28 Nov. 1692 (P.R.O.N.I., De Ros Mss, D638/18/4). 'Mr Malone' was Browne's nephew Edmund Malone, who represented the Limerick articlemen in late 1691 and early 1692. The reading of 'lord treasurer' is not absolutely certain (the letter may only be consulted on a microfilm of poor quality), but if it is correct points to a curious connection: the holder of the office was Sidney, Lord Godolphin, who was Adam Colclough's brother-in-law (Bergin, 'Irish Catholic interest', pp 38–9).

many tenants in significant arrears. Some customers of the ironworks were slow in settling their accounts.[33] The ironworks also operated fitfully, with Browne required to petition against a December 1692 proclamation forbidding the assembly of ten or more Catholics to keep them operational.[34]

The agreement Browne had reached with his creditors in 1692 required an act of parliament to formalise sale of his estate, probably because it was felt that article 13 would be more enforceable with legislative backing. The Irish and English privy councils had approved an act in 1692, and it would not have been unreasonable for Browne and his creditors to assume that success was likely when the Irish parliament next assembled.

The first session of the second Williamite parliament (August 1695 – December 1697) was made possible through the compromise negotiated by lord deputy Capell with the 1692 opposition.[35] Capell secured the support of key recalcitrant MPs such as Alan Brodrick and Robert Rochfort by appointing them and other members of the opposition to government and judicial posts, further placating them with a promise to introduce legislation for 'strengthening and securing the English and Protestant interest'.[36] Capell's instructions upon appointment as lord deputy in May 1695 made specific mention of the articles of Limerick and Galway, requiring that the articles be 'construed according to their strict meaning upon all questions or doubts which may arise, without allowing any favour to the persons comprehended in them, or extending them further than in justice and honour you are obliged to do'.[37] Implementing article 13 fell well within this remit.

The legislation agreed in 1692 also made provision for the sale of whatever portion of Browne's estate was necessary, to meet whatever debts remained after the levy had been collected. By 1695 Browne was not the only person to seek an act of parliament for the sale of an estate to meet private debts. One of the notable trends in the preparation and discussion of draft legislation during the 1690s and early 1700s is the proliferation of similar private bills. Between 1695 and 1705, nineteen sale-of-estate bills were enacted.[38] A further twenty-nine

---

[33] N.L.I., Mss 40,883/36; 40,900/3/18; 40,900/6/1–5, 14–18, 21; 40,903/2/3–4; 40,903/3/13; 40,903/5/22; 40,903/6/20; 40,906/3/6–13; 40,906/5/10–11.

[34] Proclamation, 19 Dec. 1692 (Kelly & Lyons (eds), *Proclamations of Ireland*, ii, 306–7); McCracken, 'Charcoal-burning ironworks' p. 133.

[35] McGrath, *Eighteenth-century Irish constitution*, pp 94–9; Hayton, *Ruling Ireland*, pp 52–5. Though technically one session, parliament actually sat from 27 Aug.–14 Dec. 1695, and 27 July–3 Dec. 1697 (Hayton, 'The long apprenticeship', p. 23).

[36] Henry, Lord Capell, to Sir John Trenchard, 14 July 1694 (quoted in C.I. McGrath, 'Securing the Protestant interest: the origins and purpose of the penal laws of 1695' in *I.H.S.*, xxx (1996–7), p. 33).

[37] Instructions to Capell, 5 May 1695 (*C.S.P.D.*, *1694–5*, p. 459).

[38] Ormond (7 Will. III, c. 1 [1695]); Browne (7 Will. III, c. 2 [1695]); Waller (7 Will. III, c. 5 [1695]); Jones (7 Will. III, c. 7 [1695]); Domville (9 Will. III, c. 2 [1697]); Ormsby (9 Will. III, c.

bills were considered, but not enacted. Of these unsuccessful bills, six were intended to supplement earlier private acts, with Browne accounting for five. In fact, no fewer than seven bills relating to the sale of Browne's estate were introduced into the Irish parliament between 1695 and 1705, with two enacted. A further unsuccessful bill was introduced to the commons in June 1709, while two draft bills were prepared by the Irish privy council in 1692, but not introduced to parliament. The sale of Browne's estate thus prompted ten separate legislative measures in a seventeen-year period.

'An act for securing the debts owing to the Protestant creditors of Colonel John Browne' received the royal assent on 7 December 1695.[39] As with its 1692 predecessor, the 1695 bill was intended to give legislative force to article 13, as well as an indenture signed by Browne and his creditors. The negotiations that produced this indenture were completed by the summer of 1695 and Browne was in Dublin during August and September to monitor the bill's passage through parliament, where it appears to have been initiated. No record of a petition from Browne to parliament to have heads of a bill drawn up is found in the commons' journals, implying that a member or members of the house initiated the bill. Private bills were, typically, drafted outside the confines of parliament or privy council and then presented to either forum for approval.[40] Several of Browne's creditors sat in the lower house, three of whom (Richard Aldworth, Sir Arthur Langford and Edmund Reynell) obtained a protection for Browne in the commons to 'attend the prosecution of a bill to secure his creditors'. Soon after, John Bingham, MP for County Mayo, petitioned successfully for a proviso naming himself as creditor due to a debt of £850 for which no court judgment had ever been obtained.[41] William Sprigge appears to have managed the bill in

---

3 [1697]); Parsons (9 Will. III, c. 4 [1697]); Jephson (9 Will. III, c. 5 [1697]); Stopford (9 Will. III, c. 9 [1697]); Barry (9 Will. III, c. 13 [1697]); Parsons (10 Will. III, c. 1 [1699]); Ormond (2 Anne, c. 1 [1704]); Hamilton (2 Anne, c. 3 [1704]); Stopford (2 Anne, c. 4 [1704]); Aylmer (4 Anne, c. 2 [1705]); Hackett (4 Anne, c. 3 [1705]); Magill (4 Anne, c. 4 [1705]); Browne (4 Anne, c. 6 [1705]); Dawson (4 Anne, c. 7 [1705]). All chapter numbers refer to private acts. Four of these acts (Parsons, 1699; Stopford, 1703; Ormond, 1704; and Browne, 1705) were enacted to supplement earlier private acts, making a total of fifteen individual cases. For further details of each act, see Bergin, 'Irish legislative procedure', ii, 24, 30–1, 44–50, 94–5, 103–4, 160–2, 185–8, 209, 232–5, 247–9, 310–12, 346–7.

39 7 William III, c. 2 (private); C.J.I., ii, 137; L.J.I., i, 577–8.

40 The Irish privy council discussed 'the act for John Browne's debt' at a meeting in June 1695. This was probably the same bill as had been transmitted in September 1692, and does not appear to have been the bill that was introduced to the Irish parliament in August 1695 (T.N.A., SP 63/357, ff 77–8; C.S.P.D., 1694–5, p. 514).

41 C.J.I., ii, 48, 55–6, 61, 65 (31 Aug., 10, 16, 19 Sept. 1695). Gaps in the proceedings on several bills indicate that the journals for this period are not always wholly reliable as a source for indicating where bills took their rise (Bergin, 'Irish legislative procedure', i, 74).

committee, which was approved by parliament and the Irish privy council and transmitted to the English government on 24 October.[42]

The bill attracted a significant level of lobbying from agents in London. Robert Huntington, former provost of Trinity College, successfully employed lobbyists at the English privy council to obtain a proviso in the bill, securing a debt of £260 against Browne. Browne and his creditors may also have employed agents to counter the claims of the articlemen. While the bill was before the privy council, the articlemen submitted two petitions objecting to its provisions. The bill engendered a division among the Galway articlemen, prompting some of them to join beneficiaries of the other articles of surrender in opposing it. Porter and Coningsby, as they had done in 1692, provided political support for the bill.[43] An investigation by Capell and the Irish privy council revealed the weakness of the articlemen's case. Their report to Shrewsbury concluded by recommending the proposed legislation in unambiguous terms:

> Upon the whole we submit it to your lordship's consideration whether after all these agreements, transactions and proceedings a bill of this nature, which is entirely for the advantage of Protestants, of whom many are members of the present house of commons, shall be obstructed from passing upon any the pretensions above named. We shall only add that this is a bill of general expectation, and the passing thereof will most certainly be highly grateful to the parliament.[44]

In the eyes of the Irish privy council, Browne's bill was a measure for securing the Protestant interest. Rejection at the English privy council would not sit well with members of the commons, particularly Aldworth (a member of the Irish privy council and chief secretary to Capell), Reynell, Langford, Sprigge, Bingham, Abel Ram (eldest son of Sir Abel Ram), James Sloane, Richard St George, William Crow, Richard Thompson, Gideon Delaune and Roger Moore – all of whom were either creditors or trustees for creditors to Browne.

The articlemen's objections were not heeded by the English privy council, which inserted Huntington's proviso and returned the bill with one other very minor amendment.[45] The bill had three readings in the commons on consecutive days in early December, with Colonel Garrett Moore and Arthur French securing the protection of the house for a fortnight 'to enable them to attend the passing of Colonel Browne's bill, and settling the accounts relating to his Protestant creditors'.[46] Sent to the lords on 6 December, a minor scare ensued

---

[42] B.L., Add. Ms 9175, f. 22v.

[43] See above, pp 130–3.

[44] Capell and the Irish privy council to Shrewsbury, 15 Nov. 1695 (T.N.A., SP 63/357, f. 150; C.S.P.D., 1695 & Addenda, p. 102).

[45] T.N.A., PC 2/76, f. 222.

[46] C.J.I., ii, 130–5 (4–6 Dec.).

when the lords objected to the lack of an endorsement to the engrossed bill. This procedural defect was quickly corrected, allowing for the royal assent the following day.[47]

A contemporary manuscript copy of the act survives.[48] No copies of the private bill transmitted by the Irish privy council on 29 September 1692, or that proposed for the English parliament at the end of 1692 are extant, making comparison with these bills impossible. The 1695 act gave legislative force to a tripartite indenture drawn up between Browne, his creditors and all four members of the court of exchequer, who were to act as trustees for the sale of Browne's estate. In this respect it mirrored the failed dual-purpose bill of 1692, though the 1695 act was far more detailed, naming several of the creditors and the amounts owed to them. An original copy of the indenture also survives, dated 23 August 1695. More than fifty creditors are named in the indenture, which also specified the executors and assignees of creditors who had died since lending to Browne.[49]

Much of the tripartite indenture was directly inserted into the draft bill. Within the act two main concerns were legislated for: Catholic payments to Browne for the Jacobite debt, which were to be assigned to his creditors, and the sale of his estate to satisfy his remaining debts. As the 1692 dual-purpose bill had done, the indenture and the 1695 act gave an account of Sarsfield's undervaluation of the debt owed to Browne by the Jacobite administration, declaring £18,173.0s.8d. the true amount owed. The first half of the act dealt with payment of this sum. Reference to the 1692 agreement between the Irish government and the majority of the articlemen for a levy of one year's quit-rent in satisfaction of this sum was made, alongside an alteration in the composition of the trustees to whom the quit-rents were to be paid:

---

[47] 7 William III, c. 2 (private); *C.J.I.*, ii, 134–7 (6–7 Dec.); *L.J.I.*, i, 571–8 (6–7 Dec.).

[48] N.L.I., Ms 40,915/2. The 8th marquess of Sligo also made a typescript copy in the twentieth century (Ms 40,883/15). The document from which both transcripts were made, while extant in the 1980s, has since been mislaid (Sean Murphy, 'The Sligo papers, Westport House, Co. Mayo: a report' in *Anal. Hib.*, no. 33 (1986), p. 26; N.L.I., Westport Papers Collection List, p. 160). Private acts were usually not printed by parliament after enactment. Contemporary copies of private acts should generally be treated with caution, as they may not (even when entitled 'An act ...') be true copies of the act as passed. It was common for petitioners to parliament to have a draft of the act printed for the benefit of members – such drafts might subsequently be altered in parliament or at the privy councils. The extant copy of Browne's act, however, includes the amendments known to have been made at the English privy council and can thus be taken as accurate.

[49] '1695 tripartite indenture', 23 Aug. 1695 (N.L.I., Ms 40,889/24/4). The precise number of Browne's creditors is not certain, due to the manner in which the list of creditors is intermingled with trustees. It is occasionally unclear as to whether a person named is a creditor or joint trustee with others. Additionally, the children of deceased creditors, who are not named, inherited their parents' claims against Browne, thus increasing the number of his creditors.

And the said John Browne having formerly assigned over the said value of one year's quit-rent to certain trustees for the use of the said creditors, which trustees the said creditors have agreed to change and alter and have desired the said John Browne to cancel the said former assignment (which is accordingly done) and to make a new assignment thereof.[50]

The new trustees were Philip Savage, Robert Doyne, Sir Henry Echlin and Nehemiah Donnellan (chancellor, chief baron and barons of the exchequer respectively), replacing Sir John Topham, Henry Monck, James Grace and Edmund Reynell. All of the previous trustees were creditors to Browne, or trustees for creditors. Of the new trustees, only Savage was personally involved with Browne's affairs, serving as co-trustee for the debt owed to George Percival. Topham was required to surrender all bonds entered into by him, as trustee, with Catholics for their quit-rent payments. John Talbot, having already paid his portion, was exempted from further payment. All remaining Catholic estate holders were required to give security for payment within six months of 7 December 1695, following which two years were allowed for full payment. Where a dispute arose over the amount to be paid, the chief governor and six or more of the privy council were to be the final arbiters. In the event of non-payment, collectors were authorised to distrain sufficient property to meet payment.

John Bingham's petition to parliament resulted in a proviso naming him as creditor to Browne for £850. His claim dated from the Williamite war, during which Browne used 'mine coals and iron' to manufacture supplies for the Jacobites:

Which ought therefore in conscience to be provided for and secured to the said John Bingham upon the fund intended by the said agreement for the said John Browne's creditors, and could not on 3 October 1691 be ascertained to the said John Bingham on ... Browne's account.

The connection between the Browne and Bingham families extended back to the employment of John Browne's great-grandfather by Bingham's uncle, Sir Richard Bingham. Relations between the families had been strengthened by the marriage of John Browne's older brother George to Alicia Bingham (John Bingham's niece and Sir Henry Bingham's aunt).[51] John Bingham's family seat was at Foxford, County Mayo, the location of one of Browne's ironworks, which accounts for their shared business interests. During the Williamite war, the families' loyalties diverged along confessional lines. While Browne supplied the Jacobite forces (requisitioning some of Bingham's goods in the process), John

---

[50] 7 William III, c. 2 (private).
[51] G.E. Cokayne, *Complete baronetage* (5 vols, Exeter, 1900–06), ii, 419.

Bingham contracted with the Williamite authorities to supply bread, cheese and biscuits to the army.[52]

The provisions of the first half of the act, outlined above, were effectively a parliamentary confirmation of article 13 of the articles of Limerick, yet the articles are not actually mentioned within the indenture or the act. The prevailing attitude among the Protestant polity towards the articles in general probably ensured a prudent avoidance of any direct mention within the bill, for fear that it would endanger its passage through the commons.

The quit-rent payments were not even close to sufficient to discharge Browne's debts. The second half of the act established the method for raising whatever money was necessary beyond the sum of £18,173.0s.8d. This part was designed to give legislative force to a bargain and sale agreed between Browne and the newly appointed trustees, detailed in the tripartite indenture. The act noted the existence of numerous mortgages on his lands in Mayo and Galway, agreed with William Pullein (£600) and Sir John Knox (£1,200), with 'most part [of the estate] … conveyed' to Sir Stephen Rice (for £7,000):

> So as the whole estate lies under several mortgages to several persons for several sums of money in the whole amounting to less than the said estate is worth if the same were bona fide to be sold in parcels at the best and highest rate that could be had for the same.

The mortgage to Rice was 'forfeited in law'. For a mere 5s., Browne conveyed the vast majority of this portion of his estate to the trustees.[53] They were given two years from 1 November 1695 to sell whatever portions of Browne's estate they chose. Within these two years, Browne and his heirs were required to consent to and appear as parties to such sales. After 1 November 1697, however, the trustees were given a further three-year period to complete sales, without requiring the consent of Browne and his heirs. Proceeds from sales of lands under mortgage were to be paid immediately to the mortgagee, until each mortgagee's principal and interest were repaid. Mortgagees were thus given first priority under the act, with all other creditors required to wait until 'the residue of the money so to be raised by sale … shall go … to the said trustees … to be distributed among the creditors of the said John Browne'.

The final provision of the act aimed to protect Browne and his co-debtors from arrest or imprisonment for debt. Colonel Garrett Moore, Edmund Malone, Ignatius Browne, John Bingham, George Kennedy (merchant), Robert Mason

---

[52] *The case of John Bingham, Esq., and Katherine Dunbarr, widow* ([Dublin, 1695]). Bingham's partner was John Dunbarr, who had evidently died by the time the petition was presented. Bingham served as MP for Castlebar in 1692, and for Co. Mayo from 1695 until his death in 1707.
[53] N.L.I., Ms 40,889/24/4.

and Valentine Browne were named within the act, with protection to extend for two years from 1 November 1695.[54] Several other details are found in the tripartite indenture. Each creditor agreed to forgive payment of one year's interest 'in respect of the late calamitous times'. Of much greater importance for Browne was the reduction of the interest rate on all debts to 5% per annum. While the ironworks and saltworks were to be sold eventually, Browne was permitted to retain ownership and operation of these enterprises, on the proviso that he provide yearly accounts and pay any profits to his creditors. A two-year moratorium was imposed on suits for distraint from creditors with respect to the lands named in the indenture. The act itself did not list all of the lands authorised for sale, nor did it list Browne's creditors. These lists are found in the indenture. The signatures of forty-three creditors are appended, yet this list is somewhat problematic. Four of the signatories (or more precisely, the signatures of their trustees) are not actually named as parties to the indenture. Of the fifty-five named parties, approximately twenty are not found among the signatures.[55] The indenture also specified that Browne was to cover the full cost of securing the act, and that the indenture would be void if no act had been passed by parliament within six months.

Browne worked closely with his creditors during the summer of 1695. Initial negotiations produced the indenture on which the act was based, while Browne and his agents supervised the progression of the bill through the Irish parliament, where his creditors paved the way for smooth progress. While the bill was under scrutiny in London, Browne employed agents to counter objections to the bill from any articlemen. The diligence of his agents is apparent from a letter written by John Stanton, a creditor based in Bristol, to one of Browne's estate managers:

> My father died the 6th of August last, and left all consigned to me. Pray write to your father to see and get himself and me secured by Mr Browne for I will not meddle about the business of parliament, as you have so often written about.[56]

The passage of the act surely came as a relief to Browne, taking the burden of negotiation with creditors out of his hands and providing a clear system of repayment. The punitive interest rate of 10% on his debts had been halved. Perhaps most importantly, article 13 of Limerick now had the force of law and the weight of the Irish administration behind it.

---

[54] Col. Garrett Moore, Bingham and Kennedy were creditors to John Browne, and co-debtors with Browne to other creditors.

[55] I have been unable to identify five of the signatories. Several other missing names may be covered by a signatory acting as trustee or assignee for several creditors.

[56] John Stanton to Robert Mason, Jr., 7 Oct. 1695 (N.L.I., Ms 40,900/6/20).

V

The administration moved swiftly to collect the quit-rent levy. Each Catholic landowner's contribution appears to have been decided by July 1696, allowing the lords justices to issue instructions to collectors detailing the amounts levied. Such judgments probably required attendance by Catholics at the privy council to supply information as to the size and value of their estates, particularly those who had not yet appeared before the court of claims. Further objections to the act were unlikely to have been entertained. Fragmentary evidence relating to the collection of quit-rent levies in Counties Galway, Limerick, Louth, Dublin and Kildare survives, occasionally giving details of the men and women on whom the levies were imposed, along with the amount.[57] Collection of the levy continued for a number of years, though each collector received instructions from the trustees for Browne's estate in November 1696 naming the creditor to whom they should remit their collections. A random lottery system governed the selection process for creditors. Richard Thompson appears to have served as clerk to the trustees, while each order to the collectors bore John Browne's endorsement: 'Allowed and approved by me'.

The surviving evidence relating to these payments is largely incomplete. Five orders to the Galway collector, Amias Bush, survive, while only one order (to Nicholas Westby, collector for County Limerick) is extant for the rest of the country.[58] Evidence relating to Kildare, Queen's County and King's County lists only the sums to be paid to creditors. Sir Patrick Bellew paid £37.5s.10½d in respect of his property in Counties Louth and Dublin.[59] Each of the five Galway orders levied part, if not all, of the money required on Clanricarde, amounting to a total of £797 out of the required £996. The remaining £199 was spread between Andrew Cheevers, John Cheevers, Lieutenant Malachy Connor, John Carroll, Captain Florence Callaghan, Captain Paul Daly, John Donnellan, Robert Dillon and Hyacinth Darcy.[60] In Limerick, £100 was levied on Colonel

---

[57] A note of money paid by Sir Patrick Bellew for Col. John Browne, 21 Nov. 1696 (Bellew of Barmeath Papers, C/2); N.L.I., Ms 40,901/2–3.

[58] N.L.I., Ms 40,901/2/16–21. This Amias Bush is probably Capt. Amias Bush, who lost his command in Col. Theodore Russell's foot regiment during Tyrconnell's Catholicisation of the Irish army. He was allowed 4s. a day from July 1689 by the English treasury in recognition of his service. He was later elected to the Irish parliament in 1707 and appointed customs collector for New Ross and Kilkenny (*C.S.P.D., 1686–7*, p. 52; *C.T.B., 1689–92*, p. 191; *H.I.P.*, iii, 333–4).

[59] 'A note of money paid by Sir Patrick Bellew for Col. John Browne', 21 Nov. 1696 (Bellew of Barmeath Papers, C/2).

[60] Clanricarde, John Cheevers, Donnellan, Carroll and Lt. Connor (who petitioned on behalf of his father, Dermot) were adjudicated within the articles of Limerick on 20 June 1692, 26 Nov., 6 Dec., 10 Dec. and 12 Dec. 1692 respectively.

[Nicholas] Purcell, James Riordan and Colonel John White with, presumably, his wife Bridget.[61]

The quit-rent levy was not always paid promptly. Of the money collected in Galway, £500 was allotted to John Stanton, all of which was to be paid by Clanricarde. By January 1699, only £283 had been paid.[62] Some discomfort for Catholics was inevitable. Thomas Barrett wrote to Browne to warn him that 'I find all the country is very fearful that owes you money; they keep off for fear of being taken'.[63] Whatever anger Browne's fellow Catholic landowners felt in relation to article 13 and the 1695 act is, however, impossible to trace beyond their opposition to the 1692 and 1695 bills. Delayed payment of the quit-rent may be interpreted as a rear-guard act of opposition to article 13, or as a sign of straitened circumstances. Lingering resentment towards Browne was evident in his agent Edmund Malone's observation that Browne had 'disobliged most gentlemen of those counties where his estate lies by too great a desire of extending the limits of his possessions beyond reason'.[64]

Implementation of the second part of the 1695 act – the sale of Browne's estate by trustees – did not actually begin until December 1698. Prior to this, Browne conducted only two transactions to cover encumbrances on his estate. A lease and release agreement was reached in February 1696 between Browne; Elinor, dowager Viscountess Mayo; and trustees for her legatees – thus fulfilling the requirements of the court judgment against Browne in 1682.[65] Agreement was also reached with Denny Muschamp on a debt to his wife Frances, dowager Viscountess Lanesborough (former wife of Sir George Lane).[66] However, Browne continued to keep accounts with his creditors and, up to 1698, pay off his debts with small, infrequent, augmentations of the quit-rent levy.[67]

Delayed implementation of the sale of estates authorised by acts of parliament was not, in England at least, uncommon.[68] In Browne's case, however, the failure of the trustees to initiate the sale of Browne's estate necessitated the introduction of a supplementary bill in the Irish parliament in November 1697. Beginning at the Irish privy council, the bill was transmitted to London on 4 September with a letter explaining that it had

---

[61] Col. Purcell and Col. White were adjudicated within the articles of Limerick on 25 and 27 May 1692 respectively (Simms, 'Irish Jacobites', pp 101, 104).

[62] N.L.I., Ms 40,901/2/16.

[63] Thomas Barrett to John Browne, 1 July 1696 (N.L.I., Ms 40,901/5/10).

[64] Edmund Malone, London, to John Bingham, 5 Mar. 1697 (P.R.O.N.I., T3134/1/11).

[65] N.L.I., Ms 40,889/25/3–4. See above, p. 24.

[66] N.L.I., Ms 40,889/25/1–2. Browne was subsequently released from this debt in March 1702 (N.L.I., Ms 40,889/28/2–3).

[67] N.L.I., Mss 40,901/2/9–15 (accounts for 1696); 40,901/3/1–7 (1697); 40,901/4/1–13 (1698).

[68] John Habakkuk, 'The rise and fall of English landed families, 1600–1800: II' in *Transactions of the Royal Historical Society*, 5th series, xxx (1980) p. 201.

been prepared by us at the request of the Protestant creditors, and is only an enlarging the time in the former act for the protecting the person of the said Colonel John Browne and for the more effectual putting the said act in execution.[69]

No amendments were made at the English privy council.[70] Edmund Malone, in London during October 1697 as agent for both John and his brother George Browne, probably kept John informed as to its progress. Following approval at the privy council, Malone wrote to Agmondisham Vesey, son of John, archbishop of Tuam, to ask him to suppress any potential opposition to the bill in the Irish parliament:

I pray prevail with Sir Henry Bingham not to oppose a small bill of privilege of Col. Browne's, which will soon come into the house of commons there from this side. I pray get him for his own dear uncle's sake and for my sake to befriend it. I protest if I could serve him in any part of the world I would heartily do it. My cousin John Bingham is deeply engaged for Col. Browne. I am in too; though it be not for much, 'tis more than I can at present spare, and if he loses his liberty it will confound us, for as I am a mortal man and a Christian, if he loses his liberty before his estate be sold it will not answer his debts. Tell Sir Henry so from me upon the sincerity of an honest man, though my uncle [Browne] I know has had vanity enough to say he would have a good estate left after his debts paid, for what reasons he knows best, but I understand his case better than he imagines, and have had reason to dive into it to my great sorrow, and I am content to be made a sacrifice if his estate at £2,500 a year, which he says 'tis let at, and all that he got by the Limerick money will pay his debts, though his estate were sold at 12 years purchase. I have given my cousin John Bingham my thoughts very candidly of matters, and 'tis much better to bring him to part freely with it and to join with his trustees in the sale which must be done forthwith, than by taking away that liberty, give him next opportunity not to be troubled at all the confusion that must follow in the disposition of that estate. I pray acquaint my lord archbishop with my proposals in this particular.[71]

Sir Henry Bingham sat in the commons for County Mayo and later purchased a significant portion of Browne's estate. He soon made trouble for Browne in parliament, though not in the manner feared by Malone as he raised no opposition to the proposed bill.

A bill 'for better securing the debts owing to the Protestant Creditors of Colonel John Browne' was introduced and read for the first time in the commons on 9 November 1697.[72] The bill quickly ran into difficulty with the appointment

---

[69] Irish lords justices and privy council to the English privy council, 4 Sept. 1697 (T.N.A., SP 63/359, f. 227; C.S.P.D., 1697, p. 352).

[70] T.N.A., PC 2/77, ff 81, 91–3 (16 Sept. 1697).

[71] Edmund Malone to Agmondisham Vesey, 14 Oct. 1697 (N.A.I., Sarsfield-Vesey papers). According to Tuam, Malone later converted to the Church of Ireland (Archbishop of Tuam to Agmondisham Vesey, 21 Dec. 1697 (N.A.I., Sarsfield-Vesey papers)). There is, however, some considerable doubt as to Malone's sincerity.

[72] C.J.I., ii, 212 (9 Nov. 1697).

of a committee on 12 November to inspect the 1695 act and report 'whether the fund granted by the said act exceeded the debt of £13,000 mentioned in the said act'. Later additions to the committee included creditors William Sprigge, Gideon Delaune and Edmund Reynell. On 13 November, Browne was granted the protection of the house to appear before the committee, which was enlarged on 18 November.[73] The remit of the committee was, presumably, to ascertain whether the quit-rent so far levied on Catholics had raised more than the sum intended. The committee's instructions referred to a debt of £13,000, whereas the 1695 act clearly specified the sum of £18,173.0s.8d. This may have been a genuine mistake or a more sinister attempt to cheat Browne out of the remainder. Either way, the prospect of the bill passing through parliament seemed to be fading.

Further trouble for Colonel Browne came from an unexpected direction when parliament initiated an investigation into another aspect of his affairs. On 17 November Sir Henry Bingham was ordered to lay a 'paper' before the commons, allegedly written by Browne and found among the papers of Patrick Tyrrell, former Catholic bishop of Meath. Bingham complied eight days later, with the alleged 'paper' revealed as a proposal for 'the utter extirpation of the Protestants and the Protestant Religion' in Ireland.[74] The timing of the revelation was hardly coincidental. By late October, word had filtered back to Dublin that the commons' Association bill had been amended at the English privy council after intensive lobbying by Irish Catholics.[75] The lords justices, Galway and Winchester, both wrote to Shrewsbury to express their disapproval, though when returned to Ireland the Association bill passed the commons on 20 November following a division (92:68).[76] Opposition in the lords was expected, with archbishop William King of Dublin noting that the penalty of praemunire for refusal to take the oath of supremacy (which Catholics could not do) was a likely sticking point:

> It seems a direct persecution to impose on [Roman Catholics] an oath to renounce an article of their faith. I think it reasonable that papists should be debarred all public trust, profit or power and kept from all such advantages as would put them in a capacity of disturbing the public peace, but think it hard to take away men's estates, liberties or lives merely because they differ in sentiments of religion.[77]

73 Ibid., 743–4 (12–13 Nov. 1697), 750 (18 Nov. 1697).
74 Ibid., 749, 760–2 (17 and 25 Nov. 1697).
75 The Association bill was prompted by a plot to assassinate William III and was closely modelled on an English act (7&8 Will III, c.26). For the Irish context see Bergin, 'Irish legislative procedure', i, 231–3; ibid., ii, 13–18; F.G. James, *Lords of the Ascendancy: the Irish house of lords and its members, 1600–1800* (Dublin, 1995), pp 60–2.
76 Galway to Shrewsbury, Winchester to same, 23 Oct. 1697 (H.M.C., *Buccleuch*, ii, 568–9); C.J.I., ii, 221 (20 Nov.).
77 William King to Lord Clifford, 20 Nov. 1697 (T.C.D., Ms 750/1/134). King later alleged that

The house of lords had form in this matter, with a significant minority expressing serious opposition to the bill for confirming the articles of Limerick. Following arrival in the lords on 24 November, the Association bill was scheduled for a second reading the following day; Bingham chose the day of the second reading to introduce his explosive 'paper'. A conference between the two houses to discuss the matter was immediately requested and granted, the commons deeming it to be a 'very proper time for so doing, when a bill is under your lordships' consideration for the preservation of his majesty's person and government'.[78] A select committee from each house attended a conference on 25 November, managed for the commons by Philip Savage and for the lords by William King. Notwithstanding efforts by the commons to sway the lords, the Association bill was rejected in the upper house on 27 November on the basis of two clauses; that for imposing the penalty of praemunire, and another excusing Quakers from taking the oaths.[79]

Aside from the general description offered above, no further detail as to the content of the alleged 'paper' is found in the journals.[80] Though he is identified by Malone as a possible opponent of Browne's bill, Bingham's introduction of the 'paper' seems to have been an attempt to garner support for the Association bill in the lords, rather than to scupper Browne's private bill. A report from the committee appointed to consider Browne's bill was delivered on 29 November, read twice and recommitted; it does not appear to have mentioned the 'paper'.[81] The following day parliament ordered the collectors of the quit-rent levy to chase any arrears and to remit collected moneys promptly. This was the last action taken on Browne's bill before parliament was prorogued.[82]

The 'paper' introduced by Bingham had been found among the papers of bishop Tyrrell, who died in 1692, which provides a *terminus ante quem* for its authorship. The decision to bring the 'paper' to parliament's attention in 1697 is made all the more curious by the fact that William King had made use of documents found among Tyrrell's effects in his *State of the Protestants of Ireland*,

the praemunire clause had been sent to England by 'a private hand', to be added at the privy council (King to Francis Annesley, 10 Jan. 1698 (T.C.D., Ms 750/1/154).

[78] *L.J.I.*, i, 658–61 (24–25 Nov. 1697); *C.J.I.*, ii, 226 (25 Nov. 1697).

[79] *L.J.I.*, i, 663–5 (27 Nov.); Galway to Shrewsbury, Methuen to same, Winchester to same, 27 Nov. 1697 (H.M.C., *Buccleuch*, ii, 581–4).

[80] It has been suggested that the 'paper' detailed a plot to kill William (R.H. Murray, *Revolutionary Ireland and its settlement* (Dublin, 1911), p. 313; Éamonn Ó Ciardha, *Ireland and the Jacobite cause, 1685–1766: a fatal attachment* (Dublin, 2002), p. 109, n. 85). However, this is not stated anywhere in contemporary correspondence or the journals. Had the 'paper' contained anything quite so incendiary, the reaction of the Irish parliament would surely have included the arrest of Browne.

[81] *C.J.I.*, ii, 229 (29 Nov. 1697). The committee's remit was expanded to permit investigation of the 'whole matter' of Browne's bill, but this does not seem to have encompassed the 'paper'.

[82] Ibid., 231 (30 Nov. 1697). Parliament was prorogued on 3 Dec.

first published in 1691. Had King noticed the paper, it would surely have been utilised by him and it is very likely that the 'paper' was a forgery. Bingham's use of John Browne as a foil to attempt to sway the lords in favour of the Association bill is even more baffling when one considers that the connections between the Bingham and Browne families ran deep. Bingham's uncle John was a co-debtor on some of John Browne's business engagements, George Browne was married to their kinswoman Alice, while Sir Henry himself had signed a petition to Sydney in September 1692, attesting to the good behaviour of George during the Williamite war.[83] Sir Henry may have banked on his ability to steer Browne's bill through parliament, with support from other creditor-MPs, even while the 'paper' was provoking controversy.

While it did not have the desired effect of ensuring passage of the Association bill, Bingham's 'paper' did enhance anti-Catholic sentiment in parliament. Resolutions in the commons, arising from the conference between both houses, spoke of frequent Catholic conspiracies, 'inhuman massacres' and rebellions since the Reformation. Several laws were identified as necessary for the security of William III and of the Protestant nation, including disqualification of Catholics from voting in elections to parliament, as well as legislation to impose (in addition to the oath of fidelity) oaths to abjure James II and his son and to renounce Papal authority.[84]

In 1698, Browne once again faced accusations of Catholic plotting, though in this instance the forum was not public and the accusations were probably not widely publicised, if at all. The allegations concerned contemporary seditious activity directed towards the restoration of James II or, failing that, preparations for the restoration of James Francis Stuart. In common with other prominent Catholics, Browne had been subjected to periodic arrest during the 1690s at times of heightened fears of a French-sponsored Jacobite invasion.[85] The accusations levelled at Browne in 1698, had they been proven, would have provoked a reaction from the Irish government beyond mere precautionary arrest. An anonymous letter sent to Thomas Tenison, archbishop of Canterbury, alleged continuing seditious activity by Browne as one of seven 'great managers' of Jacobite plotting in Ireland.[86] Four of the so-called managers are named in the 'Canterbury letter': Sir Stephen Rice, Sir Toby Butler, Denis Daly and Browne.

[83] P.R.O.N.I., T3134/1/6.
[84] C.J.I., ii, 229–30 (29 Nov. 1697).
[85] Sydney to Nottingham, 23 Jan. 1693 (C.S.P.D., 1693, pp 15–18); Cathaldus Giblin, 'Catalogue of material of Irish interest in the collections Nunziatura di Fiandra, Vatican archives' in Collectanea Hibernica, 4 (1961), p. 41; Ó Ciardha, Ireland and the Jacobite cause, pp 95–105.
[86] [Anon.] to Thomas Tenison, archbishop of Canterbury, 7 June 1698 (Lambeth Palace Library, Ms 935/38). All quotes below are from this letter unless otherwise specified. The letter has received brief attention, but has yet to be placed into its proper context (Ó Ciardha, Ireland and the Jacobite cause, p. 109).

Several merchants trading from Dublin, Waterford, Limerick and Galway were also implicated, though not named. The description offered of Irish Catholic plotting, assisted by well-known Jacobites then at the exiled court of St Germain, reflects an evolution from more usual portrayals of Catholic disloyalty. The 'Canterbury letter' alleged that plans for an invasion of Ireland by 8,000 troops from France had been thwarted by the Treaty of Ryswick. The remainder of the letter sketched a series of plots by Irish, English and Scottish Jacobites, and suggested covert Jacobite activity was behind some recent aspects of Irish parliamentary politics.

The first priority for the plotters, according to the 'Canterbury letter', was to sow discord among the Protestant polity in the three kingdoms, specifically between Episcopalians and Presbyterians. The plotters were to insinuate that the English parliament's attempts to restrain the powers of William III betrayed a desire to return to the days of the Commonwealth of the 1650s, which only James II's restoration could prevent. Irish agents in England were said to be very active, particularly Sir John Edgeworth and 'Malone'.[87] This latter was almost certainly a reference to Edmund Malone, who was instructed to

> pretend to be a mighty Williamite, when he is in the company of such, and to tell them that the chief of the Irish are, since they see what the king of France is, indirectly in our king's interest, and inclined to embrace the Protestant religion.

In Scotland, Episcopalians were to be reminded of the 'injuries done them'. Scottish Jacobites were also to be employed in Ulster, where ministers were to foment unrest among the Presbyterians by preaching adherence to the Covenant and animosity to 'Popery and prelacy', along with a refusal to pay tithes to the Church of Ireland or appear before ecclesiastical courts: 'By this means they hope they may create such feuds between the Episcopal party and Presbyterians, as may raise troubles that may favour their designs'. Simultaneously, the Irish 'managers' were to alarm the Church of Ireland bishops by spreading rumours of stirrings among the Ulster Presbyterians, and to convince them of the necessity of favouring Irish Catholics 'who will surely stand by them against the Scotch'.

---

[87] Sir John was the great-grandfather of R.L. Edgeworth, author (with Maria Edgeworth) of *Memoirs of Richard Lovell Edgeworth, Esq* (2 vols, London, 1820). According to this memoir, Sir John Edgeworth's son Francis raised a regiment for William III, which Sir John then later commanded. However, another source notes that the regiment was in fact formed in 1684 and first commanded by Arthur Forbes, earl of Granard. The regiment went to England in Nov. 1688 under Granard. Sir John was a major in the regiment, and inherited command when Granard sided with James II. Francis was a captain in the regiment, later becoming known as 'Protestant Frank' for the strength of his faith (*Memoirs of Richard Lovell Edgeworth, Esq*, i, 14–15; Charles Dalton, 'Richard Lovell Edgeworth's "Memoirs"' in *Notes and Queries*, ser. 8, viii (1895), p. 381; John Burke, *A genealogical and heraldic history of the commoners of Great Britain and Ireland* (4 vols, London, 1833–8), iv, 754).

To support this theory, the 'Canterbury letter' referred to opposition from Church of Ireland bishops in the house of lords to several bills debated in the Irish parliament, such as the bills for confirming the articles of Limerick and of Association.

Concurrently, the Irish 'managers' were to 'breed all the ill blood they can between England and Ireland'. This was to be done by arguing in favour of legislation to be passed in England restricting Irish trade, thus driving a wedge between the polities of both nations. Irish Protestant merchants would then, it was believed, join with Catholics in supporting the return of James II. The author of the 'Canterbury letter' here displayed a keen awareness of one of the central pieces of legislation passed by the 1689 parliament, which promised freedom of trade for Irish merchants to any part of Europe, Africa, Asia and America.[88] Intermarriage between Catholics and Protestants was to be encouraged, as were insincere conversions. Marriage into well-placed families by insincere converts would allow the plotters to 'come into favour, and be trusted by the English'. In addition, the Prince of Wales was to be raised as a Protestant as a hedge against his father's failure to reclaim the throne.[89] Dispensations were to be given to all Catholics who converted, while the converts were to use all their powers of persuasion to have their spouses and children brought into the Catholic fold. The alleged plot also included support for lessening troop numbers in Ireland.

The anonymous author of the 'Canterbury letter' displayed throughout a good knowledge of the principal figures in Irish Catholic and Protestant society. Tensions between the Church of Ireland bishops and aggressively anti-Catholic members of the commons, such as the Brodricks and Robert Molesworth, were recounted in depth. A far greater level of sophistication was attributed to Catholic plotting than Irish Protestants generally conceded, and represented a significant advance on the usual claim that Catholics simply planned the 'extirpation' of Irish Protestants. The manner of revelation also improved on the more typical discovery of seditious letters on the streets of Dublin, the steps of Christ Church Cathedral or among the papers of long dead Catholic bishops.[90] The 'Canterbury letter' implied that a copy had also been sent to the English lord chancellor, John, Baron Somers.

---

[88] 'An act for the advance and improvement of trade, and for encouragement and increase of shipping, and navigation.' (5 James II, c. 29). See Bergin & Lyall (eds), *The acts of James II's Irish parliament*, pp 83–7.

[89] James Francis Edward Stuart ('The Old Pretender') would, in 1714, come under pressure to convert to the Church of England from Robert Harley, earl of Oxford, and Henry St John, Viscount Bolingbroke, when Queen Anne's death was imminent.

[90] For example, see W. Jones to Sir Robert Talbot, 10 Dec. 1661 (Bodl., Carte Ms 31, f. 372); Clarendon to Rochester, 31 Aug. 1686 (S.W. Singer (ed.), *The correspondence of Henry Hyde, earl of Clarendon, and of his brother, Laurence Hyde, earl of Rochester* (2 vols, London, 1828), i, 567–9).

Leaving aside the improbability of the letter's allegations, the fact that the author of the 'Canterbury letter' chose to remain anonymous casts immediate doubt on the strength of the evidence to support his allegations: a point conceded several times by the author. The author's motivation was the promotion of further anti-Catholic legislation, so punitive in nature that it would discourage all future thoughts of plots or rebellions:

> If the managers I have mentioned could be severely handled, and it were set forth in the preamble of an act of parliament, that this was for their plotting and contriving against the government (which I cannot prove because I have it from one person no body present) this alone would secure us. It would terrify others, and we might spare the trouble and odium of making severe general laws ... There are ways of dealing with Rice, Butler and Daly, which will be one of the most necessary pieces of justice that was ever done, for it will secure all.

Failing such a law, several 'general' laws were identified as necessary for the security of Ireland: to make it treason to correspond with anyone in France except for trade; to prevent 'missionaries' entering Ireland; to prevent Protestants marrying Catholics for at least eight years; and to prevent Irish Catholics corresponding with Catholics or Jacobites in England.

The identification of Sir Stephen Rice, Sir Toby Butler, Denis Daly and John Browne as four of the 'great managers' was probably due to their prominence within the Irish Catholic community. The 'Canterbury letter' displayed a keen awareness of their importance to James II's Irish administration. Butler was described as 'crafty and inveterate', while Rice was blamed for the imprisonment of William Stewart, Viscount Mountjoy, in the Bastille in 1689.[91] Daly was noted as an articleman of Galway and was said to be well regarded by Irish Protestants as a result of his opposition to the 1689 parliament's act of repeal. In sharp contrast to descriptions of his character found elsewhere, he was referred to as a 'subtle and dangerous man'.[92]

Of all the Irish 'managers', John Browne features most prominently in the letter. He was said to have boasted that he had 'hit the nail on the head' by secretly marrying one of his daughters to the son of Colonel Roger Moore. One of Browne's sons was alleged to have been the chief messenger between the Irish 'managers' and their counterparts in France, to have had an introduction to James II and, typically, to have been 'bred among the Jesuits'. Browne himself was labelled 'the most dangerous and most intriguing of all the managers'. The 'Canterbury letter' supported this claim by providing an alternative perspective

---

[91] Mountjoy was imprisoned while on an embassy to James II from Tyrconnell, seeking permission to make terms with William in early 1689: Simms, *Jacobite Ireland*, p. 53. See also Mountjoy's entry in the *D.I.B.*

[92] For more positive opinions of Daly among Irish Protestants, see above, pp 128–9.

on article 13, in part closely mirroring protests registered by Irish Catholics against the article. In other respects, a uniquely Protestant or anti-Jacobite interpretation of article 13 was expressed.

The debt owed to Browne by the Jacobite administration for supplies provided during the Williamite war was said to have been fabricated, and the rationale proffered by Browne for article 13 (that he could not pay his Protestant creditors) was a 'plausible and cunning pretence. In this article (as I am informed by a person who was privy to the whole thing) there was a strange complication of rogueries.' The 'Canterbury letter' admitted that Browne did indeed have Protestant creditors, but alleged that the number of these creditors mysteriously increased after Limerick, once Browne requested their connivance. Reference was made to the incongruity present between Browne's claims that he could not on his own repay his creditors and his continued boasts that his estate was worth £4,000 per annum. As to the imposition of Browne's debt on the articlemen and protectees, Browne was alleged to have persuaded Sarsfield to acquiesce by signing a promissory note to provide James II (or his son James Francis Edward) with £10,000 in the event of an invasion of Ireland or England. In addition, 'the principal Irish out of whose estates this money is to be raised, are to be fully reimbursed from France'. By imposing his debt on his fellow Catholics, Browne

> might by this means be reckoned not to be in favour with his own party, but might the better strike in with the Protestants, and carry on a plot for the cause afterwards without being suspected by the Protestants.

The 'Canterbury letter' also alleged that Browne had engaged in 'frequent turns from Papist to Protestant first, and then in King James's time, from Protestant to Papist again'. Only the discovery of Browne's plans for the Protestant population, found in bishop Tyrrell's papers and read before parliament in November 1697 (see above), prevented Browne from getting an 'interest' among the Irish Protestant polity.

None of the information regarding Jacobite plotting contained in the letter should be taken seriously. Though clearly politically well informed, the allegations against Browne, Daly, Butler and Rice stretch the limits of credulity. No plausible connection between any of these men and Jacobite plotting in the 1690s has yet been identified. The very detailed allegations against Browne and his family include obvious errors of fact. None of Browne's daughters married into the Moore family, though a Roger Moore was a creditor of Browne's, which may have been the source of the accusation.[93] Neither of Browne's two sons,

---

93 Browne's daughters Bridget, Elizabeth and Mary married, respectively, Edward Bermingham, Lord Athenry (in 1687); John Bermingham (pre-1699); and Theobald Burke, future 6th Viscount

Peter or Valentine, fit the description tendered. Peter spent much of the 1690s in England, which may have allowed for insinuations that his absences from Ireland were spent at the Stuart court.

VI

The interpretation of article 13 offered by the 'Canterbury letter', while echoing some of the more rational arguments found within Catholic opposition to the article, was for the most part fantastical. By 1691, judgments for thirty-nine distinct creditors (or their agents) had been entered against Browne in the courts – he had no need to invent debts. Moreover, possible motivations for Protestants to engage in such fraud are difficult to imagine. Similarly, there is no evidence that John Browne engaged in opportunistic conversion. The Browne family had been Catholic since at least the 1640s, and the reversion of the family to Protestantism would not take place until the 1720s.

On the other hand, the 'Bingham paper' incident and 'Canterbury letter' are useful to illustrate a number of points, for both Browne and the Catholic interest in general. For the wider Catholic interest, the accusations levelled against Browne and the other 'managers' demonstrated the fragile nature of Protestant sufferance towards individual Catholics in the 1690s. Browne was one of the few Irish Catholics with a substantial support base in parliament in the form of his creditors, even if that support would have been somewhat conditional. If even he failed to gain a sympathetic hearing in that forum, Catholics could be certain of nothing. Negative connotations associated with service rendered to James II's Irish government continued to dog men like Daly, Butler and Rice; three prominent Catholics who enjoyed a better standing with the Irish government than most. Though the 'Canterbury letter' does not appear to have been taken seriously or circulated by Tenison, the Stuart court's presence at St Germain and the continued threat of invasion meant that the Jacobite past of these men could be used against them at any time. Such considerations were paramount in the formulation of the penal laws. The year 1697 was notable in this regard for the mutilated form of the parliamentary confirmation given to the articles of Limerick, the Bishops' Banishment Act and the 'Act to prevent Protestants inter-marrying with Papists'. Worse would follow in 1699 with the 'Act to prevent Papists being solicitors.'

Mayo (in 1702). It is possible that Elizabeth or Mary contracted a prior marriage, but unlikely. For their marriages see below, pp 221–4. For evidence of Browne's financial dealings with Roger Moore, see N.L.I., Mss 40,889/21/5; 40,894/5/3–8; 40,897/1/7; 40,897/2/9–10; 40,897/6/9; 40,898/1/15–16; 40,901/1/16–17; 40,901/2/3–7.

For Browne personally, his financial security remained precarious. The 1695 private act had yet to be fully implemented, while interest on his debts accrued with every passing year. Legislative protection for article 13 of Limerick had been secured in the private act, which counted as a significant achievement. Even so, Browne was in need of a second act of parliament from 1 November 1697, following the expiration of his protection from arrest for debt. As Edmund Malone observed, 'if he loses his liberty before his estate be sold it will not answer his debts'.[94] Just as important was the realisation that two of the five years allowed for the sale of his estate had already elapsed, with no progress made. Browne thus remained utterly dependent on the forbearance of his creditors and the good will of the Irish government and parliament. Any hint of Jacobite associations was potentially ruinous, turning parliament against any bills in Browne's name. It must, then, have been a considerable relief when the trustees responsible for selling his estate settled down to business in August 1698.

[94] Malone to Agmondisham Vesey, 14 Oct. 1697 (N.A.I., Sarsfield-Vesey papers).

7

'*I fear a bill relating to me be gone for England*': Implementing article 13 of Limerick, 1698–1708[1]

From September 1698 until his death in 1711, the bulk of John Browne's time was occupied by the sale of his estate and the process of clearing his debts. A second act of parliament to regulate the sale of the Browne estate was found to be necessary as early as 1697. The first two sections of this chapter examine several attempts to have this second act passed by the Irish parliament in 1698 and again during the session of 1703–4, before eventual success in 1705. Even that was not the final word on the matter, with a third act sought in 1709. The efforts of 1698 were important as they marked the first time that Browne was not actively involved in seeking the acts, which threatened to take away whatever control he still retained of his affairs. Browne fought hard against such a scenario, occasionally making a personal appearance in Dublin, though more usually relying on his eldest son, Peter, and various agents to protect his interests in Dublin and in London. Section III traces the sale of the Browne estate between 1698 and 1708, and payments made to creditors in the same period. By the time the process had concluded, almost nothing of Browne's once vast estate remained in his possession. Peter Browne became increasingly important in this process as the seventeenth century drew to a close. Peter's ambitions in life were subordinated to his family obligations as heir to the estate – or what little would remain once his father's debts were paid. Perhaps the greatest challenge facing Peter was the daunting prospect of rebuilding his family's landed interest and fortune. That work was undertaken as the sale of the estate progressed. Several purchasers of the estate clearly acted in concert with the Brownes, allowing Peter to immediately take out favourable leases as he sought to resurrect his family's fortunes.

I

A combination of factors had prevented Browne and his creditors securing a second act for the sale of the estate in 1697. For his creditors, a second act was

---

[1] Quotation taken from Col. Browne to Luke Hussey, [Oct.] 1703 (N.L.I., Ms 40,904/5/4).

desirable to speed up the sale process, which had not begun by the end of the year. For Browne, a second act was imperative to renew his freedom from arrest for debt, which expired on 1 November 1697. From the time of parliament's prorogation in December 1697 until the second act was finally obtained in 1705, Browne's freedom of movement was curtailed. Correspondence destined for Westport was intermittently sent under cover to his various agents, including Luke Hussey, Augustine Lynagh and James Lyon, particularly when sent from Dublin.[2] This was especially true during 1703, when law suits brought against Browne by Elinor Warren and Stephen Creagh necessitated orders from the court of exchequer to allow Browne appear before the court without fear of arrest.[3]

In what was probably a resumption of efforts begun in the summer of 1697, the Irish house of commons once more attempted to initiate heads of a bill for the sale of Browne's estate in December 1698. On this occasion, the attempt proved abortive at an early stage. On 2 December, the commons appointed a select committee consisting of Sir Henry Bingham, Henry Tenison and Alan Brodrick, solicitor general of Ireland, to prepare heads of a bill 'to enable and oblige the trustees named in an act passed in the last session of parliament, entitled, an act for securing the debts owing to the Protestant creditors of Colonel John Browne'.[4] The committee does not appear to have produced a report or draft bill. Trouble was, however, mounting for Browne in the lords. A petition from Reverend Gideon Johnston and his wife Frances, concerning a debt allegedly owed by Browne to them, prompted the lords to appoint a select committee of nine to investigate the matter. Johnston's petition may have prompted a motion 'in behalf of the clerks and officers of this house' to have the protection procured for Browne by Laurence Barry, earl of Barrymore, rescinded, so that the clerks and officers might 'be enabled to get the fees due to them, for passing the said John Browne's bill'. The following day, it was reported by the committee that the petitioners could not have any satisfaction until Browne's estate was sold. The committee's investigation showed that the 1695 act had given the trustees for Browne's estate power, but no obligation, to sell the estate. Accordingly, leave was given for heads of a bill 'to supply the defects of an act, entitled, an act for securing the debts owing to the Protestant creditors of Colonel John Browne'.[5] As was the case with the commons' efforts, the lords committee produced no heads of a bill. Though lords and commons tackled Browne's debts simultaneously, the two attempts to draft heads of bills do not appear to have been related. The extension of a parliamentary protection to

2 See N.L.I., Mss 40,903/4; 40,904/3/4, 8–10, 18.
3 N.L.I., Ms 40,904/1/13–14.
4 C.J.I., ii, 284 (2 Dec.).
5 L.J.I., i, 721–2 (1 Dec.).

Browne by Barrymore suggests that Browne was aware of and supported the commons' initiative. Johnston may have caught Browne off guard by using his presence in Dublin to initiate proceedings in the lords to recover debts he claimed were owed to him.[6]

The second session of the 1695 parliament ended on 26 January 1699, with the December 1698 proceedings on Browne's debt in both houses representing the last engagement on the issue before the dissolution of parliament. Despite the failure to procure a second act, the proceedings in parliament prompted immediate action on the part of the trustees for Browne's estate. The first parcel of the estate was sold to John Vesey, archbishop of Tuam, on 9 December. By the time the next Irish parliament met, on 21 September 1703, significant progress had been made. A total of £24,465 had been raised through the sale of almost 87,000 acres, with a further £3,143 raised through the sale of 2,696 acres in November and December 1703. Even so, by mid-October 1703 Browne's debts were again the subject of parliamentary scrutiny in the lords.

On 14 October, the lords received a petition from three of Browne's creditors (Gideon Johnston, George Kennedy and William Pullein), requesting an act of parliament for the specific purpose of discharging debts owed to them.[7] The lords ordered archbishop Vesey and Simon Digby, bishop of Elphin, to draw up heads of a bill for this purpose, with clauses 'for the relief of Mrs Mary Huntington', widow and relict of Dr Robert Huntington (former provost of Trinity College and bishop of Raphoe), and for William Lloyd, bishop of Killala and Achonry.[8] A week later, a clause to secure £500 for William Palmer was also ordered to be included in the bill.[9] On 25 October heads of a bill 'for the sale of Colonel John Browne's estate in the counties of Mayo and Galway, for the payment of his creditors' were presented by Elphin and ordered to lie on the table.[10] As had been the case with the lords initiative of December 1698, Browne was caught off guard by the actions of the upper house. Informing Browne of the initial progress of the Johnston petition, Edmund Malone advised his uncle to

---

[6] Browne's accounts show that he had previously owed money to Johnston, but received an acquittance from the debt in 1701 (N.L.I., Mss 40,903/3/10; 40,904/5/2). Johnston's second wife was Henrietta Dering and the couple emigrated to America in 1706, settling in Charles Town (Charleston), South Carolina, in 1708. Henrietta is commonly regarded as America's first female artist of note.

[7] See above, pp 29–30 and 164–5 for Kennedy's status as both creditor to and co-debtor with Browne. Pullein had become mortgagee to Browne in May 1692 (N.L.I., Mss 40,895/5; 40,895/6; 40,896/3; 40,896/8; 40,897/3; 40,898/1/3).

[8] L.J.I., ii, 20 (14 Oct. 1703). Proceedings in parliament may have prompted Browne to deal immediately with his debt to Lloyd; less than a month later, he was released from all obligations to Lloyd (N.L.I., Ms 40,904/1/8).

[9] L.J.I., ii, 26 (20 Oct. 1703).

[10] L.J.I., ii, 28 (25 Oct. 1703).

come immediately to Dublin to 'mind your proper defence'.[11] Browne's other principal agent in Dublin, Luke Hussey, also urged Browne to come to the city. Hussey reported that Malone and a Mr Delamare advised feeing counsel for presentation of a counter petition, while Baron Coningsby, the former lord justice and signatory to the articles of Limerick, cautioned that 'care should be taken of it in your absence, and that he would do all the service that he could'. Opposition would not be cheap: 'I shall want money to go on with it.'[12] The counter petition was presented to the lords on 26 October.[13]

Management of the affair in parliament was left to Hussey and Malone, as Browne had informed Hussey just three days previously that 'the floods and storms are excessive great so as I can scarce travel and indeed I am not well'.[14] The petition argued that great progress had been made under the terms of the 1695 private act: £26,000 had been realised from sales of Browne's lands, with a further £14,000 raised 'by virtue of the said act' – a sum that was likely to have been largely made up by the Catholic quit-rent levy. All told, almost £40,000 had been paid to Browne's creditors. Purchasers for part of the remaining estate were also in place. More pertinently, Johnston's and Kennedy's claims were challenged as fraudulent. Browne claimed to have receipts proving the discharge of any debt to Kennedy, while Johnston had never previously made any claim against Browne, 'though he always lived within ten miles of your petitioner's house in the country'.[15] William Pullein's claim was settled through the sale of land in Mayo on 25 November 1703.[16] On 29 October, a select committee was appointed to consider the draft heads, consisting of the archbishop of Tuam, the bishops of Elphin, Ferns, Killala, Limerick, and Killaloe, along with Viscount Charlemont, Viscount Lanesborough, and Baron Coningsby. While they were deliberating, Frederick Trench, one of the purchasers of Browne's estate, also presented a petition to the lords opposing the proposed heads of a bill.[17] Nevertheless the committee reported on 11 November that they had agreed on heads, at which time counsel for both sides were heard at the bar of the house. Browne's counsel was unable to convince the lords to drop the bill,

11 Edmund Malone to Col. Browne, 16 Oct. 1703 (N.L.I., Ms 40,904/3/15).
12 Luke Hussey to Col. Browne, 19 Oct. 1703 (N.L.I., Ms 40,904/3/18). The letter is addressed to Darby O'Bryan but clearly intended for Browne. 'Mr Delamare' may have been John Delamare, a lawyer and native of County Westmeath who had sat in the 1689 parliament as MP for Kells, County Meath.
13 L.J.I., ii, 29 (26 Oct. 1703).
14 Col. Browne to Hussey, 23 Oct. 1703 (N.L.I., Ms 40,904/5/2).
15 Draft petition from John Browne to the house of lords, [n.d.] (N.L.I., Ms 40,904/2/2). Though clearly a draft, with various emendations interlineated, this version of the petition is annotated in Browne's hand: 'This was presented on Tuesday, 26 October 1703'. Pullein's debt was noted as a mortgage, but the draft petition is largely illegible in the section dealing with Pullein.
16 See table 6 below, footnote to Sir Henry Bingham in sales listed for barony of Carra '1st side'.
17 L.J.I., ii, 34 (6 Nov. 1703).

though his arguments did prompt an order for the heads to be recommitted and a clause inserted allowing Browne one year to sell his remaining estate, with the trustees' consent, failing which the trustees would afterwards have two years to sell Browne's estate without his consent, to clear his debts. By 15 November it was reported that the heads, including the above clause, had been delivered to the lord lieutenant, Laurence Hyde, earl of Rochester.[18]

Gideon Johnston added to Browne's worries on 9 November by presenting a second petition to the commons. Though this situation bears certain similarities to the concurrent inquiries into Browne's affairs in both houses during December 1698, the initiator of both inquiries in 1703 was Johnston. Indeed, his petition to the commons arose from an altogether different motive to the petition presented to the lords. In an echo of the proceedings on Browne's estate in parliament during November 1697, Johnston's petition requested that the commons draft heads of a bill for selling Browne's estate 'to answer what he hath received over and above £13,000 granted him by act of parliament out of the Irish estates, restorable by the articles of Limerick and Galway'. As in 1697, £13,000 was incorrectly cited as the amount to be raised by the levy. Revenge and greed spurred Johnston's petition to the commons and deliberate attempt to undervalue the quit-rent levy, and he requested 'such a share of the money for the discovery, and for the losses he sustained by the said Colonel Browne's means'.[19] Richard Thompson, clerk of the quit-rents and to the privy council, was ordered to lay all papers relating to Browne's affairs before a select committee. The commons made two separate representations to Rochester, the lord lieutenant, requesting the papers. Rochester signalled his willingness to oblige, but the materials were never delivered to the commons and the matter is not mentioned in the journal after 27 November.[20] It is not clear why the commons never received the requested material, though it must be speculated that delivery from the lords to Rochester of heads of a bill relating to Browne on 15 November negated the urgency of the matter.

Having failed in his attempt to quash the bill in parliament, Browne turned his attention to the executive branch of government. Perhaps dissatisfied with the performance of his agents Browne managed his business at the Irish privy council personally.[21] He presented two petitions to the council in late November, both of which illustrate why Browne was opposed to the lords' bill despite his desperate need for a second act to assist in the sale of his estate.

[18] *L.J.I.*, ii, 31, 37–44 (29 Oct., 10–11, 13, 15, 24 Nov. 1703).

[19] *C.J.I.*, ii, 361 (9 Nov. 1703).

[20] *C.J.I.*, ii, 364, 369, 372–3, 391 (12, 16, 18–19, 27 Nov. 1703).

[21] Col. Browne to Luke Hussey, Nov. 1703 (N.L.I., Ms 40,904/5 (3 letters)). The letter dated 12 November places Browne at Kinturk. Hussey was then sent to Mayo, in order to gather together all relevant writings, letters and deeds and send them to Browne in Dublin.

Browne claimed that some aspects of the bill were drafted 'to the prejudice of your petitioner and to the purchasers under the late [1695] Act of Parliament'. However, though he had not initially sought the bill, Browne implied that his support for its transmission could be attained, provided certain amendments were made:

> In as much therefore as private bills for sale of men's estates without their own consent are things extraordinarily seldom favoured, and that the said heads of bill as now proposed are in many respects very grievous to your petitioner, who cannot thereunto consent unless rectified and amended.

According to Browne, as the bill stood it 'defeated' many of the sales already made by him in co-operation with the trustees. The trustees were now prevented from concluding mortgages on Browne's estate, while each future transaction was also to be subject to poundage – a requirement that had not been part of the 1695 act, nor had the trustees previously sought poundage.[22] While the bill granted Browne and his co-debtors a further year's protection from arrest, his heir Peter had been omitted from the provision. Gideon Johnston's claim, which Browne vigorously denied, was also sanctioned by the bill. Browne thus requested the removal of the poundage requirement; that the trustees should have power to sell *and* to mortgage; and that Peter also be offered protection from arrest. With regard to Johnston's claim, Browne pleaded for a stay in the case 'without proof [of the debt] first made and your petitioner heard thereunto'.[23]

The privy council dealt with the matter speedily and the bill had been sent to London by 27 November.[24] A bill 'for the sale of Colonel John Browne's estate for payment of his Protestant creditors' was referred by the English privy council to the law officers on 26 December.[25] Early in the new year William Wogan, agent in London for chief secretary Edward Southwell, informed his patron that Browne's bill 'will come too late'.[26] Nevertheless, the English law officers delivered their report to the privy council on 28 January, incorporating two substantial additions and several amendments. The additions suggest that Browne's endeavours at the Irish privy council were largely fruitless. The corollary conclusion is that Browne's agents in London enjoyed much greater success, prevailing upon the English law officers to insert the desired provisions

---

[22] Poundage most commonly refers to duty on merchandise imported or exported, but may be more generally a commission or fee based on a percentage of a particular sum of money. See table 7 for poundage as applied to the sale of Browne's estate from 1705, at a rate of 5%.

[23] Petitions of Col. Browne to the Irish privy council, Nov. 1703 (N.L.I., Ms 40,904/2/1, 3).

[24] Edward Southwell to Nottingham, 27 Nov. 1703 (T.N.A., SP 63/363, ff 49–51; C.S.P.D., 1703–4, pp 216–17).

[25] T.N.A., PC 2/79, f. 486 (26 Dec. 1703).

[26] William Wogan to Edward Southwell, 4 Jan. 1704 (B.L., Add. Ms 37,673, f. 33).

that had failed to gain credit in Dublin. Peter Browne, then resident in London, probably supervised the business. No copy of the bill is extant, making many of the more elliptical amendments as recorded in the privy council register difficult to decipher. Several seem technical in nature. One appears to extend the protection from arrest for Browne and his co-debtors to two years. The first substantive addition implemented one of Browne's primary concerns. Within the space of four years from 1 January 1704, the trustees and Browne were empowered to 'lease, let and mortgage the premises or any part thereof ... to satisfy and discharge the debts and encumbrances of the said John Browne', provided the majority of the creditors agreed. The second major addition was appended to the bill:

> And for the maintenance and support of the said John Browne and his family and for enabling him to better attend on the execution of this act ... the said trustees or any three of them ... are hereby empowered, authorised and required to pay out of the rents, issues and profits of the said estate unto the said John Browne, his heirs and assigns the sum of £200 per annum.

The trustees were also authorised to make supplementary payments, up to a limit of an additional £200 per annum, again with the consent of the creditors. In the event that Browne's debts were still not cleared by 1 January 1708, ownership of whatever portion of the estate remained unsold was to revert to Browne (or his heirs) without prejudice to any mortgages on the lands involved.[27]

These additions to the bill were a significant victory for Browne. Greater freedom regarding the method of disposing of the estate was secured, as was the small annual allowance. On the other hand, if it can be assumed that the Irish privy council transmitted the bill without the amendments requested by Browne, the victory was not total. Peter Browne remained outside the protection of the bill, while Gideon Johnston's claim was not removed. The bill passed the privy council on the day of the report and was probably among those returned to Dublin by Nottingham on 3 February.[28] It was not presented to the Irish house of lords until 2 March, where it passed all stages and was delivered to the commons by the next day.[29] By 4 March the bill had been read twice in the commons and committed. However, prorogation of parliament once again scuppered legislation relating to Browne – Ormond ended the

---

[27] T.N.A., PC 2/80, ff 33–5 (28 Jan. 1704).
[28] Francis Annesley to Ormond, 29 Jan. 1704 (H.M.C., *Ormonde Mss*, n.s., viii, 56–6); Nottingham to Southwell, 3 Feb. 1704 (T.N.A., SP 67/3, f. 84; *C.S.P.D., 1703–4*, p. 521). Nottingham later noted that all bills had been despatched by 10 February. These bills arrived in Dublin on 17 February (Nottingham to Ormond; Ormond to Nottingham 10 Feb. & 18 Feb. 1703 (T.N.A., SP 67/3, f. 85; T.N.A., SP 63/364, f. 63; *C.S.P.D., 1703–4*, pp 528, 536)).
[29] *L.J.I.*, ii, 77–82 (2–3 Mar. 1704); *C.J.I.*, ii, 412–13 (3–4 Mar. 1704).

session later that day. The bill was thus lost on a technicality.[30] However, the loss may not have been an innocent one. According to Edward Southwell, Browne intentionally engineered the delay between return of the bill from London and its introduction to parliament: the commons then 'would not leap over the forms of reading it more than once in a day, so it fell by the prorogation'.[31] It seems that the successes gained at Whitehall were not sufficient to make the bill acceptable to Browne. Given the failure to secure protection from arrest for Peter, or the deletion of Johnston's claim, this is perhaps not surprising.

II

A second private act for the sale of the Browne estate was finally enacted by the Irish parliament in the summer of 1705, receiving the royal assent in June.[32] On this occasion, it seems likely that Browne supported the initiative. No copy of the act and virtually no ancillary material survives to shed light on its genesis and progress through the legislative process. The few sources that do survive raise as many questions as are answered.

Browne appears to have come to an accommodation with Gideon Johnston by February 1705.[33] Indeed, Johnston appears have worked with Browne on this occasion, which suggests that the resolution of the dispute depended upon successful passage of the bill – a tactic previously used by Browne in negotiations with his creditors in 1692 and 1695. Writing from London on 15 February, Peter Browne informed his father that

> Your bill was sent away by post ... Mr Gideon Johnston stays here at some business of his own this fortnight. You need not apprehend that anybody would presume to alter a letter here or there for I have an exact copy as it passed here. The bill had gone away with Mr Stone but that Johnston had not money to pay the fees, which he borrowed at last from a gentleman of my acquaintance; though I would not seem to have any hand in it. The gentleman has Johnston's bond for the money. This to yourself.[34]

[30] James Kelly, *Poynings' law: the making of law in Ireland, 1660–1800* (Dublin, 2007), p. 155.

[31] Southwell to Nottingham, 4 Mar. 1704 (T.N.A., SP 63/364, f. 107; *C.S.P.D., 1703–4*, p. 558).

[32] 'An act for the sale of Colonel John Browne's estate for payment of his creditors' (4 Anne, c. 6 (private)).

[33] Col. Browne to Hussey, 15 Feb. 1705 (N.L.I., Ms 40,905/6/6).

[34] Peter Browne to Col. Browne, 15 Feb. 1705 (N.L.I., Ms 40,905/7/1). 'Mr Stone' was probably Richard Stone, MP for Newtown Limavady in the 1695 parliament and private secretary to Capell in 1695. It was his connection with Capell that saw him first employed by the Irish government to manage their legislative programme at Whitehall, a role he fulfilled for several years. While in London, Stone and other managers employed by the Irish government were also employed by individuals to lobby for private legislation (Bergin, 'Irish legislative procedure', i, 179–84).

However, the timeline presented here is problematic. The act passed by the Irish parliament in June 1705 was first introduced as heads of a bill in the Irish commons on 12 March 1705. Was the bill that Peter Browne referred to a month earlier the same measure? The language used by Peter ('I have an exact copy as it passed here') implies that the bill sent with Stone had received some type of formal endorsement in London, yet the 1705 act was not transmitted to London by the Irish privy council until 29 March.[35] The answer may lie in an attempt made by Browne to have a bill introduced to the English parliament in October 1704. In the middle of that month, Peter wrote to Luke Hussey from London to complain about his father's inertia:

> I admire I do not hear from my father in answer to the several letters I lately wrote about an act of parliament to be had here next sessions for the sale of his estate for payment of his debts, in which we might secure our liberty for some years. I believe £100 would pay the expense, but if matters were well managed there the creditors would be willing to bear at least part of the expense, if not all, and it being a bill by consent it would meet with no opposition here. I believe I have some friends in both houses who will be very willing to do me any service. The parliament meets the 24th instant about important affairs.[36]

The English parliament had been prorogued since 3 April but was due to reconvene on 24 October. No other material relating to this effort has been located, with no mention of the bill in the English parliamentary journals. Peter's letter of 15 February 1705 expressed the hope that

> Your bill will meet with no opposition for 'tis much to your advantage. You have two years to do what you please, in that time I doubt not but all matters will be settled to satisfaction, for I wish you were more easy.[37]

The earliest recorded consideration of legislation concerning Browne's debts at the English privy council is 20 April 1705, which tallies with the bill's transmission on 29 March.[38] It is possible that Peter Browne's letter is misdated and refers to the 1704 legislation, which was approved by the English privy council and returned to Dublin in February 1704. This reading might also be corroborated by a reference within the letter to a bill for the Hollow Blades corporation, which similarly progressed through the English privy council early in 1704.[39]

35 Ormond and the Irish privy council to [Sir Charles Hedges], 29 Mar. 1705 (T.N.A., SP 63/365, ff 159–60).

36 Peter Browne to Luke Hussey, 17 Oct. 1704 (N.L.I., Ms 40,904/5/20). The 'several letters' referred to are not extant.

37 Peter Browne to Col. Browne, 15 Feb. 1705 (N.L.I., Ms 40,905/7/1).

38 T.N.A., PC 2/80, f. 319.

39 For the Hollow Blades corporation, see Simms, *Williamite confiscation*, pp 151–4.

However, this measure failed on its return to the Irish parliament, which also led to a second transmission from Dublin in March 1705. In addition, Peter wrote to his cousin Patrick Magawley on 4 February 1705 to tell him that 'my father's bill is there by this. I did what I could in that matter and not a penny sent to defray the expense.'[40]

One other element that further complicates the timeline is that the Irish government began preparing a legislative programme in December and January, 1704–5, during which some fourteen failed bills from previous parliamentary sessions were considered. In 1705 the Irish government transmitted fifteen bills that had failed forerunners, of which Browne's bill was one, making it likely that the legislation was discussed by the Irish government in December 1704.[41] Two members of the commons were given leave to introduce heads of a bill relating to Browne on 10 March 1705 – Henry Tenison and Sir Henry Bingham. Tenison had previously been involved in the legislative programme's preparation in December 1704.[42] The first transmission of legislation from Dublin occurred on 8 January 1705.[43] If Peter Browne's letters are not misdated, the procedure followed relating to the 1705 Browne act was highly irregular, but in the absence of further evidence the exact chronology and methodology remains obscure.

On 15 February Browne instructed his agent Luke Hussey that he was to

> get my nephew [Edmund] Malone to Lord C[oningsby] and Peter, lest one bill should be transmitted to my prejudice. I need not mind you of the extreme care in everything, and especially at the council table … I am sure the Archbishop, Sir Henry Bingham and Mr [Gerald] Cuffe will do me all that Ned Malone advises.[44]

Tenison and Bingham presented the heads on 12 March. By 16 March, the bill had passed all stages in the commons and was delivered to the viceroy to be laid before the Irish privy council.[45] In their letter accompanying the bill to London the Irish government described it as a commons' initiative, based on the failure of the 1704 bill 'by reason of the prorogation' and that it was necessary as 'the power given by a former act passed some time ago [has] not been fully executed'. Again, no copy survives. The bill was referred by the English privy council on 20 April to the English law officers with their report delivered six

---

40 Peter Browne to Patrick Magawley, 4 Feb. 1705 (N.L.I., Ms 40,905/9/16).

41 Bergin, 'Irish legislative procedure', i, 104–7.

42 H.I.P., vi, 384.

43 Ormond and Irish privy council to [Sir Charles Hedges], 8 Jan. 1705 (T.N.A., SP 63/365, f. 25). The legislation transmitted dealt with grand juries, fraudulent devises, blasphemy and the linen industry.

44 Col. Browne to Luke Hussey, 15 Feb. 1705 (N.L.I., Ms 40,905/6/6).

45 C.J.I., ii, 445, 448, 453 (10, 12, 16 Mar. 1705).

days later, recommending several amendments. One notable amendment was the removal of the word 'Protestant' from the title, leaving it as 'An act for sale of Colonel John Browne's estate for payment of his creditors'. The use of the term 'Protestant creditors' in the title of every legislative measure pursued from 1692 onwards had always been misleading, given Sir Stephen Rice's status as principal creditor. This longstanding misnomer may have finally been corrected due to the specific mention of the Catholic Theobald, Viscount Mayo, within the bill. The recorded amendments imply that a dispute between Browne and Viscount Mayo (his son-in-law) was to be settled by the act.[46] Reference was also made in the amendments to the attempt to secure an act in 1704; it seems that the expenses of the attempt were to be paid. Approved by the English privy council, the bill was returned to Dublin on 8 May.[47]

John Browne and Garrett Moore both secured the protection of the commons as the house dealt with the returned bill. Its progress through the Irish parliament was swift and relatively smooth and it received the royal assent on 16 June.[48] The provisions of the act are generally unknown, though it is probably fair to assume that the measure approved by the English privy council closely resembled the bill approved by the same body just one year earlier. Thus it can be surmised that Browne and his co-debtors were extended at least two years of freedom from arrest, including Peter Browne. The year 1713 was mentioned in the amendments made at the English privy council, suggesting that the trustees were given until that year to complete the sale of the estate, though this would have been double the time allowed in the 1704 bill. Responsibility for the sale of the estate remained vested in trustees, consisting of the barons of the exchequer.

The tenth and final engagement by the Irish parliament with John Browne's debt, and by extension article 13 of the articles of Limerick, occurred in June 1709. The only reference located is found in the commons' journals; there is no extant material among the Westport papers. Yet another act was sought, this time by Sir Henry Bingham, Gerald Cuffe and Richard Tisdall, 'in behalf of themselves and the rest of the purchasers of the estate of Colonel John Browne'. All three men had purchased portions of the Browne estate after April 1704. On this occasion, the concern was not to supplement the provisions of the 1695 and 1705 acts. Rather, leave was granted to bring in heads of a bill for 'confirming the sales made by the trustees for sale of the said Colonel Browne's

---

[46] See below, pp 222–4, for the disputes between Browne and Viscount Mayo, who married John Browne's daughter Mary (and thus his first cousin) on 8 July 1702.
[47] T.N.A., PC 2/80, ff 319, 341–3 (8 May 1705); Sir Charles Hedges to Ormond, 5 May 1705 (T.N.A., SP 67/3, f. 110); Coningsby to Ormond, 8 May 1705 (H.M.C., *Ormonde Mss*, n.s., viii, 154).
[48] *C.J.I.*, ii, 483 (16 June 1705).

estate'. A seventeen-man committee was appointed to draft heads, which were considered by a committee of the whole house on 8 June. Sir Henry Bingham reported that progress had been made and further consideration was scheduled for the following week. No further mention of the bill or related committees occurs in the journals.[49] The intent of the bill is clear, though the motivation for its initiation is not. There may have been a question as to the legitimacy of the purchasers' title, perhaps arising from a suspected defect in either of the two previously enacted measures. A more plausible motive was to safeguard the work of the trustees, whose involvement in the sale of the Browne estate had come to an end that January. The apparent lack of interest in the matter after 8 June suggests that the purchasers' need was not pressing.

Until Gideon Johnston's petition to the lords in December 1698, Browne either supported or actively promoted all proposed legislation for the sale of his estate, in tandem with his creditors. The 1698 petition was the first of at least two parliamentary initiatives, both instigated by Johnston, that were begun without Browne's knowledge or his support. Browne was, however, represented by very capable agents in Dublin and London who organised effective opposition. Browne used Johnston's 1703 petitions to his advantage, ensuring that when a bill appeared before the English privy council in February 1704 without Browne's consent, it was amended largely (though not fully) in accordance with his wishes. Johnston's 1698 petition also provides the first indication that the creditors' joint interest in the management of Browne's estate and debt repayment had begun to fracture. This may be explained by the fact that many debts had been satisfied or were actively being engaged with by Browne and the trustees. There was also an element of fraud in Johnston's claim, particularly in his attempt to deceive parliament with respect to the Catholic quit-rent levy. As such, it is not surprising that Johnston was joined by only one other legitimate creditor, William Palmer, whose claim against Browne dated from the mid- to late-1690s.

The fracturing of the creditor group, or their disengagement from the minutiae of Browne's affairs, perhaps explains why Browne does not seem to have negotiated seriously with them after the late 1690s. The method of debt repayment had effectively been settled in 1695. The creditors thus had no pressing need for a second act – their primary concern was the implementation of the 1695 act. Browne's accounts show that most, though not quite all, of the pre-1692 debts were discharged by 1701. This also explains Browne's difficulty in having amendments made to the 1704 bill; without the self-interested support of a large body of creditors, as had existed in the commons in 1695 and 1697, desirable amendments were less likely. It is also necessary here to draw a distinction between the creditor group and the purchasers of Browne's

---

49 *C.J.I.*, ii, 598, 603 (2, 8 June 1709).

estate who petitioned parliament in 1709. The interest of the latter in a third act relating to the estate was probably a further layer of security on their investment. Browne's interest in pursuing a second act related to his desire to secure prolonged freedom from arrest for debt for himself and his co-debtors as the sale of his estate took far longer than anticipated. His opposition to the 1704 bill was prompted by a desire to thwart Johnston's claim, thereby ensuring that his still ruinous burden of debt was not further increased.

III

The sale of Browne's estate by the trustees appointed in 1695 was finally initiated in December 1698. The majority of purchasers were connected in some fashion to Browne and were based in Connacht. The comprehensive (though not complete) collection of extant sale agreements allows a clear picture of the progress of the sale to emerge. These sale agreements are complemented by a meticulous account book, kept by John Browne, which records all land transactions up to April 1704 in minute detail – profitable and unprofitable acres sold to each purchaser; the yearly rent; sale price; and the creditors to whom the revenue was disbursed.[50] After 1704, records become less clear, causing some difficulty for anyone seeking to reconstruct the process of clearing debts. What can be said with certainty is that, in 1698, Browne's estate in Counties Galway and Mayo consisted of 155,476 acres. Of this total 39,136 were profitable, with a combined annual rent of £3,456.3s.9d. This total rental income included twenty-two houses owned by Browne in Westport town, eighteen of which had gardens. Five of these eighteen houses also had parkland. Combined rent from these properties was £29.15s. By April 1704, £27,698 had been raised by the sale of 89,628 acres, with a combined annual rent of £1,816.[51]

Between April 1704 and July 1708 fifteen further sales were concluded, incorporating at least 18,431 acres, for a total of £19,990. After 1704 the records contained in the account book are slightly more problematic. For example, the figure of 18,431 acres slightly exceeds the stock of 18,180 profitable acres known to have remained available for sale. The account book no longer records the number of unprofitable acres that accompanied each sale, or the annual rent of each portion sold; however, it is clear that the acreage listed for these sales was profitable only. The explanation for the discrepancy probably lies in either faulty record-keeping or, more likely, double entries for sales completed with Sir Henry Bingham, Gerald Cuffe and William Chambers before and after April 1704. Portions of these sales may have been recorded twice.

50 N.L.I., Ms 40,915/1.
51 See tables 3 and 4.

Tables 3 and 4 record the overall progress of the sale of Browne's estate up to April 1704, at which point the sale of the estate was suspended. No land sale was completed between 23 March 1704 and 11 March 1707, the latter date marking a resumption of the process after the uncertainty surrounding procurement of a second act. As can be seen from table 5, all of the Browne estate in County Galway had been sold by June 1700. Table 4 shows that in County Mayo, 48,501 acres had been sold by April 1704, of which 14,810 were profitable. The Galway estate was sold for an average of fourteen years' purchase, while lands sold in Mayo fetched an average of fifteen and a half years' purchase. Tables 5, 6 and 7 provide a more detailed breakdown of the sale of the estate in each county. No sale was concluded for less than thirteen years' purchase. This implies that if, as has been argued, the price of land was depressed in the decade following the Williamite confiscations, it was not long rebounding in Connacht at least.[52] The rate at which individual lands were sold after April 1704 (table 7) has not been calculated, as the account book does not record the rental value of each denomination. A rough estimate of twelve years' purchase can be arrived at by utilising the known remainder of rental income in April 1704 (£1,639) and the total raised by sale of the lands between 1707 and 1708 (£19,990). The entire estate appears to have been sold by 1708, though the account book notes that Peter Browne possessed an estate of some 9,000 acres after that year. The process whereby this was achieved is examined below, alongside a more detailed discussion of the tables that follow.

Catholics and Protestants availed of the opportunity to purchase parts of Browne's estate, which for the most part occurred before the 1704 and 1709 Popery acts restricted the right of Catholics to purchase land. Table 8 shows the seven principal purchasers of the Browne estate, arranged in order of profitable acreage purchased.

These seven men were responsible for the purchase of 23,802 (61%) of the Browne estate's profitable acreage in Counties Mayo and Galway. Known associated unprofitable land amounted to 64,144 acres (55%) and it can be assumed that there was a good deal more unprofitable land included in sales agreed with Higgins, Malone and Tisdall. Richard Thompson was almost certainly the same man who leased land from Browne in the 1690s and had acted as agent for Sir Stephen Rice. He may also have been the Richard Thompson who served as MP in the Irish parliament between 1692 and 1713 and as clerk to the privy council. Other notable purchasers included Sir Henry Bingham; John Vesey, archbishop of Tuam; Sir Walter Blake; Arthur French; Gerald Cuffe; George Browne; and Josias Browne.

---

[52] Patrick Walsh, *The making of the Irish Protestant ascendancy: the life of William Conolly, 1662–1729* (Woodbridge, 2010), p. 68.

Table 3: Total acreage and sales of Browne's estate by April 1704 in Co. Galway

Barony	Profitable Acres	Unprofitable Acres	Owned/Sold	Annual Rent	Portion Sold	Purchase Money
Ballymoe Half-Barony	949	716	1,665/1,665	£142.7s	£142.7s	£2,000
Killian	940	203	1,143/1,143	£141	£141	£1,833
Leitrim	620	0	620/620	£90	£90	£1,200
Moycullen & Ballynahinch	1,198	25,860	27,058/27,058	£120	£120	£1,600
Rosse Half-Barony	2,439	8,202	10,641/10,641	£209.18s	£209.18s	£3,500
Total	6,146	34,981	41,127/41,127	£703.5s	£703.5s	£10,133[1]

[1] Average of 14½ years' purchase for this portion of the estate.

Table 4: Total acreage and sales of Browne's estate by April 1704 in Co. Mayo

Barony	Profitable Acres	Unprofitable Acres	Owned/Sold	Annual Rent	Portion Sold	Purchase Money
Gallen	1,197	1,296	2,493/2,493	£112	£112	£2,521
Erris	1,419	6,228	7,647/7,647	£150	£150	£2,000
Kilmaine	2,414	633	3,047/3,047	£237.15s.4d	£231.17s[1]	£4,318
Tirawley	7,080	23,854	30,934/30,934	£400	£400	£5,200
Carra	6,107	6,374[2]	12,481/4,380[3]	£529.7s.5d	£219.8s.3d	£3,436.17s
Murrisk	6,577	22,429	29,006/0	£615.6s	£0	£0
Burrishoole	8,196	20,545	28,741/0	£708.10s	£0	£0
Total	32,990 (18,180 unsold)	81,359 (47,668 unsold)	114,349/48,501	£2,752.18s.9d	£1,113.5s.3d	£17,475.17s[4]

Total acreage in Cos. Galway and Mayo: 155,476 (39,136 prof./116,340 unprof.). Unsold: 65,848 (18,180 prof./47,668 unprof.).

[1] This represented a total sale of Browne's lands in Kilmaine barony – the account book does not make clear the reason for the small discrepancy between the stated annual rent and the portion of annual rent sold.

[2] Browne's acreage calculations in Carra were in error. He noted 6,088 profitable, and only 5,490 unprofitable acres. His calculation of rental income was correct.

[3] Of the 4,380 acres sold, 2,700 were profitable (1,680 unprofitable). Total acreage in the barony of Carra was incorrectly calculated by Browne as 11,572 acres.

[4] Average of 15½ years' purchase for lands sold in Mayo up to April 1704.

Table 5: Sale of John Browne's Estate in Co. Galway, 1699–1700.[1]
Col. JB refers to Colonel John Browne; S. Rice refers to Sir Stephen Rice

Barony	Prof acres	Unprof acres	Total acres	Rent p.a.	Purchaser	Price	Payee	To payee	Date of Sale
Killian	940	203	1,143	£141	Parson Robert Smith	£1,833[2] 13 yrs	1. Maj. Delamar[3] 2. James Cruise[4] 3. S. Rice	1. £735 2. £582.8 3. £515.12	28 Feb. 1699
Leitrim	620	-	620	£90	Thomas Croasdaile[5]	£1,200 13 yrs	S. Rice	£1,200	2 Feb. 1699
Ballymoe ½Barony	949	716	1,712	£142.7.	Arthur French	£2,000[6] 7 yrs	S. Rice	£2,000	Jul. 1699

[1] The number of years' purchase – calculated by dividing the sale price by the annual rent and rounding to the nearest whole figure – is shown in **bold** in the 'Price' column. Many deeds relating to sales agreed between 1698 and 1708 have been preserved among the Westport papers. These have been used in assembling the tables to supply some deficiencies in the account book. The date of each sale is the element most frequently missing, while other details recorded in the account book are occasionally (though infrequently) at odds with those in the deeds. A case in point is the sale of 1,143 acres in the barony of Killian, County Galway, to Parson Robert Smith on 28 February 1699 (table 5). The account book records a sale price of £1,833, but the sale agreement specifies a price of £1,317. Similarly, land sold to Michael Cormick in the half barony of Erris, County Mayo, is recorded at a purchase price of either £2,000 (account book) or £1,600 (sale agreement – see table 6).

[2] The sale agreement for this purchase gives the purchase money as £1,317 (N.L.I., Ms 40,889/34/3–4). The reason for the discrepancy between the account book and the sale agreement is unknown.

[3] 'To Maj. Delamar for Rich. Dillon's children.' This 'Maj. Delamar' is probably Major Walter Delamere, who was adjudicated within the articles of Limerick on 18 June 1694 (Simms, 'Irish Jacobites, p. 93). Portions of the land sold to Smith had previously been mortgaged to Delamere, Richard Dillon and James Cruise (N.L.I., Ms 40,901/1/10). See also following note.

[4] 'To James Cruise in full of a mortgage due to him on said lands.' Cruise and Browne had connections from unspecified land transactions dating from 1675. In February and March 1678 the two men agreed several sales, leases and mortgages relating to land in the barony of Killian. Browne was in debt to Cruise as early as November 1678 (N.L.I., Mss 40,889/33/5–7; 40,884/5/3; 40,894/2/12; 40,895/8/3).

[5] See N.L.I., Ms 40,889/34/2 for sale agreement. Sir Stephen Rice and Col. Garrett Moore were also parties to the sale.

[6] A summary of the sales made on a later page of the account book notes that this land was sold for £2,000, suggesting 14 years' purchase. The main entry for this sale says £1,000. However, this would imply only 7 years' purchase. Arthur French leased the lands in question on 6 Aug. 1698 (N.L.I., Ms 40,889/34/1), but the sale agreement is not extant.

Barony	Prof acres	Unprof acres	Total acres	Rent p.a.	Purchaser	Price	Payee	To payee	Date of Sale
Moycullen & Ballynahinch	1,198	25,860	27,058	£120	Capt. Richard Martin[7]	£1,600 13 yrs	1. Thos. Cunneys[8] 2. Wm Skerritt[9] 3. S. Rice 4. James Power[10] 5. Col. JB	1. £428.10 2. £100 3. 100 4. £144.15.8 5. £826.14.4	7 Jul. 1699
Rosse Half-Barony	2,439	8,202	10,641	£209.18	James Napper & Thomas Smith[11]	£3,500 17 yrs	1. S. Rice 2. James Grace 3. Wm Alcock[12] 4. Eliz Johnson 5. Same 6. Gideon Delaune 7. Robert Pooly 8. Solomon Bethlemite 9. Edward Stratford 10. Lady Newcomen 11. Bryan Kelly 12. Col. Gorge 13. [?] Taafe 14. Lord Tyrconnell 15. Col. Garrett Moore 16. Murtagh Dowling 17. Thomas Sisson	1. £1,300 2. £100 3. £35.12.6 4. £424.10 5. £333.14.6 6. £80 7. £61.6.4½ 8. £100 9. £100 10. £100 11. £50 12. £100 13. £25 14. £40 15. £50 16. £300 17. £200	24 Jun. 1700

[7] Account book annotated: 'Most part of these lands in Capt. Richard Martin's hands the rest waste and sold to him at this rent for £1,600 and a release for Brendrum[?] & Knockranot[?] from French & Tully.' The sale agreement is not extant.

[8] 'To Thos Cunys in full of mortgage on these lands.'

[9] 'To William Skerritt for John Joyce.'

[10] 'To James Power for Thos. Arthur.'

[11] No sale agreement is extant for this transaction. These lands were immediately leased back to Peter Browne – see below for discussion.

[12] 'Wm Alcock for Ja: Lee [Sir James Leigh?].'

Table 6: Sale of John Browne's Estate in Co. Mayo, 1698–1707.[1]
Col. JB refers to John Browne; S. Rice refers to Sir Stephen Rice

Barony	Prof. acres	Unprof. Acres	Total acres	Rent p.a.	Purchaser	Purchase money	Payee	To payee	Date of Sale
Kilmaine	2,414	633	3,047	£231.17	1. Patrick Darcy[2] 2. George Browne[3] 3. Sir Walter Blake[4] 4. Edmond Fynn[5] 5. Arch. Tuam[6] 6. Arthur French[7]	£4,318 18 yrs (average – see footnotes for more detailed breakdown)	See footnotes for breakdown	See footnotes for breakdown (Total to S. Rice: £3,403.13s)	1698–9

[1] The number of years' purchase – calculated by dividing the sale price by the annual rent, rounded to the nearest whole figure – is shown in **bold** in the 'Purchase money' column.

[2] **Paid** £1,300 for 677 profitable acres (179 unprof.). **Annual rent:** £54.12 (24 yrs purchase). **Date of sale:** 24 Feb. 1699. **Paid to:** Dominick Blake (£370); Sir Stephen Rice (£930). See N.L.I., Ms 40,889/27/2 for sale agreement. The account book states that the purchaser was Francis Darcy – however, the sale agreement names Patrick Darcy, who is the more likely given his prior dealings with Browne regarding land in Kilmaine Barony in 1684 (N.L.I., Ms 40,897/5/8).

[3] **Paid:** £760 for 380 profitable acres (89 unprof.). **Annual rent:** £35.14s (21 yrs purchase). **Date of sale:** 16 Sept. 1699. **Paid to:** Sir Stephen Rice (£760). See N.L.I., Ms 40,889/27/1 for sale agreement.

[4] **Paid:** £778 for 389 profitable acres (145 unprof.). **Annual rent:** £36.15s. (21 yrs purchase). **Date of sale:** 2 Sept. 1699. **Paid to:** Sir Stephen Rice (£778). Annotated: 'To Sir Walter Blake by deeds dated 2 Sept. 1699 in trust for Joz. Browne.' See N.L.I., Ms 40,889/26/6 for sale agreement.

Also Paid: £140 for 68 profitable acres (0 unprof.). **Annual rent:** £10.10s (13 yrs purchase). **Date of sale:** 7 Jul. 1699. **Paid to:** Sir Stephen Rice (£140). See N.L.I., Ms 40,889/26/4–5 for sale agreement. Acres specified as plantation acres.

[5] **Paid:** £566 for 283 profitable acres (42 unprof.). **Annual rent:** £18.18s (30 yrs purchase). Date of Sale: 6 Sept. 1699. **Paid to:** Patt Darcy 'in full of a mortgage on the said lands' (£243); Sir Stephen Rice (£323). See N.L.I., Ms 40,889/26/7–8 for sale agreement.

[6] **Paid to:** Doctor Gorges (£250); Allen Swanwich[?] (£51.17s); Sir Stephen Rice (£472.13s). See N.L.I., Ms 40,889/25/6 for sale agreement. **Annual rent:** £70 (12 yrs purchase). **Date of sale:** 9 Dec. 1698. **Paid** £774 (plus a bond of £80 – note that all interest on the bond was remitted) for 570 profitable acres (178 unprof.).

[7] Annotated: 'Among the lands in the half barony of Ballymoe'. See table 5.

Barony	Prof. acres	Unprof. Acres	Total acres	Rent p.a.	Purchase money	Purchaser	Payee	To payee	Date of Sale
Tirawley	7,080	23,854	30,934	£400	£5,200 13 yrs	Richard Thompson	1. Richard Thompson[8] 2. S. Rice	1. £2,200 2. £3,000	1 Jul. 1699
Erris Half-Barony	1,419	6,228	7,647	£150	£2,000[9] 13 yrs	Michael Cormick	1. Robert Johnson[10] 2. Mortagh Dowling 3. Col. JB	1. £1,300 2. £400 3. £300	20 Jun. 1700
Gallen	1,197	1,296	2,493	£166[11]	£2,521 (£400+ £2,121)[14] 15 yrs	1. Will Chambers & Jo. Dunbar[12] 2. Richard Martin[13] 3. Frederick Trench	1. Thos. [Scurlock?] 2. Robert Johnson 3. John Nolan[15] 4. Col. JB	1. £200 2. £200[16] 3. £1,080 4. £1,041	1702

[8] **Paid:** £5,200 for 7,080 profitable acres (23,854 unprof.). Date of Sale: 30 June 1699. **Annual rent:** £400 (13 yrs purchase). **Paid to:** Browne remitted £2,200 of the purchase money to Thompson for debts owed to him. Thompson thus paid £3,000 in total for the lands. This sum was paid to Sir Stephen Rice. See N.L.I., Ms 40,889/26/1–2 for sale agreement.

[9] See N.L.I., Ms 40,889/27/5 for sale agreement, which states that the consideration money was £1,600. Browne and his heirs were to have the right to any minerals on the land. See N.L.I., Ms 40,889/27/6 for the immediate mortgage of these lands by Michael and Francis Cormick to John Browne (20 June 1700) for £1,257 and a lease for 500 years. The mortgage money was owed as a debt to Robert Johnson.

[10] 'To Robert Johnson Esq., for Mr Pa: Dennis.'

[11] The rent for lands listed in Gallen was £112. However, part of the money paid by Trench was for lands in Barony of Carra, annual rent £54.

[12] **Paid:** £400 for 260 acres. **Date of sale:** 2 May 1702. No detail as to profitability of the land can be provided due to unclear nature of notation for this sale. See N.L.I., Ms 40,889/24/4 for sale agreement, where the consideration money is noted as £390.

[13] Martin's inclusion as a purchaser may relate to his purchase of lands in Moycullen and Ballynahinch baronies in Co. Galway. There is no extant record of a sale to Martin in the barony of Gallen. There is also no sale agreement extant for Frederick Trench.

[14] Trench paid £2,121 – also included in this figure was land in Barony of Carra.

[15] 'To John Nolan in full of his mortgage on the lands of Prison.'

[16] [Scurlock?] and Johnson paid in Chambers and Dunbar purchase money. Nolan and Browne paid from Trench purchase money.

Barony	Prof. acres	Unprof. Acres	Total acres	Rent p.a.	Purchaser	Purchase money	Payee	To payee	Date of Sale
Carra ('1st Side')	1,810 (2,700)	1,227 (1,706)	3,037 (4,406)	£163.6.3 (£219.8.3)	1. Gerald Cuffe[17] 2. Sir Henry Bingham[18] 3. Dr Feilding Shaw[19] 4. John Browne of the Neale[20] 5. Richard Martin[21] 6. Frederick Trench[22]	£3,436.17 21 yrs (average – see footnotes for more detailed breakdown)	See footnotes for breakdown	See footnotes for breakdown	1702–3

[17] **Paid:** £1,302.12s for 668 profitable acres (413 unprof.). **Annual rent:** £47.6s (27 yrs purchase). **Date of sale:** 3 Dec. 1703. **Payable to:** Robert Johnson (£1,151.1s.6d.); Robert Welsh 'for a mortgage from Lord Mayo on Thinetown[?]' (£100); 'For an allowance for some leases Robert Welsh had on some of those lands from Lord Mayo' (£51.10s.6d). See N.L.I., Ms 40,889/28/7 for sale agreement.

[18] **Paid:** £1,119.6s for 574 profitable acres (314 unprof.). **Annual rent:** £49.7s (22 yrs purchase). **Date of sale:** 25 Nov. 1703. **Payable to:** Robert Johnson (£459.6s); William Pullein 'in full of a mortgage he had on part of said lands from my Lord Mayo' (£660). See N.L.I., Ms 40,889/28/6 for sale agreement.

[19] **Paid:** £720.19s for 421 profitable acres (306 unprof.). **Annual rent:** £55.13s (13 yrs purchase). **Date of sale:** 25 Nov. 1703. **Payable to:** Robert Johnson (£720). See N.L.I., Ms 40,889/28/5 for sale agreement. £100 was also due to paid to John Browne, though this is not noted in the account book nor is it included in the sale price.

[20] **Paid:** £294 for 147 profitable acres (168 unprof.). **Annual rent:** £10.10s.3d (28 yrs purchase). **Date of sale:** 6 Mar. 1702. **Payable to:** Robert Johnson (£200); Col. JB (£94). See N.L.I., Ms 40,889/28/1 for sale agreement, where the consideration money is given as £288.

[21] **Paid:** [Included in purchase of lands in Baronies of Moycullen and Ballynahinch – See table 5] for 653 profitable acres (453 unprof.). **Annual rent:** £44.2s.

[22] **Paid:** [Included in purchase of lands in Barony of Gallen] for 237 profitable acres (26 unprof.). **Annual rent:** £12.

Barony	Prof. acres	Unprof. Acres	Total acres	Rent p.a.	Purchaser	Purchase money	Payee	To payee	Date of Sale
Carra ('2nd Side')[23]	3,388	3,784	7,172	£309.19.2	Mortg. To Robert Johnson **Subseq. sold to:** 1. Gerald Cuffe[24] 2. Sir Henry Bingham[25] 3. Robert Lewis[26]	Mortg. For £4,000[27] 13 yrs	[£4,000 to Col. JB in mortgage] **Sale paymts. to:** 1. Robert Johnson 2. Robert Johnson & Peter Browne 3. Robert Johnson	1. £1,018 2. £441 3. £346	[Mortgaged in 1700]; Sold in 1707

[23] Note on the final page dealing with sale of lands in Carra Barony that: 'These lands [referring to denomination leased by Anthony Garvey] with the rest of the lands in this Barony [referring to '2nd Side' denominations] are mortgaged to Robert Johnson, Esq., by deed 22 Oct. 1700, for the sum of £4,000.' See N.L.I., MS 40,889/27/9 for mortgage agreement, where the mortgage sum is specified as £3,600, and below for discussion. See also Ms 40,902/1/11–12 for a nineteenth-century copy of the mortgage, where the sum is given as £4,000.

[24] **Paid** £1,018 for 346 profitable acres (215 unprof.). **Annual rent** £51.4s (20 yrs purchase). Feb. 1707. **Paid to:** Robert Johnson (£1,018). There is no sale agreement extant.

[25] **Paid** £441 for 235 profitable acres (2,590 unprof.). **Annual rent** £22.1s (20 yrs purchase). Feb. 1707. **Paid to:** Robert Johnson (£368); Peter Browne (£73). See N.L.I., Ms 40,889/29/1 for sale agreement relating to 53 acres in Ballybanaun. The agreement relating to the second half of the purchase is not extant.

[26] **Paid** £346 for 173 profitable acres (46 unprof.). **Annual rent** £16.6s (21 yrs purchase). Feb. 1707. **Paid to:** Robert Johnson (£346). There is no sale agreement extant.

[27] Mortgaged to Robert Johnson.

Table 7: Sale of John Browne's estate, April 1704 – July 1708

No. of Acres Sold	Purchaser	Purchase Money	Payees
672[1]	Gerald Cuffe	£1,133.6s.10d	1. Robert Johnson: £1,076.13s.10d 2. Poundage: £56.13s
514[2]	Sir Henry Bingham	£1,173	1. Robert Johnson: £973 2. Peter Browne: £148.15s 3. Poundage: £51.5s
173	Robert Lewis	£346	1. Robert Johnson: £328.14s 2. Poundage: £17.6s
668[3]	William Chambers	£923	1. Jean Fitzgerald: £166.9s 2. Thomas Fottrell: £213.11s.6d 3. William Chambers: £135.9s.4d 4. Rich. Barry & William Frith[?]: £31.4s 5. Col. JB: £20 6. John Usher:[4] £152.8s.4d 7. Jacob Peppard: £137.16s.10d 8. Poundage: £44.1s
937	Francis Bayly	£1,930	1. Lady Clanmalier: £1,833.10s 2. Poundage: £96.10s
1,055	Arthur Knox	£1,573	1. Robert Johnson: £99 2. Arthur Knox: [?] 3. Peter Browne: [?] 4. Poundage: [?][5]

[1] Probably includes lands sold prior to April 1704.
[2] Probably includes lands sold prior to April 1704.
[3] Probably includes lands sold prior to April 1704.
[4] For Jane, Lady Newcomen, wife of Sir Thomas Newcomen.
[5] Disbursements to Knox, Browne and for poundage not recorded. Applying a rate of 5%, poundage was likely to have been approx. £78.13s.

No. of Acres Sold	Purchaser	Purchase Money	Payees
4,411 (20&21 Feb. 1708)[6]	Bryan Higgins	£3,229.10s	1. Garrett Moore's executors: £2,826.10s.9d 2. John Dillon: £249.3s.7d 3. Poundage: £153.15s.8d
1,675 [8 July 1708?][7]	Gerald Burke	£2,580	1. Theobald, Viscount Mayo: £2,451 2. Poundage: £129
295 (8 July 1708)[8]	Gerald Burke	£255	1. Theobald, Viscount Mayo: £242.5s 2. Poundage: £12.15s
3,422 (1&2 July 1708)[9]	Richard Malone	£3,410	1. Edward, Lord Athenry: £2,300 2. Peter Browne: £300 3. Denis Daly, Junior: £305.6s 4. William Sprigg: £183.2s 5. Stephen Creagh: £151.1s.6d 6. Poundage: £170.10s
245	Dominick Burke	£100	1. John Bates: £52.8s 2. William Goulding: £41.7s 3. Poundage: £6.5s

[6] See N.L.I., Ms 40,889/29/3–4 for sale agreement. The lands involved were located in the baronies of Murrisk and Burrishoole. These lands were immediately leased back to Peter Browne. See below for discussion.

[7] Though the original sale agreement does not survive, related evidence suggests that the sale was completed on or just before 8 July 1708. The following day, Theobald, Viscount Mayo, settled the castle and lands of Castleburke and the purchase money from Gerald Burke's purchase of lands in the baronies of Murrisk and Burrishoole (for £2,580 and £258 respectively) on his wife and children. Mayo was owed £2,869.9s by Browne, arising from his marriage to Browne's daughter Mary. See N.L.I., Ms 40,906/1/4 for a late eighteenth-century copy of this settlement.

[8] See N.L.I., Ms 40,889/30/3 for sale agreement, where the purchase money is given as £258.

[9] See N.L.I., Ms 40,889/30/1–2 for sale agreement. Lands involved were located in the baronies of Murrisk and Burrishoole and included the fishery of the river Erriff.

No. of Acres Sold	Purchaser	Purchase Money	Payees
2,140 (8 Jul. 1708)[10]	Bryan Higgins	£1,596	1. William Palmer: £292.10s 2. Elinor Warren: £525.14s 3. Roger Moore's executors: £406.11s.6d 4. John Stanton: £143.1s 5. Edmund Reynell's executors: £49.10s.8d 6. Stephen Ludlow: £24.7s.6d 7. Theobald, Viscount Mayo: £67.1s.8d 8. Poundage: £79.10s
467	Richard Malone	£407	1. Henry Monck: £60 2. Simon Kirwan: £70 3. Percival's executors: £44 4. John Trench: £34.8s.4d 5. John Kelly: £167 6. James Sloan: £24 7. Poundage: £20
531	Walter Taylor	£535	1. William Adaire: £157.2s.4d 2. Reynell's executors: £351.12s 3. Poundage: £26.5s
1,226	Richard Tisdall	£800	1. Daniel Fitzsimons: £35 2. Mr Savage: £19.14s 3. Theobald, Viscount Mayo: £20 4. Lady Clanmalier: £131 5. Jacob Peppard: £2 6. Tho. Meredith: £400 7. Luke Hussey: £70[11] 8. Poundage: £40[12]
Total: 18,431		**Total: £19,990.6s.10d**	Poundage charged at a rate of 5% per transaction.

[10] See N.L.I., Ms 40,889/30/4 for sale agreement. Theobald, Viscount Mayo, appears as party to the sale. Purchased on behalf of Charles O'Hara, Baron Tyrawley (N.L.I., Ms 40,889/31/5).

[11] Annotated: 'Whereof £50 due still on Mr Browne by Mr Tho. Meredith's note on him.'

[12] Total disbursements: £767.14s. Annotated: £32.6s paid to Peter Browne, Esq., by Mr Meredith, and Lady Clanmalier's money paid likewise.'

Table 8: Principal purchasers of John Browne's estate

Purchaser	Profitable	Unprofitable	Total
Richard Thompson	7,080	23,854	30,934
Bryan Higgins	6,551	?	[6,551+]
Richard Malone	3,889	?	[3,889+]
James Napper & Thomas Smith	2,439	8,202	10,641
Richard Tisdall	1,226	?	[1,226+]
Michael Cormick	1,419	6,228	7,647
Capt. Richard Martin	1,198	25,860	27,058

Tables 5, 6 and 7 illustrate the division of money raised by sale of the estate among Browne's creditors. Thirty of the named recipients of payments (some of whom were paid through their agents or assignees) do not appear in any of the lists of creditors compiled before 1695 and who were protected by the legislation of that year. Some of these were no doubt acting as agents for creditors. Others were Catholic, and thus not recorded in the 1695 legislation.[53] The only Catholic to appear in the indenture related to that act was Sir Stephen Rice. As many as forty creditors identified from the lists compiled up to 23 August 1695 (the date of the indenture) are not named as recipients of payments. Again, some of these may have utilised agents or assignees but this number is not likely to have been very high. A large portion of these debts had in fact been discharged by 1701, with money raised through a combination of payments from the Catholic quit-rent and sale of the estate (from 1698).[54] Surviving evidence suggests that up to £14,000 of the Catholic quit-rent had been collected out of the £18,173.0s.8d levied.

---

[53] These are Richard Dillon (received by Major Delamere); James Cruise; John Joyce (received by William Skerritt); Thomas Arthur (received by James Power); [?] Taaffe; Richard Talbot, titular earl of Tyrconnell; Col. Garrett Moore; Dominick Blake; Patrick Darcy; Alan [Swanwich?]; Thomas [Scurlock?]; John Nolan; Robert Welsh; Jean Fitzgerald; Thomas Fottrell; William Chambers; Anne O'Dempsey, Lady Clanmalier; Theobald, Viscount Mayo; Edward, Lord Athenry; Denis Daly, junior; Stephen Creagh; John Bates; William Palmer; Stephen Ludlow; Simon Kirwan; John Trench; John Kelly; Thomas Meredith; and Lady Newcomen (who does not appear in the 1695 indenture, but her husband, Sir Thomas, owned land leased by Browne from the 1670s – payment was thus probably due for arrears of rent). Three other men also do not appear: Edward Stratford (probably related to debt owed to Robert Stratford); Richard Barry (probably related to debt owed to Matthew Barry); Arthur Knox (probably related to debt owed to Sir John Knox).

[54] See N.L.I., Ms 40,915/2 for a detailed list of creditors and the date of discharge of various debts. The majority were cleared between 1700 and 1701.

Proceedings on Browne's affairs in parliament during November 1697 saw the collectors of the quit-rent levy ordered to pay any money then in their possession and to chase arrears: £14,000 is, however, probably an over-estimate of the sum actually collected. An agreement reached between John Browne and Nicholas Westby, collector for Counties Clare and Limerick, noted that £1,501.0s.7d of the £2,635.19s.5d levied for those counties had been collected by April 1701. Of the remainder, £942.14s.10d had been returned 'insolvent' with the remaining £192 'solvent' but not yet collected. Browne had satisfied the insolvent arrears out of his own pocket. The agreement noted that Westby had retained a little over £105 of the collected levy, which Browne thus claimed and was granted. In addition, Westby was to pay the treasury £100 in satisfaction of the uncollected 'solvent' portion.[55] It would appear that Browne honoured the full sum levied by personally making up any shortfall, in the process clearing many of the debts incurred prior to 1692. The exact amount raised by the quit-rent levy imposed on Catholic landowners by article 13 of Limerick will never be known. Just over 35% of the amount levied in Counties Clare and Limerick was returned as insolvent, which is a telling figure. Perhaps local collectors connived with landowners to avoid payment; or perhaps the levy pushed struggling landowners over the edge of solvency.

Of the seventeen pre-1695 creditors known to have received payments from the sale of the estate, the most important were Sir Stephen Rice and Robert Johnson. Johnson was appointed as baron of the exchequer in December 1703 and thus a trustee for the sale of the estate from that date.[56] Between December 1698 and June 1700, Rice was assigned £11,519.5s of £19,651 raised in that time, returning a handsome profit on his loan to Browne of £7,200, albeit more than fourteen years after the original loans were agreed (see tables 5 & 6). These payments did not clear the debt owed to Rice and it is curious that none of the subsequent sales assigned money to him. Quite when the debt was cleared is not certain. A statement of accounts in 1706 noted money was still owed to Rice.[57] Even after his father's death, Peter was still dealing with Rice, who wrote in February 1713 to chastise Peter for sending him an inaccurate statement of the debt and to suggest that their lawyers meet to settle the issue.[58]

Browne's debt to Robert Johnson dated from at least 1686, when Johnson secured four judgments in the court of exchequer against Browne, totalling £1,556.[59] Though this debt may have been paid during the 1690s, the decision

55 Agreement between Nicholas Westby and Col. Browne, 8 Apr. 1701 (N.L.I., Ms 40,903/1/7).
56 C.S.P.D., 1703–4, p. 288.
57 N.L.I., Ms 40,905/1/12.
58 Sir Stephen Rice to Peter Browne, 18 Feb. 1713 (N.L.I., Ms 40,909/4/2).
59 As a justice of the king's bench, Johnson had witnessed land transactions concluded between Browne and Viscount Mayo in 1673 (N.L.I., Ms 40,889/12/6).

of Browne's nephew Garrett Dillon to follow James II to France continued to create problems. Proceeds from the sale of 7,647 acres in the barony of Erris, County Mayo, in June 1700 were paid to Johnson in part satisfaction of a debt owed to him by Dillon. The payment prefaced a much larger financial trans-action between Johnson and Browne. As made clear by the fact that so many new names appear in the tables included in this chapter, Browne accumulated numerous fresh creditors in the years that followed the surrender of Limerick, which goes some way to explaining why he remained so heavily indebted in the 1700s. In October 1700 a large portion of land in the barony of Carra, County Mayo, was mortgaged to Johnson for £4,000.[60] This mortgage explains the payment of just under £7,000 to Johnson between 1702 and 1708 (see tables 6 and 7). The debt was settled by March 1708, Johnson having earlier secured a judgment in the common pleas against Browne for £8,000.[61] Browne was well accustomed to such judgments, though the size of this one ensured that dealing with Johnson's debt became an urgent necessity. Johnson's mortgage was just one of many encumbrances on Browne's estate (mainly mortgages) imposed after the surrender of Limerick, which perhaps reflects his continued need for money throughout the 1690s and accounts for several of the payments to creditors noted in the tables.

Viewed in isolation, the tables above give the impression of a smooth, orderly sale process, with debts steadily satisfied. This was the case with the majority of Browne's pre-1692 creditors, but was not at all true in the case of creditors gained in the latter half of the 1690s and beyond. The pressure on Browne remained great, while both old and new creditors were not shy in pushing for their due. Of the pre-1692 creditors to whom Browne remained indebted, Elinor Warren was perhaps the most vociferous. Her daughter Mary wrote to Luke Hussey during the summer of 1703, warning him that her patience had run thin and that if satisfaction was not swiftly brought she had 'an iron in the fire that will burn you to the bone'. Her frustration was understandable; at the time of writing, Elinor Warren was owed more than £700 arising from a debt originating in 1684 and was suing Browne in Chancery.[62]

Some ambiguity in the process whereby the exact amount of John Browne's various debts was determined appears after 1700. The superior courts in Dublin had played a prominent role in the 1680s and 1690s. Browne continued to face legal suits pursuing debts during the 1700s, though at a much reduced rate. Once the estate began to be sold, the trustees for the sale apparently assessed the amount to be paid to each creditor, removing the role of the courts. As barons

---

[60] See table 6 – notes to Carra '2nd side'. See also N.L.I., Ms 40,905/1/9.

[61] N.L.I., Ms 40,906/3/1. See N.L.I., Ms 40,915/2, ff 63v, 64r for the settlement of the debt.

[62] Mary Warren to Luke Hussey, 9 July 1703 (N.L.I., Ms 40,904/4/25). See N.L.I., Ms 40,915/2, f. 100v for details of the debt.

of the exchequer their legal *bona fides* were beyond doubt, but there was in fact no provision in the 1695 act setting up the trustees as arbitrators. Nonetheless, their decisions seem to have been binding and may have benefited Browne – a list of his debts at the end of 1709 shows the sum allowed by the trustees to each creditor; the amount actually due (usually greater than that allowed); and a list of debts not allowed by the trustees but annotated as actually due, amounting to almost £5,000. If nothing else, these lists reveal that Browne was still heavily indebted as he approached his seventieth year.[63]

Surviving evidence relating to the workings of the trustees in this regard is fragmentary. Luke Hussey managed Browne's affairs before the trustees who met perhaps twice a year and before whom claims were made by creditors, which were then accepted or challenged by Hussey. That the Brownes sometimes preferred not to allow the trustees to make judgments on certain debts is revealed in Peter Browne's observation that he

> would not put the final determining of claims in the trustees' power, for who knows what they would do in Garrett Moore's case if they had the power, for which reason I am not for leaving it to them by any means, it being the only thing I can depend on.[64]

At a meeting of the trustees in April 1706, agents for several creditors requested an account of rental assignments received. Among those claiming before the trustees were Gregory Nolan and Mr Daly (either Denis or one of his sons) – Hussey wrote to warn Browne that he feared he would 'not find Mr Daly that friend you expect'. Hussey also noted that Nolan, an important London agent for Browne during the 1700s, claimed over £1,000 for his role in securing the 1705 act and an unspecified 'first business that miscarried'. However, Hussey believed that the trustees would reject Nolan's claim.[65] After July 1708, no further sales of the estate were made to satisfy debts and the trustees' involvement in the Browne family's affairs ceased. A limited time frame for their involvement had been included in the bill transmitted to London in 1704. In that bill, a period of four years had been suggested (up to 1 January 1708). With passage of a second act delayed until June 1705, it is reasonable to assume that the enacted measure stipulated that the trustees had power to dispose of the estate up to January 1709, at which time outright ownership probably reverted to John Browne. By

---

63 N.L.I., Ms 40,906/5/3–4.
64 Peter Browne to Col. Browne, 12 July 1707 (N.L.I., Ms 40,905/7/6). Col. Garrett Moore died in January 1706. His executors spent twenty-three years pursuing John and Peter Browne for a debt of £6,000 secured on the statute staple. The debt was finally discharged in 1729 by the guardians of John Browne, son and heir to Peter. Denis Daly, the Jacobite justice of the common pleas and Peter Browne's father-in-law, was one of the executors of Moore's estate – Peter's wife Mary had previously been married to John Moore, nephew of Garrett.
65 Luke Hussey to Col. Browne, 27 Apr. 1706 (N.L.I., Ms 40,905/8/11).

that time the involvement of the trustees was irrelevant as almost nothing of the original estate remained in Browne's hands.

IV

As the sale of their estate progressed between 1698 and 1708, the Brownes took the prudent decision to rebuild concurrently their landed interest. Peter Browne was foremost in this endeavour – John Browne's only role in the process appears to have been to oversee the sale of the estate. In this respect, there was a clear passing of family leadership to Peter, who turned thirty in 1700. At the end of the account book for the sale of the estate is a list of lands in the barony of Murrisk, comprising over 9,000 acres. Its value is not recorded, nor is the reason for this separate list apparent; it may have been what remained of the estate in 1708. On the other hand, it seems quite clear that all profitable acreage had been sold by this point. Land that thus remained in the family's outright ownership was probably of little economic value.

Steps to rebuild the family's landholdings were taken almost immediately. In June 1700, Thomas Smith and James Napper purchased John Browne's entire interest in the half-barony of Rosse, County Galway (table 5). Four weeks later, Peter Browne leased the land sold to Smith and Napper (more than 10,500 acres) for 'lives renewable forever' at an annual rent of £300.[66] The restrictions imposed on purchase of land by Catholics by the 1704 'Act to prevent the further growth of Popery' complicated matters as Peter Browne sought to re-establish the family, limiting him to leases that did not exceed thirty-one years.[67] Unlike many other Catholic families, the Brownes do not seem to have relied on purchases made 'in trust' by Protestant acquaintances. Rather, the recovery of the family was founded upon a leasehold interest, for the most part within the constraints of the penal laws, until the conversion of Peter Browne's son (also named John) to the Church of Ireland in 1729.

It seems that a concerted effort was made to sell the remainder of the estate to men who would in turn lease their purchases back to Peter Browne. Bryan Higgins, Richard Malone and Dominick Burke were of particular assistance, as were the Brownes of the Neale. On 20 and 21 February 1708, Higgins (described in later documents as an attorney at the court of common pleas) purchased 4,411 acres of the Browne estate in the baronies of Murrisk and Burrishoole for £3,229.10s (see table 7). Peter Browne leased these lands on 24 February at an annual rent of £260. He in fact agreed three separate leases, for successive terms

---

[66] N.L.I., Ms 40,915/2, f. 65r. Peter Browne's accounts indicate that the annual rent was paid in a combination of cash and cattle.

[67] 2 Anne, c. 6.

of seven, thirty and thirty-one years. If Peter Browne converted to the Church of Ireland before the lease of seven years expired (in February 1715) he was to be entitled to a lease for 62 years. However, in a further evasion of the Popery Act of 1704, just four days later Higgins and Peter Browne agreed yet another lease, which extended the thirty-one year lease for a further 30 years.[68]

Family connections also proved crucial. On 20 February 1714, Higgins conveyed his interest in this land to Dominick Burke, who was in turn purchasing in trust for George Browne, grandson of Colonel John Browne's brother George of the Neale, thus making him Peter Browne's nephew.[69] Though a purchase in trust implies that George Browne was a Catholic and thus evading the provisions of both the 1704 and 1709 acts relating to Catholic land ownership, George had himself converted to the Church of Ireland in 1711.[70] Dominick Burke had longstanding connections with the Brownes, having served as an agent for John Browne from at least 1680 – an employment he continued under Peter Browne until well into the 1710s, and possibly beyond. Burke's open purchase of 245 acres of the Browne estate after April 1704 implies that he was a Protestant (table 7).[71] The intimate involvement of the barons of the exchequer, as trustees for the sale of the Browne estate, would certainly have militated against any successful purchase of the estate by a Catholic.

Of the post-April 1704 purchasers of the Browne estate, Richard Malone proved second in importance only to Bryan Higgins. Malone was probably the noted lawyer from Baronstown, County Westmeath. Originally Catholic, he converted in the period before the Popery Act of 1704 required all converts to provide evidence of their conversion.[72] Malone purchased 3,889 profitable acres from the Browne estate, largely in the baronies of Murrisk and Burrishoole. The purchase included the valuable Erriff fishery. All of these lands, with the exception of the fishery, were conveyed to Peter Browne on a twenty-six-year lease on 10 February 1713. The relationship between the two men was certainly cordial: Malone wrote the following month to express his hope that they might share a drink during the next court circuit.[73] The Brownes also made use of old

---

68 N.L.I., Ms 40,889/29/5–9.

69 N.L.I., Mss 40,909/1/7; 40,918/13–14.

70 *Convert rolls*, p. 21

71 N.L.I., Mss 40,895/7; 40,897/2/7–8; 40,897/6/1, 12; 40,907/3, 8; 40,916/3. The exact nature of Burke's employment by Browne is unclear. He does not appear in the *Convert rolls*.

72 Richard Malone (1674–1745) was considered one of the foremost lawyers of the early eighteenth century. The earl of Galway used him as envoy on several diplomatic missions to Holland, which earned Malone the favour of William III (*D.I.B.*). He later gave legal advice in a dispute between the Clanricarde family and Sir William Ashhurst, former Lord Mayor of London and director of the Bank of England (N.L.I., Ms 40,909/2/14). His early conversion accounts for his failure to appear in the *Convert rolls*.

73 N.L.I., Mss 40,909/4/3; 40,918/12.

connections when selling portions of the estate to the Cormick family. Michael Cormick (agent to John Browne since the 1670s) and his son Francis purchased 7,647 acres in the half-barony of Erris on 20 June 1700. The sale agreement stipulated that John Browne and his heirs retained the right to all minerals. On the day of the sale, the Cormicks also mortgaged the land for £1,257 (payable to Robert Johnson) and leased it to Browne for 500 years (table 6).[74]

Peter Browne had rebuilt a substantial landed interest by the middle of 1713, comprising approximately 25,000 acres, with perhaps 11,500 classed as profitable. Peter's interest was leasehold rather than freehold; this was surely a preferable state of affairs, as leasehold removed the pressure of dealing with the many encumbrances on the recently sold estate.[75] Even without the various encumbrances, arrears of rent soon mounted for Peter. He wrote to advise his father in July 1707 that 'we can never pass such a clause as will secure us our liberty against Smith and Napper for the growing rents'.[76] Nonetheless, this leasehold provided Peter Browne and his descendants with the foundations upon which the Brownes of Westport would reposition themselves as the greatest landowners in Connacht by the end of the eighteenth century.

---

[74] The Cormick family's connection to the Bourke family (later Viscounts Mayo) stretched back to the 1610s, accounting for their connection with John Browne, who assumed ownership of most of Viscount Mayo's estate in the 1670s and 1680s (see for example N.L.I., Ms 40,890/7/15–16). A daughter of Michael Cormick (likely to have been the father of the Michael Cormick who served as agent to John Browne) married John Browne's cousin, Austin Browne, in March 1680 (N.L.I., Ms 40,895/3/11). Michael Cormick (the agent) of Inver, Co. Mayo, was commissioned as a captain in the Jacobite army. D'Alton contends that Cormick's regiment was never 'filled' but orders from Berwick in December 1690 directed Browne and Athenry to send 200 barrels of meal to Inis Boffin for the 'independent' company led by Capt. Michael Cormick. He was also specifically named in article 8 of the articles of Boffin (D'Alton, *King James's Irish army lists*, pp 940–1; N.L.I., Ms 40,899/3/10). Cormick was attainted during the Williamite war but later secured adjudication under the articles of Limerick on 16 July 1698 (Simms, 'Irish Jacobites', pp 81, 109).
[75] This consideration probably accounts for the failure of Catholics to build substantial freehold estates after the relaxation of penal legislation relating to Catholic landownership in 1782 (Louis Cullen, 'Catholic social classes under the penal laws' in T.P. Power & Kevin Whelan (eds), *Endurance and emergence: Catholics in Ireland in the eighteenth century* (Dublin, 1990), p. 58).
[76] Peter Browne to Col. Browne, 12 July 1707 (N.L.I., Ms 40,905/7/6).

8

'I am plagued with a quarrel':
The Browne family and the gentry
of Connacht, 1692–1711[1]

It is difficult to gauge the overall effect of article 13 of Limerick, and the prolonged sale of the estate, on John Browne's family and on the wider Connacht community. From 1698 Browne's eldest son Peter became increasingly involved in the management of the family's debts. Browne's four other children (Valentine, Bridget, Elizabeth and Mary) were largely peripheral figures in this business, though the marriages of two of his three daughters and their consequent dowries placed him under further financial burdens and brought Browne into conflict with their husbands. As Browne's most important legal representative in the 1690s and 1700s, Edmund Malone played a prominent role in the management of his affairs, including disputes with Lord Athenry and Viscount Mayo, Browne's sons-in-law. In Dublin, Luke Hussey's diligence was important to the management of Browne's business. This chapter examines the impact of John Browne's debts on the lives of his children, as well as the agency of his nephew Edmund Malone on behalf of several Catholic and Protestant families in Counties Galway and Mayo. The first section analyses Malone's work in London as he managed the affairs of the Brownes of the Neale, the Blakes of Moyne, County Galway, and the Veseys of County Galway, as well as Malone's occasionally tense relationship with his uncle. The lives of Browne's children are discussed in section II, through the prism of their relationship with their father. Though Peter Browne's correspondence is relatively well preserved among the Westport papers, the same cannot be said of Valentine Browne and his three sisters. Section III examines the conversion to Protestantism of two of John Browne's grandsons: Francis Bermingham, future Baron Athenry, and Peter Browne's son, John Browne, future earl of Altamont. Francis Bermingham's conversion in particular allows an insight into the pressure brought to bear on the Catholic gentry of Ireland by the penal laws.

---

[1] Quotation taken from Col. John Browne to Luke Hussey, 12 Nov. 1704 (N.L.I., Ms 40,904/5/10).

I

The main branch of the Browne family remained at the Neale after the death of Colonel John Browne's father in 1670, with the estate inherited by George Browne, the eldest son. Like his father and several of his direct descendants, George Browne never assumed the baronetcy bestowed on the family in 1636 – that title was not assumed until 1762, by George Browne's great–grandson (also named George) whose brother John was in turn elevated to the peerage as Baron Kilmaine (second creation) in 1789.[2] George Browne was linked with Colonel Browne's attempts to establish himself as an ironmaster in the early 1680s, though he does not appear to have become too heavily entangled in his brother's mounting debts. Alongside his assignment of several tracts of land to John, George Browne acted as trustee for the first of his brother's large mortgages, to Sir Robert Booth and Henry Whitfield, in 1680, and entered into several joint bonds with his brother during the 1670s and 1680s.[3] George Browne maintained a relatively low profile during the reign of James II and the Williamite war, though he was appointed as a justice of the peace in County Mayo and, during 1690, served as high sheriff for the county.[4] He did not sit in the 1689 parliament but was probably the George Browne appointed as a collector for County Mayo by that parliament's act of supply.[5] His son John was 'sometime captain' in the Jacobite army and was taken prisoner at the siege of Derry in May 1689.[6]

Writing in the mid-1680s, Sir William Petty identified the Catholics that he believed to have gained most from the Restoration land settlement. In a list that included James, duke of York, the earls of Clancarty, Tyrconnell, Inchiquin and Carlingford, 'Mr John Brown of Connaught' was also named.[7] Given that John Browne had begun to emerge as a landowner of considerable standing by the end of the 1670s, it is more likely that he was the Browne referred to, rather than his father, who had died in 1670.[8] Browne's father had, however, expanded his estate at the Neale after the Restoration, helped in no small part by his inclusion as a nominee in the act of settlement and his role as agent for part of

2 For the purchase of the baronetcy in 1636, see above, p. 19.
3 N.L.I., Mss 40,889/16/4–6; 40,894/3/7.
4 N.L.I., Ms 10, f. 286; Roger O'Flaherty to George Browne, 7 Mar. 1690 (N.L.I., Ms 40,899/2/17).
5 5 James II, c.2 (Bergin & Lyall (eds), *The acts of James II's Irish Parliament*, p. 16).
6 G.E. Cokayne, *The complete baronetage* (5 vols, Exeter, 1900–6), ii, 419.
7 *The economic writings of Sir William Petty together with the observations upon the bills of mortality more probably by Captain Gaunt*, ed. C.H. Hull (2 vols, Cambridge, 1899), ii, 615–16.
8 Bryan Coleborne, 'Jonathan Swift and the dunces of Dublin' (Ph.D. thesis, University College Dublin, 1982), p. 40, n. 17.

the Ormond estates in Connacht.[9] The size of the estate held by the Brownes of the Neale at the time of James II's accession is unknown, but was said to be worth £800 per annum at the close of the century.[10] Theobald, Viscount Mayo, expanded his family's holdings in similar fashion, from just under 25,000 acres in 1641 to almost 100,000 by 1670 – almost all of which eventually found its way into the hands of Colonel Browne.[11]

As landowners, the Brownes of the Neale had a vested interest in remaining in Ireland after the surrender of Limerick in 1691. The names George and John Browne appear many times in the outlawry lists of the Williamite war, though none of these entries can be definitely identified with the Neale Brownes. They claimed to have never been outlawed and neither appears to have been adjudicated within any of the articles of surrender. Nevertheless, George and his son John sought a royal pardon from William III in 1697, fearing that George's appointments as a justice of the peace and high sheriff exposed them to future prosecution.

George's petition to William was supported by several local Protestant gentry, including his wife Alice's nephew, Sir Henry Bingham; Alice's uncle John Bingham; John Vesey, archbishop of Tuam; and William Pullein, rector of Kiltullagh.[12] Francis Cuffe, appointed as a commissioner to inquire into Irish forfeitures in 1693, also wrote promising his support to George Browne.[13] Affidavits from these men had been gathered in 1692 in preparation for a petition to Sydney, then lord lieutenant. Sydney was, however, recalled before the petition could be presented and the attempt to gain a pardon suspended. But, as with the articlemen of Boffin, George Browne was spurred to action by the Irish parliament's preparation of a bill for confirming outlawries and attainders in the summer of 1697, and his petition was probably presented to the Irish lords justices later that year. The affidavits of support from George Browne's Protestant neighbours were said to be 'a mark of their compassion

---

[9] 14 & 15 Chas. II, c. 2, s. ccxxv; George Browne to John Browne, senior, 21 Mar. 1666 (H.M.C., *Ormonde Mss*, n.s., iii, 211–12).

[10] Deposition of Henry Stanford, 16 Sept. 1699 (N.L.I., Annesley Mss, xxiii, f. 114).

[11] Jane Ohlmeyer, *Making Ireland English: the Irish aristocracy in the seventeenth century* (New Haven, 2012), pp 307–13.

[12] P.R.O.N.I., T3134/1/6. This was probably the same William Pullein who became mortgagee to Col. Browne in 1692.

[13] Cuffe was first appointed to the commission of inquiry into the forfeitures in Ireland in December 1693, with a salary of £400 per annum, having previously served as a commissioner, later lord lieutenant, of the Ordnance in Ireland, as well as one of the commissaries general (*C.S.P.D.*, 1690–1, pp 352, 354; *C.S.P.D.*, 1693, pp 6, 22, 334, 442). This was probably the Francis Cuffe who was son and heir to Sir James Cuffe, clerk to the privy council of Connacht until its abolition in 1672. Sir James and his son Francis were allowed a pension of £300 per annum in lieu of the post of clerk (*C.S.P.D.*, 1673–5, pp 247, 260; *C.S.P.D.*, 1678 & Addenda, pp 361–2). Francis Cuffe died in late 1694/early 1695 (*C.T.B.*, 1693–6, p. 887).

and tenderness for your petitioner and of their due acknowledgements of his said services and sufferings'. George claimed that he and his family had always adhered to the English interest in Ireland and that it was only due to the encouragement of his Protestant neighbours that he accepted the positions of justice of the peace and high sheriff 'in order to their preservation and security'. During the war he provided sanctuary for his Protestant neighbours, prompting attacks on his property by rapparees who accused him of corresponding with his Protestant relations in the Williamite camp and who robbed him of goods to the value of £3,000. Without the intercession of his nephew, Garrett Dillon, 'your petitioner had certainly lost his life'. A further testament as to George Browne's good behaviour during the war was procured from James Gordon, rector for Castlebar, in July 1697.[14] Browne's appeal was successful; a warrant was issued by William to the Irish lords justices in June 1698, instructing them to pass letters patent granting a free pardon to George and his son John.[15]

Edmund Malone was integral to their success. Given his importance to the management of John Browne's affairs in London during the 1690s and 1700s, it is no surprise that Malone's legal experience and skills as a lobbyist were called upon to serve the Brownes of the Neale. In December 1697 Malone wrote to Agmondisham Vesey (son of the archbishop) from London enclosing several papers relating to George, including 'the original addresses of the Protestants of the province of Connacht for him to the Lord Sydney, and other papers of great moment to him'. The papers were to be sent to John Bingham for delivery to George, though Malone counselled Vesey that the papers would be safer if sent to the archbishop.[16] Malone's reports from London to John Bingham and George Browne in the first few months of 1698 reveal that the English parliament's investigation into grants of forfeited lands in Ireland by William III was causing some difficulty for several Irish Catholics petitioning for pardons. Writing in March, Malone complained that

> the bill about the Irish grants and forfeitures makes our application at a stand till that bill fail or receive an end, and when that's done, I would endeavour to have an ultimate resolution on cousin Blake's business, but 'tis impossible to have it before then … I vow I'll lose no time proper for it, but I must obey commands here and not run my head against a wall.

14 P.R.O.N.I., T3134/1/2–5, 9–10.
15 William III to the lords justices of Ireland, 9 June 1698 (P.R.O.N.I., T3134/1/17; N.L.I., Ms 10, f. 286; C.S.P.D., 1698, p. 293); J.G. Simms, 'Mayo landowners in the seventeenth century' in J.R.S.A.I., xcv (1965), p. 246. Simms contended that John Browne of the Neale was a prisoner of war in 1691, though this is probably a mistaken assumption that he continued to be held as a prisoner of war following his capture at the siege of Derry.
16 Edmund Malone to Agmondisham Vesey, 21 Dec. 1697 (N.A.I., Sarsfield-Vesey papers).

Malone went on to suggest that a favourable report from the Irish law officers (to whom petitions presented at Whitehall relating to Irish affairs were regularly referred) should be sought for George and John ('cousin Jack') Browne. It should be brief, 'for they complain at this court of long papers always out of Ireland, and the great length is often a great enemy to the success of such.' Malone also enclosed a letter from 'a friend' addressed to Charles Powlett, marquess of Winchester, one of the lords justices, in support of George and his son.[17]

The testaments gathered in support of the Brownes from local Protestant notables were back in Malone's hands by the end of March 1698, though he advised that he was not able to present them to the secretary of state 'because of his great indisposition'. The delay was not thought too material, 'for the king will do nothing relating to the Irish affairs of forfeiture or forfeiting persons' until parliament had disposed of the bill relating to Irish forfeitures. A report relating to the Brownes from the Irish law officers had also been delivered to Whitehall. Still Malone fretted, complaining that it had not been sent by the Irish government directly to the king and English privy council, 'where I might have more room of acting with several interests'. More encouragingly, he had been informed by several Irish and English privy councillors that there was little danger of fresh indictments for rebellion: 'the taste of the grants of forfeited estates is not so sweet as it has been, and the spring of making more forfeitures is much weakened.' He concluded with the bold promise that 'before any other [judicial] circuit, my uncle [George] and cousin Blake will have their pardon, or I shall cast my cap at it'.[18]

'Cousin Blake' was almost certainly Martin Blake, son of Francis of Moyne, County Mayo. While in London, Malone also managed petitions from Francis and Martin Blake for a pardon from William III. Malone did not have a high opinion of Martin. When he asked John Bingham to convey his gratitude to his uncle George for the calm tone of his letters, Malone wryly advised that 'if you hold not cousin Martin Blake by the chin, he'll die for fear'.[19] Malone's next report to Bingham, on 10 May, displayed greater urgency as he worried that the king's imminent departure for Holland would undermine his efforts:

I have been this month past ... seeing and pressing my friends all I could, and with as much privacy as possible, being in great dread for fear the father and son should be split asunder, upon sharp objections made against any necessity of a pardon for a young man not accused nor no way concerned. But finding these objections against Jack [John Browne] and Martin Blake to arise only from their innocence, and not their guilt, it gave me more spurs to press it on, for fear of worse objections than I could

17 Edmund Malone to John Bingham, 5 Mar. 1698 (P.R.O.N.I., T3134/1/11).
18 Edmund Malone to John Bingham, 2 Apr. 1698 (P.R.O.N.I., T3134/1/12).
19 Ibid.

214

answer, and finding an absolute necessity of furnishing it with a new pair of wheels, for fear of the misfortunes and delays incident to our affairs, or that it should lie here till winter, and that I must have left it undone, I have engaged to lay down 100 guineas, which is £110 here, on the day I receive a warrant for the father and son, and truly I would give a hundred ounces of my flesh rather than it should fail. I am in great hope to have it before the last day of this month. If I have it not by that time, I must tell you plainly that nothing but tricks could keep it from me, since no way in the world has been left untried to make it go.

Malone actually secured the pardons for the Blakes later that day, at a cost of £100 plus fees. He wrote to caution Martin that he should 'keep counsel of his affair till it be past concealing – that's to say till it be passed the great seal'.[20]

Malone's final despatch on the matter, on 7 June, was somewhat bittersweet in tone. Addressed to John Browne of the Neale, Malone expressed his distress at learning of the sudden death of his uncle George in early May.[21] However, 'God almighty has heard his prayers for the deliverance of his family': pardons for the Brownes had been granted and Malone expected to have the king's signature within a week. Richard Fitzgerald, a member of the important Fitzgerald merchant family of Waterford who maintained business interests in London and across the continent, loaned Malone £210 to cover the cost of securing pardons for the Blakes and Brownes: 'He is a person I have often obliged in business, a vintner and a very rich man here'.[22] Browne was to remit the money to London by a bill from the Dublin banker William Cairnes. Malone concluded with a familiar warning:

Though this be done in [the privy] council, where there are so many noble lords attending, yet it's not known here to many, and the more secret you keep it, the better, till you have it under the great seal of Ireland.[23]

---

[20] Edmund Malone to John Bingham; Malone to George Browne, 10 May 1698 (P.R.O.N.I., T3134/1/14). The letters to both men were written on the same sheet. The warrants were issued the next day and instructed the lords justices of Ireland to issue a free pardon to Francis and Martin Blake (*C.S.P.D.*, 1698, p. 244).

[21] At the time of writing to George Browne on 10 May, Malone had yet to receive any of three separate letters from Ireland informing him of the death of George: John Browne [of the Neale] to Edmund Malone; Martin Blake to same; John Bingham to same, 7, 9 & 10 May 1698 (P.R.O.N.I., T3134/1/13).

[22] For the Fitzgerald merchant family of Waterford, see Jan Parmentier, 'The Irish connection: the Irish merchant community in Ostend and Bruges during the late seventeenth and eighteenth centuries' in *E.C.I.*, 20 (2005), pp 31–54; L.M. Cullen, 'The two George Fitzgeralds of London, 1718–1759' in David Dickson, Jane Ohlmeyer & Jan Parmentier (eds), *Irish and Scottish mercantile networks in Europe and overseas in the seventeenth and eighteenth centuries* (Ghent, 2007), pp 251–70.

[23] Edmund Malone to John Browne of the Neale, 7 June 1698 (P.R.O.N.I., T3134/1/15).

The warrant directing the lords justices of Ireland to pardon George and John Browne was sent from London on 9 June.[24] Pardons for the Brownes were, at £135, more expensive than for the Blakes. Malone explained that this was caused by consideration of the Brownes' case at the English privy council, whereas the Blakes' pardons had been obtained through a 'briefer channel'.[25]

During his time in London in 1697 and 1698, Malone managed the affairs of at least four separate families – the Brownes of Westport, the Brownes of the Neale, the Blakes and the Veseys. His correspondence also suggests employment by the Fitzgerald merchant family in London. Malone's employment by the Vesey family is not surprising, given the close connections between the Brownes and the Protestant gentry of Connacht, but noteworthy nonetheless. Malone's personal religious affiliation during the 1690s is uncertain; in December 1697, archbishop Vesey was certain that he had converted to the Church of Ireland.[26] However, Malone appears in lists of 1705 and 1714 licensing Catholics to bear arms.[27] Malone's agency on behalf of the Veseys concentrated on Agmondisham's attempt to protect his claim to the Sarsfield estate in Lucan, County Dublin, through his marriage to Charlotte Sarsfield, niece of Patrick, earl of Lucan.[28] In spite of complications arising from the death during the war (in May 1690) of Charlotte's grandfather, also named Patrick, she had entered into possession of the estate by August 1696.[29]

Vesey's trust and confidence in Malone was demonstrated by his management of the presentation of two separate petitions relating to the Sarsfield estate, to the English parliament and to the privy council, in 1697 and 1698. Not all of Vesey's associates shared his high opinion of Malone. Writing in 1695, James Bamford berated Vesey for making use of Malone's services:

> By this time you see the ill consequence of bringing Colonel Garrett Moore into my stead ... I cannot but mind you of the misfortune you still lie under, in advising with any of the natives of this country who (be assured) have a greater regard to a finger of any of those in France than they have for you ... you must believe as I do that you

[24] P.R.O.N.I., T3134/1/17; C.S.P.D., 1698, p. 293.
[25] P.R.O.N.I., T3134/1/16.
[26] Archbishop of Tuam to Agmondisham Vesey, 21 Dec. 1697 (N.A.I., Sarsfield-Vesey papers).
[27] Proclamations, 30 Mar. 1705, 18 Mar. 1714 (Kelly & Lyons (eds), Proclamations of Ireland, ii, 574–8, 682–9.
[28] Charlotte was the daughter of William Sarsfield (older brother of the earl of Lucan), and Mary, illegitimate daughter of Charles II and sister to the duke of Monmouth. After the death of his older brother William in 1675 and William's son Charles in 1683, Patrick Sarsfield took possession of the estate. William's widow, Mary, who married secondly William Fanshaw, challenged this possession. The Fanshaw's challenge was heard in the Irish courts, but the case had not concluded by the outbreak of the Williamite war (Simms, Williamite confiscation, pp 86, 144–5).
[29] C.S.P.D., 1696, p. 156.

keep a snake still in your bosom ... let them pretend what they will, they have not a dram of kindness for an English man.

Vesey endorsed the letter with the following summary: 'In this letter Mr Bamford has given a character of my Irish friends, particularly of Mr Malone whom he principally means though he names Colonel Moore.'[30] Bamford's opinion did not, however, prevent him from personally employing Malone to pursue debts he claimed were owed to him by William Fanshaw, Vesey's father-in-law.[31]

Though letters patents had been issued granting Charlotte possession of her paternal estate, her possession was not yet secure. The transmission to Whitehall of the 1697 bill for hindering the reversal of outlawries and attainders threw the ownership of the estate into doubt. Charlotte's grandfather, Patrick Sarsfield, had not received a posthumous reversal of his outlawry, exposing him to future prosecution. While Malone steered a bill for his uncle John Browne through the English privy council in September 1697, he simultaneously represented Agmondisham Vesey and his wife. Vesey's petition to the council requested a saving proviso in the 1697 bill for hindering the reversal of outlawries and attainders, to reverse the outlawry of Patrick Sarsfield 'the elder'.[32] His case was strengthened by the support of the lords justices and privy council of Ireland, who noted that the outlawry was probably intended for the earl of Lucan: 'If the outlawry be confirmed, it will prejudice his grandchild [Charlotte Sarsfield], who is a Protestant.'[33]

The English privy council considered the bill from 16 September to 26 October.[34] Two days after it was referred to the English law officers, Malone notified the Veseys that the English attorney general was considering their case:

I trust in God if we can get a good report from the attorney general that we shall find good friends at council ... the bills were sent to [the attorney general] last night by messenger, and I go immediately after dinner with Mr Vesey's petition and order to him. My lord the papers and title are prolix and many to peruse and collect by so great a person as Mr Attorney, and the time for return of bills so very short, that your Grace's expense must of necessity be the greater ... this affair cannot move without expense every day and every hour.

---

30 James Bamford to Agmondisham Vesey, 2 Apr. 1695 (N.A.I., Sarsfield-Vesey papers). This James Bamford may be the person mentioned in April 1693 as a lessee on the former estate of Richard, duke of Tyrconnell (C.S.P.D., 1693, p. 113).

31 James Bamford to William Fanshaw, 3 Mar. 1697 (N.A.I., Sarsfield-Vesey papers).

32 T.N.A., PC 2/77, f. 81 (16 Sept. 1697).

33 Irish lords justices and privy council to the lords justices of England, 22 July 1697 (C.S.P.D., 1697, p. 263).

34 T.N.A., PC 2/77, f. 81 (16 Sept. 1697).

Malone intended to offer 100 guineas to have the proviso secured, and noted that he expected to have to 'gratify' others.[35] The attorney general earned his gratuity: when the bill was approved in council, it included the proviso and was enacted by the Irish parliament.[36]

Malone continued to act as Vesey's agent in London until mid-1698. With respect to a possible challenge from any of the earl of Lucan's surviving relations in France to possession of the Sarsfield estate, Malone informed Vesey that a bill was before the house of commons to prevent the return of any person who had followed James II to France without licence: 'It will be long enough before you are troubled with them or their likes.'[37] By the end of January 1698, Malone was able to inform Vesey of a successful conclusion to the case and requested that the balance of his fee be sent to him: 'I must think of returning in March, from an expensive place and a tiresome attendance.'[38]

However, by the end of 1697 the English parliament had worked itself into yet another of its periodic states of agitation over the 'unreasonable grants in Ireland' of forfeited estates.[39] Following several reports on the matter, leave was given to the house of commons on 7 February 1698 to introduce a bill for 'vacating all grants of estates, and other interests, forfeited in Ireland, since the 13th day of February 1689'.[40] Though this bill was strenuously opposed by the government's supporters in parliament, it eventually led to the tacking of a clause to a supply bill establishing the 1699 commission of inquiry in Ireland into forfeitures.[41] Before this tactic was employed, the proposed bill prompted several petitions seeking saving clauses from Irish Catholics and Protestants alike. Among those petitioning were Agmondisham Vesey and Charlotte Sarsfield, while Irish Catholics were among the first to present petitions seeking saving clauses, including a representation from the articlemen of Limerick and Galway on 25 February. That same day, Malone and his father, John, similarly petitioned for a saving clause.[42] The proposed bill was not passed and Vesey was not required to take any further action. The Act of Resumption of 1700

35 Edmund Malone to Archbishop of Tuam, 18 Sept. 1697 (N.A.I., Sarsfield-Vesey papers).

36 9 William III, c. 5, s. xxii.

37 Edmund Malone to Agmondisham Vesey, 21 Dec. 1697 (N.A.I., Sarsfield-Vesey papers). Malone was referring to a bill 'to hinder any of his majesty's subjects coming into this kingdom, who during the war have gone into France without licence, or been in arms under the French king, or in the service of the late King James; and to prevent corresponding with the said late king', first introduced to the commons on 13 December 1697 (C.J., xii, p. 5). One of the witnesses secured by Malone to testify in London on Vesey's behalf was a Capuchin monk, Father Dowdall.

38 Edmund Malone to Agmondisham Vesey, 27 Jan. 1698 (N.A.I., Sarsfield-Vesey papers).

39 James Sloane to Sir Joseph Williamson, 21 Dec. 1697 (C.S.P.D., 1697, p. 522).

40 See chapter 3 for this bill as it related to the articlemen and the protectees.

41 Simms, Williamite confiscation, p. 97.

42 C.J., xii, 128, 155 (25 Feb., 12 Mar. 1698). Malone was still in London in May (William Fanshaw to Agmondisham Vesey, 24 May 1698 (N.A.I., Sarsfield-Vesey papers)).

proved an entirely different matter, necessitating a private act of the English parliament to allow Vesey to continue in possession of the Sarsfield estate.[43] Malone appears to have played no part in this.

Malone did continue to play a prominent role in the affairs of John Browne. Luke Hussey undertook the principal management of the colonel's affairs in Dublin during the 1690s and early 1700s, regularly relying on the advice of a number of men, including Malone. Hussey's correspondence offers insights into some of Browne's most important business (such as the progress of petitions before the Irish government and parliament), as well as more mundane matters. He regularly supplied Browne with information regarding affairs on the continent.[44] Hussey's work ranged from securing postponements of legal suits against Browne in the courts, negotiations with potential purchasers of Browne's estate, financial transactions on the Exchange and the purchase of household materials.[45]

Edmund Malone appears to have been, for the most part, a trusted adviser to Hussey and Browne. This did not prevent an occasional strain in relations, typically occasioned by disputes over money or land title. Malone sent a sum of money to Browne in May 1703, warning that it was 'more than I have received this term, or I expect to receive the next … The best management I can propose … is to live upon my little rents and this lean chamber practice'. Malone went on to criticise Browne's financial husbandry:

> It is a most melancholy circumstance of your affairs that after such long preparation you should come from home and from so large possessions, with less money than is necessary to support you for two terms or months. I must confess any thinking man may reasonably despair of success from such a conduct.[46]

Such a rebuke may not have been entirely out of character; Peter Browne commented some years later that 'you know his pen is cutting sometimes which is often better let alone'.[47] In October 1703 Hussey warned Browne that Malone was intent on forcing the colonel to surrender deeds to Garrett Dillon's former estate:

---

43 1 Anne, c. 57 [private, Eng.]. For a general outline of Vesey's success in securing the Sarsfield estate see Simms, *Williamite confiscation*, pp 144–5.

44 Luke Hussey to Col. Browne, 16 Sept. 1701; same to same, 19 Oct. 1703; same to same, 10 June 1704 (N.L.I., Mss 40,903/5/3; 40,904/3/18–19).

45 N.L.I., Mss 40,903/4; 40,904/3; 40,904/5. The Exchange was located in the Tholsel and was described in 1697 by John Dunton as 'the place they call the 'Change, where the merchants meet every day, as in the Royal Exchange in London' (quoted in J.T. Gilbert, *A history of the city of Dublin* (3 vols, Dublin, 1854–9), i, 167). I am indebted to Patrick Walsh for this reference.

46 Malone to Col. Browne, 10 May 1703 (N.L.I., Ms 40,904/3/14).

47 Peter Browne to Col. Browne, 16 Aug. 1707 (N.L.I., Ms 40,905/7/13).

> If you should not comply he will give you all the opposition he can and will force you to it or break your measures ... he finds that you are in his power without respect and he will have his own demands without reason or justice, and if he should find that you would not comply, he will ruin all your endeavours.[48]

Malone himself informed Browne that he intended to provide for his family through the sale of Dillon's estate, though his letter gave no sense of the severe measures indicated by Hussey.[49] Malone's conduct may have been, in part, motivated by a desire to prevent Browne from further mismanaging his personal affairs. Later correspondence reveals that Browne assigned the land in question to Malone with the comment, 'I depend upon your integrity'.[50] Malone continued to act as a legal adviser to Browne until at least 1707 and was closely consulted during the progression of Browne's private act of 1705.

The nature of Malone's work in London, and the manner in which he pursued his objectives, were typical of agents and lobbyists who operated on the margins of the English court and government. In ordinary times they might hardly be worth noting, but the 1690s were not ordinary times for Irish Catholics. As they scrambled to protect their interests and secure their futures, London's importance as a forum for Catholic petitioning became ever more apparent. Malone's agency in London on behalf of Irish Catholics is unusually well documented; his correspondence sheds light on the cost of procuring pardons, as well as the uncertainty of success as the English parliament probed the Irish forfeitures. There was a marked tendency towards discretion, lest news of an intended pardon prompt opposition from Irish Protestants eager to exploit vulnerable land owners. Success often depended on various familial, regional, commercial and professional networks, regardless of former political or indeed confessional differences. As one of the first Irish Catholics known to have specialised in representing the interests of Irish clients in London, both Protestant and Catholic, Malone's reputation continued to grow.[51] Twelve years after he first appeared as an agent for the articlemen of Limerick, Malone appeared on their behalf in the Irish house of commons, alongside Sir Toby Butler and Sir Stephen Rice, as counsel arguing against the 1704 Popery Act.[52] Colonel John Browne was named as one of the Catholic petitioners.

---

[48] Hussey to 'Darby O'Bryan' [Col. Browne], 19 Oct. 1703 (N.L.I., Ms 40,904/3/18).

[49] Malone to Col. Browne, 16 Oct. 1703 (N.L.I., Ms 40,904/3/15).

[50] Malone to Col. Browne, 9 Mar. 1704; Col. Browne to Malone, 9 Mar. 1704 (N.L.I., Ms 40,904/3/16–17).

[51] For more on Irish Catholic networks in London, see Bergin, 'Irish Catholic interest'; idem., 'The world of Richard Lahy, an Irish law agent in eighteenth-century London' in Raymond Gillespie & R.F. Foster (eds), *Irish provincial cultures in the long eighteenth century* (Dublin, 2012), pp 75–92; idem, 'Irish Catholics and their networks in eighteenth-century London' in *Eighteenth-Century Life*, 39:1 (2015), pp 66–102.

[52] *An impartial relation of the several arguments of Sir Stephen Rice, Sir Theobald Butler, and*

II

Little can be said about the lives of four of Colonel John Browne's five children, especially his daughter Elizabeth and second son, Valentine.[53] His eldest son, Peter, is much better documented than his siblings. Two of Browne's three daughters married members of the Bermingham family: the eldest daughter, Bridget (sometimes Biddy or Bríd), married Edward Bermingham, who succeeded his father as Baron Athenry in 1677; Elizabeth, the middle daughter, married John Bermingham, probably John Berminham of Killbegs, cousin to Lord Athenry.[54] Mary, the youngest, married her first cousin Theobald, Viscount Mayo, in 1702. Some incidental details of the lives of the Westport Brownes and their wider family emerge from the correspondence of Luke Hussey: silk purchased in Dublin for Lady Mary Bophin's sister; arrangements for the study in Dublin of mathematics for a Mellaghlin of County Westmeath; gloves for Peter Browne; and dancing, singing and violin lessons for Browne's daughter, Bridget.[55] Lord Athenry wrote of his and Bridget's son Francis's education that 'there is a good Latin school, a French school, writing, dancing and fencing in Galway and a good priest that will take care to examine him in his learning and Christianity'.[56] The marriages of Bridget and Mary caused some difficulties for Browne, though this trouble reveals more about John Browne than the lives and personalities of his daughters.

Lord Athenry's first wife died of small pox in Dublin in August 1685.[57] On 20 June 1687 he contracted a second marriage with Bridget Browne, who brought with her a dowry of £2,000.[58] Given Browne's level of debt at this point, it is no surprise to find that payment of the dowry quickly fell into arrears. Outstanding dowry payments, combined with other debts arising from shared business interests, introduced a palpable tension into relations between Browne and his son-in-law, which Bridget's death in January 1702 did little to soften.[59] In

Councellor Malone … (Dublin, 1704). For Malone's agency on behalf of the Limerick articlemen in December 1691, see above, p. 104.

53 Viscount Mayo to Col. Browne, 21 May 1703 (N.L.I., Ms 40,904/3/9).

54 G.E. Cokayne, *The complete peerage*, ed. Vicary Gibbs (14 vols, London, 1910–59, 1998), i, 295–8. For Athenry's claim to the articles of Boffin, see above, pp 70–3. See also John Bermingham to Peter Browne, 26 Aug. & 29 Dec. 1707 (N.L.I., Ms 40,905/9/8–9).

55 N.L.I., Mss 40,902/5/10–17; 40,903/4/6; 40,905/6/11; Denis Edward Browne, 10th marquess of Sligo, *Westport House and the Brownes* (2nd ed., Westport, 1998), p. 106.

56 Athenry to Denis Daly, 3 June 1707 (N.L.I., Ms 40,905/9/17).

57 Cokayne, *Complete peerage*, i, 296.

58 A copy of the marriage articles has not been located. For details relating to the dowry still owing in 1706 and 1707, see N.L.I., Ms 40,905/3/1–17.

59 Cokayne, *Complete peerage*, i, 296. Peter Browne had written three months earlier to express relief at the recovery of his sister from 'the old distemper' (Peter Browne to Col. Browne, 6 Oct. 1701 (N.L.I., Ms 40,903/5/13)).

November of that year Hussey reported that Athenry intended to sue Browne.[60] Early the following year Browne's brother Dominick warned that

> [Athenry] is resolved to get from you all that the law will think justly due to him. His inclinations are not for harming you if he could avoid it, but when he reflects on his own condition ... for neglecting to get his just demands from you, he is compelled to go on and nothing will do till he sees a fund deposited ... truly I am weary of being here to listen to such as give him checks for his forbearance with you.

Dominick advised his brother to discharge the debt as soon as possible: 'I know you have enemies both before and behind the curtain, who may leap at the occasion to find and encourage a difference between you and your children.'[61] The next day, Athenry wrote to express his sorrow that matters had come to such a head, informing Browne that he would not negotiate a settlement, but 'let everything take its course ... I wish all mankind did wish your welfare as well as I do'.[62]

Athenry's attitude evidently softened in the following years, perhaps as a result of his brother-in-law Peter Browne's growing influence and control of his family's affairs. By the end of 1706, Browne's debt to Athenry stood at £4,000 for the dowry alone. An agreement was reached between Athenry and Peter in March 1707, whereby Athenry agreed to accept £2,300, with the balance to go to Peter.[63] The mediators were Thomas Nugent, earl of Westmeath (Athenry's trustee), and Denis Daly, former agent to the articlemen of Galway and Peter Browne's father-in-law. Relations between Athenry and the Brownes remained strained on occasion.[64] Even so, Athenry relied heavily on Peter's advice when the inheritance of his son, Francis, was put in jeopardy (see section III below).

Browne's youngest daughter Mary married her first cousin Theobald, Viscount Mayo, in the summer of 1702.[65] Their kinship necessitated a papal dispensation, received on 6 May 1702, but there seems to have been a question raised

---

[60] Luke Hussey to Col. Browne, 17 Nov. 1702 (N.L.I., Ms 40,903/6/21).

[61] Dominick Browne to Col. Browne, 13 Aug. 1703 (N.L.I., Ms 40,904/3/5). Dominick appears to have died within weeks of writing this letter (Athenry to Col. Browne, 24 Sept. 1703 (N.L.I., Ms 40,904/3/12)). See also N.L.I., Ms 40,904/1/9–10.

[62] Athenry to Col. Browne, 14 Aug. 1703 (N.L.I., Ms 40,904/3/11).

[63] N.L.I., Mss 40,905/1/7, 10; 40,905/3/1–17. Daly's connection to the Brownes went beyond the marriage of his daughter to Peter Browne. He was also one of the executors of the will of Col. Garrett Moore, to whom Col. Browne was heavily indebted. He thus frequently appears within the Westport papers in connection with the collection of payments for this debt.

[64] N.L.I., Mss 40,905/7/3; 40,905/9/3, 17.

[65] The date of the marriage is usually given as 8 July, though there is some evidence that it took place in June. The couple's first child was born before 13 April, which would suggest that June is the more probable month. Cf. Cokayne, *Complete peerage*, viii, 606; Dominick Browne to Col. Browne, 25 Aug. 1703 (N.L.I., Ms 40,904/3/6); N.L.I., Ms 40,906/1/4.

in 1703 regarding the legitimacy of the marriage.[66] However, the marriage endured until Mary's death, some time before 1731, when Mayo remarried.[67]

The extent of the estate inherited by Viscount Mayo is unclear, but most, if not all, of the family's land was in Colonel Browne's possession by 1680 and Viscount Mayo was reliant on Browne for subsistence prior to and after his marriage.[68] The christening of the couple's first child in April 1703 was the occasion of a dispute between the two men. Having initially advised that the christening should be delayed, Browne later wrote to instruct that the child should be christened with all haste. Browne's brother Dominick reported that Mayo was resolved

> to go his own way and to have his child honourably christened at his own expense. His lordship is mightily dissatisfied with your sudden change, and really you should consider the matters before you had possessed such honourable persons with doing and undoing, whereas it is expected that some special friends should be at the christening … It were better for you to have thrown £100 in the sea rather than to have writ that letter.[69]

Perhaps this dispute proved the catalyst for a deterioration in the relationship between Browne and Mayo. Peter Browne wrote in 1704 to inquire of the outcome of arbitration between the two men, but it does not appear to have gone well. Just three months later John Browne wrote to Hussey: 'let me tell you of the uproar in this country [Westport] by a shoal of subpoenas served at Lord Mayo's suit on every tenant. This is done to put me to expense.'[70]

There were a number of reasons for the breakdown in relations between the two men. One was Browne's failure, once again, to pay his daughter's dowry, while Browne also attempted to sell land mortgaged to his son-in-law, without Mayo's consent.[71] As of July 1708 Browne owed Viscount Mayo a little less than £3,000.[72] By 1709, Mayo had created further problems by converting to the established church.[73] The fact that his eldest son (also Theobald) conformed

---

[66] Dominick Browne to Col. Browne, 25 Aug. 1703 (N.L.I., Ms 40,904/3/6).

[67] Cokayne, *Complete peerage*, viii, 606.

[68] Luke Hussey to Col. Browne, 19 & 26 July 1701 (N.L.I., Ms 40,903/4/3, 7). Born in 1682, Viscount Mayo was too young to serve in the reign of James II and he was not outlawed during the Williamite war.

[69] Dominick Browne to Col. Browne, 13 Apr. 1703 (N.L.I., Ms 40,904/3/4).

[70] Peter Browne to Hussey, 17 Oct. 1704 (N.L.I., Ms 40,904/5/20); Col. Browne to Hussey, 28 Jan. 1705 (N.L.I., Ms 40,905/6/2).

[71] Viscount Mayo to Col. Browne, 21 May 1703 (N.L.I., Ms 40,904/3/9).

[72] N.L.I., Ms 40,906/1/4.

[73] 19 June 1709 is given as the date of conformity in Cokayne, *Complete peerage*, viii, 606. There is no entry for this conversion in the *Convert rolls*. However, Viscount Mayo took his seat in the Irish house of lords on 21 June 1709 (F.G. James, *Lords of the Ascendancy: the Irish house of lords and its members, 1600–1800* (Dublin, 1995), p. 52, n. 59). The conversion may have taken place earlier:

in 1726 suggests that Mayo's wife and children remained, for the time being, within the Catholic church.[74] John Browne's failure to mend relations with his son-in-law now left him vulnerable, as Viscount Mayo took his seat in the Irish house of lords and soon after petitioned Queen Anne.[75] The loss of his family's estate clearly rankled Mayo, who declared himself 'destitute of a support' for his family. Mayo accused Browne of defrauding his father, 'a gentleman of very weak capacity', of his estate. Browne was said to have been the 5th Viscount's only adviser and manager and that since Mayo's coming of age he had initiated several suits against Browne to recover his family's lands.[76] Mayo drew the queen's attention to his religion (without mentioning his recent conversion) and argued that

> should your petitioner recover the said estate or had he a fortune any way suitable to his quality it might prove a means to strengthen the Protestant interest in that Popish country [County Mayo] which would much contribute to the security of the kingdom.

Charles Dering, auditor general of Ireland, reported that Mayo had only a yearly allowance of about £100 from Browne for the maintenance of his family, and recommended the peer to the queen's bounty.[77] Browne dismissed Mayo's petition as one 'filled with misrepresentations almost from the beginning to the end'.[78] The outcome of the dispute supports Browne's version of events, as Viscount Mayo released, on 13 October 1710, all of his claims to his family's former estate, with the exception of Castleburke.[79]

There is much obscurity surrounding John Browne's second son, Valentine, though it is known that he lived at Mount Browne and married Bridget Talbot. He was still living in January 1722.[80] The only incident in his life which appears in any detail was a quarrel with Anthony Brabazon in 1704.[81] The confron-

in 1705, John Browne wrote to Hussey: 'I hear my Lord Mayo is gone and I hear he is resolved to go to church' (Col. Browne to Hussey, 5 Feb. 1705 (N.L.I., Ms 40,905/8/14).
[74] Convert rolls, pp 17, 28, 304.
[75] N.L.I., Ms 40,906/3/17.
[76] Mayo attained his majority in January 1703, perhaps not coincidentally the year in which tensions between the two men came to the surface.
[77] N.L.I., Ms 40,906/3/17. Dering's chief source of information was John Bourke, Lord Bophin, who succeeded to the earldom of Clanricarde on the death of his brother in 1709.
[78] N.L.I., Ms 40,906/3/18.
[79] On the same day Viscount Mayo signed similar releases relating to the lands purchased by Bryan Higgins and Richard Malone from John Browne, both of whom had purchased in trust for Peter Browne (N.L.I., Ms 40,918/2, 4–5). Disputes between Viscount Mayo and Peter Browne continued after John Browne's death, though their correspondence remained civil (N.L.I., Ms 40,909/4/8–10).
[80] Will of Peter Browne, 26 Jan. 1722, pr. 1724 (Patrick Moran, 'Notes on some Irish altar plate' in J.R.S.A.I., lxxvi (1946), p. 131). Mount Browne was near Westport in the barony of Burrishoole, and was demolished in the early twentieth century.
[81] Members of the Browne family of the Neale were also not averse to duelling in the

tation arose over an alleged insult delivered to Valentine's niece, Bridget 'Biddy' Bermingham, daughter of Lord Athenry. Not all of the episode is known, though a surviving letter from Valentine Browne to Brabazon accused him of having made a 'renegade attempt to address to a young lady of quality'.[82] A duel was set, though both Brabazon and Valentine accused each other of avoiding the appointed date for the duel and threatened to 'post' the other as a coward. Denis Daly (either the former judge or his son) acted as messenger between the two protagonists, with Valentine complaining on 31 October that Daly's arrival in the area had 'made such a noise in the country, that I am afraid we will be taken notice of'. Daly's response was indignant:

> You yourself alarmed the whole country, pretending that you received a message from Mr Brabazon by me, and that you were to meet him every day last week, going with a dozen men armed with guns and carbines which made such a noise that as we came through the Neale the whole town came out enquiring whether we were wounded or you killed.[83]

Daly urged Valentine to attend at Loughrea for the duel: 'I have that value for your reputation that I would have you to be going to Loughrea to hinder your being scandalised. I will prevail with Mr Brabazon not to post you till tomorrow in the afternoon.'[84] Valentine refused and wrote to Brabazon to complain of the manner in which he was informed of the venue:

> My servant, after the delivery of my letter [to Daly], was kept there for an answer till near sun set, and you then with your servants came out a horseback well armed, rascalling and abusing me, and told him you were a horseback on the way to Loughrea, and delivered my servant a letter … where I was to understand you would post me at Loughrea for a coward next day, and then flew away which I apprehended no gentleman would do, my friend being not come and me ordinarily furnished with horses and arms, as men of my religion now generally are.[85]

---

mid-eighteenth century. See James Kelly, *That damn'd thing called honour: duelling in Ireland, 1570–1860* (Cork, 1995), pp 57–62.

[82] Valentine Browne to Anthony Brabazon, 6 Nov. 1704 (N.L.I., Ms 40,904/5/12). There are four copy letters found at this shelf mark. Two are from Denis Daly to Valentine Browne and are undated, though they can be dated to between 1 and 5 November. They are distinguished in footnotes below by the annotation [first letter] and [second letter].

[83] Denis Daly to Valentine Browne, [1–5?] Nov. 1704 (N.L.I., Ms 40,904/5/12 [first letter]).

[84] Same to same, [1–5?] Nov. 1704 (N.L.I., Ms 40,904/5/12 [second letter]).

[85] A Valentine Browne, referred to as of Galway, was adjudicated within the articles of Galway on 24 June 1698 (Simms, 'Irish Jacobites', p. 107). Valentine Browne of 'Lishondin', Co. Mayo, was one of the Catholics licensed to bear arms by the Irish privy council in 1692 (Proclamation, 22 Feb. 1692). Valentine's 'friend' was Edmund Flaherty, who was to have acted as Valentine's second at the duel. Referring to the affair, Col. Browne noted that 'Ned Flaherty behaved himself well' (Col. Browne to Luke Hussey, 12 Nov. 1704 (N.L.I., Ms 40,904/5/10).

Valentine went on to deliver a cutting assessment of Brabazon's character:

> I know you well for a rascally coward, fit only to converse with the rakes of the lowest condition which have been posted at Galway ... and if your uncle [John] Browne of the Neale had not interposed, he had made a devil of you. Why did not you stand your ground either of the days, what had either you or I to do at Loughrea, the place appointed within two miles of your father's house, and it was twelve from mine. Why did you give out all the Neale and Ballinrobe that you were to send a challenge by Mr Daly; you yourself was the man that whispered it all over the country before any was sent. You will assert anything be it never so false, and will after that swear to it. As for religion you have none. Perjury is your known trade, which men of the greatest honour in this country know. This day you are of one church, the next of another, and I believe the next term will be a Quaker to avoid beating. Now that those truths are told of you, why should such a renegade attempt to address to a young lady of quality, in whose interest I must be all the days of my life, you never did any handsome action, and now that I have hitherto lived with an unspotted reputation ... you must not wipe yourself clean upon me, but leave you to be pissed upon by ... whores you converse with. And after all this said, I leave all gentlemen to judge you never designed acting honourably or handsomely by me.[86]

Whether the duel ever took place is unknown; perhaps both men exhausted themselves in their efforts to avoid each other.

Much more is known of Peter, John Browne's eldest son and heir. From the late 1690s he assumed a gradually increasing prominence in managing the sale of his father's estate; from 1704 the family accounts were maintained by Peter, rather than Colonel Browne, and Peter frequently appeared as a party to sales of the Browne estate. He spent considerable lengths of time in London during the 1690s and early 1700s, and seems to have travelled as far as Nantes on at least one occasion.

Though born in 1670, there is no evidence that Peter served in the Williamite war. No Peter Browne appears on the extant lists of outlawries, and nobody of that name was ever adjudicated within the benefit of the articles of surrender. This might imply that he spent this time abroad, perhaps pursuing his education. The first major recorded event of Peter Browne's life was his admission to Middle Temple on 12 July 1695.[87] On 18 April 1696, Peter obtained a licence allowing him to remain in London, in spite of William III's proclamation of 25 February that year banishing all Catholics from the cities of London and Westminster by 10 March.[88] However, by 1701 Peter had yet to complete his studies. It is not clear whether he attended the inns of court with any regularity in the intervening six years, though it is known that he was in

---

[86] Valentine Browne to Anthony Brabazon, 6 Nov. 1704 (N.L.I., Ms 40,904/5/12).

[87] Maynard, 'Irish membership of the English inns of court', p. 390.

[88] License to Peter Browne to remain in London, 18 Apr. 1696 (N.L.I., Ms 40,901/6/1); C.S.P.D., 1696, pp 33–63.

Ireland for lengthy periods in 1699 and 1700 to assist in the sale of his father's estate.[89] Instructed by his father in 1701 not to countenance further study of the law, he acquiesced with a hint of reluctance:

> I did propose to make some stay in this kingdom in order to qualify myself for the management of your business by the study of the law, but I find you would have me home. Since you do not resolve I should study the law I desire I may stay this winter in England to improve myself in my exercises and keeping good company.[90]

Without qualifying under the articles of Limerick, Peter would have been unable to appear in the Irish courts. However, some grounding in the intricacies of land law would have been very useful, particularly in the light of the complex nature of his father's affairs.

Letters sent by Peter from London to his father and Luke Hussey shed some light on the life of an Irish Catholic gentleman in that city during the 1700s. Colonel Browne does not appear to have been able to support his son in the manner in which he would have liked. In October 1701 Peter wrote of his stay in the country outside London 'fearing I might be put in trouble on account of the bill of exchange I drew on you from Nantes in favour of Sir John Kirwan'. In September 1703 he referred to his 'banishment' from London for five weeks due to a lack of money.[91] While in London Peter failed to contract a favourable marriage, despite his best efforts. Money was once more an issue: 'I can't propose that a fortune will drop into my mouth without keeping company with those that have it, which requires an expense; this you can't be ignorant of.'[92] Two years later Peter had yet to find success, complaining to Luke Hussey that

> 'Tis not in my power to make any steps in the advancement of fortune, having no money to support a project of that kind. My father knows what my design was and I had several assurances from thence of an immediate supply to follow it.[93]

---

[89] See chapter 7 for Peter Browne's appearance as a party to a number of sale agreements relating to Col. Browne's estate in 1699 and 1700. See also N.L.I., Mss 40,901/6/7; 40,902/5/10–12.

[90] Peter Browne to Col. Browne, 6 Oct. 1701 (N.L.I., Ms 40,903/5/13).

[91] Peter Browne to Col. Browne, 6 Oct. 1701; Peter Browne to Luke Hussey, 8 Sept. 1703 (N.L.I., Mss 40,903/5/13; 40,904/5/19). Sir John Kirwan had sat in the 1689 Irish parliament and was adjudicated under the articles of Galway. He was a member of the 'new interest', one of Galway's wealthiest merchants and had assisted the Williamites at the surrender of Galway in July 1691 (Eoin Kinsella, '"Dividing the bear's skin before she is taken": Irish Catholics and land in the late Stuart monarchy, 1683–91' in Coleman A. Dennehy (ed.), *Restoration Ireland: always settling and never settled* (Aldershot, 2008), pp 176–7; above, pp 39, 54.

[92] Peter Browne to Col. Browne, 6 Oct. 1701 (N.L.I., Ms 40,903/5/13).

[93] Peter Browne to Luke Hussey, 8 Sept. 1703 (N.L.I., Ms 40,904/5/19).

Peter had signalled his intention to propose to 'Mrs Roper', whose fortune was reputed at £4,000, but if a proposal was made nothing came of it.[94] Indeed, the considerable debts encumbered on his future inheritance appear to have been a major barrier to Peter, perhaps as much psychological as it was real: 'when I consider of the many debts I lie under and of the difficulties of my father's condition, it makes me abhor making any woman miserable.'[95]

Peter's time in London nonetheless was valuable to his father, as it allowed Peter to supervise the progress (or obstruction) of bills relating to the sale of the Browne estate in 1704 and 1705. From mid-1705, Peter spent the majority of his time at Dublin and Westport, assuming a more prominent role in the sale of the Browne estate and the management of their various businesses, including the ironworks on the estate. In or around March 1708 Peter married Mary Moore (née Daly), daughter of Denis Daly, former Jacobite judge and agent of the Galway articlemen. The union was brief: Mary died c.December 1709, leaving Peter with one son, also named John.[96] He does not appear to have remarried.

III

It was perhaps inevitable that pressure would be brought to bear on members of the wider Browne family to convert to the established church after the enactment of the Popery Acts of 1704 and 1709.[97] Peter's ambitions of rebuilding the family's estate were affected by the acts' provisions relating to landownership by Catholics, as were their relations and associates. At least three of John Browne's grandchildren converted. The conversion of one grandchild, Francis Bermingham, future Baron Athenry, was a rather complex episode in the reign of Anne involving several families associated with the Brownes. It is an unusually well documented conversion and one that throws sidelights on some of the motivations for conversion and the responses it evoked among propertied Catholics in the first decade of the eighteenth century.

The date of Bermingham's conformity is usually given as 19 June 1709.[98] This was probably the date on which Bermingham lodged his certificate of

---

94   Peter Browne to Col. Browne, 29 Nov. 1701 (N.L.I., Ms 40,903/5/17).

95   Peter Browne to Luke Hussey, 17 Oct. 1704 (N.L.I., Ms 40,904/5/20).

96   N.L.I., Mss 40,889/38/7; 40,906/5/1. This was Mary's second marriage, following the death of her first husband, John Moore, nephew of Col. Garrett Moore.

97   See C.I. McGrath, 'The provisions for conversion in the penal laws, 1695–1750' in Michael Brown, C.I. McGrath & T.P. Power (eds), *Converts and conversion in Ireland, 1650–1850* (Dublin, 2005), pp 35–47.

98   Cokayne, *Complete peerage*, i, 296. There is no entry for Francis Bermingham in the *Convert rolls*. Converts were legally required to lodge formal certificates of conversion in the court

conformity in the court of chancery. The date of his original conversion was actually 30 July 1707, when Francis was just fifteen years old, and took place without the knowledge of his father. Francis did not convert to avoid any of the restrictions placed by the penal laws on Catholic marriage to Protestants (his bride was a Catholic), or on the rights of Catholics to inherit land and wealth.[99] As an only son Francis was unburdened by the threat of gavelkind, a legal instrument introduced by the 1704 Popery Act that stipulated the subdivision of Catholic-owned estates among all male children.[100] Francis's conversion was, in fact, a desperate attempt to stave off the loss of his wife's considerable portion, threatened by an unscrupulous relative who himself had earlier converted to the established church.

Francis's bride was Mary Nugent, daughter of the earl of Westmeath. The marriage was contracted in February 1704, when Francis was twelve years old and Mary just ten. Lady Dowager Viscountess Clanmalier (Anne O'Dempsey, née Bermingham) was a party to the marriage contract and agreed to settle a marriage portion of £8,000 on her grandniece Mary. Lady Clanmalier's will, drawn up in 1706, settled a lease on lands inherited from her father on Francis in fulfilment of the settlement.[101] Lady Clanmalier's nephew, Richard, Lord Bellew, had other ideas. Lady Clanmalier and her sister Mary had inherited considerable portions of their father's estate after his death. Bellew had already inherited his mother Mary's portion of the estate and expected also to inherit Clanmalier's portion. He claimed that Lady Clanmalier had in fact settled her estate on him, in 1695 and again in 1703, but suppressed these settlements following his conversion. Bellew also claimed that leasing the lands to Francis Bermingham in order to pay Mary's portion was an evasion of the Popery Act of 1704.[102]

As a convert and member of the Irish house of lords from July 1707, Bellew was well placed to scupper Lady Clanmalier's intention to settle the marriage portion on Mary. At the end of July Peter Browne informed his

of chancery. The date of Viscount Mayo's formal conversion was 19 June 1709, while Denis Daly, Jr, lodged his certificate of conversion the day before. The closeness of the dates is hardly coincidental.

99 An act to prevent Protestants intermarrying with papists (9 Will. III, c. 3 (1697)); An act to prevent the further growth of popery (2 Anne, c. 6 (1704)). For the provisions of these acts as they related to marriage, see McGrath, 'Provisions for conversion in the penal laws', pp 39–44.

100 The gavelkind clause of the 1704 Popery Act stipulated that, if a Catholic landowner had more than one male heir, the estate could not descend intact to the eldest son, but was instead to be divided equally between each son. However, the eldest son would become eligible to inherit the entire estate if he converted to the Church of Ireland. Much the same provisions applied if there were only female children.

101 *The case of the right honourable Francis Lord Bermingham, baron of Athunry, in the kingdom of Ireland* ([Dublin,] n.d).

102 *The case of Richard, Lord Bellew* ([Dublin,] n.d.).

father that Bellew (with his wife Frances, dowager countess of Newburgh) had petitioned the house of commons, alleging that the original settlement had been suppressed because of his conversion and requesting a bill to settle the estate on himself. Peter advised that there was little chance of preventing an act of parliament and recommended that the earl of Westmeath should devote his resources to securing a favourable report from the attorney and solicitor general of England: 'I am of opinion that this business is not so well managed as it ought to be.'[103]

Bellew's conversion and membership of the lords no doubt benefited his case, especially in the light of the lord lieutenant's speech in parliament urging increased vigilance against the threat of Catholicism.[104] Peter Browne reported that 'not one man in the house spoke against Bellew's petition'. Francis's religion was clearly seen by some of his friends as an obstacle, and Peter Browne told his father that:

> I must acquaint you that Mr Thomas Daly has carried Franky ... yesterday to the Archbishop of Dublin and to the Archbishop of Tuam to make him a Protestant. He has declared himself so and was presented to the lord chancellor this morning. I thank God I am an entire stranger to all these proceedings and always declared my aversion to any such proceeding, though I doubt not but the lad had encouragement or he would never think on it, or Thomas Daly presume to do any such matter without a connivance from those who ought to take better care of him. My heart is broke for I do not believe his case is anything the better for it. The committee ... heard all my Lord Bellew's evidence which in my opinion are of no weight, though I find all the committee are for Bellew. He has made a strong faction in the house. Tomorrow they have appointed to hear our counsel. For my part these transactions are so disagreeable to my temper that I am very unwilling to meddle further in the affair. I doubt not but this news will make a speedy end of my Lord Athenry. I am now in that confusion that I know not what I write for the boy is lost. Be sure you burn this letter as soon as you read it ... I meet with so many misfortunes that I know not what to do. You are happy to be out of this town. I wish I had been in the country this month past, for I doubt not but it will be imagined that I gave the boy encouragement, which I protest before God I never did, directly or indirectly.[105]

[103] Peter Browne to Col. Browne, 29 July 1707 (N.L.I., Ms 40,905/7/9).

[104] The commons had drafted heads of bills for explaining and amending the 1704 Popery act and the 1697 act preventing Catholics from becoming solicitors within two weeks of the opening of the parliamentary session (*Irish Legislation Database, Queen's University Belfast*: http://www.qub.ac.uk/ild/). It was also contended that Bellew had 'secured all the top men of the house in the cause by good large fees' (Peter Browne to Col. Browne, 5 Aug. 1707 (N.L.I., Ms 40,905/7/11).

[105] Peter Browne to Col. Browne, 31 July 1707 (N.L.I., Ms 40,905/7/10). The archbishops referred to were William King (Dublin) and John Vesey (Tuam). Thomas Daly was the eldest son of Denis Daly, former justice of the common pleas and agent to the articlemen. Thomas Daly was also one of several Catholics who petitioned the English privy council against the bill for explaining the 1704 Popery Act (T.N.A., PC 2/82, f. 452 (15 Sept. 1707)).

Peter Browne's pessimism was well founded, for the conversion had little effect if its intent was to persuade parliament to reject Bellew's petition.[106]

The passage of Bellew's bill through all stages of the legislative process was relatively smooth. On 5 August, the Irish parliament received a counter-petition from Lady Clanmalier, Francis Bermingham and his wife Mary, presented by archbishops William King and John Vesey. On the same day, the select committee appointed to consider Bellew's petition reported that it intended to bring in heads of a bill in his favour.[107] Between 5 August and 11 August, negotiations between the two sides produced a compromise that was satisfactory to Bellew and Clanmalier. A bill for settling Clanmalier's estate on Bellew, encumbered with £3,000 for Mary Nugent's portion and which had the 'consent of all parties', was presented and agreed to by the commons on 11 August and sent to the lord lieutenant for transmission to London.[108]

In the meantime a printed summary setting out Francis's case and distributed to parliament attracted the ire of the house of lords, who resolved to investigate the printer and publisher. Peter Browne had been one of the instigators of the case, and he informed his father that 'Ned Malone is sick at heart about it. I resolve to return tomorrow out of town … for I would not be examined if I can avoid it … we are horrified and hunted down on all sides, God help us.' Luke Hussey and Peter both expressed the opinion that it might be possible to have the bill rejected at the Irish privy council.[109] Peter's attempt to avoid being called before the house of lords led to his absence from Dublin between 6 and 14 August. On his return, he discovered the compromise that had been negotiated between Bellew, Clanmalier and Westmeath. He expressed misgivings and urged Athenry to send him a power of attorney so that he could oppose the bill at the privy council. Athenry obliged, confident that the bill would not be sent to London: 'we shall make better party and be better prepared against the next time'.[110] The petition to the Irish privy council was, however, rejected on the grounds that Westmeath did not support it and that 'it was transacted by officious people that never considered the advantages of the family'.[111] Among

106 'Notwithstanding Franky's religion my Lord Bellew has carried his business in the house of commons' (Peter Browne to Col. Browne, 5 Aug. 1707 (N.L.I., Ms 40,905/7/11).

107 C.J.I., ii, 521–2 (5 Aug. 1707).

108 C.J.I., ii, 530 (11 Aug. 1707). The full title of the bill read 'An act for settling the estate of Anne Lady Viscountess Dowager of Clanmaleer on Richard Lord Baron of Duleek and for raising £3,000 thereout for the portion of Mary Nugent niece [sic] to the said Lady Clanmaleer and wife of Francis Bermingham eldest son of Edward Lord Baron of Athenree'.

109 Luke Hussey to Col. Browne, 5 Aug. 1707 (N.L.I., Ms 40,905/7/11). Peter Browne's letter of the same date is written on the reverse.

110 Athenry to Peter Browne, 15 Aug. 1707 (N.L.I., Ms 40,905/9/4).

111 Peter Browne to Col. Browne, 15, 16 & 19 Aug. 1707 (N.L.I., Ms 40,905/7/12–14); Athenry to Peter Browne, 15 Aug. 1707 (N.L.I., Ms 40,905/9/4–5 (two letters)). Quotation taken from Peter Browne's letter of 19 August. Cf. Peter Browne's contention in his letter to Col. Browne of

those whose advice Peter Browne and Athenry sought in the prosecution of Athenry's opposition were Arthur French, Gregory Nolan, archbishop William King and 'Mr Daly' (Denis or one of his sons).

The bill was transmitted to London for scrutiny by English privy council, providing Lord Athenry with another opportunity to defeat it.[112] His counsel were, however, denied the opportunity to present their case and the bill was approved without amendment on 24 September. By 11 October the bill had been introduced in the Irish house of commons, read and committed. On 13 October, Athenry made one last effort to be heard in parliament against the bill, but once again was denied. Within two weeks the bill had passed all stages in both houses and received the royal assent on 24 October.[113]

It is unclear whether Bellew's claim that he had been disinherited by Lady Clanmalier following his conversion had any foundation, though it would not have been unusual. The gavelling clause of the Popery Act of 1704 had brought the issue of Catholic fathers disinheriting sons who converted to Protestantism firmly to the attention of the Irish government. The Irish parliament in turn legislated to prevent such methods of circumventing the gavelling clause in the Popery Act of 1709.[114] The problem had, however, existed even before the gavelling clause was introduced, with the first legislative measure to prevent a Catholic from disinheriting a convert son drafted by the Irish house of commons in October 1695.[115] Bellew's act of 1707 properly falls into this category, given the accusation that he had been disinherited on the basis of his conversion. His personal religion and the prevailing desire of Irish Protestants to enact further anti-Catholic legislation, when coupled with Athenry's mismanagement of his opposition, ensured that failure for Athenry was the most probable outcome. Francis Bermingham's conversion can only be seen as driven by material opportunism and not from a desire to avoid any specific provision of anti-Catholic legislation then in operation. On the other hand, that his conversion was viewed by some as necessary to improve the chances of successful opposition to Bellew's bill is telling. So too the dismayed reaction of his kinsmen.

---

15 August that Westmeath supported Athenry's petition: 'I find my Lord Westmeath is willing … though he will have no hand against his own agreement.'

[112] T.N.A., PC 2/82, ff 432–3 (1 Sept. 1707).

[113] 6 Anne, c. 1 (private). A copy is preserved in Marsh's Library (Z.2.1.7 (56)). Athenry's opposition did not end there. Two further private acts relating to Bellew's estate were passed in 1709 and 1710, which allowed the vexed issue of Mary Nugent's portion to be raised again (8 Anne, c. 2 (private); 9 Anne, c. 3 (private); *The case of the right honourable Francis Lord Bermingham, baron of Athunry, in the kingdom of Ireland*; *The case of Richard, Lord Bellew*; *An answer to the printed case of Richard Lord Bellew* ([Dublin, ?])).

[114] 8 Anne, c. 3, ss 3–6, 9. See McGrath, 'Provisions for conversion in the penal laws', p. 45.

[115] Bergin, 'Irish legislative procedure', ii, 296. See also *Irish Legislation Database*: http://www.qub.ac.uk/ild/?func=display_bill&id=614.

Colonel John Browne's reaction to the conversion of his grandson is not known. He did not live to see the conversion of two other grandsons, including John Browne, the only son and heir of Peter. This John Browne was the first of the Westport Brownes to convert. His cousin George was the first of the Neale Brownes to convert, in 1711. Edward Synge, archbishop of Tuam, wrote to William Wake, archbishop of Canterbury, that George Browne's son (another John) had been 'bred a Protestant by his guardian and some other worthy friends'. Synge asked Wake to arrange lodgings and a tutor for Browne at Oxford University 'that he may be secure from the insinuating attempts of his Popish kindred'.[116]

IV

At the time of Colonel John Browne's death the family's restoration to its pre-eminent position in County Mayo was by no means certain. Browne's grandson John, who in due course acquired a peerage as earl of Altamont, enjoyed a political career and social elevation that was made possible by Peter Browne's success in beginning the process of rebuilding the landed interest of the Westport Brownes, in a difficult time for Catholic landowners.[117] To do so, Peter had first to assume an increasing level of control of the family's affairs. John Browne was approaching his seventieth birthday when the second intensive period of selling his estate began in 1708 and his health appears to have been precarious. That his mobility had decreased during the latter ten years of his life can be gauged from Hussey's occasional references to securing a *dedimus* for the colonel, as well as Browne's own admission in 1705 that he was 'very heavy and very unfit to undergo a fatigue'.[118]

According to family tradition, Colonel John Browne disappeared in or around 1704 to escape his creditors and was officially declared dead by an act of the English parliament in 1705.[119] Though not the case, a cursory perusal

[116] Edward Synge, archbishop of Tuam, to William Wake, archbishop of Canterbury, 15 Apr. 1725 (quoted in S.J. Connolly, *Religion, law and power: the making of Protestant Ireland, 1660–1760* (Oxford, 1992), p. 309).
[117] For an instance of Peter Browne falling foul of the penal laws, see G.E. Howard, *Several special cases on the laws against the further growth of Popery in Ireland* (Dublin, 1775), pp 11–12.
[118] Luke Hussey to Col. Browne, 19 July 1701 & 10 June 1704 (N.L.I., Mss 40,903/4/3; 40,904/3/19); Col. Browne to Hussey, 23 Oct. 1703 & 14 Feb. 1705 (N.L.I., Mss 40,904/5/2; 40,905/6/5). A year later, Browne wrote to Lord Athenry to explain that he could not attend a meeting in Athenry: 'I am ill mounted and much troubled with the travelling to Bundorragh' (Col. Browne to Athenry, 24 Mar. 1706 (N.L.I., Ms 40,905/8/6). A *dedimus* was granted to a person who was too unwell to travel to appear before a judge (Giles Jacob, *A new law dictionary* (London, 1729), p. 206).
[119] 10th marquess of Sligo, *Westport house and the Brownes*, pp 13–14.

of the family's papers might lead to this conclusion. The colonel's letters were frequently sent under cover to his agents – particularly between 1703 and 1705.[120] In an endorsement to a lease dated 2 August 1705, George Throckmorton is noted as having testified before Philip Savage and Henry Echlin, barons of the exchequer, that John Browne, gentleman, of Dublin had died some time previously.[121] However, this is certainly not a reference to Colonel John Browne; Savage and Echlin were both trustees for the sale of his estate and continued to deal with Browne in that matter up until July 1708.[122] Browne's signature appears on numerous leases and sale agreements concluded between 1705 and 1711 and letters were openly addressed to him again after 1705.[123] He wrote to his son in 1707:

> I am of opinion that if any business of mine be in parliament I had better be there than at home. Let me assure you I understand the affair as well before the parliament as before the trustees better than you can. Inform yourself and if there be any such matter in agitation you cannot be denied a parliament privilege for me to attend in Dublin.[124]

Though the exact date is not known, Colonel John Browne died in 1711. His last known act was to sign a deed settling his estate with his two sons on 19 April that year. By September 1711 Peter Browne seems to have assumed complete control of the household accounts.[125]

Peter Browne remained a Catholic until his death. His son John, however, did not. He matriculated at Christ Church College, Oxford, on 17 July 1725, aged sixteen.[126] The guardians appointed to care for him after Peter's death were his cousin George of the Neale and his uncles Denis Daly (junior) of Frenchbrook, County Mayo, and Peter Daly of Kilquane, County Galway.[127] In accordance with the provisions of the 1704 Popery Act, all three were

---

[120] An example of the restrictions on Browne's movements at this time is found in a letter from Lord Athenry to Browne. Referring to an intended meeting between them, Athenry wrote that 'Milltown is to be the place as formerly appointed, the day will be upon a Sunday so as no sheriff can harm you. Neither do I think the sheriff of this county has anything against you.' (Athenry to Col. Browne, 24 Sept. 1703 (N.L.I., Ms 40,904/3/12)).

[121] N.L.I., Ms 40,889/20/1.

[122] The last sale agreement to which the trustees were a party was concluded on 9 July 1708 (N.L.I., Ms 40,889/31/3).

[123] The last extant letter to or from John Browne would appear to be from William Godwin to Col. Browne, 9 Jan. 1709 (N.L.I., Ms 40,906/5/11).

[124] Col. Browne to Peter Browne, [June/July] 1707 (N.L.I., Ms 40,905/7/15). This letter is undated, but written on the same sheet as a letter from Col. Browne to Luke Hussey, dated 28 June 1707.

[125] N.L.I., Mss 40,984/11; 40,918/8; 40,906/5/6–8.

[126] Joseph Foster, *Alumni Oxoniensis* (4 vols, Oxford, 1891–2), i, 174.

[127] The year of Peter Browne's death is usually given as 1724. However, the codicil to his will was dated 26 January 1722 and it has been convincingly argued that he was in fact dead within three weeks of that date (Moran, 'Notes on some Irish altar plate', p. 131).

Protestants.[128] Denis Daly, junior, had conformed on 18 June 1709, with George Browne and Peter Daly following suit on 22 March 1711 and 22 October 1716 respectively.[129] All three also maintained close relations with the Catholic members of their families. In 1723 and 1724 two works were commissioned to honour the memory of Peter Browne, possibly at the behest of his son. The first was a chalice, presented to Burrishoole Abbey in 1723, with the inscription *Orate pro anima Petri Browne qui me fieri fecit pro Conventu de Burisowle, Anno Domini 1723* (Pray for the soul of Peter Browne who caused me to be made for the community of Burrishoole, A.D. 1723). The second has been described as an altar stone at Carrownalurgan ring fort, on the outskirts of Westport town. It was similarly inscribed: *Orate pro anima Petri Browne qui me fieri fecit 1723*.[130] The certificate of John Browne's conversion was enrolled in Chancery on 4 December 1729.[131] He was elected MP for Castlebar in 1743, the first of the Westport Brownes to sit in the Irish parliament. He held the seat until his elevation to the peerage successively as Baron Monteagle (1760), Viscount Westport (1768) and earl of Altamont (1771).[132] His grandson, yet another John Browne, was created marquess of Sligo on 29 December 1800 in reward for his support for the Act of Union. Westport House remained the family seat for more than 330 years. Built by Colonel Browne in the 1680s and much enhanced by the renowned architect Richard Cassels in the 1730s, the house stands as a fitting testament to a remarkable character.[133]

---

[128] 2 Anne, c. 6, s. 4. This section of the act prohibited Catholics from acting as guardians to children under the age of twenty-one.

[129] *Convert rolls*, pp 21, 60–1. The enrolment of the certificates of conformity of Denis Daly, Jr, Viscount Mayo and Baron Athenry occurred within two days of each other.

[130] Moran, 'Notes on some Irish altar plate', p. 130; 10th marquess of Sligo, *Westport house and the Brownes*, p. 17.

[131] *Convert rolls*, p. 22.

[132] The earl of Altamont's maternal grandfather was Denis Daly, the former judge in the reign of James II. Both of his grandfathers were thus prominent former Jacobites.

[133] Jeremy Ulick Browne, the 11th marquess of Sligo and a direct lineal descendent of Col. John Browne, died on 13 July 2014. After more than three centuries of remarkable continuity, the male line of the family was broken with his death and the title descended to his cousin, Sebastian Ulick Browne. Though there was an entailment on Westport House restricting its inheritance to the male line, that entailment was broken by a private act passed in Dáil Éireann in 1993, and the house was inherited by the 11th marquess's daughters (No. 1/1993: The Altamont (Amendment of Deed of Trust) Act). The house was, however, sold in January 2017 (*Irish Times*, 27 Jan. 2017).

Conclusion

I

The trajectory of John Browne's career, between the Restoration of Charles II in 1660 and the death of William III in 1702, mirrored that of the wider Catholic 'new interest'. None of his contemporaries were, however, able to match Browne's extreme levels of success and failure. Between 1666 and 1680 Browne created an enormous estate in the west of Ireland, consisting of more than 155,000 acres. Not content with this accomplishment, he also set out to establish himself as an ironmaster, rapidly accumulating debts as he sought to build a profitable business. This was to prove his undoing. Heavily indebted by the mid-1680s, Browne never again enjoyed a period of financial stability. Given time he may have been able to recover his position, but James II's reign introduced a period of instability in the three kingdoms that culminated with William of Orange's invasion of England in November 1688. Browne's subsequent support for the Jacobite cause was as wholehearted as any, though the underlying motive is clear. In the event of a Jacobite victory, James II would have written off at least a portion of those debts in payment for Browne's services. Trusting in this eventuality, and on the acquisition of a new estate from forfeited Protestant lands, Browne did not join with other prominent 'new interest' landowners who actively assisted the Williamites during the war. His loyalty ensured a place at the negotiating table in 1691 as a representative of the Jacobites, and offered an opportunity that Browne gladly took. The resulting articles of surrender set the course of the remainder of his life.

Article 13 of Limerick ensured that Browne was unique among the articlemen. The article itself was exceptional in that the legislative and executive branches of government made repeated attempts to ensure its implementation and to secure parliamentary ratification, beginning with the very first parliament of the post-war era. On their side too, the motive is clear – the vast majority of the beneficiaries of article 13 were Protestant and many were members of parliament or officeholders. Beyond the confines of his immediate family, it is difficult to know how Browne was regarded by Catholics in Connacht, or indeed the rest of Ireland. His sons-in-law clearly looked to him for advice and counsel, even if relations with both were occasionally strained. Petitions from the articlemen in the years after Limerick referred to article 13 as 'surreptitiously obtained', or having been inserted in the terms of surrender by 'sinister and indirect means', which implies a certain bitterness. The articlemen of Limerick did not offer any sustained objection to article 13, though they of course could not afford to unpick the terms on which their estates depended. The articlemen of Galway vigorously contested Browne's article in 1692 and several did so again in 1695, as did the other articlemen. Browne does not appear to have been shunned by his contemporaries but relations may occasionally have been tense. His nephew Edmund Malone reported that Browne's relentless pursuit of land had 'disobliged most gentlemen of those counties where his estate lies by too great a desire of extending the limits of his possessions beyond reason'.[1]

Browne's trajectory after the surrender of Limerick does not match that of his better-known contemporaries. The subsequent careers of Jacobite soldiers and politicians such as Patrick Sarsfield, Justin MacCarthy, Thomas Sheridan and Sir Richard Nagle are all well known, yet these men chose exile with James II after Limerick. There are no studies of Irish Jacobites who remained in Ireland after Limerick which would allow for some comparison with Browne. His rise among the landowners of Connacht typified that of the 'new interest' after 1660. A skilled lawyer, Browne epitomised the kind of Catholic sought by Tyrconnell to lead the counter-revolution of James II's reign. Some of his 'new interest' contemporaries became important members of Tyrconnell's administration, but Browne played no part in Tyrconnell's plans. Between 1689 and 1691 Browne was no less important than Sarsfield or Mountcashel to the Jacobite war effort but, as a supplier of ordnance and provisions rather than a military commander, his actions were never immortalised in popular memory and he has featured little in historical accounts.

Browne's ability as a lawyer was not matched by his business acumen. He lacked the experience and time necessary to successfully run the several ironworks he owned. His vast estate required the employment of multiple agents and generated an enormous amount of administrative work. Moreover, the acquisition of this estate seems to have lacked a coherent plan. Some contrasts with William Conolly's careful (and occasionally dishonest) estate-building strategy can be drawn.[2] The comparison is somewhat forced, for the two men came from very different backgrounds and, though they built their estates within twenty years of each other, they did so in utterly distinct political climates. Some broad similarities do, however, exist. Both profited handsomely from the turmoil of land confiscations in the aftermath of rebellion and were accused of behaving unethically in the process. Both were among the greatest, if not *the* greatest landowning commoners of their generation. Both built houses that befitted their social status. Westport House may not have been designed

---

[1] Edmund Malone, London, to John Bingham, 5 Mar. 1697 (P.R.O.N.I., T3134/1/11).
[2] N.L.I., Annesley Mss, xxiii, ff 36, 65.

on the same grand scale as Castletown, but it was probably one of the finest residences in Connacht even before its enhancement in the 1730s. Conolly built his estate with an eye to his political advancement and the improvement of his social standing. Browne's estate, though larger by a few thousand acres, appears to have been amassed with no such plan. If enhancing his prestige played a part, it was his local standing, not national, that drove his purchases. No moderately astute Catholic of the Restoration era could have expected to sit in any future Irish parliament, but Browne's acquisitions lacked even the prospect of great rents. Just under 40,000 acres of his estate were classed as profitable in 1704, with a potential rental income of only £3,500. Conolly's estate held a potential income of almost £15,000 and included properties in all four provinces.[3]

Surviving records for the administration of Browne's estate and other business interests during the 1690s and 1700s indicate that he had a poor grasp of the scale of the problem facing him from 1691. He was reported in 1697 as having said 'he would have a good estate left after his debts paid'.[4] This was a bold statement, for the reality was that he was destined to lose almost all of his land. Browne had still not cleared his debts by the time of his death, twenty years after the articles of Limerick were signed, despite the assistance of the levy raised on Catholic landowners by article 13. It must be wondered whether Browne ever considered exile on the continent, particularly in light of his debts. Garrett Dillon, Browne's nephew, had escaped his share of their debts by following James II to France. It seems probable that Browne's misplaced confidence in the resources of his estate allowed him to believe that his debts could be cleared quite quickly. Article 13 must be seen as a primary cause of this belief, for little else had changed since his financial troubles began in the early 1680s.

II

In September 1701 Luke Hussey wrote to Browne with news of the death of James II: 'Tis the talk in town that the Prince of Wales was proclaimed king of Great Britain in Versailles.'[5] Four weeks later Hussey informed Browne that the Pope had also recognised James Francis Edward Stuart's claim to the throne. Hussey also reported on an attempt by lord lieutenant Laurence Hyde, earl of Rochester, to encourage Irish Catholics to present an address of loyalty to William III. Rochester summoned 'Dr Burne' and inquired whether he had

---

3   For the acquisition of Conolly's estate, see Patrick Walsh, *The making of the Irish Protestant Ascendancy: the life of William Conolly, 1662–1729* (Woodbridge, 2010), pp 43–83.

4   Edmund Malone to Agmondisham Vesey, 14 Oct. 1697 (N.A.I., Sarsfield-Vesey papers).

5   Luke Hussey to Col. Browne, 16 Sept. 1701 (N.L.I., Ms 40,903/5/3).

any influence on the laity of the Roman Catholics in this city or county, and to desire
him to influence them to present an address to his Majesty, against the French King
and Prince of Wales, and that it was expected by the government that all the Roman
Catholics in the kingdom would present an address to the same purpose.[6]

'Dr Burne' was probably Edmund Byrne, then vicar-general and later archbishop
of Dublin. His reported response was pithy; the only people with such influence
among Catholics were the bishops, and they were banished by law.[7] Hussey's
letter concluded with speculation that an Irish parliament was expected soon
and that the disarmament and attainder acts of 1695 and 1697 would be
repealed.

Hussey's anticipation of the repeal of some of the earliest penal laws was, of
course, unfounded. When the Irish parliament reconvened in 1703, it immediately set about strengthening the penal laws and continued to do so for the next
fifty years. Hussey offered no further comment on the merits of a loyal address
and the sincerity of Rochester's motives is not certain. He may well have been
attempting to revive an old stratagem employed by viceroys of the Restoration
period. Ormond and Essex had sponsored a similar initiative in the 1660s and
1670s but both claimed to have been promoting divisions among the Catholic
interest – a tactic that was largely successful.[8]

The proclamation of James Francis Edward Stuart as James III was an ideal
time for such an address, were the leading members of the Catholic gentry
and nobility so inclined. Accusations of Jacobite plotting were intermittently
levelled at the articlemen throughout the 1690s, and would be again during
the reign of Anne.[9] The majority of the articlemen accepted William III as, at
least, their *de facto* monarch. Some, such as Colonel Henry Luttrell, actively
sought service with William's armies on the continent during the 1690s.
Having stood with James II at Salisbury plain in 1688 and proved himself
a valuable commander in Ireland during the war, Luttrell is nevertheless
remembered in infamy in Jacobite folklore following allegations of treason at
the Battle of Aughrim and the surrender of Limerick. Such was the hatred for
him among Irish Catholics, the Irish parliament suspected that revenge for
his alleged treachery during the Williamite war had motivated his murder in

[6] Luke Hussey to Col. Browne, 25 Oct. 1701 (N.L.I., Ms 40,903/5/15).
[7] Byrne was referring to a 1697 act, titled 'An act for banishing all Papists exercising any
Ecclesiastical jurisdiction, and all regulars of the Popish clergy out of this kingdom' (9 Will. III, c.
1).
[8] The fullest account of this episode is found in Anne Creighton, 'The Remonstrance of
December 1661 and Catholic politics in Restoration Ireland' in *I.H.S.*, xxxiv (2004–5), pp 16–41.
[9] Éamonn Ó Ciardha, *Ireland and the Jacobite cause, 1685–1766: a fatal attachment* (Dublin,
2002), pp 112–81.

1717, and offered a reward of £1,000 for information leading to the arrest of the killer.[10]

Luttrell was not an isolated case among the Jacobite officer corps. For some members of the Irish administration, perceptions of the articlemen were informed by their consistent engagement with the government in the pursuit of their objectives. Referring to the articlemen of Galway, Sir Richard Cox declared in 1699 that 'if it were not for their bigotry in religion, they would be as glad to be rid of [James II] as any of us can be'.[11] Thady Quin petitioned for a pardon from William III in 1699, noting that his title to his estate in County Limerick was 'grounded upon the Acts of Settlement and Explanation and it is in his interest as well as his inclination to be for an English government'.[12] Lieutenant-Colonel Maurice Hussey, a former Jacobite army officer and Limerick articleman, acted as an informant for the English government at the Jacobite court in St Germain-en-laye.[13] Colonel John Browne enjoyed close relations with his Protestant neighbours, as did many of the articlemen and protectees, who were able to secure testaments to their good behaviour during the war from such neighbours and associates. On the other hand, some articlemen undoubtedly corresponded with the exiled court.[14] Henry Oxburgh and Adam Colclough, intimately involved with lobbying by the articlemen in 1691 and 1692, both participated in the Jacobite rebellion of 1715.[15]

There is no doubting the strength of Jacobite sentiment in Ireland during the 1690s, or its endurance among many Irish Catholics until the latter half of the eighteenth century.[16] Jacobitism was, however, more attractive to dispossessed and landless Catholics. It should not be assumed that the landowning Irish Catholic elite yearned for a Stuart restoration in the decade after the surrender of Limerick. For these men, the preservation of their estates seems to have trumped all other considerations. Indeed, their desire to retain their patrimonies had helped to undermine the Jacobite war effort in 1690 and 1691. Lecky's conclusion that the Catholic nobility and gentry – mindful of

[10] Alan Brodrick to [Joseph Addison], 26 Oct. 1717 (S.H.C., Midleton papers, 1248/4, ff 83–4).
[11] B.L., Add. Ms 38,153, f. 21; D.I.B.
[12] Quin was recommended for a pardon by the Irish government. He never received one, but did obtain a *nolle prosequi* on his convictions for treason during the war (Caroline Quin, Countess of Dunraven, *Memorials of Adare Manor* (Oxford, 1865), pp 181–5). The report on Thady Quin's petition, which the Countess of Dunraven transcribed, is still extant (University of Limerick, Dunraven Papers, D 3196/A/3/1).
[13] B.L., Add Ms 72,570, ff 122–36, 142–68; H.M.C., *Downshire Mss*, i, part 1, 490–1; C.S.P.D., 1699–1700, pp 162, 181–3, 225, 234; Simms, *Irish Jacobites*, p. 97.
[14] 'Persons licensed to correspond with late King James' (C.J., xii, 186–7 (31 Mar. 1698)).
[15] Bergin, 'Irish Catholic interest', pp 44–5.
[16] Ó Ciardha, *Ireland and the Jacobite cause*; Vincent Morley, *Irish opinion and the American Revolution, 1760–1783* (Cambridge, 2002); Breandán Ó Buachalla, *Aisling ghéar: na Stíobhartaigh agus an taos léinn, 1603–1788* (Dublin, 1996).

their treatment by Charles II and James II – had no wish to put their estates in jeopardy once again remains pertinent.[17] They were hardly likely to forget quickly that, when the Catholic James II had sat on the throne, their estates were as vulnerable as at any time before.

While the careers of articlemen such as Colonel John Browne, Denis Daly, Sir Stephen Rice and Sir Toby Butler suggest aloofness from Jacobite plotting, the involvement of their contemporaries Colclough and Oxburgh in the 1715 rebellion illustrates that any attempt to apply broad generalisations to individuals with much in common is ultimately unhelpful. The landed elite acted together to preserve their estates on several occasions, but it must be conceded that each of these men adopted a pragmatic approach to his own individual situation, and that accordingly all cut their cloth to suit their measure. Survival and retrenchment largely informed the political activity of the articlemen during the 1690s. There remains much to be discovered regarding the activities and *mentalités* of the Irish Catholic elite in the decades that followed.

III

The articles of surrender were, initially at least, a foundation stone of the Williamite settlement of Ireland. The articlemen had obtained what seemed favourable terms. In the first instance, their estates were protected from forfeiture. Secondly, the articlemen of Galway and Limerick were to be entitled to continue in their respective professions. It was of course in the articlemen's interest to engage with the Williamite government to have these promises kept. Throughout the reigns of William III and Anne, and well into the Hanoverian era, the articlemen lobbied both the Irish and English governments to have the articles implemented, and to prevent any infringement on them by prospective legislation. In assessing the responses of the governments and the success of the articlemen, not only do the several terms of surrender have to be considered separately, but also the different promises made within each.

The English parliament's 1691 Oaths Act immediately abrogated article 12 of Galway, which promised the Catholic lawyers of the town 'free liberty of practice'. From the end of 1691, no Galway articleman could appear in the law courts. Both governments initially sought to remedy this situation, but neither appeared inclined to do so after 1692. Opposition from Irish Protestants frustrated an attempt by the English parliament in 1696 to provide relief for

---

[17] W.E.H. Lecky, *A history of Ireland in the eighteenth century* (5 vols, London, repr. 1913) i, 413; cf. Éamonn Ó Ciardha, '"A lot done, more to do": the restoration and road ahead for Irish Jacobite studies' in Paul Monod, Murray Pittock & Daniel Szechi (eds), *Loyalty and identity: Jacobites at home and abroad* (Basingstoke, 2010), p. 60.

the lawyers of Galway. Similarly, the imposition of the oath of abjuration on prospective solicitors from 1707 abrogated article 9 of Limerick, which provided that the only oath to be administered to Catholics was the oath of allegiance. The articles of Galway and Limerick each provided that freedom of religious practice would be allowed to the articlemen.[18] Beginning in 1697, the Irish parliament passed a series of acts intended to curtail the pastoral functions of the Catholic church, and it was not until the reign of George I that its ecclesiastical structures began to recover.

Very few of the articlemen suffered permanent dispossession. The retention of Catholic-owned estates had been the primary consideration that prompted negotiations with the Williamite army from late 1690, and was viewed as the most important of the promises made within the articles. The Irish privy council (acting as a court of claims in 1692 and 1694), and the specially appointed judges who sat between 1697 and 1699, seem to have adjudicated impartially. There is, however, evidence to suggest that the government vigorously pursued those whose claims were suspect and that their delay in hearing claims was more detrimental than has previously been thought.[19] In general Protestant opinion remained implacably hostile to the articles of surrender throughout the 1690s and beyond. Sir Francis Brewster complained that 'under the subterfuge of the articles of Limerick, Galway, etc., [Catholics] have sheltered themselves from common justice, and live splendidly and securely upon the spoils of ruined Protestants'.[20] Some Catholics in exile on the continent failed to appreciate the benefit of the articles. Captain Charles O'Malley, writing from St Germain, expressed his satisfaction that his son Teig was protected by the articles of Limerick, but refused to send him any papers relating to their estate in Ireland:

> My opinion is that you should not claim from the present administration but wait a more favourable juncture which the friends and allies of the King my master assure him and us is not far off … I besides am informed I am in the list of those proscribed by the Prince of Orange and a reward offered for me dead or alive. If this be so it would be a sufficient pretext to seize and take those papers from you by force had you them in

[18] The articles of Sligo also included this protection by virtue of article 16 of the articles signed at that town on 6 August 1691. See Appendix A.
[19] C.S.P.D., 1700–2, p. 396; C.T.B., 1700–1, p. 318. See above, pp 120–1, for the effect of the delay. See also Appendix B, hearings scheduled in 1694 for John Purcell, Thady Duffe (15 June); John Archer, George Darcy (18 June); Thomas Clinton, James Barrett (11 & 14 July); Richard Reddy, John Kennedy, Thomas Dwyer (9 & 15 Nov.); David Nagle, Thomas Levallin, James Barrett (19–23 Nov.); Richard Aylmer, George Darcy, James Magrath (29 Nov. & 10 Dec.); John Coghlan (12 Dec.).
[20] Francis Brewster, A discourse concerning Ireland, and the different interests thereof (London, 1698), p. 22.

your possession, for you see they will stop at nothing when they imposed a fine upon you for being reputed a Justice of the Peace.[21]

Other exiles were simply hostile to the articles, and to the articlemen, regarding them as traitors to the Jacobite cause. The penal laws undoubtedly hardened attitudes:

> If England can break her public faith, in regard to the wretched articles of Limerick, by keeping up a perpetual terror and persecution over that parcel of miserable unarmed peasantry, and dastard gentry we left at home, without any other apology or pretence for it but her wanton fears and jealousies, what could have been expected by the men of true vigour and spirit if they had remained in their country but a cruel war, under great disadvantages, or such a universal massacre as our forefathers have been often threatened with by the confederate rebels of Great Britain.[22]

It was the 'Act to prevent the further growth of Popery' of 1704 that most seriously undermined the articles of surrender, a point eloquently made by Sir Toby Butler:

> This parliament could not pass such as a bill, as that intituled An act to prevent the further growth of Popery, then before the house, into a law, without infringing those articles [of Limerick], and a manifest breach of the public faith … the case of the Gibeonites, 2 Samuel 21.2, was a fearful example of breaking the public faith, which above 100 years after brought nothing less, than a three years famine upon the land, and stayed not till the lives of all Saul's families atoned for it.

The act barred Catholics from inheriting or purchasing estates and limited leaseholds to thirty-one years, unless they converted. Referring to the incentive for eldest sons to convert in order to inherit the entire estate, Butler declared:

> It is but too common with the son, who has a prospect of an estate, when once he arrives at the age of one and twenty, to think the old father too long in the way … and how much more will he be subject to it, when by this act, he shall have liberty before he comes to that age, to compel and force my estate from me … Is this not against the laws of God and man? … Is this not the only way in the world, to make children become undutiful? And to bring the grey head of the parent to the grave, with grief and tears.[23]

---

[21] Capt. Charles O'Malley to Teig O'Malley, [1692?] in Owen O'Malley, 'O'Malleys between 1651 and 1725' in *Journal of the Galway Archaeological and Historical Society*, xxv (1952), p. 33.

[22] Quoted in J.M. Flood, *The life of Chevalier Charles Wogan, an Irish soldier of fortune* (Dublin, 1922), p. 138.

[23] *An impartial relation of the several arguments of Sir Stephen Rice, Sir Theobald Butler, and Councellor Malone, at the bar of the House of Commons of Ireland, Feb. 22 and at the bar of the House*

It was this act, and the subsequent Popery Act of 1709, that began the process of widespread conversion to the established church by Irish Catholics.[24] By preventing Catholics from freely disposing of their estates, a right guaranteed by the articles of surrender, the Irish parliament of Queen Anne's reign achieved the aim set out by James Bonnell in November 1691: 'the enquiry must now be how to make the best of [the articles of Limerick] and provide against the inconveniences of them.'[25]

The response of the house of commons to Butler's protest revealed the greatest weakness of the articles of Limerick. Admitting that to abrogate the articles of Galway and Limerick would indeed be a 'breach of the public faith', the commons noted that article 1 of Limerick promised the articlemen such rights as they had enjoyed under Charles II. As the commons pointed out, there was no law in force in that reign preventing future parliaments from enacting whatever legislation was thought necessary, especially 'when the public safety seemed to require and earnest press for it'.[26] With that, the most important protection written into the articles of surrender was undone.

Modern scholars have criticised the Jacobite negotiators for looking to the reign of Charles II as the benchmark by which Catholics were to be treated after the war's end. It is not entirely clear what reign they were instead supposed to look to. Irish Catholics had been subjected to some form of legal disability since the middle of the sixteenth century. Some of the articlemen grew to maturity during the difficult times of the 1640s and 1650s; the reign of Charles II was one in which these men prospered. Those of a mind to enter the legal profession met with few obstacles and were permitted to appear in the courts by royal favour.[27] It was perhaps natural for the Jacobite negotiators to look to that reign. The articlemen petitioned throughout the 1690s to have the articles confirmed by the Irish parliament. William III's subtle yet significant shift away from the promise of his lords justices to confirm the articles in full, to one of partial confirmation, allowed the Irish parliament to enact a mutilated version of the articles in 1697. Even so, article 2 of Limerick, which protected landowners' rights, was enshrined in that act. There simply was no formula of words that could have been inserted in the articles of Limerick that would have prevented the Irish parliament from choosing to utterly ignore their own legislation, as they did with the 1704 Popery Act. The advent of

---

of Lords, Feb. 28th 1703. Against passing the bill then under consideration in the said houses, intituled, An act to prevent the further growth of Popery (Dublin, 1704), pp 4, 6.

[24] For an analysis of the 1704 act, see J.G. Simms, 'The making of a penal law (2 Anne, c. 6), 1703–4' in I.H.S., xii (1960–1), pp 28–37.

[25] James Bonnell to Robert Harley, 3 Nov. 1691 (H.M.C., Portland Mss, iii, 479–81).

[26] An impartial relation of the several arguments of Sir Stephen Rice, pp 20–1.

[27] Colum Kenny, 'The exclusion of Catholics from the legal profession in Ireland' in I.H.S., xxv (1986–7), pp 349–50.

peace in Europe in 1697, removing William's need to avoid antagonising his Catholic allies, played a part in the king's decision to allow the continued enactment of penal laws, a policy that endured for the first half of the eighteenth century.

The articles of 'temporary' benefit were honoured, including the abatement of quit- and crown-rents owed for the three years that the Williamite war lasted, a small yet vital piece of financial relief for the articlemen. The only substantive promise made in the minor articles of Drogheda, Waterford, Boffin and Sligo was the retention of estates. As far as can be established, no articleman qualifying under these articles was dispossessed of his land. From the outset, the articles of Limerick were resented by Irish Protestants. That resentment ensured that the Irish parliament consistently sought to undermine the promises made within the articles. Though the English privy council occasionally objected to the provisions of various bills (notably the 1695 disarming act and the 1704 Popery act), it generally submitted to the advice of the Irish government. The introduction of anti-Catholic legislation soon became an accepted instrument of official management of parliament in Ireland. Of the promises made within the articles of surrender, only the right of the articlemen of Galway and Limerick to bear arms, and of the articlemen of Limerick to practise as solicitors, were never revoked. Temporary suspensions of the right to bear arms were imposed at times when the threat of invasion from France was real but, as late as 1740, legislation passed by the Irish parliament to supplement the disarming act of 1695 included a saving clause for the articlemen.[28] By that time, there were probably very few articlemen left to enjoy the privilege.

The memory of the Catholic resurgence of 1685–8 and ensuing war endured in Irish Protestant minds long into the eighteenth century. Addresses presented successively to Anne, George I and George II warned against the reversal of outlawries dating from the Williamite war, or allowing the descendants of dispossessed Catholics to recover their estates through the courts.[29] The same fears arose in the 1780s as support for the repeal of penal legislation gathered strength.[30] By then the penal laws had all but removed Catholic freeholders

[28] An act to explain, amend, and make more effectual an act, passed in the seventh year of the reign of his late majesty King William the Third of glorious memory, entitled, an act for the better securing the government by disarming papists (13 Geo. II, c. 6, s. 4 (1740)).

[29] Simms, *Williamite confiscation*, p. 159. For an example of legal proceedings relating to the articles of Limerick and outlawries in the eighteenth century, see Andrew Lyall (ed.), *Irish Exchequer reports: reports of cases in the Courts of Exchequer and Chancery in Ireland, 1716–1734*, Selden Society Publications, 125 (2008), pp cxix–cxx.

[30] Ó Ciardha, *Ireland and the Jacobite cause*, pp 368–78; Tadhg O'Sullivan, 'Between toleration and preservation: the Popery laws and Irish Anglicanism, 1782–1808', in John Bergin, Eoin Magennis, Lesa Ní Mhunghaile & Patrick Walsh (eds), *New perspectives on the penal laws* (E.C.I. special issue no. 1, Dublin, 2011), pp 27–52.

from the landscape. With their landed interest steadily eroded, it was perhaps inevitable that the position of the gentry and nobility as leaders of the Catholic interest in Ireland had declined dramatically by the end of the eighteenth century, their place taken by merchants, middlemen and lawyers.

Appendix A: Articles of Surrender, 1690–91

Articles given in this appendix are those that have clauses relating to the property and livelihoods of the beneficiaries. Article 17 of the less well known military articles of Limerick, discussed above (p. 137), is also included. Articles that were purely military in nature, such as those signed at Cork (28 September 1690), have not been included.

Articles of Drogheda (3 July 1690)

1. The officers and soldiers of the garrison, as also the Roman Catholic clergy, and all others that shall desire it shall have leave to march to Mallow, taking with them their own proper arms, but to leave behind them all public stores of canon, ammunition or other habiliments of war without embezzlement.
2. They shall take with them sufficient provisions for their journey and shall have a safe convoy thither with baggage and horses.
3. The Roman Catholic dwellers of the town shall not be molested in their properties.
4. All sick officers and soldiers shall have leave to stay in town till recovered, and then shall be conducted to the next garrison.
[Four further articles included, giving various assurances regarding safe passage with baggage.][1]

Articles of Waterford (25 July 1690)

[The articles of Waterford were identical to those of Drogheda. The only difference was the substitution of the word 'city' for 'town' in article 3.[2]]

Articles of Galway (21 July 1691)

William and Mary, by the grace of God,
To all whom these presents shall come, greeting. Whereas certain articles bearing date 21 July last past were made and agreed upon by our trusty and well beloved Robert [sic], Baron de Ginkel, Lieutenant General and

---

[1] B.L., Add. Ms 38,146, ff 193b–4.
[2] Ibid., ff 194–5.

Commander in Chief of our forces in our kingdom of Ireland, and the constable and Governor of our town of Galway in our said Kingdom, whereby our said General promises that we should ratify these capitulations within the space of three months from the date thereof or sooner, the tenor of which said articles is as follows:

1. That the town and fort of Galway shall be given up to his Excellency or such officer as he shall appoint on Sunday morning next by six of the clock, together with all the stores of ammunition and provision and magazines of all forts without embezzlement, and that immediately upon the signing these articles such person as the general shall appoint have leave to inspect them.
2. That all deserters that are in the town shall be given up.
3. That immediately after signing these articles all the outworks of the town shall be delivered to such officers as the general shall appoint to take possession of the same, and that the Governor shall withdraw all the cannon from the wall.
4. That till the town is surrendered as aforesaid the General may order such works and batteries to be made as he shall judge convenient, provided he does not bring them within 3 yards of the wall: nor the guns within 10 yards of the batteries, and that in the town they shall not proceed to work to fortify the same any further.
5. In consideration of the said rendition his Excellency gives leave to Lieutenant General d'Usson, Monsieur Metset, Commissary of War, and the rest of the French officers and soldiers and others of that nation now in Galway to go to Limerick with their arms, bag and baggage, whither they shall be safely conducted the nearest way; and in case that the said Lieutenant General d'Usson shall want horses to carry his equipage thither the General will furnish him with them.
6. That such of the garrison as desire it may remain in town or go to their respective homes and enjoy the benefit of this capitulation, and the rest shall march to Limerick with their arms, 6 pieces of cannon, drums beating, colours flying, match lighted, bullet in mouth, and as much ammunition and provisions as each officer and soldier can carry with him; and that they shall be furnished with draught, horses and harness for the guns if they want them, which said guns they shall have liberty to choose, provided they take none above 12 pounders.
7. That the wounded and sick officers may stay in town till they are cured, and that then they shall be sent to Limerick with a safe conduct, and in the mean time shall be provided in town with necessaries for their cure and subsistence.

8. That the Governor, constable, mayor, sheriffs, aldermen, burgesses, freemen and natives of Galway, and the inhabitants thereof, or the reputed ones by any former charter, or reputed charter of King James II granted before his abdication, or any of his ancestors, shall have a general pardon of all attainders, outlawries, treasons, felonies, praemunires and all manner of offences committed since the beginning of the late King James' reign, to the date hereof.

9. That all and every of the garrison, officers, governors, constable, mayor, sheriffs, aldermen, burgesses, freemen and inhabitants abovesaid shall enjoy and possess their estates real and personal, and all other liberties and immunities, as they held, or ought to have held, under the Acts of Settlement and Explanation; or otherwise by the laws of this kingdom, freely discharged from all crown-rents, quit-rents and all other charges to the date hereof.

10. That the names of the Roman Catholic clergy of the town of Galway be given to the General on or before Tuesday next, and that they as well as the laity of the said town, shall have the private exercise of their religion, and that the said clergy shall be protected in their persons and goods.

11. That the gentlemen of estates now belonging to the town and garrison of Galway shall have liberty to keep a gun in their houses for the defence of the same, and wear a sword and case of pistols if they think fit.

12. That all the Roman Catholic lawyers of the said town shall have the free liberty of practise that they had in King Charles II's time.

13. That such of the officers belonging to any of the regiments that are now in Galway, and not present at the signing these capitulations shall have the benefit of the same; provided they shall submit within three weeks to the Governor of Galway for the time being, who shall be appointed to the General; or that they shall have a safe conduct to go to Limerick in the manner as the said garrison has.

14. That such other persons now in the town as desire to go out with the garrison, or such part thereof as goes to Limerick, shall have liberty to do so, and carry their families and goods along with them, and that such officers' wives belonging to the said garrison as are there or in any other part of Connacht may at the same time depart with their goods, or at any other convenient time afterwards; particularly Colonel Edmund Ryley's wife, mother and family, the Lady Evagh and her daughter and Lieutenant Colonel Luke Ryley, his brother Philip Ryley, their wives and families.

15. That immediately all acts of hostility shall cease on both sides, and that if it shall happen that any provoking language shall pass between the soldiers, they shall be punished by their respective officers for the same, and not permitted to fire one upon another.

16. That for the due performance of these articles, the Governor shall immediately give the persons undernamed for hostages: Earl of Clanricard, Lord of Inniskillen, Colonel Dominick Browne, Lieutenant Colonel Bodkin, Major Dillon. Lastly, the General promises to have these capitulations ratified by their Majesties within the space of 3 months from the date hereof, or sooner if possible.

Signed and sealed [21 July 1691] by the commander in chief of their Majesties' forces, and the constable and governor of the said town interchangeably.
Baron de Ginkel

And whereas the said town of Galway has been since in pursuance of the said articles surrendered unto us! Know ye that we having considered of the said articles are graciously pleased hereby to declare, that we do, as far in us lies, ratify and confirm the same, and every clause, matter and thing therein contained. And as to such parts thereof for which an act of parliament shall be found to be necessary we shall recommend the same to be made good by parliament and shall give our royal assent to any bill or bills that shall be passed by our two houses of parliament to that purpose.
Provided always, and our will and pleasure is that these our letters patent shall be enrolled in our Court of Chancery, in our said kingdom of Ireland within one year next ensuing.[3]
17 February 1692

Articles of Sligo (6 August 1691)

[These articles were first agreed to and signed on 6 August 1691, abandoned and finally re-confirmed by the supplementary articles also transcribed below, dated 14 September 1691. See chapter 3, section II.]

Articles of war, agreed on by the honourable Sir Teague O'Regan, Knight, and the rest of the officers of the garrison of Sligo of the one part, and the Honourable Colonel Michelburne, in the behalf of himself, his General and the rest of his army of the other part.

1. That all the said garrison, viz., Governors, officers, soldiers, engineers, gunners, gunsmiths, bakers, chaplains and all others that have a mind to go, Creaghts or others, shall have their lives secured, and march out

---

[3] *The articles of Galway exactly printed from the letters-patents: wherein they are ratified and exemplified by their Majesties under the Great Seal of England* (Dublin, 1692). See also T.N.A., SP 63/354, ff 15–20.

with their arms, bags and baggage, drums beating, colours flying, match lighted, bullets in their mouths, each officer and soldier twelve charges of powder, with match and ball proportionable, and their horses and cows as well belonging to them respectively, as the garrison in general, without any molestation, and at their several and respective elections, their wives, friends and cattle to be protected in any part of the country, as well as any other person whatsoever.

2. That the said garrison may march the nearest and best way at their own elections into the city or town of Limerick, and from thence to what place they please, and not to be compelled to march above eight miles a day or nine, or to march from hence to what other place they please at their own election.

3. That all sick and wounded officers, soldiers and other persons that are not able to march at present may remain in the town of Sligo, till able to march, then to have a pass for to go where they have a mind to, and in the mean time to be subsisted for the time being.

4. That none of our army shall enter into any of the two forts of Sligo, except such as shall be appointed by the said Colonel John Michelburne to take possession of the same until the garrison be clear marched out of the gates.

5. That the said forts shall be put into the possession of such forces as the said Colonel John Michelburne shall think fit, at eight of the clock, the fifteenth day of this instant August, at which hour the said garrison shall march out: the hour before the outward gates shall be delivered to such forces as the said Colonel John Michelburne shall appoint in case relief do not come by that time to the said garrison, and in case Galway be surrendered, and not otherwise.

6. That the said Governor and his said garrison shall be allowed to carry with them two pieces of cannon, with horses and other conveniences of carrying them together, with two luggage horses for each company, and three for the Governor, with one truckle car for each company, all this to be supplied by the said Colonel John Michelburne.

7. That all such persons, parties or companies of the respective regiments of the said garrison, not now here, shall be allowed to come hither, or join the said regiments in their said march, after the surrendering of the said garrison.

8. That all persons taken prisoners by any of our army or volunteers that any way belonged to any of the said regiments of the said garrison, or any other person or persons belonging to said garrison, now in restraint with us, shall be forthwith set at liberty, before the surrender of the said garrison, and safely conveyed thereunto.

9. That such of the inhabitants of the said town of Sligo, as have a mind to

continue there, shall be protected in their bodies, liberties and goods, and shall have free liberty to exercise or use their several trades or occupations as formerly, and the people of the country in like manner.

10. That all the clergy of the said town, that have a mind to stay, shall also be protected in their bodies, liberties and goods, and shall have free liberty to exercise their functions, and the clergy of the country accordingly.

11. That there shall be a sufficient escort appointed and sent with the said garrison, to convey them to the place above mentioned.

12. That one officer from the said Colonel John Michelburne and another from the said garrison shall be sent to General Ginkel, who in the presence of said two officers shall confirm all the things in these presents mentioned, and the confirmation before the surrender.

13. That all and singular, the above mentioned articles shall be inviolably performed on both sides without any equivocations, mental reservations or fraud whatsoever, according to the true intent and meaning thereof.

14. That all acts of hostility shall cease betwixt the said garrison and our army, as soon as notice may be given on both sides.

15. That the said Governor and garrison shall use the town posture and all other privileges and advantages, in the same or thereabouts, in as ample and as free a manner as hitherto, and that until the surrender aforesaid.

16. That the said Governor, officers and soldiers, garrison town and county of Sligo, shall have the benefit of all and singular other advantageous articles that Galway or any other got, in case it was surrendered. In true performance of all and singular the premises, forthwith they do respectively pawn their honours, both parties having hereunto interchangeably put their hands and seals at the castle near Sligo, this sixth day of August, 1691.

Teague O'Regan
John Mitchelburne

Camp at Nenagh, 10 August 1691

I do approve of the foregoing articles agreed upon by Colonel Mitchelburne and Sir Teague O'Regan, for the surrender of Sligo, except the last, which I confine to those who are actually now in the said town and garrison, it not being my intention to extend their Majesties' grace and favour to such who have done them no service, nor made no application to me for it.[4]

Bar. de Ginkel

---

[4] Taken from [John Michelburne], *An account of the transactions in the north of Ireland, Anno Domini, 1691* (London, 1692), pp 37–40. Reprinted in W.G. Wood-Martin, *Sligo and the Enniskilleners, from 1688–1691* (Dublin, 1882), pp 178–81.

Supplemental Articles of Sligo (14 September 1691)

Articles of war or capitulations made, entered and agreed upon by the honourable Sir Teague O'Regan, Knight, of the one part, and the Right Honourable Arthur, Earl of Granard in the behalf of him, his General and Army of the other part.

Whereas there were former capitulations between the said Sir Teague and Colonel John Mitchelburne (colonel in the same army with the said Earl of Granard), concerning the surrender of the forts of Sligo, which capitulations bear date 6 August last past, wherein there was a clause that the said forts should be delivered or surrendered unto the said Colonel Mitchelburne, the 15th day of the said month of August in case relief would not come by that time to the said garrison, which said capitulations were confirmed by General Ginkel to one article or clause, and whereas relief did come by that day to the said garrison whereby the said capitulations became of none effect; Whereas also the said Earl of Granard and the party now commanded by him, have invested or besieged the said forts, and several cannon and small shot and skirmishes on both sides were made, did enter into the following articles or capitulations with the said Sir Teague concerning the said surrender:

1. Imprimis, that all and singular the articles, conditions and capitulations formerly entered into by the said Sir Teague and the said Colonel Mitchelburne concerning the surrender of the said forts aforesaid shall be revived and inviolably kept and performed to all intents, constructions and purposes, with the following alterations and additions and none other.

2. That the said Sir Teague shall deliver to the said Earl of Granard, or those he will appoint, one of the said forts commonly called the Sod Fort tomorrow morning [at] 7 of the clock, and shall keep the Stone Fort and his officers several lodgings in the town for six days after the surrender of the said Sod Fort, and then or sooner at the election of the said Sir Teague to deliver up the said Stone Fort to the said Earl of Granard or whom he will appoint, and in the mean time all private soldiers and others except commission officers of the standing army or militia now under the command of the Earl of Granard to withdraw from and not come into the said town of Sligo.

3. That Captain Owen O'Neile, formerly lieutenant to Captain Owen O'Neile and his company and Captain Edmund McSweeney and his company and Lieutenant Colonel John McDonnogh, all now in the said Stone Fort and not there at the perfection of the said first articles shall be now comprehended in these presents, and shall have all such advantages as any other of the said garrison has by these or the former articles.

4. That the said Sir Teague and all the said garrison shall, for their march, have 12 days provision for each officer and soldier and subsistence during their abode

before their said march, all to be supplied out of the stores now in the possession of the said Sir Teague or of the said garrison, and shall have all manner of liquor now in their possession without any control whatsoever, and, that all officers and soldiers, now or before at the perfection of the said former articles, of the said garrison, shall be permitted to march to such places as in the said first articles, notwithstanding anything or things done or committed or supposed to be done or committed by them or any of them.

5. That restitution or reparation shall be made to all officers belonging to the said garrison for all such horses as have been taken from them by the said Colonel Mitchelburne's party during any cessation of arms between the said Sir Teague and the said Colonel Mitchelburne.

6. That Major Terence McSweeney and Captain Dennis McSweeney, detained at Carrickfergus after the capitulation thereof and comprehended in the same as is alleged, shall, if such allegations be true, and that they committed no capital crimes since the said capitulation and before their being so restrained, be set at liberty and conveyed to what place in this kingdom they please.

7. That Bellaghy in the county of Sligo, Newtown and Castle Bourke in the County of Mayo, and the respective garrisons of the same, shall be comprehended in these articles if they respectively please, and have the same or such advantages of the said Sir Teague and his garrison are to have to all intents and purposes, provided the said garrisons do respectively surrender within 24 hours after due summons of surrender and the said Sir Teague [visiting] to the said garrisons which he is to do upon demand.

8. That all colonels, captains and other officers and their respective companies, troops or men entered into association or union with Colonel Edward Scott or the said garrison of Sligo, shall be comprehended within these articles and have such or the same advantages as any of the said garrison of Sligo, except such as have declined or joined the party, side or army that the said Earl of Granard is of.

9. That all the friends and relations of the said garrison of Sligo or of any other place belonging to his and their cattle, people and Creaghts shall have liberty to march with the said garrison if they please, and all soldiers and officers or any person belonging to the said garrison that are prisoners and taken prisoner since the first articles shall be discharged on both sides.

10. That Sir Teague or the officers of the said garrison, as near as they can, shall give a true list of the guns, ammunition and all other stores of war and other provisions after the perfection of these presents, and not before.

11. That Mr Kean O'Hara, Captain Henry Crofton and his son Edward Crofton, Burgesses of the said Corporation of Sligo by the late charter, are comprehended in these presents, and to have the same or such advantages with the said garrison of Sligo or with any person thereof to all intents and purposes. In

true performance of all and singular the premises for which they do respectively pawn their honours, both parties have hereunto interchangeably put their hands and seals this 14th day of September, 1691.[5]

Signed, sealed and delivered in presence of:

Granard	Toby Caulfield
T. Regan	Roger Moore
	Richard Hanoway
	Tirrell Rourke
	Derby Kelly
	Edward Scott

Articles of Boffin (19 August 1691)

Agreed between Sir Henry Bellasis, Governor of Galway, and Col. Timothy Riordan, Governor of Boffin.

1. That the island of Boffin, and the fort thereof, and the adjacent islands belonging to the Earl of Clanricard, shall be surrendered to such officers as shall be appointed by the Governor of Galway, with all the stores, ammunition, provisions and magazines of all sorts, without embezzlement, so soon as the Governor of Galway shall think fit to send thither after Captain Nicholas Blake's return from thence.
2. In consideration of the surrender as aforesaid, the garrison shall march forth with flying colours, drums beating, match lighted, bullet in mouth and as much ammunition as each officer and soldier can carry with him.
3. That the governor, officers and soldiers of the said Garrison, the Lord Athenry, Lieutenant Col. John Kelly and all the inhabitants of the said islands, shall possess and enjoy their estates real and personal, as they held, or ought to have held them under the Acts of Settlement and Explanation, or otherways, by the laws of this kingdom, freely discharged from all crown-rents, quit-rents, and all other charges to the date hereof: and that Colonel John Browne, his being in Boffin, shall not bar him from the capitulations of Galway, and that if the said Col. John Browne shall desire to go to Limerick, the Governor of Galway promises that he shall be safely conducted thither with his horses, servants and arms.
4. That the governor, officers and soldiers and other inhabitants thereof, by any grant of King James II, before his abdication, or any of his ancestors, shall have a general pardon of all outlawries, attainders, treasons, felonies,

---

[5] Utrecht Archive, Huis Amerongen, no. 3219.

praemunires and other offences committed since the said King James' reign, to the date hereof.

5. That the garrison, officers and soldiers shall be transported from thence, either to Galway, or the Shannon, in order to go to Limerick, or otherwise march over land with safe conduct, as to the Governor shall seem fittest; with arms, bag and baggage as aforesaid.

6. That the Governor of Boffin shall be furnished, if need be, with necessary horses to carry his equipage to Limerick.

7. That any of the inhabitants of the said island that shall desire it, may go or be transported to Limerick, with their goods, along with the garrison, and be as safely conducted as they; and that if they shall march by Galway, the said soldiers, if they shall need it, shall be furnished with four days provisions of bread for their march to Limerick.

8. That Captain Michael Cormick and Captain Dominick Brown, if they will, may stay and remain in the said island, and enjoy their stock, corn and other goods under safe protection, with their servants and families. And that if any of the garrison, officers and soldiers, or any of the inhabitants, shall desire to stay, they may, with the like advantage, and one priest. That if any ships shall happen to be at Boffin, at the time of the surrender, they shall have free liberty to go out of that harbour; and that the said Captain Michael Cormick and Captain Dominick Brown may go to any place in the county of Mayo, where their concerns are, and there remain, with their corn, goods and stock as aforesaid.

9. That for the due perfecting of these articles, Captain Nicholas Blake is immediately to repair to Boffin, to have them signed by Colonel Riordan the governor of that place, and in eight days to return with them so signed. And for assurance of his return, he hath given Lieut. Col. John Kelly and Capt. Richard Martin, as security.

10. The Governor of Galway promises, that the General shall have these articles and capitulations ratified, after such manner, and within such time as the articles of Galway shall be.[6]

19 August 1691

Articles of Limerick (3 October 1691)

William and Mary, by the grace of God,
To all whom these presents shall come, greeting. Whereas certain articles bearing date 3 October last past, made and agreed on between our Justices of

---

[6] George Story, A continuation of the impartial history of the wars in Ireland (London, 1693), pp 194–6.

our Kingdom of Ireland, and our General of our forces there on the one part, and several officers there, commanding within the city of Limerick in our said kingdom on the other part. Whereby our said Justices and General did undertake that we should ratify those articles within the space of eight months, or sooner; and use their utmost endeavours that the same should be ratified and confirmed in Parliament. The tenor of which said articles is as follows:

Articles agreed upon 3 October 1691, between the right honourable Sir Charles Porter, Knight, and Thomas Coningsby, Esq., Lords Justices of Ireland and his Excellency Baron de Ginkel, Lieutenant General and Commander in Chief of the English army, on the one part, and the right honourable Patrick, Earl of Lucan, Piercy, Viscount Galmoy, Colonel Nicholas Purcell, Colonel Nicholas Cusack, Sir Toby Butler, Colonel Garrett Dillon and Colonel John Browne, on the other part, in the behalf of the Irish inhabitants of the town and county Limerick, the counties of Clare, Kerry, Cork, Sligo and Mayo.

1. The Roman Catholics of this kingdom shall enjoy such privileges in the exercise of their religion, as are consistent with the laws of Ireland; or as they did enjoy in the reign of King Charles II. And their Majesties, as soon as their affairs will permit them to summon a parliament in this kingdom, will endeavour to procure the said Roman Catholics such further security in that particular, as may preserve them from any disturbance, upon the account of their said religion.

2. All the inhabitants or residents of Limerick, or any other garrison now in the possession of the Irish, and all officers and soldiers, now in arms, under any commission of King James, or those authorised by him to grant the same in the several counties of Limerick, Cork, Clare, Kerry and Mayo, or any of them; and all the Commissioned Officers in their Majesties' quarters, that belong to the Irish regiments now in being, that are treated with, and who are not prisoners of war, or have taken protection, and who shall return and submit to their Majesties' obedience, and their and every of their heirs, shall hold, possess and enjoy all and every their estates of freehold and inheritance; and all the rights, titles and interests, privileges and immunities, which they, and every or any of them held, enjoyed or were rightfully and lawfully entitled to in the reign of King Charles II, or at any time since, by the laws and statutes that were in force in the said reign of King Charles II, and shall be put in possession, by order of the Government, of such of them as are in the King's Hands, or the Hands of his tenants, without being put to any suit or trouble therein; and all such estates shall be freed and discharged from all arrears of crown-rents, quit-rents and other public charges incurred and become due since Michaelmas

1688, to the day of the date hereof. And all persons comprehended in this article shall have, hold and enjoy all their goods and chattels, real and personal, to them or any of them belonging, and remaining either in their own hands or the hands of any persons whatsoever, in trust for, or for the use of them, or any of them; and all, and every the said persons, of what profession, trade or calling soever they be, shall and may use, exercise and practise their several and respective professions trades and callings, as freely as they did use, exercise and enjoy the same in the reign of King Charles II. Provided, that nothing in this article contained, be construed to extend to, or restore any forfeiting person now out of the kingdom, except what are hereafter comprised. Provided also, that no person whatsoever shall have or enjoy the benefit of this article, that shall neglect or refuse to take the oath of allegiance made by act of parliament in England, in the first year of the reign of their present Majesties, when thereunto required.

3. All merchants, or reputed merchants of the city of Limerick, or of any other garrison, now possessed by the Irish, or of any town or place in the counties of Clare or Kerry, who are absent beyond the seas, that have not bore arms since their Majesties' declaration of February 1689 shall have the benefit of the second article, in the same manner as if they were present, provided such merchants, and reputed merchants, do repair unto this kingdom within the space of 8 months from the date hereof.

4. The following officers, viz., Colonel Simon Luttrell, Captain Rowland White, Maurice Eustace of Yermanstown, Chievers of Maystown, commonly called Mount Leinster, now belonging to the regiments in the aforesaid garrisons and quarters of the Irish army, who were beyond the seas, and sent thither upon affairs of their respective regiments, or the army in general, shall have the benefit and advantage of the second article, provided that they return hither within the space of 8 months from the date of these presents, and submit to their Majesties' government, and take the above mentioned oath.

5. That all and singular the said persons comprised in the second and third articles, shall have a general pardon of all attainders, outlawries, treasons, misprisions of treason, praemunires, felonies, trespasses and other crimes, and misdemeanours whatsoever, by them or any of them committed since the beginning of the reign of King James II. And if any of them are attainted by parliament, the Lords Justices and General will use their best endeavours to get the same repealed by parliament, and the outlawries to be reversed *gratis*, all but writing clerks' fees.

6. And whereas these present wars have drawn on great violences on both parts, and that if leave were given to the bringing all sorts of private actions, the animosities would probably continue, that have been too long on foot,

and the public disturbances last. For the quieting and settling therefore of this kingdom, and avoiding those inconveniences which would be the necessary consequence of the contrary, no person or persons whatsoever, comprised in the foregoing articles, shall be sued, molested or impleaded at the suit of any party or parties whatsoever, for any trespasses by them committed, or for any arms, horses, money, goods, chattels, merchandises or provisions, whatsoever, by them seized or taken, during the time of the war. And no person or persons whatsoever, in the second or third articles comprised, shall be sued, impleaded or made accountable for the rents, or mean rates, of any lands, tenements or houses by him or them received or enjoyed in this kingdom, since the beginning of the present war, to the date hereof, nor for any waste or trespass by him or them committed in any such lands, tenements or houses. And it is also agreed, that this article shall be mutual, and reciprocal on both sides.

7. Every nobleman and gentleman comprised in the second and third article, shall have the liberty to ride with a sword, and case of pistols, if they think fit, and keep a gun in their houses, for the defence of the same, or for fowling.

8. The inhabitants and residents in the city of Limerick, and other garrisons, shall be permitted to remove their goods, chattels and provisions out of the same, without being viewed or searched, or paying any manner of duties, and shall not be compelled to leave the houses or lodgings they now have, for the space of six weeks next ensuing the date hereof.

9. The oath to be administered to such Roman Catholics as submit to their Majesties' government shall be the oath abovesaid, and no other.

10. No person or persons, who shall at any time hereafter break these articles, or any of them, shall thereby make, or cause any other person or persons to forfeit or lose the benefit of the same.

11. The Lords Justices and General do promise to use their utmost endeavours, that all the persons comprehended in the above mentioned articles, shall be protected and defended from all arrests and executions for debt or damage, for the space of 8 months, next ensuing the date hereof.

12. Lastly, the Lords Justices and General do undertake, that their Majesties will ratify these articles within the space of 8 months, or sooner, and use their utmost endeavours that the same shall be ratified and confirmed in parliament.

13. And whereas Colonel John Browne stood indebted to several Protestants, by judgements of record, which appearing to the late Government, the Lord Tyrconnell and Lord Lucan took away the effects the said John Browne had to answer the said debts, and promised to clear the said John Browne of the said debts, which effects were taken for the public use of the Irish,

and their army. For freeing the said Lord Lucan of his said engagement, passed on their public account, for the payment of the said Protestants, and for preventing the ruin of the said John Browne, and for satisfaction of his creditors, at the instance of the Lord Lucan and the rest of the persons aforesaid, it is agreed; that the said Lords Justices, and the said Baron de Ginkel, shall intercede with the King and parliament, to have the estates secured to Roman Catholics, by articles and capitulations in this kingdom, charged with and equally liable to the payment of so much of the said debts, as the Lord Lucan, upon stating accounts with the said John Browne, shall certify under his hand, that the effects taken from the said John Browne amount unto, which account is to be stated and the balance certified by the said Lord Lucan in 21 days after the date hereof.

Char. Porter	Present [Witnesses]:
Thos. Coningsby	Scravenmore
Bar. De Ginkel	H. Maccay
T. Talmash	

And whereas the said city of Limerick has been since, in pursuance of the said articles, surrendered unto us. Now know ye, that we having considered of the said Articles, are graciously pleased hereby to declare, that we do for us, our heirs and successors, as far as in us lies, ratify and confirm the same, and every clause, matter and thing therein contained. And as to such parts thereof, for which an act of parliament shall be found necessary, we shall recommend the same to be made good by parliament, and shall give our royal assent to any bill or bills that shall be passed by our two houses of parliament to that purpose. And whereas it appears unto us, that it was agreed between the parties to the said articles, that after the words *Limerick, Clare, Kerry, Cork, Mayo*, or any of them in the second of the said articles, the words following, viz., *and all such as are under their protection in the said counties*, should be inserted, and be part of the said articles. Which words having been casually omitted by the writer, the omission was not discovered till after the said articles were signed, but was taken notice of before the second town was surrendered. And that our said Justices and General, or one of them, did promise that the said clause should be made good, it being within the intention of the capitulation, and inserted in the foul draught thereof. Our further will and pleasure is, and we do hereby ratify and confirm the said omitted words, viz., (*and all such as are under their protection in the said counties*), hereby for us, our heirs and successors, ordaining and declaring, that every person and persons therein concerned, shall and may have, receive and enjoy the benefit thereof, in such and the same manner, as if the said words had been inserted in their proper place, in the said second article, any omission, mistake or defect in the said second article, in any wise

notwithstanding. Provided always, and our will and pleasure is, that these our letters patents shall be enrolled in our Court of Chancery in our said Kingdom of Ireland within the space of one year next ensuing.[7]
24 February 1692.

Military Articles of Limerick

17. That all prisoners of war that were in Ireland the 28th September, shall be set at liberty on both sides, and the General promises to use his endeavours that those that are in England or Flanders shall be set at liberty also.[8]

---

[7] *The civil articles of Lymerick, exactly printed from the letters patents, wherein they are ratified and exemplified by their Majesties under the Great Seal of England* (Dublin, 1692). See also T.N.A., SP 63/354, ff 21–7.

[8] Story, *Continuation of the impartial history*, p. 244.

Appendix B: Hearings scheduled for adjudication under the articles of Limerick, 1694

No attempt has been made to modernise the spelling of personal names within this appendix. If a scheduled claim has been annotated in the source lists, that annotation is indicated in *italicised* type. Names that have been crossed out in the source lists are indicated with a strike through.

13 June 1694.[1]

Dominick Ryan of Dublin: *within articles*
Nicholas Forrter of same: *to be heard the first day after [?] June*
Timothy Hieven of same: *within articles*
Christopher Cusack of same: [annotation unclear]
Capt. Edward Plunkett of same: [annotation unclear]
Capt. Hugh Reily of same: *within articles*
John Walsh of same: *to be heard 6 weeks since*
Sir Daniel O'Neale of same: *to be heard 6 weeks since*
Constance Geoghegan and Mary his wife of same: *within articles*
Capt. Thomas Kelly of same: *within articles*
Valentine Andrew Hamlin of same: *non appearance*
Lieut. George Kelly of same: *within articles*
Egerton Dodd of same: *within articles*
Capt. Anthony Preston of same: *within articles*
Col. Henry Luttrell by leave of the board: *within articles*

15 June 1694 [adjourned to 18 June 1694].[2]

Redmond Ledwith of Dublin: *within articles*
Christopher Nicholson of same: *non appearance*
John Hart of same: *non appearance*
Lieut. John Purcell of same: *time till Friday to prove his taking protection*
John Dillon of same: *non appearance*
Capt. Patrick Sexton of same: *within articles*

[1] N.A.I., Wyche papers, 2/106.
[2] Ibid., 2/107.

William Russell of same: *non appearance*
Peter Manby of same: *put off for a month by his petition*
Walter Usher of same: *non appearance*
Capt. Thady Duffe of same: *this day se'ennight to prove him in protection*
John Lewis of same: *non appearance*
~~Thady Concannon of same~~: *claims the articles of Galway*
Col. Charles Geoghegan of same: *non appearance*
John Delamare: *within articles*
Cornet John Grace: *within articles* [Second annotation]: *By order*
Frances Grace: *judgement deferred till Friday next* [Second annotation]: *By order*

18 June 1694.[3]
[All claimants listed for this date are noted as resident in Co. Meath]

William Bettagh: *non appearance*
James Cusack: *within articles (delivery of the adjudication respited till Monday next)*
Nicholas Drumgold: *within articles*
Bartho[lomew] Cappack: *non appearance*
Lieut. Col. Matthew Everard: *within articles*
Sir Gerald Aylmer: *within articles*
Capt. James Hackett: *non appearance (In France)*
Edward Plunkett: *within articles*
Simon Plunkett: *within articles*
Capt. John Archer: *non appearance (took protection)*
Bartholomew Barnewall: *non appearance*
Francis White: *non appearance*
Michael White: *non appearance*
Christopher Weldon: *within articles*
Capt. George Darcy: *non appearance (took protection)*
Robert Farrell: *non appearance*

20 June 1694.[4]
[All claimants listed for this date are noted as resident in Co. Kildare]

Eustace Sherlock: *non appearance (on Friday next)* [see 22 June and 14 November 1694]
Capt. Pierce Bermingham: *within articles*

3 Ibid., 2/108.
4 Ibid., 2/109.

Capt. Cornelius Coman: *non appearance (to Friday next)* [see 22 June and 14 November 1694]

Morris Eustace: *non appearance (will not prosecute his claim)*

Capt. William Eustace: *within articles*

Capt. Richard Archbold: *within articles*

Henry Dalton: *non appearance*

Capt. Thomas Neville: *non appearance (this day sevennight)*

Thomas Nevill: [no annotation, appears to be a double entry]

Capt. Edmund Fitzgerald: *non appearance (Monday next)*

22 June 1694.[5]

Silvester Dowdall of Co. Westmeath: *non appearance*

Capt. Gareth Nugent of same: *non appearance*

Walter Tuite of same: *Monday next*

Lieut. Peter MacGawly of same: *non appearance*

William and Margaret Tirrell of same: *non appearance*

Col. Richard Nugent of same: *non appearance. In France*

Anthony Malone of same: *non appearance*

Henry Magan of same: *non appearance*

Lieut. Col. Charles Geoghegan of same: *within articles*

Edward Geoghegan of same: *non appearance. This day fortnight*

Hugh Geoghegan of same: *within articles*

Aghrey Shiels of same: *non appearance*

Edward Geoghegan of same: *not within articles*

Capt. Richard Tyrrell of same: *non appearance*

Capt. Michael Nugent of same: *within articles*

Mrs. Grace [of ?]: *within articles*

The following persons were put off till this day:

Captain John Purcell: *Wednesday next*

Eustace Sherlock: *pray to be deferred till next day*

Cornelius Coonan: *pray to be deferred till next day* [see hearings 14 November 1694, below].

11 and 14 July 1694.[6]

Capt. Robert Conly of Drogheda: *within articles*

---

5   Ibid., 1/3/2.
6   Ibid., 2/110.

Capt. Thomas Cashell of Co. Louth: *within articles*

Thomas Clinton of same: *time till after Michaelmas to prove protection. 3rd day of hearing*

Thomas Fottrell of Co. Meath: *within articles*

Thomas Harrold of [Co.] Limerick: *non appearance (adjudged formerly)*

Garrett Curnoge of same: *non appearance*

Daniel Carthy of [Co.] Limerick: *non appearance*

Philip Cantillon of same: *non appearance*

[All remaining names for these dates are of the city of Limerick]

James England: *non appearance*

Simon Hallorane, merchant: *non appearance*

Matthew Hartegan: *non appearance*

James Hehir, miller: *non appearance*

Edmond Joy, innkeeper: *non appearance*

Capt. John McGrath: *non appearance*

James Naughton, innkeeper: *non appearance*

James Synnott, merchant: *non appearance*

Francis Stritch, Esq.: *non appearance*

John Tobyn: *non appearance*

Michael White: *non appearance*

The persons following are appointed to be heard this day by special order, 14 July 1694.[7]

Capt. Dennis Kelly: *within articles*

Captain Donogh McMahon: *within articles*

Charles Everard, a minor: *not heard because in no danger*

James Barrett: *2nd sitting after Michaelmas to prove protection*

John Barrett: *the same rule*

Nicholas Power: *within articles*

Michael Gilgan: *see Robert Gilgan below*

Robert Gilgan: *to make out his [sic] father James' claim. Put off to the 4th sitting after Michaelmas*

John Gilgan: *see Robert Gilgan above*

Patrick Galwan: *within articles (to produce another witness)*

William Hoare: *within articles*

---

[7]   Ibid., 2/111.

5 November 1694.[8]
[All claimants for this date are noted as resident in Co. Clare]

Laurence Delahunty: *put off to Friday se'ennight*
Patrick Creagh: *non appearance*
George Martin: *non appearance*
Edward FitzGerald: *to mend his claim and come on upon Friday*
Daniel Neilan: *to come on tomorrow and take the oath before Ald. Smith*
Murtagh O'Brien: *non appearance*
John Magrath: *this day se'ennight. Consider about altering the place of residence*
Robert Magrath: *the same rule*
James Grady: *the same rule*
Murtagh Hogan: *within articles*
William Lysaght: *within articles*
Richard Connell: *a fortnight's time to revive his claim (dead)*
Major David Magee: *within articles*
Dermott Considen: *non appearance*
Sir Oliver Bourke, Bart.: *non appearance (to take the oath in the country before a justice of the peace and be heard 14 days hence)*
Michael O'Dea: *non appearance*
John Clanchy: *non appearance*
Monogh Grady: *non appearance*
Matthew Honan: *non appearance*
Roger O'Laghlin: *non appearance*
~~George Martin~~

9 and 15 November 1694.[9]

Major John Dalton of Co. Westmeath: *dead. Sunday se'ennight for his widow or son to present the claim*
Capt. Richard Reddy of Co. Kilkenny: *a fortnight for the King's Counsel to prove protection* [See 29 November and 10 December 1694, below]
Bryan McGuire of Co. Fermanagh: *mend the claim and come this day two weeks*
[Following names of Co. Tipperary unless otherwise stated]
Matthew Kennedy: *within articles*
Capt. John Kennedy: *3 weeks to prove him in protection*
~~John Butler~~
Thomas Dwire: *non appearance (King's Counsel can prove him in protection)*

8   Ibid., 2/112.
9   Ibid., 2/113.

John Keating: *desires to [?] the place of residence* [see 12 and 16 November]
Grany Kelly: *non appearance*
Richard Kearney: *within articles*
Daniel Meara: *within articles*
Capt. Edward Butler: *within articles*
John Ryan: *within articles*
Daniel Sullevane: *to the 21st*
Theobald Burke: *within articles*
[Following names of Co. Cavan]
Charles Doherty: *within articles*
Capt. James Reyley: *non appearance*
Turlogh Reyley: *non appearance*
Maj. Edmond Reyley: *non appearance*
Lieut. Col. Philip Oge Reyley: *non appearance*
Teige Considen: *within articles*

12 and 16 November 1694.[10]

John Keating: *within articles*
John Donnelly of Co. Tyrone: *non appearance*
Capt. Terence O'Donnelly of same: *non appearance*
Donache McLoughlin of Co. Donegal: *non appearance*
[Following names of Co. Down unless otherwise stated]
John Deery: *non appearance*
John Crelly: *to be heard among the claimants of the Galway articles*
Daniel Graham: *non appearance*
Capt. Arthur O'Lavery: *non appearance*
Roger Smith: *mend his claim and come on upon Monday*
Cornet Francis Savage: *non appearance*
Lieut. Patrick Savage: *within articles*
Lieut. Henry O'Gribben: *non appearance*
Owen O'Donnelly of Co. Armagh: *non appearance*
William Tippin of same: *mend his claim and come on upon Monday*
Patrick McCowell of Co. Monaghan: *non appearance*
Patrick Deery of same: *mend his claim and come on upon Monday*
John Harford of same: *like order*
Toole McKenna of same: *non appearance*
Lieut. James Freney of Co. Kilkenny: *within articles*
Maurice Eustace of Co. Kildare: *within articles*

10 Ibid., 2/114.

Claims to be heard by special order, 14 November 1694.[11]

John Butler of Co. Tipperary: *within articles*
Robert Gilgan of Co. Wexford: *put off*
John Gilgan of same: *put off*
James Gilgan of same: *a fortnight's time given the King's Counsel*
Michael Gilgan of same: *for his father* [no decision]
~~Thomas Spring of Ballynorisbine~~
Patrick Peppard of Co. Limerick: *within articles*
John Ryan: *a fortnight's time given to the King's Counsel* [see 29 November and 10 December 1694, below]
Teige Considen of Co. Clare: *tomorrow*
Darby Ryan: *a fortnight's time to the King's Counsel* [See 29 November and 10 December 1694, below]
Capt. Thady McNamara of Co. Clare: *within articles*
Darby O'Meara of Co. Clare: *put off for a fortnight*
Thady Mollowny of Co. Clare: *speak with the managers tomorrow*
Peter Aylmer: *non appearance*
Maurice Fitzgerald of Co. Cork: *within articles (minor)*
Capt. Thomas Nugent of Co. Westmeath: *within articles*
Roger McNamara of Co. Clare: *non appearance*
John Anketell: *put off till tomorrow*
Capt. Theobald Denn of Co. Kilkenny: *within articles*
Capt. Cornelius Coonan of Co. Kildare: *within articles*
Lieut. Godfrey Cunningham: *within articles*
George Stackpole of Co. Clare: *within articles*

19, 21, 22 and 23 November 1694.[12]

Ambrose Terry of Co. Clare: *within articles*
John Flood of Limerick: *within articles*
David Nagle of Cork: *King's Counsel further to prove him in protection the 2nd sitting after Christmas*
Capt. Pierce Nagle of same: *the same rule*
Thomas Levallin of same: *non appearance (King's Counsel ready to prove him in protection)*
John Barrett of same: *the second sitting after Christmas*
James Barrett of same: *non appearance/not within (proved in protection)*

---

[11] Ibid., 1/3/1.
[12] Ibid., 2/115.

Edmond Barrett of same: *the second sitting after Christmas*
Capt. Edmond Lally: *within articles*
Patrick Ryan: *within articles*
Kean Carroll of King's County: *within articles*
James Tobyn: *any day within a week to bring further evidence*
James Carroll of Galway: *non appearance*
John Carroll of same: *non appearance*
Andrew Cheevers and his wife of same: *put off to this day se'ennight*
Andrew and John Cheevers of same: *the same rule*
Elizabeth, Baroness Dowager of Cahir and Charles McCarthy, her son, of Co. Tipperary: *within articles*
Col. Martin O'Connor of Co. Mayo: *non appearance*
Capt. Donogh O'Connor of Co. Mayo: *non appearance*
Lieut. Malachy Connor of Co. Galway: *put off to Monday to take the oath before Sir [?]*
Andrew and Julian Crean of Co. Galway: *non appearance*
William Crean of Co. Mayo: *non appearance*

26 November and 7 December 1694.[13]

Capt. John Nolan of Co. Galway: *put off till after Christmas to produce more witnesses*
Thomas Tobyn of Co. Galway: *to come on next day*
~~Elenor Shaghnessy of Co. Galway~~
Major George Yelferton of Co. Galway: *within articles*
Edmond Nugent of Co. Westmeath: *put off till after Christmas*
Thomas White of same: *within articles*
~~Capt. Thomas Purcell of Co. Tipperary~~
John White of Co. Tipperary: *non appearance*
Morgan Ryan of Co. Clare: *within articles*
Col. Mille Reyley of Co. Mayo: *put off till Monday*
William Rooth of Co. Kilkenny: *non appearance*
Richard White of Limerick: *non appearance*
Gregory Rice of Co. Kerry: *non appearance*
Patrick Smith of Dublin: *within articles*
Thady Ryan of Ballyowen: *non appearance*
Pierce Stapleton: *non appearance*
Patrick Nihill of Limerick: *within articles*
Pierce Butler: *within articles*

[13] Ibid., 2/116.

Col. Daniel O'Donovan of Co. Cork: *within articles*
Donogh O'Grady of Co. Clare: *within articles*
James Butler of Co. Tipperary: *non appearance (put off till after Christmas)*
Bryen O'Bryen of same: *within articles*
Capt. John Anketell of Co. Limerick: *within articles*
Roger Hicky of Co. Clare: *within articles*
Edmond Hogan of Co. Clare: *within articles*
Capt. Thomas Dwire of Co. Tipperary: *within articles*
Charles Costelloe of Co. Mayo: *within articles*
Capt. Daniel O'Sullivan of Co. Kerry: *within articles*

Claims to be heard by special order, 29 November 1694.[14]

John Donnellan: *within articles*
Jeffrey McHugo: *wants one witness*
Capt. Darby O'Callaghan of Co.Clare: *within articles*
Mary Butler, daughter of Pierce, late Baron of Cahir: *within articles*
Peter Trant: *respitt. Whether Dingle was then in the Irish quarters*
Cornelius McGillicuddy: *within articles*
Col. Donough McGillicuddy: *within articles*
Sir Ulick Bourke, baronet: *within articles*
John Browne, esq.: *within articles*
Col. John Hoare of Waterford: *within articles*
Daniel Sullivan: *(put off till last day of causes next term)*
Honora, Lady Viscountess of Clare: *within articles*
Garrett Dardis of Gigginstown, Co. Westmeath: *within articles*
Daniel Finnucan of Culmeene, Co. Clare: *within articles*
James Mullowney of Tulla, Co. Clare: *within articles*
Capt. William Bourke and his wife, Co. Tipperary: *within articles*
Col. Lawrence Delahunty: *within articles*
Roger Smith of Dromgellin, Co. Down: *within articles*
Margaret Creagh, widow, of Limerick: *wants two witnesses*

29 November and 10 December 1694.[15]

Loughlin O'Hehir of Co. Clare: *within articles*
James Davoren of same: *within articles*
Thomas O'Connor of same: *within articles*

[14] N.L.I., Ms 174.
[15] N.A.I., Wyche papers, 2/117.

Donogh O'Loughlin of same: *within articles*

James Grady of same: *within articles*

Major Hugh McNemara of same: *within articles*

Capt. Cornelius McMahon of same: *within articles*

John Meara of King's County: *within articles*

Richard Aylmer of Co. Meath: ~~within articles~~ *(time to prove him in protection)*

Capt. George Darcy of Co. Meath: *(time to prove him in protection)*

Capt. Thomas Nugent of Co. Westmeath: *within articles*

Constance Donovan of Co. Clare: *within articles (prosecuted by the son Hugh upon the death of his father)*

James Nash of Co. Limerick: *within articles*

Lieut. Walter Spring of Co. Kerry: *within articles*

James Magrath of Co. Limerick: ~~within articles~~ *(time to prove him in protection)*

Nicholas Bourke of same: *within articles*

Doctor Richard O'Donovan of Co. Cork: *dead, prosecuted by his son. Put off to the next day* [see 3 and 11 December 1694, below]

Richard O'Donovan of the same: *put off to the next day* [see 3 and 11 December 1694, below]

Lieut. William O'Donovan of same: *within articles*

Capt. Daniel Regan of same: *within articles*

Redmond Fitzgerald of same: *non appearance*

Dennis Driscoll of same: *within articles*

John Carroll of Co. Tipperary: *within articles*

Major James Poore of Galway: *put off to the next day*

Capt. Edmund Burke of Galway: *within articles*

Christopher Dalton: *to the 3rd sitting next term*

Andrew Cheevers and Bridget his wife: *heard in part 22 November. Put off to the last day before Christmas*

Thomas Power: *within articles*

James Gilgan: *to the 2nd sitting after Christmas*

John Ryan: *to the 4th sitting after Christmas*

James Everard: *to the 3rd sitting after Christmas*

Capt. Richard Reddy: *within articles (heard 15 November)*

Darby Ryan: *within articles (heard 14 November)*

Alexander Eustace of Co. Kildare: *heard 22 July 1692. Lords to bring their notes of that day.*

3 and 11 December 1694.[16]

James Power: *within articles*
Richard O'Donovan: *within articles*
Dr. Richard O'Donovan: *within articles*
Laurence Nihill, merchant, of Limerick: *tomorrow*
Bartholomew Stritch, merchant, of same: *to the 3rd day of hearing next term, his and his father's*
Murtagh O'Bryen of Co. Clare: *within articles*
Thomas Rice of Co. Kerry: ~~within articles~~ *(to be considered with Spring's case)*
Roger O'Loughlin of Co. Clare: *within articles*
Philip McAdam of Limerick: *within articles*
Thomas Donnell of Co. Armagh: *within articles*
Capt. Dermot O'Bryen of Co. Clare: *within articles*
Edward Neilan of same: *within articles*
A[n]drew O'Donnell of Co. Armagh: *within articles*
~~Capt. Donogh McNemara of Co. Clare~~
~~Dominic [Hanning?] of same~~ *5th sitting after Christmas*
~~Daniel McNemara of same~~ *5th sitting after Christmas*
Margret Dun of Queen's County: *within articles*
~~Capt. Roger Carroll: After Christmas~~
Col. Cormac O'Neil of Co. Antrim: *within articles*
David Power of Co. Galway: *non appearance*
~~Capt Oliver Rochfort of Co. Kildare~~: *after Christmas, 4th day*
Turlagh O'Bryen of Co. Clare: *within articles*
Lieut. Col. Terence MacDonogh of Co. Mayo: *within articles*
Capt. Dennis Kelly of Co. Roscommon: [no annotation]
Capt. Andrew Browne of Co. Galway: [no annotation]
~~Dominic Hanaghan of Co. Clare~~: *after Christmas, 5th sitting*
Lieut. Col. Francis Bodkin of Co. Clare: *non appearance*
Bryen McGwire of Co. Fermanagh: *2nd day of hearing after Christmas*
Pierce Creagh of Co. Clare: *infant about 10 years old*
~~Cornet Patrick Stanton~~
Jeffrey McHugo: *to produce one witness*
Lawrence Nihill: [no annotation]

Claims to be heard by special order, 12 December 1694.[17]
[There is no annotation for the names on this list, with the exception of the last.]

Connor McDonogh of Co. Clare
John Lysaght of same
Lieut. Col. Richard Bourke of Co. Galway
Michael O'Dea of Co. Clare
Malachy O'Connor on behalf of his father Capt. Dermott O'Connor, deceased
John Tobyn of Co. Tipperary
Capt. Garrett Bourke of Co. Galway
Clare Kelly and Francis her son, a minor
John Coghlan: *King's Counsel to prove him in protection the 4th sitting after Christmas*

Appendix C: Proclamations of 7 July and 1 August 1690; [Sir Richard Cox], 'A copy of and answers to several complaints made by the Irish by their agent Mr Cockly against judgements given by the Justices and Council in several cases relating to the Articles of Limerick and Galway, together with the case of the protected Irish that came in upon the two first declarations after the Battle of the Boyne'.

1. Proclamation issued at Finglas, 7 July 1690

To all the people of our kingdom of Ireland, whom it may concern
William R.

As it hath pleased almighty God to bless our arms in this kingdom, with a late victory over our enemies at the Boyne, and with the possession of our capital city of Dublin, and with a general dispersion of all that did oppose us: we are now in so happy a prospect of our affairs, and of extinguishing the rebellion of this kingdom: that we hold it reasonable to think of mercy, and to have compassion upon those whom we judged to have been seduced. Wherefore we do hereby declare, we shall take into our royal protection all poor labourers, common soldiers, country farmers, ploughmen and cottiers whatsoever, as also all citizens, townsmen, tradesmen, and artificers who either remained at home, or having fled from their dwellings, shall by the first day of August next repair to their usual places of abode; surrendering up what arms they have, to such justices of the peace as are, or shall be appointed by us, not only to receive the same, but also to register the appearance of such of the said persons as shall come and submit unto our authority. For our royal intention is, and we do hereby declare, that we will not only pardon all those poor seduced people as to their lives and liberties, who shall come in by the time aforesaid, for all violences they have

274

done or committed by the command of their leaders during the war; but we do also promise to secure them in their goods, their stocks of cattle, and all their chattels personal whatsoever; willing and requiring them to coming in, and where they were tenants, there to preserve the harvest of grass and corn for the supply of winter. But forasmuch as many of them had a legal right to the tenancy of several lands; some holden from Protestants; and some held from Popish proprietors, who have been concerned in the rebellion against us: our will and pleasure is, that all those tenants who held from our good Protestant subjects, do pay their rents to their respective landlords; and that the tenants of all those, who have been concerned in the present rebellion against us, do keep their rent in their hands, until they have notice from the Commissioners of our Revenue, unto whom they are to account for the same. And as we do hereby strictly forbid all violence, rapine, and molestation to any, who shall thus come in, and remain obedient to us; for those of this or any rank or quality, who are already in our quarters, and within our power, and obedient to us; we do hereby charge and require, that they be not disquieted in any fort, without our particular command. For the desperate leaders of the present rebellion, who have violated those laws, by which this kingdom is united and inseparably annexed, to the imperial crown of England, who have called in the French, who have authorized all violences and depredations against the Protestants, and who rejected the gracious pardon we offered them in our proclamation of 22 February 1689; as we are now by God's great favour, in condition to make them sensible of their errors; so are we resolved to leave them to the event of war; unless by great and manifest demonstrations, we shall be convinced they deserve our mercy, which we shall never refuse to those who are truly penitent.

Given at our royal camp at Finglas near Dublin the seventh day of July 1690, in the second year of our reign.

2. Proclamation allowing additional time for Jacobites to surrender, 1 August 1690

To all the people of our kingdom of Ireland, whom it may concern
William R.

Although our former declaration of the 7th of July last past, hath not hitherto produced those effects of gratitude and obedience from several of our rebellious subjects which we justly expected: yet being willing to [be] compassionate [to] those who are misled, and to extend our farther grace, as well in granting unto some a longer time to lay hold of the advantages already offered, as to enlarge our clemency unto others. We do now farther declare, that as to all poor labourers, common soldiers, country farmers, ploughmen, and cottiers whatsoever; as also to all citizens, townsmen, tradesmen, and artificers who remained at home, or who having fled from their dwellings, shall by the five and twentieth day of this instant August, repair to their usual place of abode; surrendering up what arms they have, to such justices as are, or shall be appointed to us, not only to receive the same, but to register the appearances of such as shall submit to our authority; we do hereby declare, that we will not only pardon them, as to their lives and liberties, for all violence they have done and committed by authority of their superiors during the rebellion, but we do also promise to secure them in their goods, their stocks and cattle, and all their chattels personal whatsoever; willing and requiring them to come in, and where they were tenants, there to preserve the harvest of grass and corn for supply of the winter. But forasmuch as many of them had a legal right to the tenancy of several lands; some holden from Protestants; and some held from Popish proprietors, who have been concerned in the rebellion against us; our will and pleasure is, that all those tenants who hold from our good Protestant subjects, do pay their rents to their respective landlords; and the tenants of all those who have been concerned in the present rebellion against us, do keep their rents in their hands, until they shall have notice from the Commissioners of our Revenue, unto whom they are to account for the same. But whereas we are farther advertised, that several of these ranks aforementioned, who have adhered to our said Declaration, do complain of ill treatment from our soldiers, and of the loss of goods and stock, on pretence that such stock and goods were formerly by them plundered from the English; and therefore praying not only the security of our General Declaration,[1] but of particular protections to be granted to such as should desire the same: as we abhor all manner of violence done to our loving subjects of what religion soever, against the tenour of our said Declaration, which being under the great seal of this our kingdom, is above all other securities: yet to gratify our said subjects, and to deter all offenders, we shall order particular protections to be granted to such as desire the same: and shall farther require upon pain of our highest displeasure, that they become effectual to all such of our loving subjects, as shall remain stedfast in their duty to us, and who have not since the publishing of our Declaration aforesaid, plundered our Protestant subjects, or sheltered under such protections as already they may have had, the goods and stocks of our enemies who continue obstinate in their disobedience; for in either of these cases, they cannot expect but to remain accountable for what they have done, unless they forthwith make restitution of all such plundered goods to the right owners; and also discover immediately to some of our justices of the peace, what goods and stock they have so concealed.

[1]   This is a reference to William's proclamation of 7 July, above.

As for others of superior rank and quality, and also such as have borne office under our enemies, whether military or civil; that which at present we do declare is this: that if any of them shall within the time aforesaid surrender themselves to our obedience, and shall be content during the rebellion in this kingdom, to betake themselves to such town or city as shall be assigned them, they shall be secure in their lives, and have the liberty of such town or city; and if they are destitute and in want, shall also have a subsistence allowed them, according to their respective qualities; and the same shall be paid them by the Commissioners of our Revenue, till by the blessings of peace we may have leisure to consider the condition of all our subjects, and those in particular, who shall have been most early in their obedience towards us. As to strangers of what nation soever they be, who have taken service in this kingdom against us, we do farther declare, that if they shall forsake the enemy, and come into our quarters within the time aforesaid, they shall not only receive our protection whilst they are in the kingdom, but forthwith have passports given them, to go directly home into their respective countries.

But if these manifestations of our grace and favour, shall not be valued as they deserve; or if any shall persist in that barbarous and unchristian way of burning and desolation, which in some places has of late been practised; we shall hold ourselves discharged of those consequences and calamities which must inevitably follow, since those who are obstinate against our mercy become the authors of their own confusion.

Given at our court at Chapelizod, this first day of August 1690, in the second year of our reign.

3. [Sir Richard Cox], 'A copy of and answers to several complaints made by the Irish by their agent Mr Cockly against judgements given by the Justices and Council in several cases relating to the Articles of Limerick and Galway, together with the case of the protected Irish that came in upon the two first declarations after the Battle of the Boyne', [mid–1692].[2]

1st complaint:
The Lords Justices and Council appointed to hear the claims and restore the

---

[2]   T.N.A., SP 63/352, ff 118–23. The title of this document is calendared in the state papers for December 1690. This is certainly wrong, as the contents make abundantly clear. I have dated it to mid-1692, on the basis that the judgment explicitly mentions the ratification of the articles under the great seal of England (ordered by William in Dec. 1691, warrant issued 25 Jan. 1692), and that the complaints were addressed to the lords justices and council, dating it to before Sydney's arrival in Ireland in August 1692. I have credited it to Sir Richard Cox due to the author's mention of having written to Ginkel to direct him to exclude the protectees from the benefit of the articles of Limerick (see *The whole works of Sir James Ware*, ed. Walter Harris, ii, 210–13). 'Mr Cockly' is a phonetic spelling of Adam Colclough's surname.

persons within the said articles, have adjudged that no person therein comprehended shall have any leases for years to which they were entitled, though as
well by the letter as by the intent of the said articles they were to be restored
thereunto, as well as to their real estates. The words whereof being as follows,
'that all the persons mentioned in the second article, shall hold possess and
enjoy their estates of freehold and inheritance, and all their right titles, and
interest, privileges and immunities which they etc., held and enjoyed etc., in
the reign of Charles II at any time since by the laws that were in force in his
reign', and afterwards it is provided by the said second article, that the persons
therein comprehended should have, hold and enjoy all their goods and chattels
real and personal, to them or any of them belonging and remaining in their
own hands, or in the hands of any in trust for them, and by the fifth article all
persons comprehended in the second or third article were to have a general
pardon, and their outlawries to be reversed. By the second clause they are to be
restored to all their interest which is the most pat word to transfer a chattel real,
and by the fifth clause they are to have a general pardon, and their outlawry
to be reversed which (had there been no more words) is sufficient to restore
them yet on a strained construction grounded on that particle of the second
clause that restores them to all their goods and chattels real or personal to them
belonging and remaining in their hands, or in the hands of any in trust for
them, whereas if these words were omitted, the other words of the articles are
sufficient, and a favourable construction of that same clause may well maintain
a restitution of all their chattels real, at least restrains not any other branch of
the articles.

Answer to the 1st complaint:
The Lords Justices and Council are by the King's letter to determine all cases
upon the articles according to the plain sense and meaning thereof, without
straining the words, either to the prejudice or favour of any persons. That they
have generally done so in the case of chattels real is most evident for these
following reasons:
1st: That the first part of the second article provides only for their estates of
inheritance and never intended to meddle with any chattel real or personal
needs not other argument to prove, than there being a subsequent part of the
second article which relates wholly to them, and says they shall only be restored
to such as are in their own possession, or in the possession of any one in trust for
them and the complainants themselves saying, that if the second clause be left
out, and a favourable construction made of the words 'right, title and interest'
in the former part of the second article, it might very well be supposed it was
intended to restore them to their chattels real, as an ample allowance that
the said second clause not being to be left out, and no strained or favourable

construction to be made by the [Lords] Justices and Council, they ought not to complain of the injustice of the judgement.

2nd: The gentlemen who solicited the putting the articles under the seal well knew the original words could by no means be reached to the meaning they intended, and therefore instead of 'right, title and interest', as it was in the original articles, they added in the letter for passing the patent the letter 's' to each word, and so made it, 'rights, titles and interests', and this way indeed it seemed much more favourable to their demands than before it was.

3rd: They insist because their outlawries are by the fifth article to be reversed, therefore they being put then in all respects in the same condition they were before their rebellion, it is hard they should have any other restraints upon them; it is true that had that been the first and only article for them, as Sir Stephen Rice the most cunning man of their party said, if he had been concerned in the treaty he would not have asked for, nor taken more, their reasoning had been just, but since in the body of the articles there are several things to be performed on their part to the King and his Protestant subjects, it is reasonable that they should give security for doing the same before their outlawries are reversed, or otherwise both will be at their mercies afterwards, which by experience is not to be allowed of, or else his Majesty being necessitated to indict them again, which for many reasons can not be thought for their interest, this of the chattels real will prove a very considerable advantage to his Majesty especially in the estates of the Dukes of York and Ormond, when by the articles there is no ground for any such demand.

2nd Complaint:

All those entitled to any remainder depending on any estate which determined during the war, are kept out of possession by the said second article in the particle they are expressly restored thereunto by these words, 'all their estates of freehold and inheritance, right, title and interest, etc.'

Answer to the 2nd complaint:

Those in remainder after estates tail whose ancestors died in rebellion were at the making of the articles in words expressly excepted as appears by the first draught of the said articles, and were at the desire of the very gentlemen that now solicit them struck out, because they said that the words of the second article did not restore any such, and that it would raise a clamour upon them, if the said words were continued in, and be of no advantage to us, since as afore is said no part of the articles could be construed to restore them, and now to have the very same men complain of great hardship that these persons are out of possession of their estates when they know it was never intended they should have them is very disingenuous, and certainly it is as just and reasonable to make use of the intention of those that treated to add these [words] which were upon this occasion left out as those which they pretend were forgot and were added by his Majesty afterwards, by which addition they got at least one third more than without it they could have pretended to.

3rd complaint:
The several Roman Catholics that submitted to their Majesties and took protections long before the surrender of Limerick were after such protection and during their being under the same indicted and outlawed for high treason, all their cattle and substance seized on, and taken away by the militia, dispossessed of their estates (some of them killed as was Mr Geoghegan[3] of Castletown's cousin german and several others of his family and many more under the same circumstances in the kingdom) for their safety being deprived both of their liberties and properties, and their lives in daily fear, and question, fled to the Irish quarters, and were there 3 October 1691 and for many months before, and consequently comprehended within the said articles; and likewise the Roman Catholic proprietors of the county of Limerick which took protection from his Majesty at the time of the first siege and when the same was raised was stripped and plundered of all their substance by his Majesty's army, yet continued still in their houses until by a subsequent proclamation they were deprived of their Majesties' protection, whereby they were necessitated to be and remain in the Irish quarters for their security and maintenance [and] continued therein until after 3 October 1691, and consequently are comprehended within the words, intent and meaning of the articles, yet are debarred from the benefit thereof, it being resolved that no person that at any time took protection shall have the benefit of the said articles, which resolution is grounded on a strained construction of a branch of the said second article, the words whereof are as follows: 'That the inhabitants and residents in the Irish quarters, and the officers and soldiers then in arms under any commission of King James, etc., in any of the counties mentioned in the said article, and all the commissioned officers in their Majesties' quarters that belonged to the Irish regiments then in being, that were treated with, and who are not prisoners of war, or have taken protection, and who shall return, etc., to be restored, etc.,' and by construction of the words 'have taken protection' they bar any person that at any time took protection, though the same by any impartial exposition extends only to such commissioned officers in their Majesties' quarters that had taken protection, and this being a law of restitution should receive a beneficial construction.

Answer to the 3rd complaint:
This case of persons that took protections seems in the way it is put to be above all others the most hard and unjust, and therefore ought to have a more full and

---

3   Edward Geoghegan. See Simms, *Williamite confiscation,* pp 80–1.

particular answer, and though this is chiefly intended to justify the proceedings of the Lords Justices and Council in the judgements they have given in this case of protections upon the articles of Limerick, yet I shall not only speak of such who have pretence to these articles, but to persons that came in upon protection in general from the time his Majesty put out his first declaration, to the end of the war, and may be they are comprehended all under these four heads.

1st: Such who upon the first and second declaration took protection and lived within our quarters till the end of the war.

2nd: Such who took protection and afterwards returned into the enemy's quarters and pretend to be comprehended within the articles of Limerick.

3rd: Such who upon the raising of the siege of Limerick the first year were when our army withdrew left without our lines, and upon our approach to the town the second time withdrew into the enemy's quarters, and likewise claim the benefit of the Limerick [articles].

4th: Such who when we had besieged the town were by force of arms brought under the power of our army, and allowed to live under the protection of it.

For the 1st it is evident they have forfeited their estates by law, and his Majesty is at present neither by declaration, proclamation or articles obliged to restore them; what they submitted upon was his Majesty's first and second declarations, which have been inviolably kept to them, by which to those of the first rank, nothing is granted but their lives, though they have by a strained construction in their favour held and enjoyed their personal estates without disturbance. Most if not all of them live in their own houses, being let to persons in trust for them at easy rents, and have certainly found much more kindness and indulgence from the Government than they can pretend to deserve from it, and I doubt not but I shall be able to make it evident:

1st: That they have no pretence or right to their estates.

2nd: That their behaviour before and since they came under the Government had by no means deserved to have such a favour granted them.

3rd: And that it is opposite to the interest of England that they should be restored.

1st: That they of right ought to have their estates, I suppose they don't pretend they will know they came in upon the declaration that reserved their real estates to the King expressly.

2nd: That they did no service by submitting, and therefore had no better conditions granted them.

3rd: That because others who held out longer had their estates must not be a reason why they should have theirs, because they delivered up the kingdom, and these gentlemen did not deliver up themselves, only as the country was conquered and brought under his Majesty's obedience by force of arms, these gentlemen were found in it, their age, their interest or their design to stay in our bosom to betray us, not allowing them to follow their friends, and when it is considered, it will certainly be found more reasonable that those of Drogheda, Waterford, Cork, Kinsale and Ballymore (the most of which places surrendered at discretion), and all such who did, have without dispute or any intercession for them forfeited their estates, should have as large articles as those at Limerick than that these gentlemen should, for they delivered up places of importance, and most of them in their submission as early, but if these now are restored they won't only be equal with any other that opposed the King in that country but in a much better condition than any of those Protestants who have with their lives and fortunes assisted his Majesty in the conquest of it.

That they do by no means deserve so to be is certain for the following reasons:
1st: They have generally the characters of persons who did with the greatest violence in the stations they were in, which was generally in the civil government, oppose the King's and promote the late King James his interest of any in the kingdom, as they passing the act of attainder, their several proclamations signed by some of them which were of the Council will demonstrate.
2nd: Their submission was not voluntary but necessary for their interest, their estates and employments, which they hoped one day again to enjoy and officiate lying near Dublin. That any of them who had sons they went along with the enemy, and that there is not a single instance of any person who had an employ in the army that submitted upon the declaration.
That they had a constant correspondence with the enemy, supplied and supported them with money and necessaries, and encouraged and raised the poorer sort of people to run out and turn rapparees.
That they had a general design to murder all our soldiers as dispersed in quarters and had begun with 20 of Col. Foulkes'[4] within four miles of Dublin by persons who owned they never in all their lives had so great advantages under any Government and by letters intercepted we found they made their best to their friends beyond the Shannon, that those that stayed and submitted did more service to the cause than those that went away. Certain it is they were much a greater plague to us, and without all question of more use to them, for as if they had been there they would have helped to devour their provisions, which was to the last degree scarce, so being with us, they did not only live upon ours, but sent great quantities into their quarters; to prove this the paper that concerns [?]

---

4   Colonel John Foulkes.

murder, Cavenagh's examination, Baggott's confession and Wm Ogan's letters are undeniable evidence.[5]

3rd: That it is opposite to the interest of England to restore them. The greatest part of the forfeitures would be remitted by so doing. The estates of the forfeiting persons under this qualification lie near the metropolis of this kingdom, which should be altogether Protestant if possible, and if this opportunity be lost, it will be impracticable to make it so, for Papist landlords will have Papist tenants, which will neither answer to the present intention either of security or improvement.

There being no forfeitures, there will be no rooms for any new colonies of foreign Protestants to come in and plant in this kingdom, which will frustrate the design of making the balance of the Protestants' side as it is now on the Popish, and till that is done England must expect, and the Protestants of Ireland fear, frequent rebellions in their country.

Where the land goes will go the interest of a kingdom, and no doubt of it, it must be great mistake in policy when there is so justifiable a pretence to lose the opportunity of changing the proprietors from Papists to Protestants, as this will be.

That while it is in the hands of Papists, it is in the hands of persons who will be always endeavouring to overturn this government, that where it is given or sold to Protestants, they will thereby be obliged by interest, the strongest tie of all others, to support it.

That it will above measures disoblige the Parliament of England to see themselves disappointed of disposing of the forfeitures for the sakes of the enemies of the government, and the Protestants of Ireland will, if these persons are restored, be in a perfect despair.

2nd: Such who took protection upon the declaration and afterwards returned into the enemy's quarters, and because there at the time of the treaty claim the benefit of the Articles of Limerick.

That they are excluded is plain by the articles being excepted in express terms, and though the complainants would have the exception only to extend the officers in our quarters, yet I humbly conceive, if it be English, it is impossible

---

5   This may be a reference to 'Mark Bagott, wch was hangd for a spye' on 20 May 1691 (*The registers of St. Catherine, Dublin: 1636–1715*, ed. Herbert Wood (Exeter, 1908; reprinted, Dublin, 2003), p. 96). However, it is more likely to have been Capt. Mark Baggot, MP for Carlow in the 1689 Irish parliament, licensed to bear arms in Feb. 1692, listed as having been arrested with other former Jacobite officers in Dec. 1692, and as a forfeiting landowner in County Dublin. A Mark Baggot was also one of the two Catholic petitioners to the English parliament included in the petition of the Protestant purchasers against the act of resumption (*C.S.P.D.*, *1693*, pp 13–15; *C.S.P.D.*, *1695 & Addenda*, p. 142; Simms, *Williamite confiscation*, p. 125; Walsh, *Making of the Irish Protestant Ascendancy*, p. 29). I have been unable to identify Cavenagh or Ogan [Wogan].

to have such a construction, for the exception comes after all the particular enumerations, and if the prisoners of war, and those that died in rebellion, are not to have the benefit of the articles, which they don't pretend to, though they seem to deserve better from their party than these persons, unless their staying behind in our quarters to have afterwards an opportunity to desert and betray us was looked upon a greater service than the losing of life and liberty in their cause, and if so they most certainly deserve less from us, no doubt on it those that took protection and afterwards went into the enemy's quarters ought to be excluded.

But admit there were no words into this purpose, I must here again say that it is unquestionably reasonable that those that treated for his Majesty should be allowed to add what was intended if omitted, as well as those that treated for the enemy, and if so I will aver that it was so far from our intention to allow any such apostates the benefit of articles, that upon notice that many persons were flocking into Limerick for that purpose we wrote to the General positively to except them, and when we came to treat, ourselves put in these words, for that end, and they being expressly and fully, I humbly conceive, in the body of the articles excepted, and it being the manifest intention of the parties concerned in the treaty that they should be so, how can there be any room for a just complaint against any judgement in this case.

Such who were left without the line being those I suppose said to be turned out of his Majesty's protection by a proclamation, this I guess is Mr Fitzgerald's case, the lawyer, the only one in the like circumstances I know of.[6]

Mr Fitzgerald did when the King was at Limerick take a protection from Sir Robert Southwell, and upon our army's marching from the siege of that place, had a guard allowed him to secure his house and goods; however, as he pretends some of the Deans did plunder him of great part of his stock and moveables, which is the reason he gives that he continued at his own house which happened to be without our lines and therefore he says he was by a proclamation published afterwards put out of his Majesty's quarter and protection, and consequently was forced to seek the latter from the enemy.

Now when it is considered that Mr Fitzgerald always was looked upon as one of the most violent men of his party, that he only took the protection to secure his own interest, that notwithstanding he had a guard at his house, who were answerable for the violence done him, and could have informed him where

---

[6] James Fitzgerald's claim to the articles of Limerick was rejected on 8 July 1692 (Simms, 'Irish Jacobites', p. 95). He was among those who petitioned the English parliament in 1698 seeking a saving proviso in the bill for resuming grants of forfeited lands; a printed copy of this petition survives (C.J., xii, 144 (5 Mar. 1698); *The case of James Fitz-Gerald esq; counsellor at law; upon a petition to the commons of England in parliament assembled* (London, 1698)).

the persons were that plundered him, yet he never was to complain and seek reparation as others in his circumstances did in the like cases and had it.

That upon the proclamation mentioned which encouraged all persons to come within our lines that it might be in our power to protect them, he instead of that stayed in the enemy's quarters and assisted them with necessaries, and that upon the approach of our army to the second siege he left his habitation which then came in our quarters again, and went into rebellion with the enemy.

That notwithstanding the enemy for fear we should fall on his house and make a garrison of it, burned the same, yet he did not think fit to leave them, though ever so hardly used, and come to us, though much the more plentiful quarter, but on the contrary chooses to live in a cellar with the Irish.

I say all these things considered Mr Fitzgerald will be found to have no better an excuse for his apostasy than the rest of the gentlemen that took protection, and afterwards deserted us, and went into the Irish, besides the exception being expressly against him, could not by the [Lords] Justices and Council be moderated though they had found.

Lastly, those who after we besieged Limerick by the excursions and quarters of our horse came to live under us and our protections.

These gentlemen, like the rest, have no pretence to be restored either by the words of the articles, or the intention of the parties that treated; the persons heard for and comprehended in the articles being such that were in their quarters and under their protection in the counties of Kerry, Cork, Clare and Mayo, which allowed we had likewise quarters in the same counties as indeed we had, and several persons living in them who had before been by force reduced to their Majesties' obedience without any other terms than discretion, and did no service upon their surrender and therefore ought to have no benefit by it, it being at the opening of the treaty proposed by the [Lords] Justices that nobody should be treated with, but such who were at that time without our lines or protection, it being never our intention to give such advantageous terms to any who had not power to pretend to them, and for these reasons soever that exception made of the prisoners of war, such who died in rebellion and those who had formerly taken protection, looking upon it to be out of the power of such to do service equivalent to the favours granted them by the articles, and any of the Irish residing in any other part of our quarters may as well insist to be restored, as these gentlemen who have no other pretence for it but being nearer the place of treaty than those who lived in the more remote parts of the kingdom, and if the submitting early of those who pretend to have come in upon the first declaration be the only reason why they ought to have their estates. Certainly the holding out to the last day, and brought in by force at last can't by the same way of arguing be an inducement to give these gentlemen theirs.

There yet remains to answer a general argument for all persons concerned in the complaint that the articles are a law of restitution and therefore ought to be construed in favour of the persons restored. But when it is considered this will be found not a law of pardon and restitution granted *ex gratia*, but a bargain made between a King and his subjects who had rebelled against him, and who with their swords in their hands insisted upon having such terms, or otherwise they would not submit, and therefore on the one side the King will make good every part of the agreement according to the plain words of the same, so on the other hand if any part of it be dubious, and will bear two constructions, it ought to be made in favour of the crown rather than of such subjects who by such means came by it, unless it is believed that the Irish want encouragement to rebel which nobody that is acquainted with that country even in its present circumstances can imagine.

Bibliography

1. Manuscript Material
2. Printed Primary Material
3. Pamphlets
4. Guides, Calendars and Reference Works
5. Secondary Sources

1. Manuscript Material

Barmeath Castle, Co. Louth
Bellew of Barmeath papers (private collection)

Bodleian Library, Oxford
Carte Ms 31	Correspondence, etc., of the Duke of Ormond, 1660–2
Carte Ms 69	Miscellaneous Irish papers, 1660–88
Carte Ms 113	Miscellaneous papers, 17th and 18th centuries
Carte Ms 146	Copies of letters from the Duke of Ormond, 1677–80
Carte Ms 181	Correspondence of James II, etc.
Clarendon Ms 88	
Rawlinson D. 921B	Miscellaneous papers

British Library
Add. Ms 4,761	Papers relating to the revenue and trade of Ireland, 1629–1713
Add. Ms 9,715	Southwell papers
Add. Ms 13,956	Survey of forfeited estates in Co. Galway, [1701]
Add. Ms 21,136	Southwell papers
Add. Ms 34,195	Papers relating to the Tower Establishment, Crown Loans, etc, 1576–1763
Add. Ms 35,838	Hardwicke papers, 1567–1720
Add. Ms 36,662	Letters to Sir William Dutton Colt, 1691–2
Add. Ms 37,673	Letters from William Wogan to Edward Southwell, 1703–18
Add. Ms 38,145	Letter book of Richard Talbot, 1689–90
Add. Ms 38,146	Letter book of Sir Robert Southwell, 1690
Add. Ms 38,153	Letters from Sir Richard Cox to Sir Robert and Edward Southwell, 1687–1706
Eg. Ms 2618	Egerton papers

Lambeth Palace Library, London
Ms 935

London Metropolitan Archives
MJ/SP/XX/51   Book of Recognizances, 1698

Marsh's Library, Dublin
Z.2.1.7 (107)   'Reasons humbly offer'd against the heads of a Bill intituled heads of a Bill for Explaining and amending an Act intituled an Act to prevent the further growth of Popery', [1709?]
Z.3.1.1

The National Archives, London
PC 2/66, 71–81 Registers of the privy council of England
PC 4/1   Minutes and associated papers of the privy council of England
SP 32   State Papers Domestic, William and Mary
SP 34   State Papers Domestic, Anne
SP 44   State Papers, Entry Books
SP 63/350–65   State Papers Ireland, 1681–1705
SP 66, Case B   Parchment documents, including Irish bills
SP 67   State Papers Ireland, Entry Books

National Archives of Ireland
2/446/37 (2)   Calendar of Patent Rolls, 1685–1688
2/446/54 (2)   Book of Protections, 1695–6
Sarsfield–Vesey papers
Wyche papers, series 1 & 2

National Library of Ireland
Annesley Mss
Microfilm, pos. 264

Mahon Papers
Ms 47,873/1

Mount Bellew Papers:
Ms 31,889   Petition of Christopher Bellew for the benefit of the articles of Limerick, 1698

O'Hara Papers
Ms 20,386
Ms 36,386/1–5

Reports on private collections, i, no. 4.

Sarsfield Papers
D. 26,059   Commission to Justices Denis Daly and Bryan O'Neill to go on the
             assizes in Cork, Feb. 1691

Various Papers:
D 16,250 – D 16,261
Ms 10   *Collectanea de Rebus Hibernicis* (transcripts of seventeenth- and
             eighteenth-century material by Walter Harris)
Ms 13,653   Drafts of proclamations of William III on Irish affairs, 1689–91
Ms 20,665   Draft petition to James II against repealing the Restoration land
             settlement, 1689

Westport Papers:
Mss 40,883–41,112

Public Record Office of Northern Ireland, Belfast
Annesley Papers
D1854/2   Records of the forfeiture inquiry commissioners and the forfeiture
             trustees, 1699–1703 (consulted in the National Library of Ireland
             on microfilm, pos. 264)

De Ros Mss
D/638/12
D/638/18

Kilmaine Papers
T3134   (photocopies of originals held at Shelfield House, Warwickshire)

Royal Irish Academy, Dublin
24 G 1–7   'The reduction of Ireland'
24 Q 34   'A book of postings and sale of the forfeited and other estates and
             interests in Ireland … [1703]'

Shelfield House, Warwickshire
Kilmaine Papers (Deposited with the Library of Trinity College Dublin in 2014)

Staffordshire Record Office, Stafford
Stafford Papers
D641/2/K/2/3 'The examination of Col. John Browne's clause in the Articles of Limerick …'
D641/2/K/2/4 Stafford–Howard family correspondence, 1691–1733
[All references to this material have been very kindly supplied to me by Dr John Bergin]

Surrey History Centre, Woking
Midleton Papers
1248/1–7 [Consulted in transcript form. I am grateful to Professor David Hayton and Michael Page for their kindness in allowing me to consult these transcripts.]

Somers-Cocks Papers
371/14/F Papers relating to Irish political affairs, 1694–1709

Trinity College Dublin
Ms 744 Appendices to the report of the forfeiture inquiry commissioners, 1699
Ms 749/1–13 Correspondence of George Clarke, secretary of war in Ireland, 1690–2
Ms 750 William King's letter books
Ms 1688 Sermons by Anthony Dopping, bishop of Meath

Utrecht Archive
Huis Amerongen
Ms 3219–21 [Some of this material may be consulted in the National Library of Ireland on microfilm p. 3721. I am also grateful to Dr Evelien Schillern for providing me with material not found on the microfilm.]

2. Printed Primary Material

Annesley, Francis, Hamilton, James, Langford, Henry and Trenchard, John, *The report of the Commissioners appointed by Parliament to enquire into the Irish Forfeitures, delivered to the House of Commons the 15th of December, 1699* (London, 1700).
The Articles of Galway, exactly printed from the letters–patents: wherein they are ratified and exemplified by their Majesties under the Great Seal of England (Dublin, 1692).

Barry, J.G. (ed.), 'The groans of Ireland' in *Irish Sword*, ii (1956–7), pp 130–6.

Bergin, John and Lyall, Andrew (eds), *The acts of James II's Irish parliament of 1689* (Dublin, 2016).

Berwick, Edward, *The Rawdon papers* (London, 1819).

Brewer, J.S. and Bullen, William (eds), *Calendar of Carew manuscripts, preserved in the Archiepiscopal library at Lambeth, 1589–1600* (London, 1869).

Burke, W.P., *The Irish priests in the penal times, 1660–1760* (Waterford, 1914).

Chamney, Anne and O'Byrne, Eileen (eds), *The convert rolls* (revised ed., Dublin, 2005).

Chandler, Richard (ed.), *The history and proceedings of the House of Commons, from the Restoration to the present time* (14 vols, London, 1742–4).

The civil Articles of Lymerick exactly printed from the letters patents: wherein they are ratified and exemplified by their Majesties under the Great Seal of England (Dublin, 1692).

Clarke, J.S. (ed.), *The life of James the Second, king of England* (2 vols, London, 1816).

Cronin, John, Loeber, Rolf and Murtagh, Harman (eds), 'Prelude to confiscation: a survey of Catholic estates in Leinster in 1690' in *Journal of the Royal Society of Antiquaries of Ireland*, lxxxi (2001), pp 61–139.

Cunningham, Bernadette, 'Clanricarde letters' in *Journal of the Galway Archaeological & Historical Society*, xlviii (1996).

Curtis, Edmund and McDowell, R.B. (eds), *Irish historical documents, 1172–1922* London, 1943).

Danaher, Kevin and Simms, J.G. (eds), *The Danish force in Ireland, 1690–91* (Dublin, 1962).

The Eleventh, Twelfth, and Thirteenth, and the Fourteenth and Fifteenth reports from the Commissioners … respecting the public records of Ireland (London, 1825).

Fagan, Patrick (ed.), *Ireland in the Stuart papers* (2 vols, Dublin, 1995).

Giblin, Cathaldus, 'Catalogue of material of Irish interest in the collection Nunziatura di Fiandra, Vatican archives' in *Collectanea Hibernica*, 1 (1958), pp 7–34.

Gilbert, J.T. (ed.), *A Jacobite narrative of the war in Ireland, 1688–1691* (Dublin, 1850, reprinted Shannon, 1971).

Grey, Anchitell, *Grey's debates in the House of Commons* (10 vols, London, 1769).

Hatchell, George (ed.), *Abstract of Grants of Lands and other Hereditaments under the Commission of Grace, 36–37 Charles II, and 1–4 James II, 1684–1688* (Dublin, 1839).

Hogan, James and Tate, Lilian (eds), 'Letter book of Richard Talbot' in *Anal. Hib.*, no. 4 (1932), pp 99–138.

Hogan, James (ed.), *Négociations de M. le comte d'Avaux en Irlande, 1689–90* (Dublin, 1934).

— (ed.), *Négociacions de M. le comte d'Avaux en Irlande, 1689–90: supplementary volume with indexes by Lilian Tate* (Dublin, 1958).

Hull, C.J. (ed.), *The economic writings of Sir William Petty together with the observations upon the bills of mortality more probably by Captain Gaunt* (2 vols, Cambridge, 1899).

Kelly, James with Lyons, Mary Ann (eds), *The proclamations of Ireland, 1660–1820* (5 vols, Dublin, 2014).

Kelly, Patrick, 'The improvement of Ireland' in *Anal. Hib.*, no. 35 (1992), pp 45–84.

Lyall, Andrew (ed.), *Irish Exchequer reports: reports of cases in the Courts of Exchequer and Chancery in Ireland, 1716–1734*, Selden Society Publications, 125 (2008).

McNeill, Charles (ed.), 'Letters from the Earl of Tirconnell to the Lord President' in *Anal. Hib.*, no. 1 (1930), pp 38–44.

Macpherson, James (ed.), *Original papers, containing the secret history of Great Britain from the Restoration, to the accession of the House of Hannover* (2 vols, London, 1775).

MacSwiney of Mashanaglass, Marquis, 'Some unpublished letters of the Count d'Avaux in the National Library of Ireland' in *Proceedings of the Royal Irish Academy*, 40C (1931–2), pp 296–307.

Melvin, Patrick (ed.), 'Sir Paul Rycaut's memoranda and letters from Ireland, 1686–1687' in *Anal. Hib.*, no. 27 (1972), pp 125–82.

—, 'Letters of Lord Longford and others on Irish affairs, 1689–1702' in *Anal. Hib.*, no. 32 (1985), pp 37–111.

Mulloy, Sheila (ed.), *Franco-Irish correspondence: December 1688–February 1692* (3 vols, Dublin, 1983–4).

Ohlmeyer, Jane and Ó Ciardha, Éamonn (eds), *The Irish statute staple books, 1596–1687* (Dublin, 1999).

O'Kelly, Charles, *Macariae Excidium: or, the destruction of Cyprus, being a secret history of the war of the revolution in Ireland, 1688–1691*, ed. J.C. O'Callaghan (Dublin, 1850).

Routledge, F.J. (ed.), *Calendar of the Clarendon state papers preserved in the Bodleian Library, v, 1660–1726* (Oxford, 1970).

Sharpe, Richard (ed.), *Roderick O'Flaherty's letters to William Molyneux, Edward Lhwyd, and Samuel Molyneux, 1696–1709* (Dublin, 2013).

Simington, R.C., *Books of survey and distribution, ii: Co. Mayo* (Dublin, 1956).

—, *The transplantation to Connacht, 1654–58* (Dublin, 1970).

Simms, J.G., 'The original draft of the civil articles of Limerick, 1691' in *I.H.S.*, viii (1952–3), pp 37–44.

—, 'Irish Jacobites' in *Anal. Hib.*, no. 22 (1960), pp 11–230.

Singer, S.W. (ed.), *The correspondence of Henry Hyde, earl of Clarendon, and of his brother Laurence Hyde, earl of Rochester* (2 vols, London, 1828).

Tallon, Geraldine (ed.), *Court of claims: submissions and evidence, 1663* (Dublin, 2005).

Troost, Wouter, 'Letters from Bartholomew van Homrigh to General Ginkel, earl of Athlone, 1692–1700: from the Huisarchief Amerongen, Amerongen Castle, near Utrecht' in *Anal. Hib.*, no. 33 (1986), pp 59–128.

Publications of the Irish and English Parliaments:

Ireland:

A collection of the protests of the Lords of Ireland, 1634–1771 (Dublin, 1772).

Journals of the house of commons of the kingdom of Ireland (3rd series, 32 vols, Dublin, 1782–95).

Journals of the house of lords of the kingdom of Ireland (8 vols, Dublin, 1779–1800).

The statutes at large passed in the parliaments held in Ireland (20 vols, Dublin, 1786–1801).

England:

Journals of the house of commons [of England] (London, 1547–)

Journals of the house of lords [of England] (London, 1578–)

Historical Manuscripts Commission:

Buccleuch Mss, vol ii.

Downshire Mss, vol i.

Egmont Mss, vol ii.

Finch Mss, vols iii–iv.

House of Lords Mss, new series, vols ii–iv.

Leyborne-Popham Mss.

Ormonde Mss, new series, vols iii–viii.

Portland Mss, vol. iii.

Stuart Mss, vol. i.

3. Pamphlets

An account of the capitulation and surrender of Limerick (London, 1691).

An account of the present state Ireland is in, under King James: and the deplorable condition of the Protestants (London, 1690).

An account of the sessions of parliament in Ireland, 1692 (London, 1693).

An account of the surrender of Limerick (London, 1690).

An account of the transactions of the late King James in Ireland. Wherein is contain'd the act of attainder passed at Dublin in May, 1689 (London, 1690).

The acts of that short session of parliament held in Dublin, May 7, 1689 (Dublin, 1756).

Anno regni Jacobi II … at the parliament begun at Dublin the seventh day of May, Anno Domini 1689 [An act of supply for his Majesty for the support of his army] (Dublin, 1689).

Anno V. Jacobi II Regis ([Dublin, 1689]) [A compilation of 15 of the acts of the 1689 parliament, lacking a title page].

Articles of war agreed upon between his Grace the Duke of Schonberg, and Teige O'Regan, for the surrender of Charlemont, the twelfth of May, 1690 (Edinburgh, 1690).

Brewster, Francis, A discourse concerning Ireland and the different interests thereof (London, 1698).

Boate, Gerard, Ireland's natural history (London, 1652).

The case of all persons comprized in the Articles or capitulations of the City of Waterford, fort and castle of Bophin, and the towns of Sligo and Drogheda in the kingdom of Ireland, humbly submitted to the consideration of the honourable the Knights Citizens and Burgesses in Parliament assembled [London, 1700].

The case of James Fitz-Gerald esq; counsellor at law; upon a petition to the commons of England in parliament assembled (London, 1698).

The case of John Bingham, Esq., and Katherine Dunbarr, widow [Dublin, 1695].

The case of John Burke … humbly offered to the consideration of the Honourable the House of Commons (London, 1701).

The case of Richard, Lord Bellew ([Dublin,] n.d.).

The case of several of his majesties subjects in Ireland, commonly called Protectees, most humbly offered to the consideration of both houses of parliament [London, 1699].

The case of the creditors of Sir Abel Ram, Kt, deceased, humbly presented to the honourable, the knights, citizens and burgesses in parliament assembled ([Dublin, 1695]).

The case of the right honourable Francis Lord Bermingham, baron of Athunry, in the kingdom of Ireland ([Dublin,] n.d).

Davenant, Charles, Discourses on the publick revenues, and on the trade of England (London, 1698)

A diary of the siege and surrender of Lymerick with the articles at large, both civil and military (Dublin, 1692).

The Duke of Tyrconnel's speech to the garrison and magistrates of the city of Lymerick, upon their late debates, for the surrender of the said place (London, 1691).

An elegy on the much lamented death of Denis Daly, one of the late King James's

Judges in this kingdom, who departed this life, at his lodgings in High–Stret Dublin, on Saturday the 11th of this instant March 1720–21 (Dublin, 1721).

An exact account of the late action at the town of Dundalk, against the Irish, by their Majesties forces, commanded by Sir John Lanier, together with the articles of surrender of Moss-Town (London, 1690).

An exact and impartial account from Ireland, of the death of the late earl of Tyrconnell, who died in the city of Limerick, on Tuesday the 18th of this instant August (London, 1691).

An exact journal of the victorious progress of their Majesties forces under the command of Gen. Ginckle, this summer in Ireland ... together with the total defeat of the Irish at Agrim and Thomond Bridge: And lastly, of the capitulation and surrender of Limerick (London, 1691).

An exact relation of routing the Irish army under Sarsfield, and of the hostages agreed on, in order to a capitulation for surrender of Limerick into their Majesties hands (London, 1691).

A full and further account of the surrender of Galway, with the articles contained therein (Edinburgh, 1691).

A full and true account of all the proceedings in Ireland, since his Majesties first embarking for that kingdom, to his present march to besiege Limerick (London, [1690]).

A full and true relation of the taking Cork, by the right honourable the earl of Marlborough, Lieut. General of their Majesties forces: together with the articles of their surrender (Edinburgh, 1690).

An impartial relation of the several arguments of Sir Stephen Rice, Sir Theobald Butler, and Councellor Malone, at the Bar of the House of Commons of Ireland ... against passing the Bill then under consideration intituled An Act to prevent the further growth of Popery (Dublin, 1704).

An impartial relation of the surrender and delivery of the famous city of Dublin to the French, by the late King James, with some great and remarkable passages, what happened betwixt Teague O'Regan, and the English General, at the surrender (London, 1690).

The journal of the proceedings of the parliament in Ireland, with the establishment of their forces there (London, 1689).

A journal of the proceedings of the pretended parliament in Dublin, from the 7th, to the 20th of this instant May (London, 1689).

King, William, *The state of the Protestants of Ireland under the late King James's government* (4th ed., London, 1692).

Leslie, Charles, *An answer to a book, intituled, The State of the Protestants in Ireland under the late King James's government* (London, 1692).

A letter from an English officer in his Majesty's army in Ireland, giving a true account of the progress of affairs in that kingdom: together with what past at the surrender of Waterford and Duncannon (London, [1690]).

A list of such of the names of the nobility, gentry and commonalty of England and Ireland ... by an act of a pretended parliament assembled in Dublin in the kingdom of Ireland, the 7th of May, 1689 before the late King James, attainted of high treason (London, 1690).

London Gazette, 28–31 July 1691.

Marsh, Francis, *An address given to the late King James, by the titular archbishop of Dublin* (London, 1690).

Michelburne, John, *An account of the transactions in the North of Ireland, Anno Domini, 1691 ... with a particular relation of the manner of besieging and taking the town of Sligoe* (London, 1692).

The most acceptable and faithful account of the capitulation the Irish Governor of Charlemont made to D. Schonbergh's forces (London, 1690).

Reasons for his Majesties issuing a general pardon to the rebels of Ireland, that will submit: without exemption of the considerable and influencing men among them (London, 1689).

A relation of the surrender of Limerick (London, 1691).

A relation of the victory obtained by the King in Ireland, at the passage of the Boyne, on the first day of this instant July, 1690. And of the surrender of Drogheda (London, 1690).

Story, George, *A true and impartial history of the most material occurrences in the kingdom of Ireland during the last two years* (London, 1691).

—, *A continuation of the impartial history of the wars in Ireland* (London, 1693).

A short memorial humbly offered in behalf of the Old English of Ireland. Praying to be govern'd by the parliament of England (London, 1700).

The state of the case of Denis Daly, and Edmund Malone, Esqrs; and of a few other lawyers, of the town of Gallway, in the Kingdom of Ireland (Dublin, 1696).

The state of the Papist and Protestant proprieties in the kingdom of Ireland in the year 1641 ... and how the properties stand this present year 1689 ... (London, 1689).

Tutchin, John, *The British muse: or tyranny exposed: a satyr* (London, [1702?]).

A true account of the whole proceedings of the parliament in Ireland, beginning March 25, 1689, and ending the 29th of June following (London, 1689).

Villare Hibernicum, being an exact account of all the provinces, counties, cities, arch-bishopricks, bishopricks, towns, castles, fortifications, garrisons and most considerable villages and places of strength which have been reduced by his Majesties arms (London, 1690).

4. Guides, Calendars and Reference Works

Ball, F.E., *The judges in Ireland, 1221–1921* (2 vols, New York, 1927).

Bosworth, N., Good, J.M. and Gregory, O., *Pantologia: a new cyclopedia, comprehending a complete series of essays, treatises and systems ... of human genius, learning and industry* (12 vols, London, 1808–13).

Brady, John, *Catholics and Catholicism in the eighteenth-century press* (Maynooth, 1965).

Browne, Josiah, *Reports of cases, upon appeals and writs of error, in the High Court of Parliament, from the year 1701 to the year 1779* (7 vols, London, 1779–83).

Calendar of State Papers, Domestic, 1673–5; 1678 & Addenda; 1683 to 1686–7; 1690–1 to 1703–4.

Calendar of State Papers, Ireland, 1660–2; 1663–5 & Addenda; 1669–70.

Calendar of Treasury Books, 1681–5 to 1714.

Calendar of Treasury Papers, 1556–1696; 1697–1702.

Carolina chronicle: the papers of Commissary Gideon Johnston, ed. Klingberg, F.J. (Berkeley, 1946).

Clesham, Brigid, 'The Westport estate papers' in *Cathair na Mart*, xxvi (2008), pp 90–105.

Cokayne, G.E., *The complete baronetage* (5 vols, Exeter, 1900–06).

—, *The complete peerage*, ed. Gibbs, Vicary *et al* (14 vols, London, 1910–59, 1998).

Cruickshanks, Eveline, Handley, Stuart and Hayton, D. W. (eds), *The history of parliament: the house of commons, 1690–1715* (5 vols, Cambridge, 2002).

D'Alton, John, *Illustrations, historical and genealogical of King James's Irish army list (1689)* (Dublin, 1855, repr. 1997).

Englefield, D.J.T., *The printed records of the parliament of Ireland, 1613–1800: a survey and bibliographical guide* (London, 1978).

Foster, Joseph, *Alumni Oxonienses* (4 vols, Oxford, 1889–91).

—, *The register of admissions to Gray's Inn, 1521–1889* (London, 1889).

Howard, G.E., *Several special cases on the laws against the further growth of popery in Ireland* (Dublin, 1775).

Jacob, Giles *A new law dictionary* (London, 1729).

James, E.T., James, J.W., and Boyer, P.S. (eds), *Notable American women: a biographical dictionary* (Radcliffe, 1971).

Johnston–Liik, E.M., *History of the Irish Parliament, 1692–1800: commons, constituencies and statutes* (6 vols, Belfast, 2002).

MacLysaght, Edward, 'Dunsandle papers' in *Anal. Hib.*, no. 15 (1944), pp 392–405.

Murphy, Sean, 'The Sligo papers, Westport House, Co. Mayo: a report' in *Anal. Hib.*, no. 33 (1986), pp 15–46.

Russell, C.W., and Prendergast, J.P., *The Carte manuscripts in the Bodleian library, Oxford* (London, 1871).

Simington, R.C., 'Annesley Collection' in *Anal. Hib.*, no. 16 (1946), pp 39–73.

Simms, J.G., 'Report on the compilation of a bibliography of source material for the history of Ireland, 1685–1702' in *Anal. Hib.*, no. 22 (1960), pp 1–10.

Steele, Robert (ed.), *A bibliography of royal proclamations of the Tudor and Stuart Sovereigns, 1485–1714* (2 vols, Oxford, 1910).

White, Newport B., 'George Clarke's Irish war correspondence' in *Anal. Hib.*, no. 10 (1941), pp 247–9.

Online Databases

British History Online (http://www.british-history.ac.uk/)
Dictionary of Irish Biography, online ed. (http://dib.cambridge.org/)
Early English Books Online (http://eebo.chadwyck.com/home)
Eighteenth-Century Collections Online (http://find.galegroup.com/ecco/start.do?)
Irish Legislation Database, Queen's University Belfast (http://www.qub.ac.uk/ild/)
Oxford Dictionary of National Biography, online ed. (http://www.oxforddnb.com/)

5. Secondary Sources

Allen, R.C., 'The price of freehold land and the interest rate in the seventeenth and eighteenth centuries' in *Economic History Review*, n.s., xli (1988), pp 33–50.

Andrews, J.H., 'A note on the later history of the Irish charcoal iron industry' in *Journal of the Royal Society of Antiquaries in Ireland*, lxxxvi (1956), pp 217–19.

—, 'Notes on the historical geography of the Irish iron industry' in *Irish Geography*, iii (1956), pp 139–49.

—, 'Sir Richard Bingham and the mapping of western Ireland' in *Proceedings of the Royal Irish Academy*, 103C (2003), pp 61–95.

Arnold, L.J., 'The Irish court of claims of 1663' in *I.H.S.*, xxiv (1984–5), pp 417–30.

—, *The Restoration land settlement in County Dublin, 1660–1688: a history of the administration of the Acts of Settlement and Explanation* (Dublin, 1993).

Barnard, T.C., 'Sir William Petty as Kerry ironmaster' in *Proceedings of the Royal Irish Academy*, 82C (1982), pp 1–32.

—, 'An Anglo–Irish industrial enterprise: iron–making at Enniscorthy, Co. Wexford, 1657–92' in *Proceedings of the Royal Irish Academy*, 85C (1985), pp 101–44.

—, 'Historiographical review: Farewell to old Ireland' in *Historical Journal*, xxxvi (1993), pp 909–28.

—, 'Lawyers and the law in seventeenth-century Ireland' in *I.H.S.*, xxviii (1992–3), pp 256–82.

—, A new anatomy of Ireland: the Irish Protestants, 1649–1770 (London, 2003).

—, 'Conclusion: Restoration Ireland' in Dennehy (ed.), Restoration Ireland, pp 179–93.

—, 'The Irish in London and the "London Irish", ca. 1660–1780' in O'Shaughnessy (ed.), Networks of aspiration: the London Irish of the eighteenth century (Eighteenth-Century Life special issue, 39:1 (2015), pp 14–40).

Bartlett, Thomas and Hayton, D.W. (eds), Penal era and golden age: essays in Irish history (Belfast, 1979).

Bartlett, Thomas and Jeffery, Keith (eds), A military history of Ireland (Cambridge, 1996).

Bartlett, Thomas, 'The O'Haras of Annaghmore c.1600–c.1800: survival and revival' in Irish Economic and Social History, ix (1982), pp 34–52.

Beckett, J.C., The making of modern Ireland, 1603–1923 (London, 1981).

Bergin, John and Kinsella, Eoin, 'Hurling matches in London (1733–1818) and New York (1781–2)' in Archivium Hibernicum, lxviii (2015), pp 19–67.

Bergin, John, Magennis, Eoin, Ní Mhunghaile, Lesa and Walsh, Patrick (eds), New perspectives on the penal laws (E.C.I. special issue no. 1, Dublin, 2011).

Bergin, John, 'The Irish Catholic interest at the London Inns of Court, 1674–1800' in E.C.I., xxiv (2009), pp 36–61.

—, 'The world of Richard Lahy, an Irish law agent in eighteenth-century London', in Gillespie & Foster (eds), Irish provincial cultures in the long eighteenth century, pp 75–92.

—, 'Irish Catholics and their networks in eighteenth-century London' in O'Shaughnessy (ed.), Networks of aspiration: the London Irish of the eighteenth century, pp 66–102).

Blake, M.J., 'A map of part of the county of Mayo in 1584' in JGAHS, iv (1908), pp 145–8.

Bosher, J.F., 'The Franco–Catholic danger, 1660–1715' in History, lxxix (1994), pp 5–30.

Bottigheimer, K.S., 'The Restoration land settlement in Ireland: a structural view' in I.H.S., xviii (1972–3), pp 1–21.

Boyce, D.G., Eccleshall, Robert and Geoghegan, Vincent (eds), Political thought in Ireland since the seventeenth century (London, 1993).

Boyce, D.G., Eccleshall, Robert and Geoghegan, Vincent (eds), Political discourse in seventeenth- and eighteenth-century Ireland (Basingstoke, 2001).

Brady, Ciaran (ed.), Worsted in the game: losers in Irish history (Dublin, 1989).

—, 'Introduction: historians and losers' in idem (ed.), Worsted in the game, pp 1–8.

Brady, John and Corish, Patrick, 'The Church under the penal code' in A history of Irish Catholicism, iv (Dublin, 1971).

Brown, Michael, McGrath, C.I. and Power, T.P. (eds), *Converts and conversion in Ireland, 1650–1850* (Dublin, 2005).

Browne, Denis Edward, 10th marquess of Sligo, *Westport House and the Brownes* (2nd ed., Westport, 1998).

Burke, John, A *genealogical and heraldic history of the commoners of Great Britain and Ireland* (4 vols, London, 1833–8).

Burke, Oliver, *Anecdotes of the Connaught Circuit: from its foundation in 1604 to close upon the present time* (Dublin, 1885).

Burns, R.E., 'The Irish penal code and some of its historians' in *Review of Politics*, xxi (1959), pp 276–99.

—, 'The Irish Popery laws: a study of eighteenth-century legislation and behavior' in *Review of Politics*, xxiv (1962), pp 485–508.

Childs, John, *The Williamite wars in Ireland, 1688–1691* (London, 2007).

Clarke, Howard B. and Devlin, Judith (eds), *European encounters: essays in memory of Albert Lovett* (Dublin, 2003).

Connolly, S.J., 'Religion and history' in *Irish Economic and Social History*, x (1983), pp 66–80.

—, *Religion, law and power: the making of Protestant Ireland, 1660–1760* (Oxford 1992).

—, *Divided kingdom: Ireland, 1630–1800* (Oxford, 2008).

Creighton, Anne, 'The Remonstrance of December 1661 and Catholic politics in Restoration Ireland' in *I.H.S.*, xxxiv (2004–5), pp 16–41.

—, '"Grace and favour": the Cabal ministry and Irish Catholic politics, 1667–73' in Dennehy (ed.), *Restoration Ireland*, pp 141—60.

Crofton, H.T., *Crofton memoirs* (York, 1911).

Cullen, Louis, 'Catholics under the penal laws' in *E.C.I.*, i (1986), pp 23–36.

—, 'Catholic social classes under the penal laws' in Power and Whelan (eds), *Endurance and emergence*, pp 57–84.

—, 'Economic trends, 1660–91' in Moody *et al* (eds), A *new history of Ireland*, iii, pp 398–407.

—, 'The two George Fitzgeralds of London, 1718–1759' in Dickson, Ohlmeyer, & Parmentier (eds), *Irish and Scottish mercantile networks in Europe and overseas in the seventeenth and eighteenth centuries*, pp 251–70.

Cunningham, John, *Conquest and land in Ireland: the transplantation to Connacht, 1649–1680* (London, 2011).

Dalton, Charles, 'Richard Lovell Edgeworth's "Memoirs"' in *Notes and Queries*, 8th series, VII (1895), p. 381.

Darcy, Eamon, Margey, Annaleigh & Murphy, Elaine (eds), *The 1641 depositions and the Irish rebellion* (London, 2012).

[Davis, Thomas Osborne], 'Irish state papers, no. 1: acts of the Irish parliament of 1689' in *The Dublin Magazine* (Jan., 1843), pp 25–42; [idem], 'Irish state papers, no. 1 (continued): statutes of 1689; act of repeal of the acts of settlement and explanation, with an introduction' in *The Dublin Magazine* (Feb., 1843), pp 75–90; [idem], 'Proceedings of the parliament in Ireland in 1689: introduction, containing an examination of the legality of its constitution as compared with other parliaments of the same epoch' in *The Dublin Magazine and Citizen* (April, 1843), pp 170–5; [idem], 'Irish state papers, no. 1 (concluded): statutes of 1689; act of attainder … with an introduction on the authenticity and effect of the statute' in *ibid.*, pp 182–95; [idem], 'Retrospect of the parliament of 1689, and its acts' in *ibid.*, pp 196–201.

Davis, Thomas Osborne, *The patriot parliament of 1689, with its statutes, votes and proceedings*, ed. Duffy, Charles Gavan (3rd ed., Dublin, 1893). [An abridged collection of the previously listed essays by Davis]

Dennehy, Coleman (ed.), *Restoration Ireland: always settling and never settled* (Aldershot, 2008).

Dickson, David, *New foundations: Ireland, 1660–1800* (2nd ed., Dublin, 2000).

Dickson, David, Ohlmeyer, Jane and Parmentier, Jan (eds), *Irish and Scottish mercantile networks in Europe and overseas in the seventeenth and eighteenth centuries* (Ghent, 2007).

Dolley, Michael, 'The Irish coinage, 1534–1691' in Moody, Martin & Byrne (eds), *A new history of Ireland*, iii, pp 408–19.

Doyle, Thomas, 'Jacobitism, Catholicism and the Irish Protestant elite, 1700–1710' in *E.C.I.*, xii (1997), pp 28–59.

Edgeworth, Maria and Edgeworth, R.L., *Memoirs of Richard Lovell Edgeworth, Esq* (2 vols, London, 1820).

Farrell, Brian (ed.), *The Irish parliamentary tradition* (Dublin, 1973).

Finnegan, Francis, 'The Irish "Catholic convert rolls"' in *Studies*, xxxviii (1949), pp 73–82.

Fitzpatrick, Brendan, *Seventeenth-century Ireland: the war of religions* (Dublin, 1988).

Flood, J.M, *The life of Chevalier Charles Wogan: an Irish soldier of fortune* (Dublin, 1922).

Froude, J.A., *The English in Ireland in the eighteenth century* (3 vols, London, 1872–4).

Genet-Rouffiac, Nathalie and Murphy, David (eds), *Franco-Irish military connections, 1590–1945* (Dublin, 2009).

Genet-Rouffiac, Nathalie, 'The Wild Geese in France: a French perspective' in Genet-Rouffiac & Murphy (eds), *Franco-Irish military connections, 1590–1945*, pp 32–54.

Geoghegan, Vincent, 'Thomas Sheridan: toleration and royalism' in Boyce, Eccleshall & Geoghegan (eds), *Political discourse in seventeenth- and eighteenth-century Ireland*, pp 32–61.

Gibney, John, *Ireland and the Popish Plot* (Basingstoke, 2009).

Gilbert, J.T., *A history of the city of Dublin* (3 vols, Dublin, 1854–9).

Gillespie, Raymond and Moran, Gerard (eds), *'A various country': essays in Mayo history, 1500–1900* (Westport, 1987).

Gillespie, Raymond and Foster, Roy (eds), *Irish provincial cultures in the long eighteenth century: essays for Toby Barnard* (Dublin, 2012).

Gillespie, Raymond, 'Mayo and the rising of 1641' in *Cathair na Mart*, no. 5 (1985), pp 38–44.

—, 'Lords and commons in seventeenth-century Mayo' in Gillespie & Moran (eds), *'A various country'*, pp 44–66.

—, *Seventeenth-century Ireland: making Ireland modern* (Dublin, 2006).

Glickman, Gabriel, *The English Catholic community, 1688–1745: politics, culture and ideology* (Woodbridge, 2009).

Guy, Alan J., 'The Irish military establishment, 1660–1776' in Bartlett & Jeffrey (eds), *A military history of Ireland*, pp 211–30.

Habakkuk, John, 'The rise and fall of English landed families, 1600–1800: II' in *Transactions of the Royal Historical Society*, 5th series, xxx (1980), pp 199–221.

Harris, Tim, 'What's new about the Restoration?' in *Albion*, xxix (1997), pp 187–222.

—, *Revolution: the great crisis of the British monarchy, 1685–1720* (London, 2006).

Hastings, Caitríona, 'A history of Holy Trinity Church, Westport' in *Cathair na Mart*, no. 27 (2009), pp 5–27.

Hart, A.R., *A history of the king's serjeants at law in Ireland: honour rather than advantage?* (Dublin, 2000).

Hayton, D.W., 'The Williamite revolution in Ireland, 1688–1691' in Israel (ed.), *The Anglo-Dutch moment*, pp 185–213.

—, (ed.), *The Irish parliament in the eighteenth century: the long apprenticeship* (Edinburgh, 2001).

—, *Ruling Ireland, 1685–1742: politics, politicians and parties* (Woodbridge, 2004).

—, *The Anglo-Irish experience, 1680–1730: religion, identity and patriotism* (Woodbridge, 2012).

Hogan, Daire and Osborough, W.N. (eds), *Brehons, serjeants and attorneys: studies in the history of the Irish legal profession* (Dublin, 1990).

Irwin, Liam, 'The Irish presidency courts, 1569–1672' in *Irish Jurist*, n.s., xii (1977), pp 113–14.

—, 'The suppression of the Irish Presidency system' in *I.H.S.*, xxii (1980–1), pp 21–32.

Israel, J.I. (ed.), *The Anglo-Dutch moment: essays on the Glorious Revolution and its world impact* (Cambridge, 1991).

James, F.G., 'The Irish lobby in the early eighteenth century' in *English Historical Review*, lxxxi (1966), pp 543–57.

—, 'The active Irish peers in the early eighteenth century' in *Journal of British Studies*, xviii (1979), pp 52–69.

—, *Lords of the ascendancy: the Irish house of lords and its members, 1600–1800* (Dublin, 1995).

Jordan, D.E., *Land and popular politics in Ireland: County Mayo from the Plantation to the Land War* (Cambridge, 1994).

Kearney, H.F., 'Richard Boyle, ironmaster: a footnote to Irish economic history' in *Journal of the Royal Society of Antiquaries in Ireland*, lxxxiii (1953), pp 156–62.

Kelly, James, McCafferty, John and McGrath, C.I. (eds), *People, politics and power: essays on Irish history 1660–1850, in honour of James I. McGuire* (Dublin, 2009).

Kelly, James, *Poynings' Law and the making of law in Ireland, 1660–1800* (Dublin, 2007).

—, *That damn'd thing called honour: duelling in Ireland, 1570–1860* (Cork, 1995).

Kelly, Patrick, '"A light to the blind": the voice of the dispossessed élite in the generation after the defeat at Limerick' in *I.H.S.*, xxiv (1984–5), pp 431–62.

—, 'Nationalism and the contemporary historians of the Jacobite war in Ireland' in O'Dea and Whelan (eds), *Nations and nationalisms*, pp 89–102.

—, 'Ireland and the Glorious Revolution: from kingdom to colony' in Beddard, Robert (ed.), *The revolutions of 1688* (Oxford, 1991), pp 163–90.

Kenny, Colum, 'The exclusion of Catholics from the legal profession in Ireland' in *I.H.S.*, xxv (1986–7), pp 337–57.

Kenyon, J.P., *Robert Spencer, earl of Sunderland, 1641–1702* (Westport, Connecticut, 1975).

King, Peter, 'The production and consumption of bar iron in early modern England and Wales' in *Economic History Review*, lviii (2005), pp 1–33.

Kinsella, Eoin, '"Dividing the bear's skin before she is taken": Irish Catholics and land in the late Stuart monarchy, 1683–91' in Dennehy (ed.), *Restoration Ireland*, pp 161–78.

—, 'In pursuit of a positive construction: Irish Catholics and the Williamite articles of surrender' in *E.C.I.*, 24 (2009), pp 11–35.

Lecky, W.E.H., *A history of Ireland in the eighteenth century* (5 vols, London, repr. 1913).

Lenihan, Pádraig, *1690: Battle of the Boyne* (Stroud, 2003).

—, *Consolidating conquest: Ireland, 1603–1727* (Harlow, 2008).

McBride, Ian, 'Catholic politics in the penal era: Father Sylvester Lloyd and the Delvin address of 1727' in Bergin *et al* (eds), *New perspectives on the penal laws*, pp 115–47.

MacCarthy-Morrogh, Michael, 'Credit and remittance: money problems in early seventeenth-century Munster' in *Irish Economic and Social History*, xiv (1987), pp 5–19.

MacCuarta, Brian (ed.) *Reshaping Ireland, 1550–1700: Colonization and its consequences* (Dublin, 2011).

Maguire, W.A. (ed.), *Kings in conflict: the revolutionary war in Ireland and its aftermath, 1689–1750* (Belfast, 1990).

—, 'The estate of Cú Chonnacht Maguire of Tempo: a case history from the Williamite land settlement' in *I.H.S.*, xxvii (1990–91), pp 130–44.

McCracken, Eileen, 'Charcoal-burning ironworks in seventeenth and eighteenth century Ireland' in *Ulster Journal of Archaeology*, 3rd series, xx (1957), pp 123–38.

—, 'Supplementary list of Irish charcoal-burning ironworks' in *Ulster Journal of Archaeology*, 3rd series, xxviii (1965), pp 132–6.

McGrath, C.I., 'Securing the Protestant interest: the origins and purpose of the penal laws of 1695' in *I.H.S.*, xxx (1996–7), pp 25–46.

—, *The making of the eighteenth-century Irish constitution: government, parliament and the revenue, 1692–1714* (Dublin, 2000).

—, 'English ministers, Irish politicians and the making of a parliamentary settlement in Ireland, 1692–5' in *English Historical Review*, cxix (2004).

—, 'The provisions for conversion in the penal laws, 1695–1750' in Brown *et al* (eds), *Converts and conversion in Ireland*, pp 35–59.

—, 'Government, parliament and the constitution: the reinterpretation of Poynings' Law, 1692–1714' in *I.H.S.*, xxxv (2006–7), pp 160–72.

—, *Ireland and empire, 1692–1770* (London, 2012).

McGuire, James, 'The Church of Ireland and the Glorious Revolution of 1688' in Art Cosgrove and Donal McCartney (eds), *Studies in Irish history presented to R. Dudley Edwards* (Dublin, 1979), pp 137–49.

—, 'The Irish Parliament of 1692' in Bartlett and Hayton (eds), *Penal era and golden age*, pp 1–31.

—, 'Richard Talbot, earl of Tyrconnell (1630–91) and the Catholic counter-revolution' in Ciaran Brady (ed.), *Worsted in the game: losers in Irish history* (Dublin, 1989), pp 72–83.

—, 'James II and Ireland, 1685–1690' in Maguire (ed.), *Kings in conflict*, pp 45–57.

—, 'The Treaty of Limerick' in Whelan (ed.), *The last of the great wars*, pp 127–38.

—, 'A lawyer in politics: the career of Sir Richard Nagle, c.1636–1699' in Devlin and Clarke (eds), *European encounters*, pp 118–31.

Kevin McKenny, 'The Restoration land settlement in Ireland: a statistical interpretation' in Dennehy (ed.), *Restoration Ireland*, pp 35–52.

Maynard, Hazel, 'The Irish legal profession and the Catholic revival, 1660–89' in Kelly *et al* (eds), *People, politics and power*, pp 28–50.

Miller, John, *James II* (2nd ed., London, 2000).

—, 'The earl of Tyrconnel and James II's Irish policy' in *Historical Journal*, xx (1977), pp 803–23.

—, 'Thomas Sheridan (1646–1712) and his "narrative"' in *I.H.S.*, xx (1976), pp 105–28.

Monod, Paul, Pittock, Murray and Szechi, Daniel (eds), *Loyalty and identity: Jacobites at home and abroad* (Basingstoke, 2010).

Moody, T.W., Martin, F.X., and Byrne, F.J. (eds), *A new history of Ireland*, iii: *early modern Ireland, 1534–1691* (Oxford, 1976).

Moran, Gerard (ed.), *Galway: history and society* (Dublin, 1996).

Moran, Patrick, 'Notes on some Irish altar plate' in *J.R.S.A.I.*, lxxvi (1946).

Morley, Vincent, *Irish opinion and the American Revolution, 1760–1783* (Cambridge, 2002).

—, *The popular mind in eighteenth-century Ireland* (Cork, 2017).

Morrill, John, 'The causes of the Popery laws: paradoxes and inevitabilities' in Bergin *et al*, *New perspectives on the penal laws*, pp 55–73.

Muldrew, Craig, 'Credit and the courts: debt litigation in a seventeenth-century urban community' in *Economic History Review*, n.s., xlvi (1993), pp 23–38.

Mulloy, Sheila, 'Galway in the Jacobite war' in *Journal of the Galway Archaeological and Historical Society*, xl (1986), pp 1–19.

—, 'Inisbofin – the ultimate stronghold' in *Irish Sword*, xvii (1987–8), pp 105–15.

—, 'Mayo and the Jacobite war, 1689–91' in *Cathair na Mart*, no. 8 (1988), pp 30–39.

—, 'Military history of the western islands (with special reference to Inishbofin)' in *Cathair na Mart*, no. 9 (1989), pp 101–19.

—, 'The transfer of power: Galway, 1642–1702' in Moran (ed.), *Galway: history and society*, pp 223–4.

Murphy, David, *The Irish brigades, 1685–2006* (Dublin, 2007).

Murray, R.H., *Revolutionary Ireland and its settlement* (Dublin, 1911).

Murtagh, Diarmuid and Murtagh, Harman, 'The Irish Jacobite army, 1689–91' in *Irish Sword*, xviii (1990–2).

Murtagh, Harman, 'Waterford and the Jacobite war, 1689–1691' in *Decies: Journal of the Waterford Archaeological and Historical Society*, 8 (1978), pp 2–6.

Ó Buachalla, Breandán, 'Irish Jacobitism in official documents' in *Eighteenth Century Ireland*, viii (1993), pp 128–38.

—, 'James our true king: the ideology of Irish royalism in the seventeenth century in Boyce, Eccleshall & Geoghegan (eds), *Political thought in Ireland*, pp 7–35.

—, 'Irish Jacobitism and Irish nationalism: the literary evidence' in O'Dea, M.

and Whelan, Kevin (eds), *Nations and nationalisms: France, Britain and the eighteenth-century context* (Oxford, 1995).

—, *Aisling ghéar: na Stíobhartaigh agus an taos léinn, 1603–1788* (Dublin, 1996).

O'Brien, Gerard (ed.), *Catholic Ireland in the eighteenth century: collected essays of Maureen Wall* (Dublin, 1989).

Ó Ciardha, Éamonn, *Ireland and the Jacobite cause, 1685–1766: a fatal attachment* (Dublin, 2002).

—, '"A lot done, more to do": the restoration and road ahead for Irish Jacobite studies' in Monod, Pittock, & Szechi (eds), *Loyalty and identity*, pp 57–81.

O'Connor, Thomas (ed.), *The Irish in Europe, 1580–1815* (Dublin, 2001).

O'Dowd, Mary, *Power, politics and land: early modern Sligo, 1568–1688* (Belfast, 1991).

Ó hAnnracháin, Tadhg, 'The strategic involvement of continental powers in Ireland, 1596–1691' in Pádraig Lenihan (ed.), *Conquest and resistance*, pp 25–52.

Ohlmeyer, Jane, '"Making Ireland English": the early seventeenth-century Irish peerage' in MacCuarta (ed.), *Reshaping Ireland, 1550–1700*, pp 131–46.

—, *Making Ireland English: the Irish aristocracy in the seventeenth century* (New Haven, 2012).

O'Malley, Sir Owen, 'O'Malleys between 1651 and 1725' in *JGAHS*, xxv (1952–3), pp 32–47.

Osborough, W.N., 'The regulation of the admission of attorneys and solicitors in Ireland, 1600–1866' in Hogan and Osborough (eds), *Brehons, serjeants and attorneys*, pp 101–51.

—, 'Catholics, land and the Popery Acts of Anne' in Power and Whelan (eds), *Endurance and emergence*, pp 21–56.

O'Shaughnessy, David (ed.), *Networks of aspiration: the London Irish of the eighteenth century* (*Eighteenth-Century Life* special issue, 39:1 (2015)).

O'Sullivan, Tadhg, 'Between toleration and preservation: the Popery laws and Irish Anglicanism, 1782–1808', in Bergin *et al* (eds), *New perspectives on the penal laws*, pp 27–52.

Parmentier, Jan, 'The Irish connection: the Irish merchant community in Ostend and Bruges during the late seventeenth and eighteenth centuries' in *E.C.I.*, xx (2005), pp 31–54.

Perceval-Maxwell, Michael, 'Sir William Alexander of Menstrie (1567–1640)' in *International Review of Scottish Studies*, xii (1982), pp 14–25.

—, 'The Irish Restoration land settlement and its historians' in Dennehy (ed.), *Restoration Ireland*, pp 19–34.

Power, T.P. and Whelan, Kevin (eds), *Endurance and emergence: Catholics in Ireland in the eighteenth century* (Dublin, 1990).

Power, T.P., 'Conversions among the legal profession in Ireland in the eighteenth century' in Hogan and Osborough (eds), *Brehons, serjeants and attorneys*, pp 153–73.

Quin, Caroline, Countess of Dunraven, *Memorials of Adare Manor* (Oxford, 1865).

Rapple, Rory, 'Taking up office in Elizabethan Connacht: the case of Sir Richard Bingham' in *E.H.R.*, cxxiii, no. 501 (2008), pp 277–99.

Simms, J.G., 'Land owned by Catholics in Ireland in 1688: historical revision ix' in *I.H.S.*, vii (1950–1), pp 180–90.

—, 'Williamite peace tactics, 1690–1' in *I.H.S.*, viii (1952–3), pp 303–23.

—, *The Williamite confiscation in Ireland, 1690–1704* (London, 1957).

—, 'Connacht in the eighteenth century' in *I.H.S.*, xi (1958–9), pp 116–33.

—, 'Irish Catholics and the parliamentary franchise, 1692–1728' in *I.H.S.*, xii (1960–1), pp 28–37.

—, 'The making of a penal law (2 Anne, c.6), 1703–4' in *I.H.S.*, xii (1960–1), pp 105–18.

—, *The Treaty of Limerick* (Irish History Series, no. 2, Dundalk, 1965).

—, 'Mayo landowners in the seventeenth century' in *J.R.S.A.I.*, 95 (1965), pp 237–47.

—, 'Sligo in the Jacobite war, 1689–91' in *Irish Sword*, vii (1965), pp 125 – 35.

—, *Jacobite Ireland, 1685–91* (Dublin, 1969).

—, 'Marlborough's siege of Cork, 1690' in *Irish Sword*, ix (1969), pp 113–23.

—, 'The bishops' banishment act of 1697 (9 Will. III, c. 1)' in *I.H.S.*, xvii (1970–1), pp 185–99.

—, *War and politics in Ireland, 1649–1730*, eds. Hayton, D.W. and O'Brien, Gerard (London, 1986).

—, 'Kilkenny in the Jacobite war, 1689–91' in idem, *War and politics in Ireland*, eds. Hayton & O'Brien, pp 149–60.

Stapleton, Patricia, '"In monies and other requisites": the 1641 depositions and the social role of credit in early seventeenth-century Ireland' in Darcy, Margey & Murphy (eds), *The 1641 depositions*, pp 65–78.

Troost, Wouter, 'William III and the Treaty of Limerick (1691–97): a study of his Irish policy' (Published PhD thesis, Leiden, 1983).

—, 'William III and religious tolerance' in Whelan (ed.), *The last of the great wars*, pp 39–54.

Waldman, Felix, 'Anthony Dopping's restoration to the Irish privy council: a correction' in *Notes and Queries*, no. 255 (2010), pp 69–70.

Wall, Maureen, 'Catholic loyalty to king and Pope in eighteenth-century Ireland' in *Proceedings of the Irish Catholic Historical Committee* (Dublin, 1960), pp 17–24.

—, 'The Penal Laws, 1691–1760' (Irish History Series, no. 1, Dundalk, 1976).

Walsh, Patrick, *The making of the Irish Protestant Ascendancy: the life of William Conolly, 1662–1729* (Woodbridge, 2010).

The whole works of Sir James Ware concerning Ireland, revised and improved, ed. Walter Harris (2 vols, Dublin, 1764).

Whelan, Bernadette (ed.), *The last of the great wars: essays on the war of the three kings in Ireland* (Limerick, 1990).

Wood-Martin, W.G., *Sligo and the Enniskilleners, from 1688–1691* (Dublin, 1882).

Theses:

Aydelotte, J. E., 'The Duke of Ormonde and the English government of Ireland, 1678–85' (PhD thesis, 2 vols, University of Iowa, 1975).

Bergin, John, 'Irish legislative procedure after the Williamite Revolution: the operation of Poynings' Law, 1692–1705' (PhD thesis, 2 vols, University College Dublin, 2005).

Coleborn, Bryan, 'Jonathan Swift and the dunces of Dublin' (PhD thesis, University College Dublin, 1982).

Creighton, Margaret Anne, 'The Catholic interest in Irish politics in the reign of Charles II' (PhD thesis, Queen's University, Belfast, 2000).

Doyle, T.G., 'The politics of the Protestant ascendancy: politics, religion and society in Protestant Ireland, 1700–1710' (PhD thesis, University College Dublin, 1996).

Maynard, Hazel, 'Irish membership of the English Inns of Court, 1660–1699: lawyers, litigation and the legal profession' (PhD thesis, University College Dublin, 2006).

Murphy, Brian, 'The Waterford Catholic community in the eighteenth century' (MA thesis, University College Dublin, 1997).

Nolan, Frances, 'Jacobite women and the Williamite confiscation: the role of women and female minors in reclaiming compromised or forfeited property in Ireland, 1690–1703' (PhD thesis, University College Dublin, 2015).

O'Sullivan, Harold, 'Land ownership changes in the County of Louth in the seventeenth century' (PhD thesis, 2 vols, University of Dublin, 1991).

Walsh, Philip, 'The Blakes of Ballyglunin: Catholic merchants and landowners of Galway town and county in the seventeenth and eighteenth centuries' (PhD thesis, University College Dublin, 2017).

Index

acts and bills
 Irish
  act of settlement (1662) 3, 19,
   21–2, 36, 39, 88, 211, 240, 249,
   255
  Viscount Mayo's private bill (1662)
   21–2
  act of explanation (1665) 3, 22,
   240, 249, 255
  act of repeal of acts of settlement
   and explanation (1689) 5, 18,
   34–9, 40, 50, 51, 61, 128n, 174
  act of attainder (1689) 34, 37, 92,
   282
  act for improvement of trade (1689)
   173
  act of supply (1689) 35, 211
  bill for Colonel John Browne's
   Protestant creditors (1692)
   156–7, 160, 162
  bill to confirm articles of Limerick
   (1692) 107, 111
  bill of indemnity (1692) 89, 105,
   111–15, 129, 157
  'dual-purpose bill' about articles
   of Galway and Colonel John
   Browne's creditors (1692) 105,
   114, 129–30, 132, 154–6, 157n,
   162
  act for Colonel John Browne's
   Protestant creditors (1695) 119,
   130–2, 148, 160–9, 177, 179, 181,
   183, 188, 189, 203, 206
  act disarming papists (1695) 118,
   239, 245
  act banishing bishops and regular
   clergy (1697) 239
  act to confirm articles of Limerick
   and establish third court of claims
   (1697) 97, 117–18, 119, 122,
   137, 170, 173, 176, 244
  act to hinder reversal of outlawries
   and attainders (1697) 71–2, 74,
   75, 78, 109n, 118, 212, 217–18,
   239
  act to prevent Protestants marrying
   Papists (1697) 176
  association bill (1697) 169–71, 173
  bill for Colonel John Browne's
   Protestant creditors (1697)
   167–71
  act to prevent Papists being
   solicitors (1697) 176
  bills for Colonel John Browne's
   Protestant creditors (1698) 178,
   179–85, 189
  Lord Bophin's private bill (1699)
   138, 141–2
  bill for Colonel John Browne's
   Protestant creditors (1703–4)
   181–5, 187, 188, 189–90, 206
  act to prevent further growth of
   popery (1704) 118, 119
  act for Hollow Blades corporation
   (1704) 186
  act for Colonel John Browne's
   creditors (1705) 119, 178, 179,
   185–8, 206, 220
  act for settling Lady Clanmalier's
   estate on Lord Bellew (1707)
   229–32
  act to prevent the further growth
   of popery (1704) 191, 207, 208,
   220, 228, 229, 232, 235, 243–4,
   245
  act amending act to prevent the
   further growth of popery (1709)
   118, 119, 125, 139, 191, 208, 228,
   232, 244
  bill for purchasers of Colonel John
   Browne's estate (1709) 160,
   188–9
  act amending act disarming papists
   (1740) 245
 English
  act about oaths (1691) 104, 118,

119, 127, 128, 129, 130, 134, 148, 156, 241, 258
bill about Irish forfeitures (1692) 117
bill amending act about oaths (1696) 134
bill about Irish forfeitures (1698) 213–14, 218, 284n
bill about Jacobites in exile (1698) 218
act of resumption (1700) 9, 74–5, 81, 87, 89, 92–4, 109n, 120, 139, 143, 218–19, 283n
act for relief of Protestant purchasers of forfeited estates (1701) 139
'Bophin Act' (1702) and acts explaining same 138–40, 142
private bill sought by Colonel John Browne (1705) 138–40, 142
private acts unsuccessfully sought by protectees 94
parliamentary ratification of articles of surrender 66, 107, 111, 117–19, 122
promised under articles of Galway 250
promised under articles of Limerick 260
private acts and bills 12, 94, 119, 138–40, 142, 148, 159–60, 177, 181, 185, 219, 220
see also parliament of England; parliament of Ireland; penal laws
Adaire, William 202
Albemarle, earl of see van Keppel, Arnold Joost
Albeville, marquis d' see White, Ignatius
Alcock, William 195
Aldworth, Richard 86, 160, 161
Altamont, earl of see Browne, John, earl of Altamont
Anketell, Captain John 268, 270
Anne, queen of England, Scotland and Ireland 1, 224, 244, 245
Antrim, earl of see MacDonnell, Alexander, 3rd earl of
Archbold, Captain Richard 264
Archer, Captain John 263
Arthur, Thomas 195
article 13 (of the articles of Limerick)

see under Browne, Colonel John; Catholics; Limerick; privy council of England; privy council of Ireland
articlemen (those claiming the benefit of articles) 1, 6–10, 11, 12, 13–14, 66, 81, 93, 94, 97, 104, 122, 142–4, 147–9, 152, 155–7, 161, 162, 165, 236–7, 239, 240–45
see also Drogheda; Galway; Inis Boffin; Limerick; Sligo; Waterford
articles of surrender 1, 6, 9–11, 13, 17, 65–6, 71, 74, 79–80, 91, 95, 106–7, 109, 112, 115, 119, 140, 141, 142, 147–9, 161, 241–5
see also under Drogheda; Galway; Inis Boffin; Limerick; privy council of England; privy council of Ireland; Sligo; Waterford
Athenry, Barons see Bermingham, Edward; Bermingham, Francis
Athenry, Co. Galway 54
Athlone (town) 48, 53, 75
Athlone, earl of see Ginkel, Godard van Reede
Aughrim, battle of 39, 53–4, 55, 75, 123, 239
Aungier, Francis, 1st earl of Longford 99–100
Avaux, comte d' see Mesmes, Jean-Antoine de
Aylmer, Dame Ellen 86, 87
Aylmer, George 105
Aylmer, Sir Gerald 263
Aylmer, Peter 268
Aylmer, Richard 271

Baggott, Mark 99, 283
Bamford, James 216–17
Barnewall, Bartholomew 263
Barnewall, Matthias, 10th Baron Trimlestown 58
Barnwall, Richard 93
Barrett, Edmond 269
Barrett, James 265, 268
Barrett, John 265, 268
Barrett, Thomas 167
Barry, Laurence, 3rd earl of Barrymore 179–80
Barry, Richard 200

Bates, John 201
Bath, John 73
Bayly, Francis 200
Beckett, Mr (lawyer) 23
Bellasis, Sir Henry 71, 72, 255
Bellew, Frances, Lady Bellew and
    dowager countess of Newburgh
    230
Bellew, John, 1st Baron Bellew of Duleek
    121
Bellew, Sir Patrick 39, 40, 107, 110–11,
    166
Bellew, Richard, 3rd Baron Bellew of
    Duleek 229–32
Bennet, Sir Henry 22
Bermingham, Anne see O'Dempsey,
    Anne, Viscountess Clanmalier
Bermingham, Bridget (daughter of
    Colonel John Browne) 175n,
    210, 221, 225
Bermingham, Bridget (granddaughter of
    Colonel John Browne) 225
Bermingham, Edward, 13th Baron
    Athenry 12, 29, 32, 43, 71–3, 80,
    110, 132, 201, 210, 221–2, 230,
    231–2, 255
Bermingham, Francis, 14th Baron
    Athenry 13, 210, 221, 228, 230
Bermingham, John 35, 221
Bermingham, Mary 231
Bermingham, Captain Pierce 263
Berwick, James FitzJames, duke of 43
Bethlemite, Solomon 195
Bettagh, William 263
Bingham, Alicia 163
Bingham, Sir Henry 163, 168, 169–71,
    176, 179, 187, 188–9, 190, 191,
    198, 199, 200, 212
Bingham, John 30, 153, 160, 161, 163–4,
    168, 171, 212, 213, 214
Bingham, Sir Richard 18, 163
Bird, James 73
Birmingham, Joan 18
Blake, Dominick 196, 203n
Blake, Francis 214–16
Blake, Martin 132–3
Blake, Martin ('cousin') 213, 214–16
Blake, Captain Nicholas 255, 256
Blake, Sir Walter 39, 132, 191, 196
Blathwayt, William 68

Blayney, William, 6th Lord Blayney,
    Baron of Monaghan 61
Bodkin, Lieutenant Colonel [John] 250
Bodkin, Lieutenant Colonel Francis 272
Boffin see Inis Boffin
Bonnell, James 88, 91, 102, 244
Booth, Sir Robert 21, 24, 211
Bophin, Lord see Bourke, John
Bourke, Elinor, Viscountess Mayo 23,
    24, 167
Bourke, Captain Garrett 273
Bourke, John, Baron Bourke of Bophin
    and 9th earl of Clanricarde 121,
    125, 135, 137–42
Bourke, Luke 23–24
Bourke, Maud (wife of Colonel John
    Browne) 21, 22
Bourke, Michael, Baron Dunkellin and
    10th earl of Clanricarde 142
Bourke, Miles, 2nd Viscount Mayo 19
Bourke, Miles, 5th Viscount Mayo
    23–24, 224
Bourke, Nicholas 271
Bourke, Sir Oliver 266
Bourke, Richard, 8th earl of Clanricarde
    52, 78, 132, 166–7, 250, 256
Bourke, Lieutenant Colonel Richard 273
Bourke, Theobald, 3rd Viscount Mayo
    17, 21
Bourke, Theobald, 4th Viscount Mayo
    19, 21–3, 24, 212
Bourke, Theobald, 6th Viscount Mayo
    12, 24, 188, 201–2, 203n, 210,
    221, 222–3, 224, 229
Bourke, Theobald, 7th Viscount Mayo
    223
Bourke, Sir Ulick 42, 270
Bourke, Colonel Walter 21, 35, 140
Bourke, William, 7th earl of Clanricarde
    21, 22, 71, 135
Bourke, Captain William 270
Boyle, Michael, archbishop of Dublin
    21
Boyle, Roger, 1st earl of Orrery 22
Brabazon, Anthony 224–6
Brenan, John, archbishop of Cashel 58,
    60
Brewster, Sir Francis 25, 49, 242
Brodrick, Alan 97–8, 138, 141, 159, 179
Brodrick, Thomas 140, 141–2

Browne family
  Brownes of Kilpatrick 18
  Brownes of the Neale 4, 13, 18, 207, 210–13, 216, 226, 233, 234 *see also* Browne, George (brother of Colonel John); Browne, George (grandson of Colonel John's brother George); Browne, George (great-grandson of Colonel John's brother George); Browne, John, of the Neale
Browne, Captain Andrew 272
Browne, Bridget *see* Bermingham, Bridget (daughter of Colonel John Browne)
Browne, Colonel Dominick 132, 250, 256
Browne, Sir Dominick 18
Browne, Dominick (brother of Colonel John) 26, 33, 72, 222, 223
Browne, Edward 68
Browne, Elizabeth 210, 221
Browne, George (brother of Colonel John) 17, 35, 163, 168, 170, 191, 196, 208, 211, 212–16
Browne, George (grandson of Colonel John's brother George) 208, 233, 234, 235
Browne, George (great-grandson of Colonel John's brother George) 211
Browne, George (nephew of Colonel John) 35
Browne, Lieutenant Colonel George (nephew of Colonel John) 42, 44
Browne, Ignatius 164
Browne, Colonel John
  accused of Jacobite plotting 12, 148, 169–76
  and article 13 of articles of Limerick and debts 1, 5, 6, 11–12, 17, 24–5, 28–32, 36, 41, 57, 60–1, 110, 129, 130–1, 147, 210, 211, 221–2, 228, 236, 238, 259–60
  Clarendon's assessment of 33
  creditors 1, 6, 11–12, 27, 29–32, 36, 50, 55, 110, 129–32, 147–50, 152–69, 175–81, 183–6, 188–9, 203–6, 233
  deputy lord lieutenant of Co. Mayo 43

England, unlicensed visit to (1689) 35, 50
estates
  acquisition of 1, 17, 21–4, 29, 38, 49–50
  sale of 12, 148, 159–60, 162, 167–8, 178, 180, 182–3, 185–209, 226–8, 234
  as exemplar of 'new interest' 4, 11, 17–18, 237
  and Galway surrender 55
  and Inis Boffin surrender 55
  ironworks 5, 24–7, 29, 31, 33, 35, 36, 40, 41, 43–4, 46–50, 61, 150–2, 153, 154, 158–9, 163, 165, 228, 237
  difficulties in managing 46–7, 48
  as lawyer 18, 19–20, 22, 32–3, 58, 237
  lobbying by or on behalf of 1, 7, 11, 17, 104, 131, 147, 155, 157–8, 161
  member of Jacobite commission (1690) 52, 53
  as negotiator at Limerick 11, 17, 30, 41, 55–61, 62, 149, 236, 244
  and parliament of 1689 35–6, 38, 40, 43, 50
  regiments raised by, for James II 17, 44–5, 46–7, 50
  supplier of materiel to Jacobite army 5, 41, 44, 149–51, 237
  wife (Maud Bourke) 21, 22
Browne, John, of the Neale (nephew of Colonel John) 211–12, 214–15
Browne, John (father of Colonel John) 18–19, 211
Browne, John (great-grandfather of Colonel John) 18–19
Browne, John, earl of Altamont (grandson of Colonel John) 207, 210, 233, 235
Browne, John, of the Neale, Baron Kilmaine 211
Browne, John, marquess of Sligo (great-great grandson of Colonel John 235
Browne, Josias 191
Browne, Josias (grandfather of Colonel John) 18
Browne, Mary 18, 210

Browne, Peter (eldest son of Colonel
John) 12, 176, 178, 183–8, 191,
195, 199, 200, 201, 202, 204,
206–10, 219, 221–3, 226–35
Browne, Valentine 30, 165
Browne, Valentine (son of Colonel John)
176, 210, 221, 224–6
Burke, Dominick 201, 207–8
Burke, Captain Edmund 271
Burke, Gerald 201
Burke, Theobald 267
Burne, Mr (lawyer) 23
Bush, Amias 166
Butler, Captain Edward 267
Butler, James, 1st duke of Ormond 3, 99,
101, 105, 212, 239, 279
petitioned by Colonel John Browne 23
Butler, James, 2nd duke of Ormond 184
Butler, James, of Co. Tipperary 270
Butler, John 266
Butler, John, of Co. Tipperary 268
Butler, Mary 270
Butler, Pierce 269
Butler, Pierce, 2nd Viscount Ikerrin 21
Butler, Piers, Viscount of Galmoy 58, 60,
88, 257
Butler, Sir Toby (Theobald) 56, 58, 60,
61, 104–5, 110, 157, 171, 174,
175, 176, 220, 241, 243–4, 257
Butler, Colonel Walter 105
Byrne, Edmund, archbishop of Dublin
239

Cahir, Elizabeth McCarthy, Dowager
Baroness 269
Cairnes, William 215
Caldwell, Sir James 49
Callaghan, Captain Florence 166
Cantillon, Philip 265
Capell, Arthur, earl of Essex 239
Capell, Henry, Baron Capell of
Tewkesbury 117–18, 122, 130,
131, 133, 159, 160
Cappack, Bartholomew 263
Carroll, James 269
Carroll, John 166, 269, 271
Carroll, Kean 269
Carroll, Owen 87, 93–4
Carroll, Captain Roger 272
Carthy, Daniel 265

Cashell, Captain Thomas 265
Cassels, Richard 235
Catholics
landownership 1, 2–4, 6, 8, 11, 13–14,
30, 35, 41, 55, 60, 62, 78, 94, 98,
139, 142, 228, 233, 240, 244 see
also
levy imposed on by article 13 of
Limerick 1, 11, 12, 55, 129, 130,
147–8, 149, 152, 154–6, 159, 162,
166–7, 170, 181, 182, 189, 203–4,
238
'new interest' landowners 1–5, 6, 11,
13, 17, 18, 20, 32, 33–8, 40, 51–2,
54, 55, 62, 236, 237
see also penal laws
Caulfield, Toby 255
Caumont, Antonin Nompar de, comte de
Lauzun 51
Cavenagh, – 283
Chambers, William 190, 197, 200
Charles II, king of England, Scotland and
Ireland
grants land to Colonel John Browne
23
and Irish Catholics 1–3, 8, 21, 127,
144, 241, 244
Cheevers, Andrew 166, 269, 271
Cheevers, Bridget 271
Cheevers (Chievers), Edward, Viscount
Mount-Leinster 258
Cheevers, John 166, 269
Church of Ireland
conversions to 13, 21, 142, 144, 168n,
173, 176, 207–8, 210, 216, 223–4,
228–31, 232–3, 235, 243–4
defection from 19, 44n, 77n
Churchill, John, earl of Marlborough 80
Clanchy, John 266
Clanricarde, earls of see Bourke, John;
Bourke, Michael; Bourke,
Richard; Bourke, William
Clare, Dowager Viscountess see O'Brien,
Honora
Clarendon, earl of see Hyde, Henry
Clarke, George 56
Clinton, Thomas 265
Coghlan, John 273
Colclough, Patrick 106
Colclough ('Cockly'), Adam 46, 89–90,

100, 104–6, 113, 149, 157, 240, 241, 277
commissioners of forfeiture (Williamite) 121, 212
  1699 commission of inquiry 75, 78, 79n, 80n, 94, 120, 139, 141, 218
commissioners of the revenue
  Jacobite 38, 58
  Williamite 98, 134, 275, 276, 277
commissioners of the treasury (Jacobite) 38, 39, 46, 105, 150
Concannon, Thady 263
Coningsby, Thomas, earl of Coningsby 52, 57, 59, 66, 99, 107, 149, 154, 155, 157, 161, 181, 187, 257, 260
Conly, Captain Robert 264
Connell, Richard 266
Connor, Lieutenant Malachy 166, 269
Conolly, Luke 73
Conolly, William 140, 237–8
Considen, Dermott 266
Considen, Teige 267, 268
Coonan, Captain Cornelius 264, 268
Coote, Thomas 140
Cordon, Major 58
Cork, surrender of garrison 80–1
Cormick, Francis 197, 209
Cormick, Captain Michael 35, 72, 80, 194, 197, 203, 209, 256
Costelloe, Charles 270
Cotter, Sir James 105
courts of claims
  1663 3
  1689–90 (intended Jacobite court) 37–8
  1692 (Irish privy council) 10, 65–6, 78–80, 84, 89, 94, 109–11, 120–2, 127, 135, 153–5, 242
  1694 (Irish privy council) 10, 65–6, 78–80, 84, 94, 109, 120–2, 127, 242, 262–73
  1697–9 10, 65–6, 78–80, 84, 94, 97, 109, 120–2, 127, 137, 140, 143, 242
Cox, Sir Richard 74, 83, 90–92, 94, 100–1, 105, 122, 141, 240, 277
Cranisbrough, Peter 68
Creagh, Margaret 270
Creagh, Sir Michael 52
Creagh, Patrick 266

Creagh, Pierce 272
Creagh, Stephen 179, 201
Crean, Andrew 269
Crean, Julian 269
Crean, William 269
Crelly, John 267
Croasdaile, Thomas 194
Crofton, Sir Edward 38, 77, 254
Crofton, Sir Henry 75, 76–80, 127n, 284
Cromwellian land confiscation and grants see under land confiscations
Crow, William 161
Cruise, James 194
Cuffe, Francis 212
Cuffe, Gerald 187, 188, 190, 191, 198, 199, 200
Cunneys, Thomas 195
Cunningham, Lieutenant Godfrey 268
Curnoge, Garrett 265
Cusack, Christopher 262
Cusack, James 263
Cusack, Colonel Nicholas 58, 60, 257

Dalton, Christopher 271
Dalton, Henry 264
Dalton, Major John 266
Daly, Charles 21
Daly, Denis 18n, 126, 133–4, 139, 171, 174, 175, 176, 206, 222, 225–6, 228, 232, 241
  agent for the Galway articlemen 104, 125, 128–9, 131–2, 136, 140, 142
  appointment as judge (1686) 20, 32, 33
  as leader of Jacobite peace party 52, 53–5, 123
Daly, Denis, junior 201, 203n, 225–6, 234–5
Daly, Mary 228
Daly, Captain Paul 166
Daly, Peter 234–5
Daly, Thomas 230
Darcy, Francis 196
Darcy, Captain George 263, 271
Darcy, Hyacinth 166
Darcy, Patrick 196
Darcy, Patrick (Confederate era lawyer) 20
Dardis, Garrett 270
Davis, Sir John 21

Davis, Thomas (historian) 37–38
Davoren, James 270
Deery, John 267
Delahide, Thomas 73
Delahunty, Captain Laurence (or
    Lawrence) 266, 270
Delamare, John 181, 263
Delamere, Major Walter 194
Delaune, Gideon 161, 169, 195
Denn, Captain Theobald 268
Dennis, Patrick 197
Dering, Charles 224
Digby, Simon, bishop of Elphin 180
Dillon, Frances 60
Dillon, Garrett 30, 213, 219–20, 257
    business partner of Colonel John
        Browne 17, 29, 205, 238
    as lawyer 17, 33
    member of 1689 parliament 36
    as negotiator of the articles of Limerick
        56, 58–60
Dillon, Henry, 8th Viscount Dillon of
    Costello-Gallen 21, 26, 35, 58,
    60, 125, 132
Dillon, John 201, 262
Dillon, Luke, of Clonbrock 121
Dillon, Major 250
Dillon, Richard 194
Dillon, Robert, of Clonbrock 121, 166
Dillon, Robert, 6th earl of Roscommon
    61
Dillon, Theobald, 7th Viscount Dillon of
    Costello-Gallen 21, 26, 60
Dodd, Egerton 264
Doherty, Charles 267
Donnell, Thomas 272
Donnellan, John 166, 270
Donnellan, Nehemiah 163
Donnelly, John 267
Donovan, Constance 271
Donovan, Hugh 271
Dopping, Anthony, bishop of Meath
    101–2
Dover, Henry Jermyn, earl of 45, 48
Dowdall, Silvester 264
Dowling, Murtagh (Mortagh) 195, 197
Doyne, Robert 163
Driscoll, Dennis 271
Drogheda 27
    articles of 1, 65, 67, 127, 245, 282

claimants under 73, 74, 79–80, 118
ratification and implementation of
    73–5, 77, 81, 94, 118, 143
text 247
surrender of 67, 282
Drumgold, Nicholas 263
Duffe, Captain Thady 263
Dun, Margret 272
Dunbar, John 197
Dunn, Thady 144
d'Usson, Lieutenant General [Bonrepaus]
    248
Dwire, Captain Thomas 266, 270

Echlin, Sir Henry 33, 163, 234
Edgeworth, Sir John 172
England, James 265
Enniskillen (Inniskillen), Roger Maguire,
    styled Lord 250
Essex, earl of see Capell, Arthur
Eustace, Alexander 271
Eustace, Maurice (Morris) 258, 264,
    267
Eustace, Captain William 264
Evagh (Iveagh?), Lady 249
Everard, Charles 265
Everard, James 271
Everard, Lieutenant Colonel Matthew
    263
Evers, John 73

Fanshaw, William 216–17
Farrell, James 136
Farrell, Robert 263
Feilding, Colonel Robert 44–5, 47,
    50–1
Finch, Daniel, earl of Nottingham 52,
    68–70, 88–9, 107, 112, 113–15,
    125, 129, 155, 156, 184
Finnucan, Daniel 270
Fitton, Alexander 58
Fitzgerald, Captain Edmund 264
Fitzgerald, Edward 266
Fitzgerald, James 90–1, 284–5
Fitzgerald, Jean 200
Fitzgerald, John 67–8
Fitzgerald, Maurice 268
Fitzgerald, Redmond 271
Fitzgerald, Richard 68
Fitzgerald, Richard (2) 215

Fitzgerald merchant family of London 215–16
FitzJames, James, duke of Berwick 43
Fitzpatrick, Thomas 46, 48
Fitzsimons, Daniel 202
Fleming, Ignatius 73
Flood, John 268
Forbes, Arthur, 2nd earl of Granard 253, 254, 255
Forrter, Nicholas 264
Fottrell, Thomas 200, 265
Foulkes, Colonel John 280
France and the French 29, 54, 172, 174, 175, 218, 245
  gunsmiths from 47
  Irish regiments sent to 44–5, 47, 49, 51
  steel from 44
  Tyrconnell in 43, 52
French, Arthur 54, 104, 121, 123, 125, 127, 132–3, 135–7, 140, 142, 161, 191, 194, 196, 232
Freney, Lieutenant James 267
Frith, William 200
Fynn, Edmond 196

Galmoy, Piers Butler, Viscount of 58, 60, 88, 257
Galwan, Patrick 265
Galway 39
  articles of 1, 6, 71, 77, 83, 127–8, 140, 252, 255, 256
    claimants under 65, 72, 78, 79, 85, 87, 89, 108, 109, 110, 118, 120, 127, 129, 131–8, 141, 155–6, 161, 218, 237, 240, 263, 267
    ratification and implementation 66, 67, 81, 104, 111–12, 114, 119, 123–5, 127–38, 142, 159, 241–2, 244, 245
    text 247–50
  Catholic inhabitants well affected to English interest 141, 240
  defence and negotiations for surrender 43, 48, 49, 51–5, 70, 75–6, 78, 123, 125, 141, 251
  Inis Boffin garrison granted safe conduct to 256
Galway, Francis 127
Galway, Henry de Ruvigny, earl of 169

Galwey, John 86, 104, 106, 113, 157
Galwey, William 92
Garvey, Anthony 199
Geoghegan, (Lieutenant) Colonel Charles 263, 264
Geoghegan, Constance and Mary 264
Geoghegan, Edward (1) 264, 280
Geoghegan, Edward (2) 264
Geoghegan, Hugh 264
Geraghty, Bryan 49
Gibbon, Richard 49
Gilgan, James 268, 281
Gilgan, John 265, 268
Gilgan, Michael 265, 268
Gilgan, Robert 265, 268
Ginkel, Godard van Reede, earl of Athlone 53–7, 60, 76, 77, 102, 103, 107, 110, 123, 125, 126, 131, 135, 136, 137, 138, 142, 149, 247, 250, 252, 253, 257, 260
Godolphin, Francis 86
Gordon, James 213
Gorge, Colonel 195
Gorges, Dr Robert 21, 196
Gorges, Samuel 33
Gormanston, 7th Viscount see Preston, Jenico
Goulding, William 201
Grace, Mrs 265
Grace, Frances 263
Grace, James 156, 163, 195
Grace, Cornet John 263
Grace, Oliver 86, 87
Grady, James 266, 271
Grady, John 52–3
Grady, Monogh 266
Graham, Daniel 267
Granard, Arthur Forbes, 2nd earl of 253, 254, 255

Hackett, Captain James 263
Hallorane, Simon 265
Hamlin, Bartholomew 73
Hamlin, Valentine Andrew 262
Hanaghan, Dominic 272
Handcock, William 99
Hanning, Dominic 272
Hanoway, Richard 255
Harford, John 267
Harley, Robert 102

Harrold, Thomas 265
Hart, John 264
Hartegan, Matthew 265
Hehir, James 265
Herbert, William, 1st duke of Powis 44
Hicky, Roger 270
Hieven, Timothy 264
Higgins, Bryan 191, 202, 203, 207–8
Hoare, Colonel John 270
Hoare, William 265
Hogan, Edmond 270
Hogan, Murtagh 266
Hollow Blades corporation 186
Honan, Matthew 266
Huntington, Mary 180
Huntington, Dr Robert 161, 180
Hussey, Luke 179, 181, 186, 187, 202,
        205, 206, 210, 219–20, 221, 222,
        223, 227, 231, 233, 238–9
Hussey, Lieutenant-Colonel Maurice
        240
Hyde, Henry, 2nd earl of Clarendon
        32–33, 40
Hyde, Laurence, earl of Rochester 182,
        238

Ikerrin, Pierce Butler, 2nd Viscount 21
Inis Boffin
    articles of 1, 65, 245
        claimants under 67, 70, 71, 72,
            79–80, 104
        ratification and implementation
            68, 71–2, 75, 81, 94, 118, 143,
            156
        text 255–6
    Colonel John Browne and surrender
        55
    defence and negotiations for surrender
        43, 55, 70–1
iron industry in Ireland 25–7, 49
    see also under Browne, Colonel John;
        Protestants
Iveagh, Viscount Magennis of see
        Magennis, Brian
Iveagh(?), Lady ('Evagh') 249

James, F.G. (historian) 10
James II 41, 67, 105, 148, 150, 151, 171,
        172, 173, 174, 175, 205, 218, 236,
        237, 255, 257, 258, 282

and Colonel John Browne 44, 45, 46,
    48, 50
death 238
as duke of York 101, 211, 279
in exile 242
in France 34, 53, 62, 205
and Irish Catholics/Catholic attitudes
    to 1–2, 7–8, 13, 40, 62, 88,
    240–1
and Irish parliament of 1689/Irish land
    settlement 33–5
municipal charters granted by 77,
    127n, 249, 254
proclamations 7n, 37, 38, 82
succeeds to throne 5, 40
James III / James Francis Edward Stuart
    / Prince of Wales 106, 171, 173,
    175, 238, 239
Jermyn, Henry, earl of Dover 45, 48
Johnson, Elizabeth 195
Johnson, John 46
Johnson, Robert 134, 197, 198, 199, 200,
    204–5, 209
Johnston, Frances 179
Johnston, Reverend Gideon 179–83,
    184–5, 189–90
Jordan, Captain William 45
Joy, Edmond 265
Joyce, John 195

Kearney, Richard 267
Keating, John 267
Kelly, Bryan 195
Kelly, Clare 273
Kelly, Captain Dennis 265, 272
Kelly, Derby 255
Kelly, Francis 273
Kelly, Lieutenant George 262
Kelly, Grany 267
Kelly, John 72, 202
Kelly, Colonel John 71–2, 73, 80, 255,
    256
Kelly, Captain Thomas 262
Kennedy, George 29, 30, 164, 180, 181
Kennedy, Captain John 266
Kennedy, Matthew 266
Kilmaine, Baron see Browne, John, of the
    Neale
King, William, archbishop of Dublin
    37–8, 141, 169–71, 230, 231, 232

Kirwan, Sir John 39, 54, 123, 227
Kirwan, Simon 202
Knox, Arthur 200
Knox, Sir John 164

Lacy, Thomas 92
Lally, Captain Edmond 269
land confiscations
    Cromwellian 2–3, 4, 8, 19, 20, 25, 35,
        237
    Jacobite 35, 37–9, 40
    Williamite 2, 6, 8, 9–10, 73, 88, 98–9,
        191, 237, 245
Lane, Sir George, 1st Viscount
    Lanesborough 167
Lanesborough, dowager Viscountess see
    Muschamp, Frances
Langford, Sir Arthur 160, 161
Lauzun, Antonin Nompar de Caumont,
    comte de 51
Lecky, W.E.H. (historian) 8, 240
Ledwith, Redmond 264
Lee, Ja: (Sir James Leigh?) 195
Leigh, Francis 86–87
Leigh, Sir James 195
Levallin, Thomas 268
Levinge, Sir Richard 108–9, 128, 142
Lewis, John 263
Lewis, Robert 199, 200
Limerick 67, 72–3, 125
    articles (or 'Treaty') of 1, 6, 9–11, 65,
        66, 83, 241–5
        claimants under 77, 79, 80, 83,
            84–5, 86, 87, 89, 108, 109, 110,
            144, 194, 218, 227, 240, 262–73,
            280–4
        protectees and 81, 84, 88–91,
            280–1, 283, 284–5
        ratification and implementation
            67, 71, 81, 95–122, 127–8, 129,
            130–2, 136–7, 143, 159, 182, 220,
            241–2, 244, 245
        text 256–61
    article 13 1, 6, 11, 31–2, 57, 59–61,
        125, 129, 147–209, 236–7, 238
    opposition of articlemen to 11, 104,
        111, 128, 130–2, 133n, 147–8,
        149–53, 154–8, 167, 174–5, 236–7
    see also under privy council of
        England; privy council of Ireland

defence and negotiations for surrender
    43, 44, 48, 51–2, 55–62, 70, 81–3,
    127
    first siege 81, 82
    safe conduct to, granted to other
        Jacobite garrisons 248, 249, 251,
        255, 256
Lloyd, William, bishop of Killala and
    Achonry 180
Loghra, Marcus 46
Longfield, Robert 86, 116
Longford, earl of see Aungier, Francis
Louth, Baron see Plunkett, Oliver
Lucan, 1st earl of see Sarsfield, Patrick
Ludlow, Stephen 202
Luttrell, Colonel Henry 103, 104–5, 113,
    117, 157, 239–40, 262
Luttrell, Colonel Simon 258
Lynagh, Augustine 179
Lynch, Henry 52
Lynch, Sir Roebuck 22
Lyon, James 179
Lysaght, John 273
Lysaght, William 266

McAdam, Philip 272
McCarthy, Charles 269
MacCarthy, Donough, 4th earl of
    Clancarty 80
McCarthy, Elizabeth, Dowager Baroness
    Cahir 269
MacCarthy, Justin, Viscount Mountcashel
    7n, 44, 47, 80, 237
McCowell, Patrick 267
MacDonnell, Alexander, 3rd earl of
    Antrim 116
MacDonnell, Colonel Alexander,
    governor of Galway 53
McDonnogh, Lieutenant Colonel John
    76, 253
McDonogh, Connor 273
MacDonogh, Lieutenant Colonel Terence
    272
McElligott, Colonel Roger 80
MacGawly, Lieutenant Peter 264
McGillicuddy, Cornelius 270
McGillicuddy, Colonel Donough 270
McGrath, Captain John 265
McGuire (McGwire), Bryan (Bryen)
    266, 272

McHugo, Jeffrey 270, 272
Mackay (Maccay), Hugh 260
McKenna, Toole 267
McLoughlin, Donache 267
McMahon, Captain Cornelius 271
McMahon, Captain Donogh 265
McNamara, Roger 268
McNamara, Captain Thady 268
McNemara, Daniel 272
McNemara, Major Hugh 271
McSweeney, Captain Denis 76, 254
McSweeney, Captain Edmund 76, 253
McSweeney, Major Terence 76, 77, 80, 254
Magan, Henry 264
Magawley, Patrick 187
Magee, Major David 266
Magennis, Brian, Viscount Magennis of Iveagh 58
Magennis, Daniel 116
Magennis, Phelim 116
Magrath, James 84, 271
Magrath, John 266
Magrath, Robert 266
Maguire, Dominic, archbishop of Armagh 58, 60
Maguire, Roger, styled Lord Inniskillen (Enniskillen) 250
Malone, Anthony 264
Malone, Christopher 60
Malone, Edmund (Ned) 13, 30, 60n, 126, 133–4, 164, 170, 177, 221, 231, 237
    as agent for Colonel John Browne 17, 158, 167–8, 180–1, 187
    as lawyer and agent in London 17, 86, 93n, 104, 106, 172, 210, 213–20
    supposed convert to Church of Ireland 216
Malone, John 86
Malone, Richard 191, 201, 202, 203, 207, 208, 224n
Manby, Peter 263
Marlborough, earl of see Churchill, John
Martin, George 266
Martin, Oliver 123
Martin, Peter 33, 52
Martin, Captain Richard 132, 195, 197, 198, 203, 256

Mary, queen of England, Scotland and Ireland (wife of James II) 43, 47
Mary, queen of England, Scotland and Ireland (wife of William III) 41, 93, 113, 155, 156–7
Mason, Robert 154, 164
Mayo, Viscounts (family of) 4, 21–24, 209n
    see also Bourke, Elinor; Bourke, Miles; Bourke, Theobald
Meade, Sir John 33, 98
Meara, Daniel 267
Meara, John 271
Meredith, Thomas 202
Mesmes, Jean-Antoine de, comte d'Avaux 43, 47
Methuen, John 138, 140–1
Metset, Monsieur, Commissary of War 248
Michelburne, Colonel John 75–6, 250, 251, 252, 253, 254
Molesworth, Robert 173
Mollowny, Thady 268
Monaghan, William Blayney, 6th Lord Blayney, Baron of 61
Monck, Henry 156, 163, 202
Moore, Colonel Garrett 30, 35, 133, 161, 164, 188, 194, 195, 201, 206, 216–17
Moore, Mary 228
Moore, Michael 73, 74
Moore, Colonel Roger 60, 161, 174, 175, 202, 255
Mount-Leinster, Viscount see Cheevers (Chievers), Edward
Mountcashel, Viscount see MacCarthy, Justin
Mountjoy, Viscount see Stewart, William
Mullowney, James 270
Murphy, James 27
Muschamp, Denny 167
Muschamp, Frances, dowager Viscountess Lanesborough 167

Nagle, David 268
Nagle, Captain Pierce 268
Nagle, Sir Richard 33, 44, 58, 237
Napper, James 195, 203, 207, 209
Nash, James 271
Naughton, James 265

Neale, the, Co. Mayo 4, 13, 18, 207, 208, 210–13, 215–16, 225–6, 233, 234
Neilan, Daniel 266
Neville, Captain Thomas 264
'new interest' (of Irish Catholic landowners) *see under* Catholics
Newcomen, Jane, Lady 195, 200
Nicholson, Christopher 264
Nihill, Laurence (Lawrence) 272
Nihill, Patrick 269
Nolan, Gregory 206, 232
Nolan, John 197
Nolan, Captain John 269
Nottingham, Daniel Finch, earl of 52, 68–70, 88–89, 107, 112, 113–15, 125, 129, 155, 156, 184
Nugent, Mr (lawyer) 23
Nugent, Edmond 269
Nugent, Captain Gareth 264
Nugent, Mary 229, 231
Nugent, Captain Michael 264
Nugent, Colonel Richard 264
Nugent, Thomas, Baron Nugent of Riverston 24n, 32, 52, 53
Nugent, Thomas, 4th earl of Westmeath 58, 222, 229, 230, 231
Nugent, Captain Thomas 268, 271

O'Brien, Honora, Dowager Viscountess Clare 270
O'Brien (O'Bryen), Murtagh 266, 272
O'Bryen, Bryen 270
O'Bryen, Captain Dermot 272
O'Bryen, Turlagh 272
O'Callaghan, Captain Darby 270
Ó Ciardha, Éamonn (historian) 8
O'Connor, Captain Dermott 273
O'Connor, Captain Donogh 269
O'Connor, Colonel Martin 269
O'Connor, Malachy 273
O'Connor, Thomas 270
O'Conor Don, the 78
O'Dea, Michael 266, 273
O'Dempsey (née Bermingham), Anne, Viscountess Clanmalier 200, 202, 229, 231–2
O'Donnell, Andrew 272
O'Donnelly, Owen 267
O'Donnelly, Captain Terence 267

O'Donovan, Colonel Daniel 270
O'Donovan, Doctor Richard 271, 272
O'Donovan, Richard (junior) 271, 272
O'Donovan, Lieutenant William 271
O'Flaherty, Roderick 39
Ogan, William 283
O'Grady, Donogh 270
O'Gribben, Lieutenant Henry 267
O'Hara, Charles, 1st Baron Tyrawley 202
O'Hara, Kean 76–7, 254
O'Hehir, Loughlin 270
O'Kelly, Colonel Charles 42, 51
O'Laghlin, Roger 266
O'Lavery, Captain Arthur 267
O'Loughlin, Donogh 271
O'Loughlin, Roger 272
O'Malley, Captain Charles 242
O'Malley, Gráinne 21
O'Malley, Teig 242
O'Meara, Darby 268
O'Neale, Sir Daniel 264
O'Neill, Colonel Cormac 116, 272
O'Neill, Captain Owen 76, 253
Ordnance Office 45, 46, 47, 48, 50, 51
O'Regan, Sir Teague 75–6, 77–8, 250, 252, 253–4, 255
Ormond, dukes of *see* Butler, James
Orrery, 1st earl of *see* Boyle, Roger
Osborne, John 23, 97–8, 99
O'Sullivan, Captain Daniel 270
Oxburgh, Colonel Henry 105, 240, 241

Palmer, William 120–1, 180, 189, 202
Parker, Benjamin 26
parliament of England 39n, 104, 115–16, 138, 157–8, 172, 213, 216, 218, 219, 283n *see also* acts and bills
parliament of Ireland
   of James II (1689) 2, 5, 8, 35–7 *see also under* Browne, Colonel John
   of William III and Anne 1, 10, 11–12, 14, 144n, 170, 171, 220
   see also acts and bills; penal laws
penal laws 6, 10, 13, 66, 119, 142, 143–4, 148, 176, 207
   and incentives for conversion 210, 228–35
   see also under acts and bills, Irish
Peppard, Jacob 200, 202
Peppard, Nicholas 73

Peppard, Patrick 268
Peppard, Thomas 73, 74
Percival, – 202
Percival, George 163
Petty, Sir William 25–6, 27, 48, 211
Plowden, Francis 58
Plunkett, Edward 263
Plunkett, Captain Edward 262
Plunkett, James 39
Plunkett, Oliver, 8th Baron Louth 58
Plunkett, Patrick 73, 74
Plunkett, Simon 263
Pooly, Robert 195
Poore, Major James 271
Porter, Sir Charles 57, 59, 66, 77, 107,
    112, 115, 117, 118, 122, 128–9,
    131, 149, 154, 155, 157–8, 257,
    260
Porter, John 22, 68, 80
Porter, Matthew 68
Porter, Thomas 68
Power, David 272
Power, James 195, 272
Power, John 81
Power, Nicholas 265
Power, Richard, earl of Tyrone 80–1
Power, Thomas 271
Powis, 1st duke of see Herbert, William
Powlett, Charles, 6th marquess of
    Winchester 169, 214
Poynings' Law 10
Preston, Captain Anthony 264
Preston, Jenico, 7th Viscount
    Gormanston 52
Pritchett, Walter 93
privy council of England 12, 21, 114,
    122, 133, 168, 245
  and article 13 of Limerick 130–2, 148,
    156–8, 159, 161, 167, 183–4, 186,
    187–8, 189
  and articles of surrender 67, 70, 74,
    78, 89, 100, 105, 112, 114, 130–2,
    134, 136, 143
  lobbying by Irish Catholics 10, 113,
    117, 131, 132, 161, 169, 214, 215,
    216–18, 230n, 232
privy council of Ireland 8, 10, 12, 40, 67,
    102, 108, 120, 121, 132, 138, 161,
    191, 231
  and article 13 of Limerick 130, 148,
    154, 155–6, 159, 160, 162, 163,
    166, 167, 182–4, 186, 187
  and articles of surrender 73, 74, 78,
    111, 116, 117, 129, 134, 143, 242
  as court of claims see under courts of
    claims
protectees 66, 81–94, 98n, 103, 105n,
    110, 114, 122, 130, 148, 149, 175,
    240, 257
Protestants
  employed in Colonel John Browne's
    ironworks 45, 47
  interest, security of 12, 91, 92, 94,
    101, 122, 140, 159, 161, 169–71,
    172–5, 176, 224 see also penal
    laws
  lobbying in London 10, 115–17, 134,
    216–19
  opposition to the articles of surrender
    95, 97, 98–102, 111, 112, 116,
    122, 135, 164, 240, 241–5
  owners of ironworks 49
  and Restoration land settlement 3, 4,
    20, 28, 35, 37
  support for the articlemen and
    protectees 39, 77n, 85, 88,
    109–10, 137, 140–2, 143, 212–13,
    214, 240
  see also Church of Ireland; see also
    under Browne, Colonel John
Pullein, Frances, widow of Samuel,
    archbishop of Tuam 22
Pullein, William 164, 180, 181, 198n,
    212
Pulteney, John 120
Purcell, Captain John 264
Purcell, Lieutenant John 262
Purcell, Colonel Nicholas 58, 60, 105,
    117, 157, 166, 257
Purcell, Captain Thomas 269
Pyne, Sir Richard 86

Quin, Thady 87n, 240

Raby, Baron see Wentworth, Thomas
Ram, Sir Abel 50, 60
Ram, Abel (junior) 161
Reddy, Captain Richard 266, 271
Regan, Captain Daniel 271
Regan, T. see O'Regan, Sir Teague

Reily, Captain Hugh 264
Restoration land settlement 2–4, 5, 7n, 13, 17, 18, 20, 21, 28, 33–7, 39, 40, 88, 105, 211–12, 240, 249, 255
Reyley, Captain James 267
Reyley, Colonel Mille 269
Reyley, Lieutenant Colonel Philip Oge 267
Reyley, Major Edmond 267
Reyley, Turlogh 267
Reynell, Edmund 156, 160, 161, 163, 169, 202
Reynell, Sir Richard 21, 104, 156
Rice, Gregory 269
Rice, John 105
Rice, Sir Stephen 21, 24, 31–2, 101, 105, 154, 164, 171, 174, 175, 176, 188, 191, 194, 195–7, 203, 204, 220, 241, 279
Rice, Thomas 272
Riordan, James 167
Riordan, Colonel Timothy 71, 255, 256
Riverston, Baron see Nugent, Thomas, Baron Nugent of Riverston
Rochester, earl of see Hyde, Laurence
Rochfort, Captain Oliver 272
Rochfort, Robert 159
Rooth, William 269
Roscommon, 6th earl of see Dillon, Robert, 6th earl of
Rourke, Tirrell 255
Russell, William 263
Ruvigny, Henry de, earl of Galway 169
Ryan, Darby 268, 271
Ryan, Dominick 264
Ryan, John 267, 268, 271
Ryan, Morgan 269
Ryan, Patrick 269
Ryan, Thady 269
Ryley, Colonel Edmund 249
Ryley, Colonel Luke 249
Ryley, Philip 249
Ryves, Sir Richard 33

St George, Sir Oliver 38
St George, Richard 161
Sarsfield, Charlotte 216
Sarsfield, Patrick, senior 216, 217
Sarsfield, Patrick, 1st earl of Lucan 49, 51, 52, 53, 56, 58–9, 60, 61, 76, 84, 92, 106, 147, 149–51, 156, 162, 175, 216–19, 237, 257, 259–60
Savage, Mr 202
Savage, Cornet Francis 267
Savage, Lieutenant Patrick 267
Savage, Philip 163, 170, 234
Schomberg, Frederick de, 1st duke of Schomberg 37, 40, 41, 113
Scott, Colonel Edward 254, 255
Scravenmore, Heer van see van der Duyn, Adam
Scurlocke, Thomas 153, 197
Sexton, Captain Patrick 264
Shaghnessy, Elenor 269
Shapcote, Mr (lawyer) 23
Shaw, Dr Feilding 198
Shaw, Robert 54
Sheldon, Lieutenant-General Dominic 58
Sheridan, Thomas 32, 237
Sherlock, Eustace 263, 264
Shiels, Aghrey 264
Shrewsbury, 1st duke of see Talbot, Charles
Simms, J.G. (historian) 9–10, 84–5, 120, 122
Sisson, Thomas 27–8, 32, 195
Skerritt, William 195
Sligo 82
   articles of 1, 65, 76–7, 245
      Crofton, Sir Henry (sole claimant under) 75, 76–80, 127n, 284
      ratification and implementation 68, 73, 75, 78, 81, 94, 118, 143
      text 250–5
   defence and surrender of 43, 48, 75–6
Sloane, James 116–17, 161, 202
Smith, Patrick 269
Smith, Robert 194
Smith, Roger 267, 270
Smith, Thomas 195, 203, 207, 209
Somers, Sir John, Baron Somers 157, 173
Southwell, Edward 183, 185
Southwell, Sir Robert 284
Spencer, Robert, 3rd earl of Sunderland 33
Sprigge, William 160, 161, 169, 201
Spring, Thomas 268
Spring, Lieutenant Walter 271

INDEX

Stackpole, George 268
Stanton, Edmond McThomas 49
Stanton, John 165, 167, 202
Stanton, John McHubert 49
Stanton, Cornet Patrick 272
Stantons of Birmingham 27, 29
Stapleton, Pierce 269
Stewart, William, 1st Viscount Mountjoy 174
Stone, Richard 185–6
Story, George 54, 56, 71n
Stratford, Edward 195
Stritch, Bartholomew 272
Stritch, Francis 265
Sullevane, Daniel 267
Sullivan, Daniel 270
Sunderland, 3rd earl of see Spencer, Robert
Swanwich, Allen 196
Sydney, Henry, 1st Viscount Sydney 52, 69, 87, 88–9, 106, 108, 110, 112–16, 121, 125, 154, 155, 156, 157, 171, 212, 213
Symms, Robert 46
Synge, Edward, archbishop of Tuam 233
Synnott, James 265

Taaffe, – 195
Talbot, Mr, of Malahide 88
Talbot, Barbara 33
Talbot, Bridget 224
Talbot, Charles, 1st duke of Shrewsbury 117, 161, 169
Talbot, Frances, duchess of Tyrconnell 60
Talbot, John 163
Talbot, Richard, earl and duke of Tyrconnell 47–8, 58, 82, 99, 128n, 174n, 211
  appeals to Queen Mary for money during war 43, 47
  and Colonel John Browne 18, 33, 147, 150, 237, 259
  Catholicisation of Irish administration 32, 33
  in France 43, 52, 62
  and land settlement 32–5, 40
  and siege of Limerick 51, 52–3
  and war 41–3
Talbot, William, earl of Tyrconnell 104, 195

Talmash (Tollemache), Thomas 260
Taylor, Walter 202
Temple, Sir John 21, 23
Tenison, Henry 179, 187
Tenison, Thomas, archbishop of Canterbury 171, 176
Terry, Ambrose 268
Thompson, Richard 31, 154, 161, 166, 182, 191, 197, 203
Thomson, John 21
Throckmorton, George 234
Tippin, William 267
Tirrell, William and Margaret 264
Tisdall, Richard 188, 191, 202, 203
Tobyn, James 269
Tobyn, John 265, 273
Tobyn, Thomas 269
Tollemache (Talmash), Thomas 260
Topham, Sir John 61, 155, 156, 163
Trant, Peter 270
Trench, Frederick 181, 197
Trench, John 202
Trimlestown, 10th Baron see Barnewall, Matthias
Tuite, Walter 264
Tyrawley, 1st Baron see O'Hara, Charles
Tyrconnell, Frances Talbot, duchess of 60
Tyrconnell, earl and duke of see Talbot, Richard
Tyrconnell, William Talbot, earl of 104, 195
Tyrone, earl of see Power, Richard
Tyrrell, Patrick, bishop of Meath 169, 170, 175
Tyrrell, Captain Richard 264

Uniack, Margaret 121
Usher, John 200
Usher, Walter 263

van der Duyn, Adam, Heer van Scravenmore ('s-Gravemoer) 260
van Keppel, Arnold Joost, earl of Albemarle 138, 140, 141
Vesey, Agmondisham 168, 213, 216–19
Vesey, John, archbishop of Tuam 168, 180, 187, 191, 196, 212, 213, 216–17, 230, 231

Waddington, Sir Henry 49

Wake, William, archbishop of Canterbury 233
Walsh, John 264
Warburton, Mr (lawyer) 23
Warren, Elinor 179, 202, 205
Warren, Mary 205
Waterford 22, 215
    articles of 1, 65–71, 127, 245
        claimants under 66–7, 68, 73, 79–80, 118
        ratification and implementation 67–70, 74–5, 81, 94, 104, 143, 156
        text 247
    defence and negotiations for surrender 67, 69–70, 282
Wauchope, Major General John 58, 60
Weldon, Christopher 263
Welsh, Robert 198
Wentworth, Thomas, Baron Raby 121
Westby, Nicholas 166, 204
Westmeath, earl of *see* Nugent, Thomas, 4th earl of Westmeath
Westport, Co. Mayo 4, 22, 26, 29, 49, 50, 179, 190, 228, 235
Westport House 26, 29, 235, 237–8
White, Francis 263
White, Ignatius, marquis d'Albeville 51, 52
White, John 269
White, Colonel John 167
White, Michael 263, 265
White, Richard 269
White, Captain Rowland 258
White, Thomas 269
Whitfield, Mr (lawyer) 23
Whitfield, Henry 24, 211
Whitshed, Thomas 99
William III, king of England, Scotland and Ireland 5, 88–9, 90, 93, 102, 151, 226, 236, 242
    alleged plot to assassinate 169, 171–2

and articles of surrender 62, 66–72, 73–4, 77, 80, 95, 98, 101, 104, 106–7, 108, 113, 115, 116–17, 122, 136–8, 140, 143, 149, 244–5, 250, 252, 257–8, 259, 260, 278, 279–82, 284, 286
    policy on articles and articlemen 81, 94, 95–102, 106–7, 108–9, 122, 136, 143, 286
    Catholic attitudes to 51–4, 65, 172, 238–9
    Catholics in service of 106, 239
    changing peace policy 51–3, 82
    coronation 41
    in Holland 106, 136, 214, 215
    invasion of England 5, 34, 236
    land confiscation under 9–10, 93, 98, 100–1, 109, 110, 111
    land grants by 74, 81, 87, 92, 106, 138, 213, 214, 217, 218
    oath of allegiance to 103, 119, 137, 171, 242, 258, 259, 266, 269,
    and personal pardons 13, 39, 66, 72, 75, 78, 84, 85–7, 91, 92, 94, 97, 98, 106, 121, 133, 136–7, 212–16, 220, 240
    proclamations encouraging Jacobite surrender 54, 66, 67, 80, 81–2, 85, 88, 91, 94, 125, 149, 274–7 *see also* protectees
Winchester, 6th marquess of *see* Powlett, Charles
Wogan, William 183
Wotton, Peter 73
Württemberg-Neuenstadt, Carl Rudolf, duke of 57, 59
Wybrantz, Peter 23
Wyse, Thomas 68, 80

Yeadon, John 23
Yelferton, Major George 269